STUDIES IN COMMONWEALTH POLITICS AND HISTORY

No. 6

General Editors: Professor W. H. MORRIS-JONES
Institute of Commonwealth Studies
University of London

Professor DENNIS AUSTIN
Department of Government
University of Manchester

Sri Lanka —
Third World Democracy

About the Series

Legatee of a vast empire, the Commonwealth still carries the imprint of its past. And in doing so it may be said to have a collective identity which, in a very varying degree, each of its members exhibits. This, we believe, can sustain a collective inquiry into the political history and institutions of countries which were once governed within the British Empire and we note signs of a revival of interest in this field. In recent years 'area studies' have been encouraged, but there is also a sense in which the Commonwealth is itself a region, bounded not by geography but history, and imperial history in particular. Seen thus the region cannot exclude areas into which empire overspilled as in the Sudan, or areas now outside the Commonwealth such as South Africa and Burma, or the unique case of Ireland. No account of the dilemmas which face the government of Canada or Nigeria or India—or indeed of the United Kingdom—which examines the present in relation to the past can be complete which omits some consideration of this 'imperial dimension'. Without in any sense trying to claim that there is a 'political culture' common to all Commonwealth conntries it is certainly the case that some of the institutions, some part of the political life, and a certain element in the political beliefs of many Commonwealth leaders, can be said to derive from the import of institutions, practices and beliefs from Britain into its former colonies.

Nor is the Commonwealth merely a useful category of study. It is also a community of scholars, many of them teaching and writing within the growing number of universities throughout the member countries who share an interest in the consequences of imperial experience and have common traditions of study.

The present series of books is intended to express that interest and those traditions. They are presented not as a guide to the Commonwealth as a corporate entity, but as studies either in the politics and recent history of its member states or of themes which are of common interest to several of the countries concerned. Within the Commonwealth there is great variety—of geographical setting, of cultural context, of economic development and social life: they provide the challenge to comparative study, while the elements of common experience make the task manageable. A cross-nation study of administrative reforms or of legislative behaviour is both facilitated and given added meaning; so also is an examination of the external relations of one or more member states; even a single country study, say on Guyana, is bound to throw light on problems which are echoed in Sri Lanka and Jamaica. The series will bring together—and, we hope, stimulate—studies of those kinds carried out by both established and younger scholars. In doing so, it can make its distinctive contribution to an understanding of the changing contemporary world.

Mr. Jupp's study of Sri Lanka is very representative of the intention behind this series. It examines the complicated interplay of political forces during successive changes of government in the former island of Ceylon—now Sri Lanka. Always seemingly at risk, yet never fully subdued, democratic forms in Sri Lanka have survived during the post-colonial years since independence in 1948. Their survival has run parallel with the indigenisation of political life under a variety of local pressures, a process which Mr. Jupp has traced with scholarly precision and a wealth of interesting detail. The volume is likely to stand as a definitive study of politics in the unusual setting of a "third-world democracy".

List of books in the series

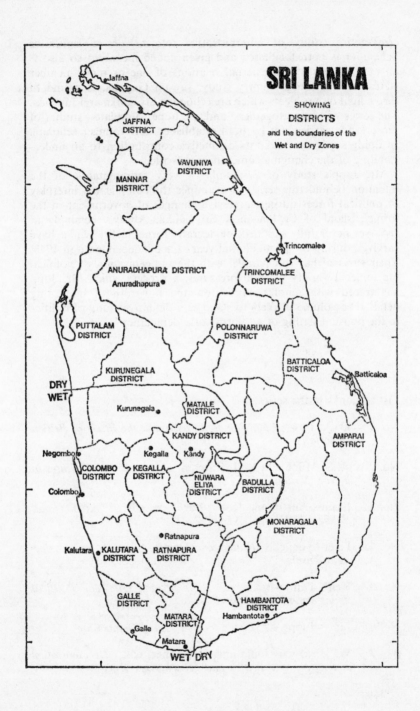

SRI LANKA

SHOWING

DISTRICTS

and the boundaries of the
Wet and Dry Zones

Jaffna

JAFFNA
DISTRICT

VAVUNIYA
DISTRICT

MANNAR
DISTRICT

Trincomalee

ANURADHAPURA DISTRICT

Anuradhapura

TRINCOMALEE
DISTRICT

PUTTALAM
DISTRICT

POLONNARUWA
DISTRICT

KURUNEGALA
DISTRICT

BATTICALOA
DISTRICT

Batticaloa

DRY
WET

Kurunegala

MATALE
DISTRICT

Negombo

KANDY DISTRICT

Kegalla

Kandy

AMPARAI
DISTRICT

COLOMBO
DISTRICT

KEGALLA
DISTRICT

NUWARA
ELIYA
DISTRICT

BADULLA
DISTRICT

Colombo

MONARAGALA
DISTRICT

Ratnapura

Kalutara

KALUTARA
DISTRICT

RATNAPURA
DISTRICT

GALLE
DISTRICT

HAMBANTOTA
DISTRICT

Hambantota

MATARA
DISTRICT

Galle

Matara

WET DRY

Sri Lanka—
Third World Democracy

James Jupp

FRANK CASS

First published 1978 in Great Britain by
FRANK CASS AND COMPANY LIMITED
Gainsborough House, Gainsborough Road,
London, E11 1RS, England

and in the United States of America by
FRANK CASS AND COMPANY LIMITED
c/o Biblio Distribution Centre
81 Adams Drive, P.O. Box 327, Totowa, N.J. 07511

British Library Cataloguing in Publication Data

Jupp, James
    Sri Lanka.— (Studies in Commonwealth politics and history; No. 6).
    1. Sri Lanka — Politics and government
    I. Title II. Series
    320.9549'303   JQ655.A1

ISBN 0-7146-3093-4

Printed in Great Britain by
The Bourne Press, 3—11 Spring Road, Bournemouth

To

Janet, Julie, Judy, Steve and Ira

who always make New York

seem like home

Contents

Acknowledgments

My interest in Ceylon (as it then was) began in 1956 when I first visited the island shortly after the general election which returned S. W. R. D. Bandaranaike. It has continued until the present and in July 1977 I was able to witness yet another of the regularly held elections which have distinguished Sri Lanka from many other states in the region. Throughout the past twenty years I have enjoyed the friendship of politicians, academics and journalists without whom it would have been impossible to have completed this work. Most important among these have been Anil and Susil Moonesinghe and their families, whose hospitality was always extended to me even at the shortest notice. Continuing discussions with Jeanne Moonesinghe have proved invaluable over the past twenty years. Among many other friends I number Donovan Mold-rich, who gave me access to the files of the *Times of Ceylon,* Jeyaratnam Wilson, Ranjith Amerasinghe, Kumari Jayawardene, Michael Roberts and Ian Goonetilleke. Everyone who works in Sri Lanka remarks on the ease of dealing with local politicians and all my contacts with them have borne this out. All those listed at the end of the book gave me their time without hesitation and regardless of party or factional allegiance.

While working in North America I have been privileged to discuss Sri Lanka with Professor Howard Wriggins, with Bob Kearney, Calvin Woodward and Charles Blackton. The small group of overseas scholars working on Sri Lanka are as friendly and charming as the country they are studying and it has been a pleasure to meet them at conferences of the Association for Asian Scholars or at the Columbia University Centre for South Asian Studies.

In Britain I owe a special debt to Professors Morris-Jones

and Dennis Austin who act as editors of the series in which
this book appears. The University of York has always given
me generous leave, both to visit Sri Lanka and to study in
North America, where most of the overseas scholars are
concentrated. I have particularly to thank Professor Graeme
Moodie in this respect, together with those colleagues who
took over the burden of teaching during my absences. The
University of York was also instrumental in getting me a
Social Science Research Council grant to visit Sri Lanka in
1969, during which time I was able to interview most of the
politicians quoted in this work.

No research is possible without the help of libraries,
universities and institutions of learning. I have been especially
indebted to the University of Sri Lanka, with its excellent
collection of local material, the *Times of Ceylon,* the Central
Bank of Ceylon and the many parties, trade unions and other
local organisations which have freely given me access to
material. University libraries most heavily used have included
the London School of Economics, Columbia University, the
University of York, the University of Waterloo, the School of
Oriental and African Studies, the University of Leeds and
the University of Toronto. I have also had invaluable assistance
from the librarians of the British Museum, the Colombo
Museum, the Commonwealth Office, the Royal Commonwealth Society, the New York Public Library, the Institute
of Commonwealth Studies and the Commonwealth Institute.

In sum, it has been a pleasure to work with the politicians
of Sri Lanka, with those who comment upon them, with
interested academic colleagues in Britain, North America and
South Asia and with the staff of my publisher, Frank Cass.
My hope is that by introducing new readers to the problems
of Sri Lanka as well as to its often unique political life, I will
help it to gain the friends it deserves in a world which has
often seemed indifferent or unsympathetic during its thirty
years of independence.

London, January 1978   JAMES JUPP

Glossary of Terms and Abbreviations

A.C.B.C.	All-Ceylon Buddhist Congress
Ayurveda	Indigenous medicine
B.B.P.	Bandaranaike Bosath Pakshaya
Bhikkhu	Buddhist monk
B.J.B.	Bauddha Jathika Peramuna (Buddhist National Front)
Boddhisatva	One who will become a Buddha
C.F.L.	Ceylon Federation of Labour
C.F.T.U.	Ceylon Federation of Trade Unions
C.P.	Ceylon Communist Party
C.T.U.F.	Ceylon Trade Union Federation
C.W.C.	Ceylon Workers Congress
Dakayaka	Lay temple trustee
Devale	Shrine for a god
Dissawa	Kandyan noble title
D.M.K.	Dravida Munnetra Kazhagham
D.W.C.	Democratic Workers Congress
E.B.P.	Eksath Bhikkhu Peramuna (Monks' United Front)
F.P.	Federal Party (Ilankai Tamil Arasu Kadchi)
Grama Sevaka	Local administrative officer
Hartal	General protest strike (especially in 1953)
I.S.F.	Islamic Socialist Front
Jathika V.P.	Jathika Vimukthi Peramuna (National Liberation Front)
J.V.P.	Janatha Vimukthi Peramuna (People's Liberation Front)
Kachcheri	District administrative headquarters

xiii

Kapurale	Lay guardian of a shrine for a god
L.P.P.	Lanka Prajathantrawadi Pakshaya
L.S.S.P.	Lanka Samasamaja Pakshaya (or Party)
Mahanayake Thero	Chief Abbot
Maha Mudaliyar	Chief Headman
M.E.P.	Mahajana Eksath Peramuna (Peoples' United Front)
Mudaliyar	Low Country Headman
Nikaya	Buddhist sect
Perahera	Religious procession (especially at Kandy)
Pirivena	Buddhist seminary
Samanera	Buddhist monastic novice
Sangha	The Buddhist clergy
Satyagraha	Passive resistance
S.L.F.P.	Sri Lanka Freedom Party (Sri Lanka Nidahas Pakshaya)
S.L.F.S.P.	Sri Lanka Freedom Socialist Party
S.M.P.	Samajawadi Mahajana Peramuna (1960) *or* Sinhala Mahajana Peramuna (1968–70)
S.M.S.	Sinhala Mahasabha
Swabasha	Indigenous language
U.L.F.	United Left Front
U.N.P.	United National Party (Eksath Jathika Pakshaya)
V.L.S.S.P.	Viplavakari Lanka Samasamaja Pakshaya (Revolutionary L.S.S.P.)

Chronology of Events in Modern Sri Lanka History

1505–1656	Portuguese occupation of coastal areas
1656–1796	Dutch occupation of coastal areas
1796–1802	Dutch possessions administered by British East India Company
1802	British Crown Colony established in coastal areas
1815	Kandyan convention establishes united Ceylon under British rule
1818	Rebellion of Kandyan chiefs
1833	Colebrooke-Cameron reforms create Legislative Council with local nominees
1840	Land Ordinance enables expansion of coffee plantations
1848	Last Kandyan revolt
1869	State education system begins
1897	Land Ordinance completes expansion of tea plantations
1911	Legislative Council includes elected 'unofficials'
1915	Communal rioting and arrest of leading Ceylonese
1917	Ceylon Reform League established
1919	Ceylon National Congress created from Reform League
1921	Twenty-three 'unofficials' in the Legislative Council
1924	Further expansion of the elective principle for the Legislative Council
1928–9	Donoughmore Constitutional Commission
1931	State Council elected by universal suffrage—59% vote

1934–5   Malaria epidemic and founding of the Suriya
            Mal movement
1935   Trade Union Ordinance
            December: Lanka Samasamaja Party (LSSP)
            founded
1936   Elections to State Board—two LSSP members
            returned
            'All-Sinhalese' Council of Ministers set up
1937   Sinhala Mahasabha founded by S. W. R. D.
            Bandaranaike
1940   Arrest of LSSP leaders for opposition to the war
1942   Rice ration scheme introduced
1943   Ceylon Communist Party formed
1944   Universal free education introduced. Tamil Con-
            gress formed
1944–5   Soulbury Constitutional Commission
1945   *March:* State Council passes 'Free Lanka Bill'
1946   *June–September:* United National Party (UNP)
            formed
1947   Ceylon Independence Act gives effect to Ceylon
            (Constitution) Order in Council of 1946. General
            elections to the House of Representatives return
            the UNP led by D. S. Senanayake
1948   *February* 4: Independence Day
            Ceylon Citizenship Act passed, determining
            status of Indian Tamils
1949   Federal Party founded by S. J. V. Chelvanayakam
1951   *July:* S. W. R. D. Bandaranaike resigns from
            UNP and founds Sri Lanka Freedom Party
            (SLFP)
1952   D. S. Senanayake dies and is replaced as Prime
            Minister by Dudley Senanayake
            May: General Elections return the UNP with
            an enlarged majority
1953   *August:* Hartal against rice ration cuts. Dudley
            Senanayake resigns as Prime Minister and is
            replaced by Sir John Kotelawala
            Revolt in the Temple published
            Rice-rubber agreement signed with China
1955   SLFP adopts policy of 'Sinhala Only'

1956   *February:* Kelaniya sessions of UNP adopt
            'Sinhala Only'
            Mahajana Eksath Peramuna (MEP) formed
            Betrayal of Buddhism published. Buddha Jayanti
            begins in May
            April: Election returns MEP coalition headed by
            S. W. R. D. Bandaranaike
            July: Official Language Act passed. Communal
            rioting

1957   *March:* Buddha Sasana Commission set up
            July: Pact between Bandaranaike and Chel-
            vanayakam to protect Tamil interests
            October: J. R. Jayawardena marches to Kandy
            against the B-C Pact
            British leave Trincomalee and Katunayake bases
            Select Committee on the Constitution set up

1958   *April:* B-C Pact abrogated after organised
            protests by *bhikkhus*
            May: Race riots. Emergency powers operate
            until March 1959
            Paddy Lands Act passed to secure tenure of rice
            farmers
            October: LSSP withdraws its support from
            Bandaranaike's government

1959   Ceylon Constitution (Amendment) Act increases
            constituencies to 151
            June: Philip Gunawardena and P. H. William de
            Silva excluded from Cabinet
            September 25: Bandaranaike assassinated. Daha-
            nayake forms government
            December: Parliament dissolved. Dahanayake
            forms Lanka Prajathantrawadi Pakshaya and is
            expelled from SLFP. C. P. de Silva becomes
            SLFP president

1960   *January 2:* First working day in 'Sinhala Only'.
            Federal Party calls a hartal
            March: General election returns UNP as largest
            party but without an overall majority. Dudley
            Senanayake forms government

1960   *April:* Government defeated in parliament. Representatives dissolved and elections called. Mrs Bandaranaike assumes presidency of SLFP
             May: Electoral agreement between the SLFP and the LSSP
             July: General election returns the SLFP. Mrs Bandaranaike nominated to the Senate and forms government
             Catholic parents occupy Church schools, protesting against nationalisation

1961   *February:* Federal Party satyagraha causes military occupation of Jaffna
             April: Federal Party 'postal service' leads to arrest of Tamil M.Ps.
             Village headman system abolished

1962   *January:* Strike leads to military takeover of Colombo harbour
             Discovery of planned coup by officers of the army and police force
             Sir Oliver Goonetilleke replaced as Governor-General by W. Gopallawa
             July: Trials of alleged plotters held under the Criminal Law (Special Provisions) Act. LSSP conference votes to withdraw support from government
             August: Opposition to rice ration cuts leads to resignation of Felix Dias Bandaranaike as Finance Minister

1963   *February:* US aid cancelled after nationalisation of oil installations
             August: United Left Front launched by LSSP, CP and MEP
             September: Press Commission set up
             Maoist split begins in the Ceylon Communist Party

1964   *March:* Parliament prorogued by Mrs Bandaranaike who begins negotiations with Philip Gunawardena and N. M. Perera

1964   *June:* LSSP special conference votes to enter coalition with SLFP and splits. LSSP expelled from Trotskyist Fourth International
    December: SLFP–LSSP Coalition government defeated in parliament by 74 votes to 73 after defection of C. P. de Silva and others

1965   *March:* General election leads to return of the UNP-led 'National Government' of Dudley Senanayake
    July: US aid restored after compensation is paid to oil companies
    December: Privy Council quashes sentences on 1962 coup defendants and declares the law under which they were tried to be invalid
    Janatha Vimukthi Peramuna (JVP) secretly established as a faction of the Maoist Communist Party

1966   *January 8:* Regulations for 'reasonable use of Tamil' introduced, causing Opposition demonstrations
    February: Discovery of a planned coup by Army N.C.Os. leads to arrest of Ven. Henpitegedara Gnanaseeha and Army commander Richard Udugama

1967   *June:* Indo-Ceylon Agreement Act settles status of Indian Tamils
    November: Rupee devalued by 20% following British devaluation

1968   *June:* Proposals to establish District Councils published. R. G. Senanayake forms the Sinhala Mahajana Peramuna
    July: District Council proposals abandoned by the government

1969   *April:* Federal Party withdraws support from the government
    September: Release of Gnanaseeha and Udugama

1970   *April–May:* Police investigate activities of the JVP 'Guevarists'. Rohan Wijeweera of the JVP arrested but released in July

1970   *May 27:* General elections return the Coalition of the SLFP, the LSSP and the Communists under Mrs Bandaranaike
July: Parliament becomes a Constituent Assembly
August: Police Insurgent Unit set up to investigate the JVP

1971   *March:* US embassy attacked and state of emergency declared. Rohan Wijeweera and many others arrested
April 5: JVP revolt breaks out with attacks on police stations. Fighting continues into May and incidents into August
September: Senate abolished. Peoples Committees established
December: Draft constitution for Sri Lanka laid before parliament

1972   *April:* Ceiling established on disposable incomes. Criminal Justice Commission established to deal with insurgency and currency offences
May: Tamil United Front formed
May 22: Republic of Sri Lanka established under new constitution
June: Trials of JVP leaders before the Criminal Justice Commission begin
August: Land Reform Act passed

1973   *April:* Death of UNP leader Dudley Senanayake
July: Public ownership of 'Lake House' newspapers

1974   *January:* Completion of final citizenship agreement with India
August: Completion of land reform under the Act of 1972
December: Judgement in the trial of JVP leaders

1975   *May:* UNP civil disobedience campaign to protest delay of elections until 1977
September: LSSP Ministers forced out of the Coalition government
October: Nationalisation of plantations completed

1976   *February:* Sir Oliver Goonetilleke sentenced in
            absentia for currency offences
            March: Plantation management transferred to
            state corporations
            May: Tamil Liberation Front, pledged to
            separation, replaces Tamil United Front
            July: Conference of Non-aligned Nations held
            in Colombo

1977   *February:* Communists expelled from the Coali-
            tion
            July 21: General elections return the UNP, led
            by J. R. Jayawardena, in a landslide victory
            October: Constitution amended to create an
            executive president

CHAPTER 1

The Politics of
Independent Ceylon

Ceylon became independent on 4 February, 1948 in auspicious conditions. Its plantation economy, unlike that of Southeast Asia, had not been ravaged by war and was producing profitably and with great benefit to the trade balance. Its people enjoyed a subsidised price for a weekly measure of rice under a rationing scheme introduced in 1942.[1] Its political structure was intact, it had not been invaded and there was no revolutionary element in the transfer of power. For many years it had been ruled with a very small police force and army and was to continue with one of the smallest military budgets of any country in the world.[2] It had enjoyed a large degree of internal self-government, based since 1931 on a State Council elected by universal suffrage. In this respect it was unique throughout the then colonial world. The Ministers who took office had already served in a democratically elected legislature, several of them as political heads of departments. Of the ninety-five Members of Parliament returned in 1947 to make up the newly created House of Representatives, twenty-nine had already served in the State Council, and many State Councillors were to continue active in independent politics. In the Cabinet of 1965 there were five former State Councillors, including the Prime Minister, Dudley Senanayake: even in 1970 there was still one original State Councillor left in Ministerial office, N. M. Perera, Minister of Finance and leader of the Lanka Samasamaja Party. In addition, four other Ministers had originally been elected to parliament in 1947 while Ceylon was still under British rule.

There was no clear-cut break in development in 1948. Nor, indeed, had there been any since the country was united under British rule in 1815 by treaty with the nobility of Kandy. Already by 1833 there was a nominated Legislative Council including three non-British members. It was gradually expanded until, by 1911, four elected members were added, though on an extremely limited franchise. By 1923 'unofficial' members outnumbered those appointed by the Governor, eleven of them elected on the basis of different communities and twenty-three for territorial constituencies. Despite periodic risings in the former Kandyan kingdom and serious rioting in 1915 which led to the arrest of several prominent Ceylonese,[3] the progress towards self-government in the first century of British rule was a copy-book model. This gave some pride not only to the Colonial Office but also to the educated élite in the capital, Colombo, who provided the 'unofficial' element in the various legislatures. This élite was English-speaking, often English educated and 'modernised' in the sense that its position came from business, plantation ownership and professional training rather than from the system of feudal obligation still significant in the Kandyan areas. Although this small political class had been very hesitant about the wisdom of universal suffrage, its position was not seriously disturbed by its introduction, since the Ceylon (State Council) Order in Council of 1931, which was the basis of the Donoughmore Constitution, barred election to anyone who "is unable to speak, read and write the English language".[4]

The reforms of 1931 did not upset the hold of the educated élite on politics, nor has it been seriously challenged yet. It did, however, disturb the elaborate communal balance which the British had maintained ever since 1833. The majority community, the Sinhalese Buddhists, naturally had the most votes under universal suffrage and tended to elect co-religionists. The other groups, making up over one-third of the population, were correspondingly at a disadvantage.[5] It could be argued, and indeed was, that they had been particularly well looked after until 1931. Christians, and especially Protestants, had been favoured in government employment not only under the British but by the Dutch who controlled the coastal areas from 1656 to 1796. Catholics, whose origins date back to the Portuguese occupation of 1505, while unable to reach the social heights of Protestants, had a well developed school system which received generous state subsidies. The small Burgher community, also a relic of the Dutch period, enjoyed great advantages because English was its mother tongue. The Ceylon Tamils, many of whom were also Christians, had developed a tendency towards advanced education and entry into the public services. Even the Muslims, whose élite was mainly engaged in trade, had been granted Legislative Council representation as a community since 1889. A large part of the country's trade was in the hands of Indians, while its plantations, banks and major services were owned by the British. All of these elements were favoured by the colonial government in various ways. Communal representation, which was abolished in 1931, had given them access to political power as well as to business, education, the public service, judiciary and armed forces.

The political élite was inter-communal, many previously Buddhist families becoming Anglican as a recognition of acceptance into the Establishment. The use of English in business, government and law, encouraged the growth of a replica of the English public school system, with its pinnacle in Oxford or Cambridge. Even after independence leaders of the various communities worked together quite harmoniously because they were socially and educationally equal. Ceylon had been more influenced by English culture than any other Asian colony, an influence which helped to obscure the growth of communalism and the deep resentments felt by many Buddhists against the Westernisation of their culture and the restriction of opportunities to those who had become assimilated to the tiny British community. Such trends can now be detected, with hindsight, as early as 1915. The riots of that year between Sinhalese and Muslims provoked the British into their only major repression of local political leaders and were an early witness to the growth of communalism, Sinhalese Buddhist revivalism, labour unrest and the rise of a mildly but unmistakably nationalist group. These developments grew until they shaped contemporary Ceylon politics.

Out of the communal problem there developed a sense of Sinhalese identity which the Anglicisation of the richer minority had repressed. The imprisonment of D. S. Senanayake, W. A. de Silva, D. B. Jayatillake and others in 1915 created a group which, as the Ceylon National Congress, was to dominate politics into the period of independence. They were closely associated with D. R. Wijewardena, founder of a commercially viable Sinhalese language press.[6] The influence of Anagarika

Dharmapala, a Buddhist revivalist and of Piyadasa Sirisena, a Sinhala writer, was also significant.[7] All these men came from commercially successful families who were part of the Colombo middle classes. The labour movement, too, was of middle-class inspiration through men like John Kotelawala, father of a later Prime Minister, and A. E. Goonesinha, founder of the Ceylon Labour Party.[8] They were radicals and modernisers, in the sense both of being against British colonialism and culture and of coming from the modern sector of the economy rather than from the Kandyan aristocracy. They were, however, by no means revolutionary or socialist. Marxism was brought to Ceylon only in the early 1930's by students returning from England who founded the Lanka Samasamaja Party.

Establishing Independence 1945–1953

The British, largely as a by-product of their much greater concerns in India, gave serious consideration to the political future of Ceylon during the Second World War when the country became the headquarters of Southeast Asia Command. Elections had been postponed in 1940 and the group of Trotskyists in the Lanka Samasamaja Party, who opposed the war, had been imprisoned. On 26 May 1943, full internal responsible self-government was promised on the basis of a new constitution to be approved by three-quarters of the State Council 'unofficial' members. This was too limited for the Ceylon National Congress, which had become more radical by 1943. Although a constitutional scheme was prepared by the Board of Ministers, they withdrew it in August 1944, and pressed for full Dominion status. In March 1945, the State Council passed by a large majority the Free Lanka Bill, originally moved by S. W. R. D. Bandaranaike as Minister for Local Administration. Thus, when the constitutional commission under Lord Soulbury arrived in Ceylon, it was faced with non-cooperation by the majority of elected representatives. By the time it reported, the demand for self-government had been ratified by the legislature.[9] The commissioners were, however, able to hold private discussions with two of the most important Sinhalese in the island, D. S. Senanayake, leader of the State Council, and Sir Oliver Goonetilleke, the Civil Defence Commissioner.

The election of a Labour government in Britain improved the prospect of self-government and Senanayake was able to bring back from London the assurance that "His Majesty's Government will co-operate with the people of Ceylon so that such (i.e. Dominion) status may be obtained in a comparatively short time." On this basis the political leaders in the State Council accepted the Soulbury constitution which had, in any case, been based on recommendations made by D. S. Senanayake advised by Sir Ivor Jennings, then Vice-Chancellor of the University of Ceylon. The new House of Representatives was elected over the period 23 August to 20 September 1947 and a Cabinet, consisting largely of leaders of the Ceylon National Congress (now merged into the United National Party), was appointed. D. S. Senanayake, as Prime Minister, was ready to take full independence at the beginning of 1948. The whole operation took place in an atmosphere of subtle negotiation, backed by verbal criticism and fairly gentle pressure. The leader of the Ceylon Tamils, G. G. Ponnambalam, who had been one of the most vocal critics of the scheme drawn up by the all-Sinhalese Board of Ministers, agreed to serve as a Minister under Senanayake.[10] The only radical critics of the new constitution were the three Marxist groups, the Lanka Samasamajists, the Bolshevik Leninists and the Communists.

At every step the elected Sinhalese politicians had shown themselves to be gradualist and constitutional. Despite wartime imprisonment and later illegal escape to India, the revolutionary element was brought into the constitutional structure of which it still disapproved. N. M. Perera and Philip Gunawardena, who had been elected to the State Council as Samasamajists in 1936, were re-elected for their former districts. They were joined by a large bloc of fellow Marxists, providing the only effective opposition to the United National Party and its allies, the Tamil Congress and independent M.P.s. This pattern of revolutionaries facing the constitutional conservatives was to continue until after D. S. Senanayake's death in 1952. Outside parliament, the Left was supported by militant labour action, concentrated particularly on the Colombo harbour area and bringing a general strike in 1947 in which sections of the public service were involved. The Left also worked with the Ceylon Indian Congress which was both a political party and a trade union representing the Indian Tamil estate workers in the tea industry. This was potentially a strong alliance, directed economically and politically against the British and those the Left regarded as their local agents, the UNP government.

Senanayake had also to deal with the 'Indian problem' which had been occupying politicians for over twenty years. Indian Tamil estate workers were the largest proletarian force in the island and Indian Tamils were also very important among Colombo harbour and municipal workers. The voting quali-fications of Indian Tamils had always been a controversial point: the estate workers, as British subjects, were allowed to vote and controlled six seats and 75,000 votes through the Ceylon Indian Congress. Senanayake solved this problem by the simple expedient of disfranchising the Indian Tamils. The Marxist Left was probably deprived of some electoral support by this action, while the Left in general suffered by the disappearance of the Ceylon Indian Congress from parlia-ment.

The continuing rise in the value of plantation commodities as a result of the Korean war helped to lessen economic discon-tent. The war also hardened the conservative element in the United National Party which began to draw closer to the United States. When D. S. Senanayake died in March, 1952, his son Dudley Senanayake went to the polls immediately in very favourable circumstances, and the UNP won an absolute majority. S. W. R. D. Bandaranaike had resigned from the UNP in 1951, but his new Sri Lanka Freedom Party did little better than the Samasamajists. The UNP had the support of most Catholic and Muslim leaders and, with the Tamil Congress, even had a following in the Tamil Northern Province. Despite this, a number of forces existed in Ceylon society which, while apparently dormant, were to break out into a powerful reaction which would permanently prevent the UNP from becoming the natural majority party. The economic situation, too, began to change for the worse with the ending of the Korean war and the beginning of the long term decline in the terms of trade which has dogged the economy ever since.[11]

The most important disturbing forces were the militant work-ing class in Colombo and the Western province, and militant Sinhalese Buddhist nationalism in most rural areas. The first showed its power in the *hartal* (general strike) of 12 August 1953 caused by the removal of the subsidy on rice. The strike, in which troops were called out and an emergency and curfew called for the first time since 1915, demoralised the government which was already internally divided between the followers of Dudley Senanayake and those of his more conservative kinsman, Sir John Kotelawala. The prime minister resigned and a period of increasingly repressive conservatism followed.

Change of Government 1953–1959

After the resignation of Dudley Senanayake, a major force in society, the Sinhala Buddhist revivalists, moved decisively and in many cases permanently away from the UNP. Buddhism was preparing throughout the world for the Buddha Jayanti year, which marked 2500 years of Buddhism. Locally, Buddha Jayanti was also believed to coincide with the arrival of Vijaya and his Sinhalese band in Lanka in 543 B.C. and was to be celebrated from May 1956. Kotelawala, who had gained enthusiastic Western support for his criticisms of Communism and neutralism at the Bandung conference in 1955, seemed quite insensitive to the dangers of holding an election during the national and religious celebrations. Although petitioned by most Buddhist lay and clerical leaders to postpone the elections, which he was constitutionally entitled to do as his term did not expire until 1957, Kotelawala showed himself to be politically inept as well as quite out of touch with the national sentiment.[12] Meanwhile, organised campaigns leading up to the Buddha Jayanti year had focused attention on Buddhist grievances against Christians and on Sinhalese grievances against the English-speakers. Thus language and religion became major political issues. Kotelawala was at a grave disadvantage compared with Bandaranaike who had been fighting on both fronts for over twenty years. The detachment of most Buddhist revivalists from the UNP made it much easier for basically conservative rural opinion leaders to give their support to the socialist Sri Lanka Freedom Party. The overt pro-Americanism of Kotelawala also made it easier for the Marxists to reach a tactical arrangement with what many of them had characterised as a communalist or "national bourgeois" party, led by an aristocratic landowner and lifelong critic of Marxism. Even in Catholic areas, where the Buddhist revivalists and socialists were regarded as hostile to the Church, the language issue was strong, and there had always been a substantial Christian element among Bandaranaike's followers, including the bulk of his Anglican family.

The most effective organisations opposing the UNP were not the branches of the SLFP, which were hastily thrown together by a weakly-financed and decentralised machine, but the Buddhist and language pressure groups and committees of monks. These were largely inspired by two books published in expectation of Buddha Jayanti, D. C. Wijewardena's *Revolt in the Temple* of 1953 and the Buddhist Commission of Enquiry's *Betrayal of Buddhism* in 1956. Both emanated from the Buddhist revivalists around the All-Ceylon Buddhist Congress and made essentially the same points against Anglicisation, colonialism and Christianisation. The Ven. Mapitigama Buddarakkitha joined with other monks in forming the Eksath Bhikkhu Peramuna, or monks' united front. Although the Mahanayake Theros of the Malwatte and Asgiriya monasteries both advised against monks becoming involved in politics and, by inference lent their support to the government, the great majority of monks ignored them and followed the EBP in its support for Bandaranaike.[13] The EBP presented its ten point programme (the *Dasa Panatha*) at a mass rally in Colombo in February 1956 attended by S. W. R. D. Bandaranaike and the labour leaders Philip Gunawardena and A. E. Goonesinha.[14] During the election itself "every meeting was addressed by members of the *Sangha*. Leading and popular *bhikkhus* went from meeting to meeting, from electorate to electorate. Some of the *Pirivenas* in Colombo and the provinces were turned into election head-quarters. The older monks went from house to house. The small *samaneras* did other work such as writing of election cards, drawing of posters, flags and other odd jobs."[15]

The campaign of the monks meshed with the associated campaign by language enthusiasts (drawn mainly from the Sinhala teachers and journalists) and with Philip Gunawardena's strong trade union organisation. These came together to form the Mahajana Eksath Peramuna with the SLFP.[16] The two Marxist parties, the LSSP and the Communists, while avoiding conflicts with the MEP, disagreed with it on language. Until

1960 the LSSP continued to stand for parity between Sinhalese and Tamil. The composition of the MEP made language policy the primary issue, but the additional organised Buddhist drive behind the MEP and its acceptance by the Marxists and the major trade unions made it invincible. It won the elections in April 1956 with 51 seats of the 95 and reduced the UNP to a derisory eight seats. In the North and the East, in reaction against Sinhalese nationalism, S. J. V. Chelvanayakam's Federal Party wiped out most of its opponents to return a bloc of ten Tamil M.P.s pledged to protect their language against any changes to the benefit of Sinhalese.

The defeat of the UNP was due to its failure to understand the forces moving in the villages after less than ten years of independence. It "antagonised the vernacular educated middle-class who were in the forefront of the cultural and religious revival".[17] The new and inexperienced government was now faced with satisfying the demands which had created it and with tackling the steadily deteriorating economic stituation caused by the ending of the commodity boom and the failure of the UNP to limit imports. Moreover the government was committed to socialist measures at home and to a reorientation abroad which would take it away from the Western alliance so strongly supported by the previous prime minister. In the three short years of the Bandaranaike government much more was started than could be finished. The government immediately legislated that "the Sinhala language shall be the one official language of Ceylon".[18] Against a background of communal rioting in irrigation and resettlement colonies and the threat of mass opposition in the Northern and Eastern provinces, Bandaranaike concluded a pact with the Federal Party leader, Chelvanayakam, in July, 1957[19] and the Federal Party agreed to cancel its proposed *satyagraha* (civil disobedience). Rioting between Sinhalese and Tamils broke out again in May, 1958 after the pact was abandoned under pressure from Sinhalese politicians and Buddhist monks. So widespread and vicious was the rioting, involving several hundred deaths and the large-scale transfers of people between Jaffna and Colombo, that military rule was imposed on the Tamil areas; the Federal Party and the Jathika Vimukthi Peramuna (a Sinhalese communalist party) were declared illegal, a press censorship and curfew was

imposed and effective power passed into the hands of the
Governor-General, Sir Oliver Goonetilleke.[20] The emergency
continued until March 1959 and began the practice of ruling for
months, and eventually years, under emergency powers.

While communal tension characterised the first two years of
the new government, it was also faced with difficulties in achieving its economic objectives. Some important socialist measures
were introduced, including the nationalisation of bus companies
and the Colombo harbour, and the creation of state corporations
in chemicals, textiles and small industries. What caused most
political opposition was Philip Gunawardena's Paddy Lands
Act of 1958, which aimed at securing the tenure of rice farming
tenants and the setting up of cultivation committees to control
production. This was resisted by the larger owners of paddy
land and, together with Philip's support for striking members of
his own trade unions, was seen as sufficient cause for his
removal. After a series of representations by Ministers against
Gunawardena for his alleged complicity in industrial strife, a
threatened "strike" by the majority of the Cabinet forced him
out and an all-SLFP government was formed without
Gunawardena or P. H. William de Silva who formed a separate
party taking the name of the Mahajana Eksath Peramuna. In
these conditions of growing political confusion Bandaranaike
was assassinated on the verandah of his own home by the monk
Talduwe Somarama on 25 September, 1959.[21]

The manner of Bandaranaike's death and the nature of his
victory in 1956, ensured that his name would be associated with
all subsequent reforms. Both the Marxists and the UNP, who
had been hostile critics of Bandaranaike at the time of his death,
subsequently claimed to be carrying on his tradition. The
Marxists emphasised his socialism and hostility to the UNP,
while the latter stressed his opposition to Marxism. Bandaranaike
was the only politician to die violently in the otherwise peaceful
evolution of the political system. The notion that he had sacri-
ficed his life for the good of the people had a great appeal in a
popular culture where such sacrifice was characteristic of the
boddhisatva or Buddha-to-be. Despite his Anglican and English-
speaking family background, Bandaranaike had tried—from his
initial election in 1931—to identify himself with the aspirations
of the Buddhist Sinhala rural majority in a sense which was

unique among State Councillors. Unlike his conservative fellow Ministers before independence, he symbolically dissociated himself from Western culture by adopting an admittedly artificial "national dress". He was the first member to address the Representatives in Sinhala after independence. Thus Bandaranaike had adopted the characteristic role of the national populist leader some years before the developments between 1953 and 1956 transformed Sinhala Buddhist revivalism into the major electoral force in Ceylon. Yet, by adopting democratic socialism in a form similar to that adopted by Nehru and the Congress Socialists in India, Bandaranaike was able to draw the cosmopolitan and previously alienated Marxists into a consensus about the shape of radical politics in Ceylon. By defeating the UNP he was also able to liberate the group within that party which wished to move away from the Westernised conservatism of Sir John Kotelawala. Thus, without ever working out a detailed and coherent ideology of his own, Bandaranaike was able to dictate the future shape of political argument in Ceylon and, in a sense, to determine that it would be transformed into Sri Lanka in due course.

Chaos and Confusion 1959–1962

The assassination of Bandaranaike completed the disintegration of his government and, for the time being, of the SLFP. All those involved in the conspiracy had been members of Bandaranaike's own party.[22] The great majority of those mentioned in court were known personally to Bandaranaike and several were at the heart of SLFP politics. They represented a segment of the party which had been resolutely opposed to Philip Gunawardena and had resisted the socialist aspect of Bandaranaike's programme. The ensuing chaos could scarcely be contained by the unanimous party choice of prime minister, Wijayananda Dahanayake, previously leader of the House and Minister for Education. Dahanayake had wandered through several parties and was to wander through several more. He had neither the organisational backing nor the social standing to reunite the SLFP, and his government disintegrated within less than three months. Dahanayake dissolved parliament without consulting his ministers, called an election for March, 1960 and proceeded

c

to rule for the intervening three months without the need to prop up his rapidly vanishing parliamentary majority.

The entire party system seemed to be dissolving. Dahanayake formed a caretaker Cabinet, only four of whose members had previously held ministerial office. In the confusion caused by a rapid proliferation of new parties there were growing accusations against him of planning a coup. Leaders of all parties called on the Governor-General to resummon parliament if any attempt were made to postpone the elections and to command the army and the public services to disobey illegal orders from the government.[23] In fact, Dahanayake had no political base from which such a threat could materialise even if he had seriously intended it. The elections took place as planned and Dahanayake's Lanka Prajathantrawadi Pakshaya secured only four seats with its leader losing his own. The newly elected UNP government of Dudley Senanayake rested on such a weak basis however, that the new prime minister had to resign when the Speech from the Throne was defeated.[24] Despite representations from most of the major parties, the Governor-General then dissolved parliament rather than call upon the SLFP to try to form a government.[25]

By the end of April, 1960 all the classic ingredients for a collapse of government and a revolutionary or military takeover seemed to exist. However, the armed forces did not move, the elections were not suspended, the parties did not collapse, and the Marxists did not revolt. By the end of the year Ceylon once again had stable parliamentary government. No major party wished to alter the rules of the game. N. M. Perera and his supporters in the LSSP were resolute in defending the parliamentary system and in bringing the Marxists into an electoral alliance with the SLFP.[26] The cohesion of the SLFP was saved by Mrs. Sirimavo Bandaranaike's assuming the leadership, although from the Senate rather than as an elected parliamentarian.[27] The UNP had no intention of frustrating the electoral process and presumably hoped by dissolving parliament to gain a working majority. Although the Federal Party was to launch a passive resistance campaign in 1961, it was still ready to use parliamentary tactics. When faced with the prospect of abandoning a system within which all the principal political actors had spent their entire lives, no important group could be found ready to jump into the void. The electors, too, by their massive turnout on two occasions during 1960, and their reaffirmation of support for the major parties and rejection of communalist extremes, showed that they fully endorsed the attitudes of the politicians. The SLFP returned to power less than a year after it had seemed totally fractured and discredited.

After the confusions of 1960 the SLFP government settled down to two major battles. The Catholic community was resisting the nationalisation of its school system, while the Federal Party quickly realised that 'Sinhala Only' would be just as resolutely pursued as before. The Tamil resistance was much the more determined, as it was organised under a single political party, while Catholic loyalties were not unanimous and they were not effectively mobilised by the UNP. A *satyagraha* campaign began at Jaffna in February, 1961 which resulted in military occupation of the town and of the Northern and Eastern provinces,[28] military intervention seemed to worsen the crisis and, in April, Federal Party M.P.s began acting as 'postmen' for a new independently stamped postal service set up by the party leaders in Jaffna. Talks with the government failed completely, and by the end of the month a state of emergency was declared for the North and the East, a press and radio censorship imposed, and Chelvanayakam (together with twelve Federal Party M.P.s and one Tamil Congress M.P.) were under arrest.[29]

By the end of 1961, therefore, there were again some of the classic preconditions for a breakdown of parliamentary government. A state of emergency which was to last for two years, had restricted press freedom, while the actions of troops in the Tamil areas had caused fears of a permanent military involvement in politics. The Marxist parties were reducing their support for the government, criticising in particular the powers exercised by Felix Dias Bandaranaike, nephew and parliamentary secretary of the prime minister, who they suspected of planning a coup.[30] The estate workers, who had been politically dormant for some years, had been aroused by the support for the Ceylon Tamil *satyagraha* expressed by V. E. K. S. Thondaman for the Ceylon Workers' Congress. At this point, with the UNP, the Federalists, the Marxists and most unions moving into confrontation with the government, a plot to stage a military coup within the army

and the police force was uncovered.[31] While Dudley Senanayake
and Sir Oliver Goonetilleke had both been given pseudonyms
by the plotters, they argued their complete innocence. Nevertheless, Sir Oliver was replaced as Governor-General by William
Gopallawa, a distant relative of Mrs. Bandaranaike, at the end
of February. Another of the prime minister's relatives, Colonel
Stanley Ratwatte, became leader of the Army volunteers, while
in the following year a further relative, Richard Udugama,
assumed command of the Ceylon Army. Arrests continued
throughout February, 1962 and trials were begun in July
under the hastily passed Criminal Law (Special Provisions)
Act.[32]

Towards a Two-Party System 1962–1970

The arrest of the conspirators, the resignation of Sir Oliver
Goonetilleke and, temporarily, of Felix Dias Bandaranaike,[33]
the ending of American aid[34] and the eventual petering out of
Federal Party threats of further civil disobedience, seem random
events. Nevertheless, they marked a basic shift in Ceylon
politics away from communalism as the major issue and from
chaos and confusion in the parties towards a system which by
1970 was clearly divided into two political blocs, one mildly
reformist and the other radically socialist. Economic issues became increasingly important. Communal and religious cries
rose to a frenzy around election time but were no longer the
essential stuff of politics. A glance at what happened in 1962
helps to explain why this should be so. The first Buddhist
Governor-General was appointed. The first Buddhist commander of the armed forces came into office and Catholic
dominance in the army and police was ended. Christian control
over major sectors of education was already very limited. Ceylon
had no choice but neutralism, with a bias towards Russia and
China, after the break with the United States over nationalisation of oil installations, and the agitation against the budget,
which caused Felix Dias Bandaranaike to resign, once again
underlined the inviolability of basic welfare provision, international advisers notwithstanding. Finally, but of most immediate importance, the possibility of Tamil separation receded
and the Ceylon Tamils prepared to accept 'Sinhala Only with

the reasonable use of Tamil', knowing that no significant Sinhalese party supported parity any more.

Bandaranaike had altered the issues in Ceylon politics and future controversy would centre on socialism, which was still unattained, rather than on Sinhalese domination, which was far advanced. Yet confusion still persisted. The Sri Lanka Freedom Party still had to reorganise itself in such a manner as to hold together in crises and to replace the considerable number of leaders who had defected or been expelled during 1960. Its relationship with the Marxists, which had been seriously damaged, had also to be restored as the mechanics of maintaining an effective majority left little alternative. Moreover the ruling group in the SLFP was not outstanding and Mrs. Bandaranaike had difficulty in finding a Minister of Finance who could survive one Budget. This became increasingly acute as the economic situation continued to get worse. By 1964 there was a slight decline in Gross National Product per head and import restrictions were at their most rigid. These problems brought the Marxists together temporarily in a United Left Front embracing the LSSP, the Communists and the MEP of Philip Gunawardena, an alliance based not merely on parliament, where the Left had only one sixth of the seats, but more importantly, upon the trade unions. The Federalists continued to agitate for the use of Tamil regionally and declared New Year Day, 1964, a day of mourning.[35] Thus all the forces seemed to be regrouping for an attack on a still weakened SLFP, and the UNP visibly improved its organisation.

In this atmosphere of crisis, with renewed talk of dictatorship and revolution, Mrs. Bandaranaike had parliament prorogued for four months in March, 1964,[36] to avoid a possible defeat in the House and to negotiate with the Left parties for the kind of support which her husband had enjoyed between 1956 and the end of 1958. By the beginning of June the negotiations were complete and three Samasamajists entered the Cabinet. The result was to split the United Left Front and the LSSP, to bring Samasamajists into office for the first time, to give Mrs. Bandaranaike the co-operation of most of the Leftwing unions and to supply her with a Minister of Finance in N. M. Perera.[37]

Although the Coalition did not last long as a government, it remained the basis for radical politics despite its electoral defeat in March 1965. In retrospect it seems a natural alliance, polarising the radical and conservative elements at last. As a government, however, the Coalition was to be faced with three potential threats, from the trade unions, from organised Buddhist opponents of N. M. Perera's Budget and from an alliance of the newspapers, the UNP and conservative sections of the SLFP objecting to plans to nationalise the press. It was this latter alliance which was to bring down the Coalition and put the UNP into power for the next five years. On 3 December, 1964 thirteen SLFP M.P.s defected under the leadership of C. P. de Silva, the Minister of Lands. The vote in the House which overthrew Mrs. Bandaranaike was 74 to 73 and the resulting bitterness against the SLFP defectors and the two 'revolutionary' Samasamajists who joined them[38] can be imagined. Despite the narrow margin, the vote was unmistakably one of confidence and Mrs. Bandaranaike announced the dissolution of parliament. She also decided to step down from the Senate, from which leadership had proved difficult and to contest her husband's former electorate of Attanagalla. The election of March 1965 saw the leaders of the Buddhist clergy clearly aligned against the Coalition because of its Marxist element: so wide was the UNP's range of support that it extended from the Sinhala communalists to the Ceylon Workers Congress. And the result was a 'National Government' with a majority of over forty and support from six parties, some of which were normally bitter enemies.

The next five years were remarkably stable. Western aid was restored and with guidance from the World Bank and under the direction of Gamini Corea, Permanent Secretary of the Planning Ministry, the economy began to improve in conventional terms. Rice production started to rise rapidly with the introduction of new methods. Yet the problem of unemployment remained acute, the terms of trade continued to deteriorate and the population continued to rise more rapidly than in most countries. While the National Government brought stability and relative communal harmony, it could not hold the loyalty of the voters. Nor was it allowed to resolve the communal problem on lines desired by its partner, the Federal Party. On 8 January, 1966 the three Coalition parties, the SLFP, LSSP and Communists, organised a day of public mourning and a march to demand regulations for the 'reasonable use of Tamil'. In the renewed atmosphere of tension there was an attempt at an army coup in the following month. Although this was farcical and incompetent the government took the opportunity of suspending and later arresting Major-General Richard Udugama, the SLFP appointed commander, and the Ven. Henpitegedara Gnanaseeha, a monk active in SLFP politics.[39] They, together with other defendants, were not released until 1969 when no evidence was found to convict them.

These events proved to be the end of serious dissension, rather than the beginning of a new round, although the UNP retained emergency powers for over three years. There were strikes against devaluation in 1967 and regular disturbances at the universities. These were, however, quite normal and do not affect the generalisation that constitutional government was never seriously challenged. The UNP made genuine efforts to come to terms with the Ceylon Tamils. Yet despite relative harmony and economic improvement the UNP began to lose support at local elections from 1968, probably due to the intractable problem of unemployment which had been with every government since 1952. The government was badly defeated in the elections of May 1970 when the three Coalition parties gained nearly half the votes and three-quarters of the seats. Their Common Programme was radical socialist and three Samasamajists and one Communist sat in the Cabinet. The changeover was perfectly peaceful. In ten years Ceylon had moved a long way from confusion, communal strife and near collapse.

Ceylon becomes Sri Lanka

Mrs. Bandaranaike's victory on 27 May, 1970 fully justified the decision taken six years before to forge a permanent alliance between the Sri Lanka Freedom Party, the Samasamajists and the Communists. Never before had there been so many officially committed Marxists in parliament. There was a strong contingent of socialists and admirers of Russia or China in the governing party as well.[40] The new government strengthened the friendly ties with China which had existed since 1953, broke relations with Israel, recognised the Provisional Government of South Vietnam and began to look towards Eastern Europe for technical assistance. None of this altered Ceylon's continuing reliance on the World Bank or on tea exports to Britain, nor was the pro-Chinese orientation allowed to damage relations with India and the Soviet Union. In general the political atmosphere was more sympathetic to the Communist world than previously, even if the reality of Ceylon's trading position made it very much a dependency of the international capitalist system.

Conservatism and pro-Westernism were seriously, perhaps permanently, damaged. The United National Party held its vote well and gained slightly more support than the SLFP. The Coalition tactic of eliminating split contests was completely effective in reducing the UNP to a derisory seventeen seats. Moreover it lost much of its talent. Its two remaining national figures, Dudley Senanayake and J. R. Jayawardena, conflicted openly within a short period of the defeat. While the Federal Party retained most of its following, the SLFP for the first time began to build a viable base among the Tamils. Mrs. Bandaranaike could claim to have a government which was every bit as 'national' as that which it replaced. The Federal Party and the UNP, who made up most of the Opposition, were no longer on good terms and the Federalists were to isolate themselves even further by refusing to participate in the Constituent Assembly set up to draft a new constitution. With a two-thirds majority and an ineffectual and divided opposition, Mrs. Bandaranaike seemed able to offer the strongest government seen in Ceylon since Dudley Senanayake's landslide victory of 1952. Yet just as in that previous period, there were forces outside the parliamentary arena which made it difficult, and for a time impossible, to rule effectively and to achieve the promises made at the election.

The government had, apparently unknown to itself, been placed on probation by a well organised and largely secret youth front, the Janatha Vimukthi Peramuna.[41] This group had not contested elections and was thus unnoticed by the press and by most politicians until just before the 1970 election. Student protest groups had arisen in Ceylon many times and most of their leaders had subsequently become lawyers, politicians and even ministers. Police attention began to focus on the JVP in preparation for the 1970 election when it was normal to report on groups likely to cause disturbances at the polls. The Criminal Investigation Department believed that "the group has a very strongly organised network of saboteurs spreading through the country. It is believed that all members of this group are either university students or unemployed graduates and belong to the age group of 18 to 52".[42] With the change of government very little was done about the JVP until August, 1970 when an 'insurgent unit' was set up by the police.

The JVP ran a successful campaign of public rallies for several months at which the general theme was that the youth who had put Mrs. Bandaranaike into power now expected her to fulfil promises to find employment for them. An increasing threat was that provocative acts would goad the movement into retaliation.[43] Had it not been for an armed attack on the American embassy on 6 March, 1971, and the consequent declaration of a state of emergency and the arrest of the JVP leader, Rohan Wijeweera, the JVP might have been able to build its clandestine strength even more effectively. That the revolt which broke out on 5 April was ostensibly without a central leadership is an indication of the skill with which the JVP had built up its system of contacts, had indoctrinated thousands of youth through classes, lectures and camps, had gathered uniforms and weapons, pinpointed strategic targets and penetrated the police, military and government systems.[44]

The aftermath of the revolt was tragic. It is generally believed that at least five thousand were killed, including many in the Kegalle district. Fifteen thousand were interned in camps. The education system ceased to function and the Vidyodaya and Vidyalankara universities became internment camps. Economic disruption was estimated at 400 million rupees and what external aid was made available by the Chinese and others was used to expand the armed forces or to repair the damage. The economy declined once more and the payments balance became acute. Democratic institutions were damaged despite the government's declared intention to restore normal conditions. Local authority elections were suspended and the first by-elections for parliament were not held until over a year after the end of the revolt. Censorship continued throughout 1971 as did the Colombo curfew. Arrests were still being made at the end of 1971. The size of the armed forces was trebled and the police force

doubled. Because of the large number of internees awaiting trial
the government thought it necessary to bypass the normal legal
procedures which had proved so ineffective in dealing with the
coups of 1962 and 1966. After two-and-a-half years of exhaustive and publicly recorded trial, judgement was finally
handed down in December 1974. In contrast to the summary
death suffered by many JVP activists and suspects in 1971, the
leaders were treated with considerable leniency with the
maintenance of the convention that no-one engaged in political
activity, however radical, should be executed. Those detained
without trial were released for rehabilitation and some returned
to active politics, often in the Youth Leagues of the LSSP or
the Communist Party. A small minority reverted to planning
further guerilla operations, but the greatly improved security
arrangements which the 1971 insurgency had prompted, proved
quite capable of limiting the potential of such groups as were
formed.

The new republic of Sri Lanka proceeded to carry out the
programme of the Coalition, which extended its own life until
1977 under the provision of the new constitution which made
the electoral interval a maximum of six years. The United
National Party took exception to this extension and launched
civil disobedience campaigns in 1973 and 1975 which threatened
the stability of the system, prolonged government under
emergency regulations, but did not lead to the suspension of
democratic procedures, nor even to the postponement of the
many by-elections which the SLFP consistently lost. Potentially
more disruptive was the opposition of the Tamil parties to a
constitution which enshrined unitary government. Overcoming
their historic differences the Federal Party, some of the Tamil
Congress, Tamil separatists and the Ceylon Workers Congress
came together in 1972 to form a Tamil United Front which, in
the light of the increasing futility of asking for federal government, reformed in 1976 as a Tamil Liberation Front pledged to
the creation of a separate Tamil state. Both movements were
met with repression, especially of their militant youth wings,
while the murder of the former mayor of Jaffna, Alfred
Durayappah, in 1975, suggested that those who co-operated with
the Sinhalese dominated Coalition were risking more than their
political popularity. Despite attempts by Mrs. Bandaranaike to

make friendly gestures towards the Ceylon Tamils, the political isolation of the Jaffna peninsula and the growing problems of its educated youth, seemed as threatening as the continued frustrations of the younger members of the majority community.[45]

The Coalition was intended to be something more than the guardian of Sinhalese interests and it moved progressively towards achieving the socialist objectives which had attracted the LSSP and the Communists. The major remaining private sectors of the economy were progressively nationalised, culminating in 1975 with the final extinction of the British-owned plantation sector. By 1976 plantations, agency houses, banking, insurance, most of the press and much of wholesaling and retailing were under the control of state corporations or co-operatives. Important individuals in the Sinhalese and Indian business communities had been placed on trial before the Criminal Justice Commission for currency offences. Land redistribution and the transfer of assets to state plantation corporations were well advanced, while income ceilings and compulsory saving schemes attempted to divert private resources towards public objectives. None of this necessarily meant that the Ceylonese upper classes were eliminated, nor that private ownership of land, retailing, minor commerce, entertainment and small industries did not remain and even expand. The leadership of all major parties was firmly in the hands of the professional classes, themselves substantial owners of private property. Yet Sri Lanka had more of the characteristic features of a socialist society than any other non-Communist state in Asia, while still retaining a functioning parliamentary democracy. Within the governing Coalition, as in the Opposition parties, there were widely differing views on the extent to which democracy and socialism were to be maintained or even extended. By 1976 the UNP leader, J. R. Jayawardena, having defeated the group surrounding relatives of the Senanayakes, was able to declare that the major "conservative" party in Sri Lanka was, in fact, socialist and had no intention of reversing any of the socialist measures introduced by the Coalition, however critical it might be of what it considered undemocratic or unconstitutional trends. Within the Coalition itself the SLFP began to develop quite distinct Left and Right wings, around

the persons of Mrs. Bandaranaike's daughter, Sunethra
Rupasinghe and her son, Anura. By mid-1975 the latter was
dominant and growing unease about the entrenching of LSSP
influence in the Ministries under its control led to the exclusion
of the LSSP from the government and its loss of effective
political power after five years in office.

The new society which was being created was thus socialist
and democratic, yet under the control of still-Anglicised
politicians and public servants, with the governing party more
firmly dominated by the Bandaranaikes and Ratwattes than
ever before, families which had enjoyed the most important
political positions under the British since the middle of the
nineteenth century.[46] While the position of the Sinhala language
and the Buddhist religion were constitutionally entrenched, the
new political arrangements did nothing in themselves to rectify
the economic problems revealed by the rising of 1971. International indebtedness grew, particularly with the increasing cost
of imported fuel, while the levels of unemployment rose steadily
in line with trends in the developed world on which Sri Lanka
depended for most of its markets. World inflation and recession
after 1973 simply made matters very much worse for economies
like that of Sri Lanka, even where its previous dependence on
the stagnant British economy was progressively reduced. Efforts
to reorient trade and aid towards the Arab oil producers had
some success while the continuing relationship with China was
a stabilising influence in limited areas of trade. Yet nothing
could prevent the steady erosion of the relatively sound economic position reached by the late 1960s. The Sri Lanka government, while it could nationalise foreign enterprises within the
country, could not control their operations overseas nor have any
influence on the policies of international agencies or multi-
national corporations. Sri Lanka became less "dependent" on
its former colonial power throughout the decade leading up to
the 1977 elections, but this in no way diminished its total
vulnerability to world economic trends. It was not enmeshed in
costly military alliances, yet its own internal security position
made a shift towards higher defence costs inevitable after 1971.
It was not sought out as an investment area by multi-national
corporations, yet its very unattractiveness to foreign capital
raised as many problems as such investment might have

brought. Whatever astrologers might have said, the Republic of Sri Lanka which was inaugurated under the new Constitution on 22 May, 1972, had much less to be optimistic about than the new state of Ceylon created in 1948. The achievement of the formal aspects of the "Bandaranaike revolution", which the new Constitution marked, were less important than the creation of a viable and self-reliant economy on which to base the future.

NOTES

1. For discussions of the economic and political effects of the subsidised rice ration see: D. R. Snodgrass: *Ceylon—an Export Economy in Transition*; Homewood, Ill.; 1966, pp. 78–9 (and pp. 160–163 for the Guaranteed Price Scheme for paddy purchase begun in 1948); H. Wriggins: *Ceylon—Dilemmas of a New Nation*; Princeton, 1960, pp. 74–76; F. Nyrop: *Area Handbook for Ceylon*; Washington, 1971, pp. 252–3 and the ILO Report: *Matching Employment Opportunities and Expectations*; Geneva, 1971, pp. 205–6.
2. For many years Ceylon spent less than 3% of its Budget on defence; see e.g. Central Bank of Ceylon; *Annual Report*; Colombo, 1968; Table 22. For evidence of the tiny number of British troops in Ceylon before the First World War see L. Woolf: *Growing*; London, 1961.
3. See R. N. Kearney *et al.*: "The 1915 Riots in Ceylon—a Symposium'; *Journal of Asian Studies* XXIX, 2; February 1970.
4. Ceylon (State Council) Order in Council, 1931; s.9 (b); see also the *Report of the Special Commission on the Constitution 1928 (Donoughmore Report)*. Cmd. 3131; and S. Namasivayam: *The Legislatures of Ceylon*; London, 1951.
5. For more on communal politics see Chapters 2 and 5.
6. See H. A. J. Hulugalle: *The Life and Times of D. R. Wijewardene*; Colombo, 1960.
7. Anagarika Dharmapala (David Hewavitarane) came from the prosperous family which founded the Don Carolis Furniture Company and had its origins near Matara. He adopted the title *anagarika* in 1886 and worked with the American Theosophist Colonel Olcott in founding the Buddhist Theosophical Society schools. He was interned by the British from 1915 to 1920 and died in 1930.
8. See Kumari Jayawardene: *The Rise of the Labor Movement in Ceylon*: Durham, N.C., 1972.
9. See *Report of the Commission on Constitutional Reform 1945 (Soulbury Report)*; Cmd. 6677 (Colombo reprint 1969); Sir Charles Jeffries: *Ceylon—the Path to Independence*; London, 1962 and his *OEG—Sir Oliver Goonetilleke*; London, 1969.
10. Ponnambalam stood out for the so-called '50–50' arrangement whereby half the new legislature would be drawn from the non-Sinhalese minorities.

11. Table 2 (p. 11) of the ILO Report (*op. cit.*) shows annual average terms of trade (export prices divided by import prices x 100) as follows: 1952–6: 142; 1957–60: 144; 1961–7: 119; 1968–70: 88.
12. Although Wriggins: *op. cit.*, p. 330, argues that the UNP probably estimated that opposition to them would be more effectively organised during Buddha Jayanti. I. D. S. Weerawardena: *Ceylon General Election 1956*; Colombo, 1960, believed that the campaign against a Buddha Jayanti election was 'in a sense a part of the anti-UNP campaign' (p. 18).
13. For a full account of the monks' involvement in 1956 see D. E. Smith (ed.): *South Asian Politics and Religion*; Princeton, 1966, esp. Chapters 21 and 22.
14. The *Dasa Panatha* are reproduced by I. D. S. Weerawardena: *op. cit.* at p. 146. They were: to practice non-violence, to oppose injustice, to implement the Buddhist Commission Report, to make Sinhala the only official language, to defend democracy against fascism and communism and acts of the UNP government, to promote national arts and ayurvedic medicine, to give Buddhism its rightful place without restricting freedom of religion, to manage public affairs, to bring happiness to all, to distribute wealth more fairly, to refuse state assistance to institutions not promoting communal harmony or peace and equality among peoples.
15. From a feature series "Background to Politics"; *Ceylon Observer* 17/7/1962.
16. Groups in the MEP included the Viplavakari Lanka Samasamaja Party of Philip Gunawardena, the Basha Peramuna of W. Dahanayake and a group of independents including I.M.R.A. Iriyagolle, T. B. Subasinghe, Hugh Fernando and Lakshman Rajapakse. They had nothing much in common except strong local, personal followings.
17. I. D. S. Weerawardena: *op. cit.* pp. 233–4. For other accounts of the 1956 election see H. Wriggins: *op. cit.* Chapter 9; and R. N. Kearney: *Communalism and Language in the Politics of Ceylon*; Durham N.C., 1967, Chapter 4.
18. The Act is reproduced in Kearney *op cit.*, Appendix One.
19. The Bandaranaike—Chelvanayakam Pact is reproduced by Kearney as Appendix Two.
20. See Tarzie Vittachi: *Emergency '58*; London, 1958, esp. pp. 68–82 and A. J. Wilson: "The Governor-General and the State of Emergency; May 1958–March 1959"; *Ceylon Journal of Historical and Social Studies* II (1959), 2.
21. See L. G. Weeramantry: *Assassination of a Prime Minister*; Geneva, 1969. Somarama was ordained a monk in 1929 and educated at the Vidyodaya and Vidyalankara *pirivenas*. He worked for Mrs. Wimala Wijewardena (SLFP) in the Kelaniya election of 1952 and became a lecturer at the Ayurvedic College in Colombo in 1957.
22. Mentioned in the trial proceedings though not necessarily directly involved were two Ministers, Stanley de Zoysa and Mrs. Wimala Wijewardena, de Zoysa's two brothers (one of whom was third in

command of the police force), H. P. Jayawardene, president of the Advisory Board of Indigenous Medicine, Dr. Carolis Amerasinghe, chairman of Kolonnawa Urban Council and, most important of all, Ven. Mapitigama Buddarakkitha, founder of the Eksath Bhikkhu Peramuna. Jayawardene and Buddharakkitha eventually received life sentences. Also involved, though not convicted, were Lionel Goone-tilleke a former police officer, Newton Perera a police officer, Ossie Corea and Anura de Silva. See the *Report of the Bandaranaike Assassination Commission*: S.P. III—1965.

23. *Ceylon Observer* 25/1/1960.

24. *Ceylon Observer* 28/3/1960.

25. For a discussion of the constitutionality of this decision see A. J. Wilson: "The Governor-General and the Two Dissolutions of Parliament—December 5, 1959 and April 23, 1960"; *Ceylon Journal of Historical and Social Studies* III: 2; July–December 1960.

26. *Ceylon Daily News* 29/4/1960 and *Ceylon Observer* 1/6/1960.

27. *Times of Ceylon* 25/5/1960.

28. See G. Ponniah: *Satyagraha and the Freedom Movement of the Tamils in Ceylon*; Jaffna, 1963.

29. See Chapter 5.

30. Felix Dias Bandaranaike was made responsible for the military operations to counter the *satyagraha*, which aroused bitter feelings because of the behaviour of the military towards civilians.

31. Charges were eventually made against twenty-four. The most import-ant arrested were C. C. Dissanayake (DIG Police), John Pulle (ASP Police). Sidney de Zoysa (DIG Police), Colonel Maurice de Mel (Army), Col. F. C. de Saram, Lt. Col. B. R. Jesudason, Lt. Col. W. Abraham, Lt. Col. J. H. V. de Alwis, Lt. Col. Noel Matthysz, and D. J. F. D. Liyanage a Ceylon Civil Servant. In addition four Majors, four Captains and eight police officers were arrested while Col. de Mel's brother Royce remained at large until the trial, which eventually lasted for four years.

32. This allowed the suspension of *habeas corpus* and the nomination of judges by the government. It was retrospective and as such was con-demned by the International Commission of Jurists and ultimately was judged unconstitutional by the Privy Council. See *Law Quarterly Review* vol. 82, no. 237, July 1966, pp. 289–91 and H. W. R. Wade: *Annual Survey of Commonwealth Law 1966*, pp. 57–59. The Privy Council decision led the UNP government to abandon proceedings in 1966.

33. As Minister for Finance, Felix Dias Bandaranaike proposed a cut in the rice ration in his August 1962 Budget. The major unions and the LSSP agitated for his resignation which was achieved.

34. The government's nationalisation of oil installations without agreed compensation brought into operation the "Hickenlooper Amend-ment" which provided for the automatic cancellation of American aid to any country expropriating the property of American nationals. Aid

was resumed in 1965 after the UNP government renegotiated the terms of compensation.

35. *Ceylon Observer* 2/1/1964.

36. *Ceylon Observer* 13/3/1964.

37. Mrs. Bandaranaike in an interview with the *Ceylon Observer* (20/9/1964) said that the LSSP "plays a dominant role among the urban working class", that government corporations could not function without working-class co-operation, and that there were no basic differences between the two parties as the LSSP had "eschewed revolution".

38. Meryl Fernando and Edmund Samarakkody.

39. The group behind the coup were said at the trial to be "extreme Buddhist elements in the Army". (*Ceylon Daily News* 31/7/1969) It subsequently emerged that Rohan Wijeweera who later founded the Janatha Vimukthi Peramuna, was marginally involved under the pseudonym of "Dr. Tissa". Most of those allegedly taking part were of low rank.

40. At Ratnapura in August, 1970 a rally was addressed by the SLFP Mayor, its own and ten other M.P.s and two junior ministers, Ratne Deshapriya Senanayake and Ratnasiri Wickramanayake. Pictures of Mao, Trotsky and Guevara were displayed and the rally demanded the nationalisation of all foreign assets. All sponsors were in the SLFP and were subsequently reprimanded by Mrs. Bandaranaike (*Ceylon Daily News* 13/8/1970).

41. For a full analysis of the JVP see Chapter 10.

42. *Sun* (Colombo) 30/4/1970.

43. Rohan Wijeweera said at a Hyde Park, Colombo rally of the JVP that "we will strike when we are provoked to do so by the armed forces which are now trying to accuse us of conspiracy". *Ceylon Daily News* 28/2/1971.

44. See Urmilla Phadnis: "Insurgency in Ceylon Politics—Problems and Prospects"; *Institute for Defense Studies and Analysis Journal* (New Delhi) 3: 4, April 1971.

45. For an up-to-date discussion of the Tamil political situation see Walter Schwarz: *The Tamils of Sri Lanka*; Minority Rights Group, London; 1975.

46. Of the eight Low Country Sinhalese nominated to the Legislative Council between 1843 and 1911, only one was not a member of the Dias Bandaranaike/Obeyesekera families. See K. M. de Silva (ed.): *History of Ceylon*, vol. 3; Colombo Apothecaries, Colombo; 1973; p. 248.

CHAPTER 2

Politics and Society

Sri Lankan politics is best undertsood against a background of consistent Western penetration into a feudal agricultural society, having an ancient civilisation, itself previously disrupted by invaders from the equally ancient culture of Tamil South India. The Island's recorded history begins with the invasion of Vijaya and his North Indian band over two thousand five hundred years ago. Constant interaction with the Tamils forms the basis of current fears of Sinhala isolation in a Dravidian sea. Knowledge of the great civilisations of Anuradhapura and later Polonnaruwa strengthen the belief that Sri Lanka was a major culture while the British were still primitive farmers. These cities, too, were destroyed by Tamil invasion, heightening the sense of continuous conflict. The modern exposition of history in Sinhalese school texts has thus become a major element socialising the majority population into the belief that it is at once the inheritor of a more ancient culture than any of its invaders and, at the same time, is continually threatened. The whole tenor of Buddhist teaching for over a thousand years has been in this tradition. Both through formal education and transmitted legends, the Sinhalese Buddhist believes himself to be the guardian of a social system which might have been the most advanced in the world had it not been for foreign intervention.

What has been stressed less readily in recent years, is that there is no aspect of local culture which is not profoundly affected from elsewhere. This is true of Buddhism, which is totally permeated with Hindu practices and beliefs, including animal reincarnation, the intercession of many gods and the caste basis of the major Buddhist sect. It is true of the racial composition of the Sinhalese, who have been subjected to centuries of Tamil interbreeding such that the very term "race" is seldom used and has very little real meaning.[1] While Sinhalese and Tamil certainly have racial stereotypes about each other these can rarely be sustained in actual situations of confrontation. During the communal riots of 1958, for instance, the only test which could be applied to suspected Tamils by roving Sinhalese hooligans was that of language, as there were few visible signs of difference.[2] Similarly, the Muslim peasants of the East Coast or the Catholics of the West, are not visibly distinctive from those Tamils and Buddhist Sinhalese amongst whom they live. Even the Burghers, the most self-consciously "pure" of the minorities, vary considerably in their skin, eye or hair colouring.

This racial and religious intermingling has not, however, produced a single Ceylonese nation and in recent years the consciousness of the past has exacerbated differences between the various communities left behind by successive invasions. There has been a recrudescence of consciousness of language, religion, national community and caste. These factors were always present but the colonial system tended to obscure them by its creation of an English-educated professional class based to some extent on merit rather than status. Despite this apparent return to pre-colonial concerns, the influence of Europeans for over four hundred and fifty years has been unmistakable and irreversible. The most militant national revivalists are themselves the products of British education and of nineteenth century liberal, radical, nationalist and evangelical notions. The continuing influence of aristocracy, whether the Kandyan *dissawas* or the Low Country *mudaliyars,* reflects the British adaptation of a system which resembled an idealised version of their own and which they used as the cheapest way of preserving order. The very wealth of the upper classes themselves, while it may derive from land originally held on feudal tenures has depended since the abolition of compulsory labour obligations (*rajakariya*) in 1832, on the plantation economy introduced originally by the Dutch and greatly expanded by the British. In no important respect, whether it be the education system, transport, plantations, banking and exporting, universal suffrage, parliamentary institutions or political parties, has Sri Lanka remained a traditional society. On the contrary it is a largely modernised society in its economic and political arrangements, but one in which the bulk of the people still live, think, act and worship in traditional ways. Even those ways are rarely, if ever, directly traceable in their pure form to classical Sri Lanka.

The degree to which modern practices have penetrated can be illustrated by the extent of the welfare state in Ceylon. Already, before independence, political pressures and the necessities of wartime had produced free, universal education and a free health scheme based on dispensaries and public hospitals. Subsidised rice, including a free weekly measure for all rice rationbook holders, ensured that the basic food was available to all. The suppression of malaria during the war, coupled with the health and food subsidy policies, raised the expectation of life to European levels by the early years of independence. The education system, while not effectively compulsory, raised the literacy level to 75% by 1965. Labour regulations adopted initially in 1935 gave Ceylon an elaborate arbitration system, while further measures adopted by the Bandaranaike government after 1956 gave some degree of financial protection against unemployment and retirement. By 1960 Ceylon could claim to have the most effective welfare state in Asia and one which, in some basic respects, was superior to those of North America or parts of Western Europe.[3] The fact that much of this was vitiated by rising unemployment and depressed incomes does not invalidate the point that the Ceylon peasant and worker was fully enmeshed in welfare economics and social provisions unthinkable in a traditional society. Families still looked after their own members while astrologers and interceders with the gods flourished side by side with state provision of welfare, education and basic protection.

This intermingling of indigenous, external and modernising influences has given politics three dimensions. There has been a marked attempt to use politics for the reassertion of non-Western values and institutions. There has been an emphasis on communalism as a way of asserting the rights of the Sinhala Buddhist majority over groups whose privileges derived from past invasions. There has also been a powerful movement to preserve and advance the social measures of wholly Western inspiration introduced between 1940 and 1960. The issues in local politics are responses to these different levels of historical experience.

Communities

More than two millenia of invasion and foreign penetration have left Sri Lanka with a highly complex communal structure. It is the only country in the world with substantial representation from the four major religions of Buddhism, Hinduism, Christianity and Islam. Its population includes two major ethnic divisions, the Indo-Aryan and the Dravidian, while its tiny aboriginal Veddah group is probably of Australoid type. The Census only recognises a limited number of communities, a term which it does not define, but which in normal Ceylonese parlance includes elements of race, religion and culture. These officially acknowledged communities are Low Country Sinhalese (4,470,000 in 1963 or 42.2%), Kandyan Sinhalese (3,043,000; 28.8%), Ceylon Tamils (1,165,000; 11%), Indian Tamils (1,123,000; 10.6%), Ceylon Moors (627,000; 5.9%), Indian Moors (55,000; 0.5%), Burghers and Eurasians (46,000; 0.5%), Malays (33,000; 0.3%) and Others (20,000; 0.2%).[4] The last category includes Europeans and Chinese. Some of the distinctions made here are necessarily vague, although presented in strict statistical classes. There are many Sinhalese-speaking people of Tamil origin in the Chilaw and Negombo areas, a few Sinhalese-speaking Hindus and some small but economically important Indian groups who are neither Tamils nor Moors. Nevertheless the communities as described formed the basis of much social and educational policy, including the distribution of parliamentary constituencies, and the selection of Nominated Members of the House of Representatives and Senators.

The raw figures for communities disguise a great deal of complexity. Not only are some communities blurred at their edges, but within themselves they contain important sub-groups which are often self-contained and endogamous. Thus while it is true that marriage between communities is almost unknown,[5] it is equally true that marriage, the disposal of property and the distribution of political favours may be as rigidly controlled within a community as between it and another. Were this not so it is probable that political parties would have formed purely

on a communal basis with very little leeway for partisan competition within an area dominated by one community. While
there are strong communal bases for some parties and most
candidates, there is still considerable competition within communities, whether between language groups, religions, castes,
families or ideological groupings.

The largest community, the Low Country Sinhalese, represent
those most subject to European influence. The majority of
Christians belong to this community but it is still overwhelmingly
Buddhist, particularly in the Southern Province where it is
least intermingled with others. Its geographical spread is from
Chilaw in North Western Province, where it is largely Catholic,
to Hambantota District in Southern Province where it is wholly
Buddhist. The Western Province, including Colombo, has the
largest numerical concentration of Low Country Sinhalese.
They form slightly less than half the population within the
Colombo municipal limits, being much more strongly concentrated in the outer suburbs of Dehiwela-Mount Lavinia, Kotte
and Kolonnawa. They are also preponderant in the large
coastal towns of Negombo, Moratuwa, Panadura, Kalutara
and Galle, form the largest single community in Kandy and are
a significant element in Trincomalee. Thus not only have the
Low Country Sinhalese been subject to European contact since
1505, but a large part of them live under urban influences. Not
surprisingly, they have furnished the leadership of the Marxist
parties, the United National Party and, to a lesser extent, the
Sri Lanka Freedom Party. The Low Country Sinhalese have
been predominant in the professions and what there is of
Sinhalese business. They are not a monolithic community,
since they contain a large Christian element and are strongly
affected by politically significant caste divisions.

The Kandyan Sinhalese are those living under Kandyan,
rather than Roman-Dutch law and inhabiting the inland area of
the Kandyan kingdom, which remained independent until
1815.[6] They are almost entirely Buddhist and rural, forming
less than one-third of the population of Kandy town and being
mixed with substantial Muslim or Low Country elements even
in smaller towns like Badulla, Matale or Kegalle. Kandyan
social structure still reflects the hierarchical system formally
abolished by the British in 1832. Dominant families still receive

obeisance from inferiors, monastic lands form an important economic enclave and primitive beliefs and practices are common. Poverty is widespread, particularly in the Dry Zone Kandyan areas of North Central and Uva Provinces.[7] Landlessness became an increasing problem and in 1951 a full-scale enquiry was published from which the Paddy Lands Act of 1958 eventually emerged. Sociological surveys among Kandyans suggest that they, too, are influenced by non-peasant ways, in particular in seeking employment to supplement their income.[8] Not surprisingly, many of the politicians coming from the Kandyans have belonged to aristocratic families. Yet, despite its traditional aspects, which include a high level of illiteracy, the Kandyan area is the scene of hard fought political struggles and massive electoral turnout.

The Ceylon Tamils are the only community to sustain parties with purely communal appeals, in particular the Tamil Congress whose rules confine membership to Tamils.[9] The Federal Party, although appealing to Muslims as well, has done so on the basis that they speak Tamil and therefore have a common interest. Ceylon Tamils are highly concentrated in Northern Province where only Jaffna town has sizeable communities of Moors and Indians. They are also strongly represented in Eastern Province, form a bare majority of the population of Trincomalee town; and also maintain a sizeable community in Colombo of about one-eighth of the population. Thus while most Ceylon Tamils are rural dwellers they are as subject to urban influences as the Low Country Sinhalese, have as high a level of literacy, have been under continual European influence in Jaffna for three hundred years and contain a large Christian minority. Like the Low Country Sinhalese they have developed a professional and political élite. Indeed the first "educated Ceylonese" elected to the Legislative Council in 1911 was the Tamil Sir Ponnambalam Ramanathan. Jaffna Tamils, migrating to Colombo, were able to secure positions in law, the public service and politics, making them a privileged group in the eyes of many Sinhalese.

The Indian Tamils are the least privileged of any community, despite periodic claims to the contrary by Sinhalese politicians.[10] The great bulk of them are tea plantation workers, whose families were brought to Ceylon from South India between 1850 and 1940. Under the Citizenship Act of 1948 even those born in Ceylon of parents born in Ceylon, were still regarded as aliens and deprived of the vote. They have no local government influence, being barred from electing Village Councillors, and find it difficult to leave the estates. Many areas of employment, particularly in state agencies, are barred to Indian Tamils. Schools were controlled by the estates, despite repeated promises to bring them under state control and little over half of Indian Tamils are literate, the lowest level for any community. Under the Indian and Pakistani Residents (Citizenship) Act of 1949, provision was made for registration of permanent residents and after various abortive conferences with the Indian government the repatriation of nearly half the Indian Tamil population was agreed in 1964 and legislated for in 1967. Both registration and repatriation were very slow until 1971 and under-employment and overpopulation on the estates were becoming a serious problem.

The rest of the Indian population off the estates may be divided between Indian Tamils forming a manual labouring class in Colombo, Kandy, Jaffna and Trincomalee, and Indian Moors and others, who are mainly in trade. The latter group, while also liable to deprivation of citizenship, have long exercised control over retail trade and importing. The small communities of Chettiars, Borahs, Sindhis and Malayalis were particularly entrenched in textile and food importing. Most of the nationalisation measures introduced in importing since 1956 have been directed against them but their position remains very strong. As businessmen and aliens they play a cautious role in politics although many were said to contribute to United National Party funds after 1949 in order to secure Temporary Residence Permits or Distinguished Citizenship enabling them to remain in Ceylon.

The Ceylon Moors, too, are mainly engaged in trade although there is a large peasant population in Eastern Province, where they are one third of the inhabitants. Most other Moors are town dwelling, being particularly concentrated in central Colombo, Galle, Kandy and Jaffna. The Muslim population also includes the Malays, who live mainly in Colombo and Hambantota. These speak either Malay or English, while most Moors speak Tamil though those from the Western and Southern Provinces more normally speak Sinhalese. Thus the

Muslims, while not divided by caste, are divided between language groups, between peasants, merchants and workers, and between those of Arab, Indian and Malay origin.

The only other significant community, the Burghers, are no more homogeneous than the rest despite their small numbers. The highest class from which many professionals, public servants and politicians have come, are those registered by the Dutch Burgher Union as of pure European descent on both sides. Their language is English but religiously they are divided between Catholics and the Dutch Reformed Church. Nearly all Dutch Burghers are urban dwelling, mainly in Colombo and Mount Lavinia, well educated and prosperous. There are, however, other groups, more properly called Eurasians, and the Portuguese Burghers, some of whom still speak Portuguese three hundred years after their ancestors were driven out. These are not so economically fortunate. In recent years about half the Burgher population has emigrated to Australia, Britain and Canada, having lost their particularly favoured position under the British. Nevertheless Burghers are still represented in parliament, the professions, the judiciary and police and form a vocal section of the middle-class Christian population of Colombo.

Each of these communities is divided. Caste is important among the Sinhalese and vital among the Tamils. Religion divides both these communities whereas for the Muslims it represents almost the only common bond. In recent years language has become the most important dividing line of all. It gave political solidarity to Tamils of all castes and even produced some tentative alliances between Ceylon and Indian Tamils, who are otherwise quite distinct. The appeal of Sinhala Only, raised by Bandaranaike in 1956, was as strong to Christians as to Buddhists. Indeed the major responsibility for public policies designed to carry through the slogan rested between 1960 and 1964 with a Muslim Minister for Education and with two Christian Cabinet Ministers, Sam C. P. Fernando and Felix Dias Bandaranaike. For ten years, from the passing of the Official Language Act in 1956, until the promulgation of the Reasonable Use of Tamil regulations in 1966, language was more important in determining communal political allegiances than anything else.

While the struggle over language policy divided the Sinhalese from the Tamil, its origins lay in attempts to limit the privileges of yet another "community", the English-educated. These were drawn from all racial, religious and caste groups, mainly on the basis of wealth and service to the colonial power. Since their entire middle-class was not only literate in English, but used it almost as a mother tongue, Colombo, Jaffna and Kandy were all dominated by a cultural minority which had considerable solidarity based on a common culture. Not until July 28, 1948 was the first Sinhala speech made in the legislature.[11] So entrenched was English among the educated that Sir Ivor Jennings could write *after* independence that "since a knowledge of English is spreading downwards through the social classes, it is easier to imagine the triumph of English than that of the national languages."[12] From this "sub-community" of less than 10% of the population, came virtually all the political leaders, all the professionals and most of the important businessmen and plantation owners. Despite the victory of 1956 and the consequent legalisation of Sinhala Only, it was not until 1970 that a Cabinet Minister was chosen, in Tikiri Banda Tennekoon, Minister for Social Services, who had not been educated wholly or largely in English. The politically effective, whether politicians or public servants, gained their knowledge of institutions and practices through the English language and almost entirely from Britain. This has been as potent a factor in local politics as any other.

Religion

Sri Lanka has large numbers of Buddhists (66.3%), Hindus (18.5%), Catholics (6.8%), Muslims (6.7%) and Protestants (1.6%). With the exception of the Protestants these have all been established for over four hundred years and embrace many rural communities. It is part of local history, as taught in schools and reiterated by politicians, that Buddhism has pride of place. This it gains not merely because two-thirds of the people adhere to it but, more emotively, because Sri Lanka is seen as having preserved Therevada Buddhism in its purest form, sending out missionaries to Burma and Thailand, and receiving reciprocal support from them in later centuries.

Because of their isolation from other Buddhist centres, the Sinhalese have clung fiercely to their religion, believing it to be in constant peril from the Christianity of the colonisers and the Hinduism of the Tamils. This sense of beleaguerment reinforces the associated fears of the Sinhalese when faced with their linguistic isolation from other Indo-European cultures. The Tamils are not only historic enemies, but also pose religious and cultural threats. The often paranoid belief that "Buddhism is in danger", uttered by clerical and lay leaders alike, must be understood against this background.[13] There is little concern with Islam, which is even more isolated. Little real hostility is currently expressed against Hinduism, though it is often difficult to disentangle anti-Tamil feeling into its components of fear of Indian domination and ancient fears deeply embedded in the national culture of the Sinhalese.[14]

To say that the bulk of Sinhalese are fiercely "Buddhist" is to obscure the complexity of the religion which has three aspects, "modern", "conservative" and "primitive". Until 1956 the modern form, expressed through the revival of Buddhist ideology under Colonel Olcott, the Mahabodhi Society and the Theosophists, was probably the most important politically. This "modern" Buddhism, which is less than a century old, has been compared with the Protestantism of the British colonisers.[15] Its political expression was mainly through the All-Ceylon Buddhist Congress, founded in 1918 from the already established Young Men's Buddhist Association whose Protestant inspiration is evident from its name. The temperance movement and the revivalism of Anagarika Dharmapala, a disciple of Olcott, gave an ideology to this movement.[16] This essentially puritan morality has not yet succeeded in achieving prohibition of alcohol but it did lead to the abolition of horse racing in 1960 and inspires the film censorship and the general tone of critics of Western culture. Its main victim, politically, was Sir John Kotelawala, whose styles of government and life ran counter to this tradition.

The "Protestant Buddhists" have had their stronghold in the Colombo middle-classes, in politics through the Senanayake family, in the public service through N. Q. Dias, former permanent secretary for Defence, and later High Commissioner in India, and in education through G. P. Malalasekera and L. H.

Mettananda, principal of Ananda College, the leading Buddhist public school. It is they who have engaged most directly in struggles against the Catholics, who have likewise been important in politics, the public service and education. Many of their objections to the Catholic Church are very similar to those made by Protestant Christians, in particular that Catholics "represent a foreign power", that they proselytise through their schools, and that they conspire to control positions in government and politics through priestly direction and lay obedience. The Buddhist-Catholic conflict, which reached its height between 1959 and 1962, is thus a struggle between the two most "modern" religious groupings in Ceylon. The Catholics, as a minority, have seen their school system effectively placed under State control, in 1960, and their strong position in the armed forces and police reduced as the result of the 1962 coup. However, the Church, in accordance with international developments, has proceeded to "nationalise" itself, with the Mass in Sinhalese and Tamil and with Cardinal Cooray and other Church leaders dealing directly with Buddhist clerics.

The "conservative" aspect of Buddhism, with which the modernisers sometimes clash, centres on the monastic life, with its feudal land-holdings and vague organisational structure.[17] This, in turn, is divided between the largest and most conservative sect, the Siam Nikaya (founded in 1753), with its pinnacle in the Kandyan monasteries of Malwatte and Asgiriya, and the reformed Amarapura (1802) and Ramanya (1865) sects, which are mainly Low Country and, unlike the Siam sect, open to monks drawn from all castes. None of these have politically effective hierarchies however as "the Sangha, or monastic order, is divided into several sects, with no supreme patriarch and there is very little disciplinary authority which can be imposed on the individual monk outside of his own monastery."[18] The political importance of the conservative Siam Nikaya, has grown with the increased significance of Kandyan electorates since 1956, although individual monks had taken part in election campaigns and party politics since the 1930's. Apart from protecting their substantial property and their own succession processes,[19] the monastic leaders see themselves as having a duty to protect Sinhalese Kandyan culture against Western or Tamil encroachments.

The "primitive" aspect of Buddhism is that associated with the *devales*, most of which are of Hindu origin though containing images worshipped as gods by Buddhists. They are often housed in the temple precincts and protected by lay *kapurales*. By far the most important is the Kataragama *devale* of Skanda, to which members of all four main religions make pilgrimages. Kataragama is visited by political leaders no less regularly than Anuradhapura or the Temple of the Tooth at Kandy and in 1965 Philip Gunawardena began his election campaign "for a Buddhist government" there.[20] The *devales* gain political importance mainly as devices for appealing to the peasantry. When appearing in support of a Communist candidate in the July, 1960, election, C. P. de Silva said: "The blue of the Vishnu Deva and the red of the Kataragama Skanda Deva have come together onto a common platform,"[21] thus tying in traditional religious symbolism with that of the partisan colours of the SLFP and the Marxists.

Caste

All societies, however "modern", tend to divide politically over race, religion or language. Sri Lanka does not differ in that respect from the United States, Canada, Ulster or Belgium. It is also "traditional" in that the caste system continues to be socially divisive and to affect promotion, election and recruitment. Fundamentally influenced from India for two thousand years, Sri Lanka has two generalised systems of caste, one among the Sinhalese and one among the Tamils. The latter is more rigid, being sanctified by Hinduism whereas Buddhism and Christianity are theoretically opposed to caste. Only the Muslims have kept free of caste, although some vestiges of Tamil caste divisions may be found on the East Coast. The essential characteristic of caste, that it is endogamous, also holds for the Muslims and Burghers who act as though they, too, were castes even if formally they are not. Thus society is divided not only by language and community but by caste, to the extent for example, that Catholics are more likely to marry outside their religion than outside their caste.[22] Inter-communal marriage is probably more common among the educated élite than cross-caste marriage. Cross-caste marriage is virtually unknown in rural areas and was specifically controlled by caste courts in North Central Province until fairly recently. People may, however, "change" caste by moving to another village.

The Sinhalese caste system has two major aspects, the Kandyan and the Low Country. In the Kandyan areas it derives directly from the functional and political divisions of the Kandyan kingdom. Thus there are some subcastes which still carry with them political obligations. In the Low Country some of the most important castes are of fairly recent origin and possibly do not predate the original contact with the Portuguese in 1505.[23] Despite these distinctions it would be wrong to assume that caste was more politically important in the traditional Kandyan areas. On the contrary, several Low Country castes have a strong sense of identity which welds them into effective voting blocs, whereas in Kandyan districts candidates tend to come from traditionally power-wielding sub-castes and families and thus gain support for ascriptive rather than solidaristic reasons. Caste becomes important not only as a point of identity for voters, but as an element of continuity with a feudal past which is still far from dead. It further helps to bind together politically and socially powerful families by virtue of endogamy. Wealth and power are preserved within a large but carefully controlled family circle of caste members.

No statistics of caste are kept and there is some doubt as to how many castes there are and where they are to be found.[24] Within the approximately two-dozen distinct castes there are several sub-castes and within those, patrilineal groups distinguished by their *ge* names[25] as well as aristocratic sub-castes. These latter retain important feudal privileges with regard to temple administration as well as *de facto* local authority, the legal basis for which was abolished before independence. By far the largest caste, the Goyigama, probably includes over half the Sinhalese and is therefore likely to be electorally dominant even if it were not also traditionally dominant. In a Low Country village in 1953 Bryce Ryan found that "leaders both in and out of office are, and always have been, Goyigama. There is no challenge to their monopoly of honours nor is there likely to be for some years."[26] The most powerful Goyigama sub-caste of all are the Radalas, of which Mrs. Bandaranaike's family, the Ratwattes, are members. "Where the Radala exists, caste differentiation generally is at its maximum, for around him adhere the various service castes and with him, too, traditional modes of conduct persist."[27]

By their numbers and status the Goyigama naturally play a dominant role in politics. Every Prime Minister has been a Sinhala Buddhist Goyigama. However, there is no monopoly of power among the Sinhalese, comparable to that enjoyed by the equivalent Vellala caste among the Tamils. The Low Country Karawas and Salagamas are very caste conscious and have wealthy and enterprising leaders. The Karawa and the associated Tamil Karaiyyar are coastal dwelling,[28] often Catholic and probably decisive in over a dozen electorates, from Point Pedro in the Northern Province to Devinuwara in the Southern. In some areas this dominance is secured not by a numerical majority, but by the possibility of forming an alliance with the Salagama and Durawa castes against the Goyigama. None of these castes is committed to one party nor do caste leaders refrain from competing against each other. C. P. de Silva, an authoritative figure in the Salagama caste, fought hard against his uncle, Colvin de Silva of the LSSP, in the Agalawatte by-election of 1967. At Balapitiya in 1968 both candidates were Salagama relatives and C. P. de Silva organised for the UNP against the SLFP. Despite bitter tension, the winning candidate, Lakshman de Silva, was sufficiently caste conscious to urge at the poll declaration: "Do not create any disturbance I appeal to you. They may be our political rivals but we are all relatives."[29]

In contrast to the Tamil system, in which about one quarter of the Ceylon Tamils are untouchables, that is, *harijans* or "minority Tamils", there are only limited remnants of untouchability among the Sinhalese and the caste hierarchy is not very clearcut.[30] A member of the lowly Hinna caste, A. E. Goonesinha, was leader of the Ceylon Labour Party for many years and a Cabinet Minister. Even among the Tamils a Senator was appointed specifically to represent the minority. In the Northern province, however, the situation is still acute, and untouchables are often refused entry to Vellala temples. Many Tamil untouchables turned to Christianity or, to a lesser degree, to Buddhism to escape these restrictions. The bulk of Indian Tamils are also low caste and some carry out many municipal scavenging tasks which Sinhalese will not undertake, making them an important element still in the Colombo working class.

The Class Structure

While caste is a "boundary line of communal life"[31] there is also a well developed class system which no longer corresponds to traditional or feudal hierarchies even in the Kandyan villages. The entire economy was drastically restructured by European influences for over four hundred years. The estates of coffee and later tea in the nineteenth century completely disrupted hill country life, planting a large alien population on the hillsides, bringing roads and railways and a market economy and depriving villagers of their forest land. Even the Dry Zone Kandyan areas, which have been least touched by the cash economy, began to be drawn into it by peasant colonisation schemes from the 1930s and by the spread of bus services and of schools and dispensaries from the 1940s. There is hardly any remote part of Sri Lanka in which people cannot be distinguished by their money income as well as by caste or community. In the villages the growing problem of landlessness, which dates at least from the plantation period if not before, divides the peasants into two distinct groups, those who work for others and those who work for themselves. In one Kandyan village, Bryce Ryan found that "there is no caste bitterness ... but there is intense bitterness of the landless towards the landed."[32]

The creation of a class of landless labourers has its corollary, the acquisition of land by all who can afford it. Many of the richest Low Country families have engaged in plantation agriculture, particularly in rubber and coconut. Through the Low Country Products Association, founded in 1908, they built up considerable solidarity which was to be transmitted into political power by the Ceylon National Congress and the United National Party. With the withdrawal of British capital after 1948 Sinhalese came to acquire many tea estates as well, though the largest and best were still under British ownership. The desire for land was common to all, from the richest businessman to the smallest teacher or public servant. In their survey of Pata Dumbara near Kandy, N. K. Sarkar and S. J. Tambiah found that "the estate owners, the salaried classes and the businessmen constitute the owning class in the rural areas. They are also the class which enjoys the highest income."[33] They noted particularly the "landgrabbing" role of *boutique*-keepers (small village shopkeepers) and teachers. This underlines the complex character of the Sri Lankan propertied classes and the lack of distinction between business, landowning and the professions. It is almost invariably true that the higher professionals are also landed estate owners and it is this which gives them a rural political base. The lawyer, teacher or public servant is thus not simply an urbanised salary earner but may still exercise some political authority on his estate.

Possibly two-thirds of Sinhalese peasants own no rice-producing paddy land, with about half of these share-cropping on various traditional tenures. These form the bulk of the rural population and the political appeal of measures like the Paddy Lands Act of 1958, which guaranteed tenure for share croppers, was considerable. The politically powerful class in the villages, including the Buddhist monasteries which own about 10% of paddy land, tend to resist such measures, however verbally committed they may be to "socialism". The responsibility for solving landlessness has been squarely placed with the Government since the 1930s, with colonisation schemes based on irrigation, guaranteed prices for rice and attempts to secure employment for Ceylonese citizens on tea estates being some of the measures which leave the vested interests of land owners alone. Only with the fixing of a land ceiling in 1972 was a major land reform undertaken. The peasantry, despite the high and increasing degree of landlessness, did not take to direct action before 1971 and Marxist parties have been electorally unsuccessful in most Kandyan areas. But landlessness does seem to lie behind much of the communalism found in rural areas. The feeling against Indian Tamils in the Kandyan districts, probably signified a displacement of resentment against the original acquisition of forest lands by the Ordinances of 1840 and 1897. The rioting which broke out in colonisation schemes in 1956 and 1958 also reflects the fact that these resettlement schemes are at the margin of "traditional" Tamil lands. One of the con-

tinuing demands of the Federal Party has been for all colonisation in such lands to be confined to Tamils who are desperately
overcrowded in the arid Jaffna peninsula.

The rural labouring class is drawn from the landless and
suffers a high degree of unemployment.[34] The urban workers,
too, have strong rural connections. Many Colombo Sinhalese
workers commute either daily or weekly from surrounding
semi-rural areas where coconut growing or fishing provide only
limited incomes. They tend to settle in fringe areas of the city,
leaving the centre to traders, the middle-classes and Indian
Tamil or Muslim workers. Recent public policy in this sphere
has been directed towards increasing the Sinhalese element
particularly on the Colombo waterfront where, after nationalisation in 1958, the proportion of Indian Tamil workers drastically
declined. Other public employers such as the railways, buses and
local government are areas of patronage appointment which also
favour Sinhalese. The working class, off the estates, is becoming
increasingly Sinhalese and rural in origin, having nothing in
common with the Indian Tamils who still make up half the
wage paid work force. Marxist parties based on trade unions
have gradually lost their cross-communal character of the 1940s
and become Sinhala dominated.

While over half the workforce is engaged in agriculture and
only one-fifth in manufacturing, transport or similar industries,
there is considerable professional, clerical, sales and service
employment. Most of the servants are villagers, while the largest
group of professionals (about 95,000) are teachers, most of
them also villagers living in rural areas. In Colombo and other
major towns, there remains a clerical element which is highly
unionised and militant and responsible for most of the non-
estate strikes which are a regular feature despite a complex and
legalistic arbitration system.[35] When the Marxist parties talk
of the "workers" it is often to this element that they are referring.
Estate, transport and clerical workers make up the three major
components of the "class-conscious" workers, rather than the
very small numbers engaged in manufacturing.[36] Of these, the
estate workers are almost completely insulated from the rest of
the population.

The Political Class

The class structure of Sri Lanka is relevant when analysing the mass backing for parties or trade unions. As in most other political systems, the effective participants in politics tend to come from a fairly narrow social range. The professions, and particularly law, public service and teaching, are strongly represented. Plantation owners and businessmen also play a major direct role, although most of the richest local businessmen do not stand for elected office.[37] The Buddhist clergy, particularly since 1956, has an important influence although it, too, is prevented from holding formal political power. These classes tend to be interrelated, as the border line between the professions, estate owners and businessmen is by no means clearcut. Even the clergy may be involved in business as individuals. The major monastic orders protect their role as landowners, supported by lay *dakayakas* (temple guardians) who are also from the middle classes. All Siam sect bhikkhus are Goyigama and Radala influence is strong at Malwatte and Asgiriya. The small scale of local politics, the complex network of caste and family relationships and the long periods which leading politicians have spent in office, all help to give the political class a great deal of potential homogeneity. The leaders of the SLFP, the UNP, the LSSP and the Communist Party, for example, all lived within a mile of each other in the Borella constituency of Colombo in 1970. Sir Oliver Goonetilleke became recruited to the political élite from which his middle-class background might have excluded him, because he moved close to the Senanayake home home at Borella.[3]

The existence of a small, proximate, and often interrelated political class was already apparent by 1920. Even then it was not synonymous with the Colombo upper-class, being more predominantly Buddhist and Goyigama, whereas the richest and most powerful men of the colonial times were often Christian Karawas, Burghers or Ceylon Tamils. The background of public school (St. Thomas's, Royal College and Ananda) and university (Oxford, Cambridge, London or Colombo Law College) preserved the inter-communal and Westernised aspect of the élite long after universal suffrage had increased the Sinhala Buddhist proportion in the legislature to something closer to its strength in the general population.[39] The very creation of the United National Party, with its Tamil andMuslim initial support, was possible because the élite was still thinking in terms of a common class and cultural background. The leadership normally spoke English not merely in public but often at home as well. The great majority had enjoyed a public school or university education which made them as socially and intellectually distinguished as the British parliament which handed authority to them in 1948.

In the most exhaustive analysis of the political élite yet made it has been argued that a great change took place in 1956, and that a new, emerging élite has grown up which is markedly less Westernised, more traditionalist and "essentially middle-class".[40] There is something to be said for this approach, but it tends to impose a rigid theoretical framework on a process which has been very gradual and often more apparent than real. The notion that "it is entirely possible to locate every member of the contemporary political élite along a 'Westernised-traditional' continuum"[41] is very attractive but quite untrue. Some of the most rabid communalists, for example R. G. Senanayake, Philip Gunawardena, or the Tamil separatist C. Suntheralingam, were not only educated abroad but were also in Ceylon politics for very many years, changing their policies and their dress but still by no means becoming rural middle-class "traditionalists". The fact that S. W. R. D. Bandaranaike donned national dress, while Dudley Senanayake did not, is not necessarily more relevant than the fact that one went to Oxford and one to Cambridge. There has been a marked change in the symbolism of politics but less in the sources from which politicians are drawn. In 1956 "from the point of view of education and occupation the preponderant majority of the candidates came from the middle-middle and upper-middle classes. Parliamentary leadership therefore continues to remain in the hands of this class."[42] Even in 1970 three-quarters of M.P.s could speak English although in their public addresses they chose not to.

The generalisation that the political élite is now primarily Sinhala Buddhist, lower caste, Swabasha educated, of traditional rural background and middle-class cannot, despite Singer's analysis, be made in any meaningful way. The proportions of lawyers (20–30%), businessmen (11–16%), landed gentry (21–24%) and public servants (9–13%) elected to parliament has not markedly changed since 1947 although the wealth of those concerned may not be as great as when the election of notables, rather than party candidates, was more common.[43] One third of M.P.s still have a tertiary education, although increasingly within Sri Lanka, reflecting the establishment of a national university in 1942, a trend which restrictions on overseas travel since 1960 will make more apparent in later years. Half the M.P.s retain a permanent home in the Western province, the cradle of most pre-independence Sinhalese politics. The conspiratorial and paranoid style of local politics may even be traceable to this continuing proximity and constant social contact. This has been especially true for the party leaders, who not only live in Colombo 7, but have faced each other in the legislature for periods of up to thirty-five years. This leads to a personalism which, in the West, is supposed to be created by television but in Ceylon is maintained not only by the press but by the political actors themselves. First names and initials are commonly used within a social circle which, 1956 notwithstanding, is still very small and cosy.

The impact of the 1956 electoral shift shows itself in the admission to local office, especially in Village Councils, of the elements who supported Bandaranaike, the ayurvedic doctors, school teachers, small shopkeepers, locally-based landowners, and minor public servants, most of them *swabasha* educated. It is at the local level and in party recruitment that one can justify the claim that "the revolution of 1956 worked through the election which put the MEP into power, and indicated the shift of political power from the westernised bourgeoisie into the hands of the national bourgeoisie and petit-bourgeoisie who lived in small towns and villages."[44] Only the passing of a whole generation of pre-independence leaders can project these elements into effective national leadership.

The Political Families

Within the narrow confines of the political class, there exist even smaller circles based on the complex network of relationships created by the caste system and the common practice of cross-cousin marriage. Of the six Prime Ministers of Ceylon, three belonged to one family group (D. S. Senanayake, Dudley Senanayake and Sir John Kotelawala) and two (Mr. and Mrs. Bandaranaike) belonged to another. Only W. Dahanayake, who, as a school teacher, was also the first "middle-class" Prime Minister, was outside the orbit of these families. As S. D. Bandaranaike, himself a cousin of the late Prime Minister said on joining the Maoist Ceylon Communist Party in 1968, the SLFP seemed "only interested in a game of musical chairs by which a Bandaranaike (SLFP) or a Senanayake (UNP) can alternatively come to power."[45] The estates and electorates controlled by members of the two groups run side by side in the Low Country between Colombo and Kurunegala, though the fortunes of D. S. Senanayake and Sir John Kotelawala were made from plumbago mining rather than land. Bandaranaike's father was a *Maha Mudaliyar*, and his marriage into the Radala Ratwattes in 1940 brought together the Low Country and Kandyan aristocracy, his wife, Sirimavo, being the daughter of a *Dissawa*, a high Kandyan title.[46]

The UNP earned itself the title "Uncles and Nephews Party" at an early stage. Even in 1970, when Dudley Senanayake relinquished the post of Leader of the Opposition, he handed it over to his kinsman J. R. Jayawardena. Jayawardena was related to D. C. Wijewardena, and thus by marriage to Mrs. Wimala Wijewardena, who fought against him at Kelaniya in 1952. He was also related to R. G. Senanayake who, in alliance with Mrs. Wijewardena, pushed him out of the seat in 1956. R. G. Senanayake, in turn was a cousin of Sir John Kotelawala, whose mother's sister had married F. R. Senanayake, the brother of D. S. Senanayake. This family tree, then, includes the founders of the Ceylon National Congress, three Prime Ministers, two Cabinet Ministers, and the author of *The Revolt in the Temple*, the most coherent exposition of Sinhala Buddhist revivalism. The latter, D. C. Wijewardena, was the brother of the founder of Associated Newspapers of Ceylon which launched the mass circulation Sinhala press. A further relative, E. L. Senanayake, was Mayor of Kandy and a Cabinet Minister under Dudley Senanayake. Even the extreme Left has a branch of the tree in Edmund Samarakkody, leader of the Revolutionary Samasamaja Party which broke away from the LSSP in 1964.

The Bandaranaike family tree is equally complicated, particularly in its Kandyan reaches. Bandaranaike and S. D. Bandaranaike were foundation members of the SLFP, while another kinsman, J. P. Obeyesekere, took over the "family seat" of Attanagalla after Bandaranaike's assassination, duly handing it back to Mrs. Bandaranaike in 1965. Bandaranaike's nephew, Felix Dias Bandaranaike, took the other half of the seat, Dompe, after the 1959 redistribution and served in Mrs. Bandaranaike's Cabinets of 1960 and 1970. There were at least eight relatives of the Bandaranaikes elected to the Parliament of 1970, all for the SLFP. After the Coalition victory of 1970, Mrs. Bandaranaike's daughter, Sunethra Rupasinghe, became increasingly important as her mother's political secretary and the leader of a Leftwing group around the journal *Janavegaya*. The Prime Minister's son, Anura, also became leader of the SLFP Youth Leagues, but was associated politically with his cousin, Felix Dias Bandaranaike, on the Rightwing of the party. The Bandaranaikes, too, have had revolutionary members, in Susil Siriwardena and S. D. Bandaranaike, who were both tried for connections with the JVP revolt of 1971. Relatives of Mrs. Bandaranaike who have attained political importance include the Governor-General William Gopallawa, the commander of the army from 1962 to 1966, Major-General Richard Udugama, elected to parliament for the SLFP in 1970, Hector Kobbekaduwa, Minister of Agriculture in 1970, C. S. Ratwatte M.P. and his wife, Mrs. Mallika Ratwatte M.P., who replaced him for Balangoda after he was unseated on an election petition. It was during her election that a UNP rally was asked: "Is the Balangoda electorate the heirloom of the Ratwatte family?"[47]

This question draws attention to the existence of a number of "family seats" normally held by representatives of the largest estate owning family in the district, a phenomenon which had naturally arisen before independence. Sir John Kotelawala recalled, of his first election at Kurunegala in 1931, that "I had vast permanent interests in the district for which I sought election and the interests of a large number of people there, both in the planting and plumbago-mining areas, were linked with my own."[48] This sort of relationship continued in some areas. Maithripala Senanayake, a Minister in Mrs. Bandaranaike's Cabinet of 1970, was related to four of the other five

North Central province M.P.s, including the Chief Government
Whip, K. B. Ratnayake. The three seats of Mulkirigala, Beliatta
and Tissamaharama in Southern province are normally contested and frequently won by, members of the Rajapakse family,
though they change parties and thus, sometimes, lose the seats.
Altogether, at the time of dissolution in 1969, one-eighth of all
Sinhala M.P.s were members of the four families mentioned
above (i.e. Senanayake-Jayawardena-Wijewardena-Kotelawala,
Bandaranaike-Ratwatte-Obeyesekera, Maithripala Senanayake
and Rajapakse). The important role of extended families does
not necessarily mean that these families act together politically.
Suspicion that Mrs. Bandaranaike's uncle S. L. Ratwatte was
supporting his nephew A. C. L. Ratwatte as UNP candidate in
a Kandy municipal election, led to his expulsion from the
SLFP in 1963, though he denied the charge.[49] The expectation
that relatives will assist each other does not always stretch
across party lines. In the July 1960 election, Mrs. Vivienne
Goonewardena of the LSSP referred to her uncle, Philip
Gunawardena, as "the number one enemy of the country and
the Sinhalese nation."[50] Shortly afterwards a serious breach
occurred between Philip and his brother Robert. Family
quarrels are as typical of Sri Lanka as mutual family assistance
and add a further complication in the determination of
political alignments.
  The major families are, in part, carrying on a feudal tradition
of obligation. When the loyal villagers of Udugaha Pattu
presented an address to S. W. R. D. Bandaranaike on his
return from Oxford in 1925, they spoke as "those who look to
you and to your family as their natural leaders."[51] Forty years
later George Rajapakse M.P. could still say: "If our family
has done any service to the people of Ruhunu it was not with
the hope of getting votes, but strictly because our family is
bound to serve and protect them."[52] This attitude is even more
marked in the SLFP than in other parties as it often controls
many of the remaining "family seats". However, the experience
in 1970 of two prodigal sons, S. D. Bandaranaike and R. G.
Senanayake, who stepped outside the party ranks and were
savagely defeated, suggests that the notables are becoming less
important than their parties.

Social patterns and politics

The Ceylonese who comes to politics whether as a voter or a leader, is already socially identifiable in many different ways, each one of which will influence his attitudes and behaviour. He will belong to a particular language group, religion, caste, occupation, social strata and family. His culture, which has built up its conventions over two thousand years, will help him to interpret politics in terms of these other influencing factors. Thus a Low Country Sinhala Karawa Christian University educated, professional, Colombo dwelling politician may be totally Westernised in all significant respects, yet be willing to accept astrology, Buddhist dominance, Sinhala communalism and the intervention of the *devales* in order to appeal to his electorate.[53] Similarly a Kandyan Radala will have to appeal to trade unionists, a Tamil Vellala to untouchables or a Burgher to Muslims. Marxists will bow before monks and Catholics go on pilgrimages to Kataragama. The complexity of local politics is largely a reflection of the constant interpenetration of all these cultural variants over the past four centuries. The spread of education, rather than homogenising local culture, may very well make it more divisive by teaching historical myths in which the major races and religions fought with each other. The growth of wage paid employment, rather than creating social classes which cut across communities, may lead to competition between communities for the best jobs. The caste system, though less rigorous than the Indian, projected the Goyigamas into politics and the Karavas into business, just as communal traditions gave rise to the Ceylon Tamil public servant, the Indian Tamil estate worker, the Borah or Sindhi businessman, the Muslim jeweller or the Malay policeman.

Thus it is hardly surprising that politics have been characterised by factionalism, conspiracy, eclectic ideology and personalism. These are present in all political systems, but the local social situation emphasises them. Loyalty to family cuts across loyalty to party, which is further weakened by communalism. A complex ideology like Marxism, which has a long history of factionalism in the West, must be twisted out of recognition not only to satisfy the voters, as happens everywhere, but even to describe the local circumstances in any meaningful way.

Most of it is only comprehensible to the English-educated, which partly explains the social character of Marxist leadership and the adherence to Marxist unions of clerical workers, bank employees, public servants, school teachers and other theoretically unsympathetic lower middle-class groups. Competition between Ceylonese and British or Indian businessmen turns traders and factory owners into "socialists" who can also espouse extreme nationalism, the two being quite compatible rationalisations of the need to "nationalise" business control. Every appointment, every political ideology comes to be judged personally and communally, in terms of the social character and past history of the individuals or groups concerned.

In the light of these seemingly endless complications caused by centuries of foreign influence, it is surprising that politics have emerged from total confusion into relative simplicity since 1948. The voter has come to distinguish between parties generally on "the Left" and "the Right" by conventional European usage. The parliamentary system remains in force, and power alternates between members of a slowly growing élite which still retains major links with the important families of colonial times. There are obviously forces at work which slow down and restrain the potentially disruptive influences which modernisation necessarily brings. Buddhism has absorbed modern reforming notions without basically altering its medieval structure. Politics has absorbed universal suffrage without totally dislodging the traditional hierarchy of deference and obligation. Money wages have created a class system without ending caste divisions or even seriously disturbing them.

The Ceylonese have clearly become adept at synthesising and this, in itself, is vital for the success of a plural democracy. Ceylon seemed able to absorb influences and institutions, to change them, to retain much of its own myths and culture and yet not show intolerable tensions or mass alienation. The explanation, in so far as one can be provided, cannot be separated from economic factors and in particular the continuing ability of the soil to provide an adequate subsistence level both through indigenous agriculture and plantation-derived exports. The traditional social structure, too, preserves stability by its combination of complex hierarchy with relative permissiveness. The Sinhalese villager knows his superiors, his equals and his inferiors and acts politically in the light of this knowledge. Yet this is not a rigid caste system so much as an adaptive system in which families may move up or down over several generations. Moreover it is common practice, by changing names and homes, to slide out of a lower caste into a higher by taking advantage of opportunities provided by the money economy.

The question whether the Buddhist religion is particularly conducive to adaptation is less easily tackled. Bryce Ryan argues that the "basic principles of Therevada Buddhism are consistent with both loose structuring and smooth social transition. Buddhism has no deep alignment with any particular secular order of society."[54] This may be so in theory, but it is equally true that Buddhism preaches non-violence yet Sri Lanka has one of the world's highest murder rates. There are some aspects of Sinhalese Buddhism, in particular its belief that the Kandyans are a chosen race surrounded by enemies, which make for disharmony and political authoritarianism. What seems more probable is that a society which has always been subject to foreign penetration, yet which has also possessed much fertile land, has developed a form of Buddhism which is both adaptive and benign. This has helped the peasant to adjust to a political system based on foreign institutions. This is controlled by an English-speaking upper-middle class always ready to compromise with popular beliefs in order to stay in power, beliefs which largely concede the right of that class to enjoy office.

There is no reason to suppose that popular beliefs in the natural superiority of rulers need be permanent. Electoral tactics have been based on catering both to the patron-client, superior-inferior dimension of popular attitudes and to the equally strong mass resentment against the privileges of the established rulers and the desire for social changes which will advance the indigenous peasant masses. Thus there is always an ambivalence within local politics between conservatism and radicalism, which cuts across conventional party lines. The Bandaranaikes' "aristocratic socialism", whereby two of the oldest established upper-class families have taken the responsibility for creating a democratic socialist republic sympathetically aligned to the "Third World", epitomises the contradiction. The insurrection of 1971 suggests that among youth, the poor and the politically ineffectual, there is a growing questioning of the right of the upper classes to dominate all political life. The failure of Ceylon Marxism to cater for the underprivileged and its equal reluctance to open political positions to the young, led to a mass movement towards the JVP. For the first time the lower ranks of the working class and even some sections of the poorer peasantry, were able to organise themselves rather than to be organised by their betters. Their conclusion, backed by many thousands of teenagers, was that their demands would only be met by self-assertion rather than by accepting leadership from above.

NOTES

1. "No matter what the racial origin, little remains today of the original stock, except a belief in it." N. K. Sarkar: *The Demography of Ceylon*; Colombo, 1957; p. 191.
2. See Tarzie Vittachi: *Emergency '58*; London, 1958.
3. ECAFE: *Economic Survey of Asia and the Far East; 1970*; p. 100 shows that Ceylon spent 15·7% of government expenditure on social services, against 2·4% for Malaysia and had the highest expenditure (% of GDP) on education and health in the region. For further brief comparisons between Ceylon and Malaysia see Y. Levy: *Malaysia and Ceylon*; Sage Publications, Beverly Hills, 1974.
4. *Statistical Pocket Book of Ceylon*; Colombo, 1968; Table 10.
5. In 1963 only 1·4% of marriages were contracted between individuals of different ethnic groups. R. F. Nyrop: *Area Handbook for Ceylon*; Washington, 1971; p. 77.
6. Kandyans are defined in the Report of the Kandyan Peasantry Commission; S.P. XVIII—1951.
7. Two-thirds of the population lives in the Southwestern Wet Zone at a density of over 700 to the square mile. This includes the great majority of Low Country Sinhalese.
8. See N. K. Sarkar and S. J. Tambiah: *The Disintegrating Village*; Colombo, 1957.
9. *Constitution of the All-Ceylon Tamil Congress*; Colombo, 1944. Pt. 4(a).
10. *The Statistical Abstract of Ceylon—1966;* Colombo, 1969; Table 44 shows that only coconut plantation workers (male) received smaller monthly wages than tea plantation workers (male), although this excludes food and rent concessions available on the tea estates. See also Edith Bond: *The State of Tea*; War on Want, London; 1974.
11. This was S. W. R. D. Bandaranaike's speech on the Appropriation Bill 1948-9.

12. Sir W. Ivor Jennings: *Nationalism and Political Development in Ceylon*; New York, 1950; p. 14.

13. K. Malalgoda: "Millenialism in Relation to Buddhism"; Ceylon Studies Seminar Paper No. 4; Peradeniya, 1968; p. 10.

14. See for example the controversy about declaring the Koneswaram Hindu temple area of Trincomalee as a "protected area" in 1968, which aroused strong Sinhalese objections and was abandoned.

15. See G. Obeyesekere: "Religious Symbolism and Political Change in Ceylon"; *Modern Ceylon Studies* 1:1, January 1970 and S. J. Tambiah: "Buddhism and this worldly activity"; *Modern Asian Studies* 7:1, January 1973.

16. See Anagarika Dharmapala's major work *Return to Righteousness* (ed. A. Guruge; Colombo, 1965).

17. See R. Gombrich: *Precept and Practice—Traditional Buddhism in the Rural Highlands of Ceylon*; Oxford, 1971.

18. D. E. Smith: *South Asian Politics and Religion*; Princeton, 1966; p. 29. Until 1972 there was no official register of monks and individuals frequently assumed the role of a monk without any justification.

19. See H. D. Evers: "Monastic Landlordism in Ceylon"; *Journal of Asian Studies* 28:4; August 1969.

20. The launching of the 1818 Kandyan rebellion similarly began with pledges at Kataragama. In 1971 the JVP occupied Kataragama for three weeks, a fact which was kept hidden by the Ceylon government for fear of its impact on the Sinhalese Buddhists.

21. *Ceylon Daily News* 18/7/1960.

22. Interview with Father Tissa Balasuriya in July, 1969.

23. M. D. Raghavan: *The Karava of Ceylon*; Colombo, 1961 suggests (p. 8) that the Karava were well established by the 10th Century and originated in South India. The frequency of Portuguese names among Karava, Salagama and Durava underlines their coastal concentration and early contact with Europeans.

24. For a list of Ceylon castes see R. F. Nyrop: *op. cit.* Table 7 (Sinhalese) Table 8 (Ceylon Tamils) and Table 9 (Indian Tamils).

25. The *ge* name, rather than the surname, indicates a person's caste and his social location within the larger castes. For a discussion of *ge* names see E. Leach; *Pul Eliya*; Cambridge, 1961.

26. Bryce Ryan: *Sinhalese Village*; Miami, 1958; p. 123.

27. Bryce Ryan: *Caste in Modern Ceylon*; New Brunswick, 1953; p. 99.

28. Michael Roberts: "The Rise of the Karavas"; Ceylon Studies Seminar Paper No. 5; Peradeniya, 1969.

29. *Ceylon Observer* 19/12/1968.

30. Public discrimination against lower castes was banned by the Prevention of Social Disabilities Act of 1957.

31. Bryce Ryan: *Caste in Modern Ceylon*; p. 16.

32. Ibid. p. 211.

33. Sarkar and Tambiah: *op. cit.* p. 26.

34. The ILO Report (*Matching Employment Opportunities and Expecta-*

tions; Geneva, 1971) argues that agriculture "provides much less than a reasonable amount of work." (p. 85).

35. Two of the most politically militant unions have been the Ceylon Mercantile Union and the Government Clerical Service Union, employing private and public clerks respectively.

36. There are approximately 120,000 workers employed directly in manufacturing.

37. Less than 100,000 people pay income tax and approximately 10,000 declare incomes equivalent to more than £1,000 per annum (*Statistical Abstract of Ceylon*; Colombo; 1969; Table 190).

38. Sir Charles Jeffries: *OEG—Sir Oliver Goonetilleke*; London, 1969; p. 28.

39. See *Ceylon Daily News Parliaments of Ceylon*.

40. Marshall Singer: *The Emerging Elite*; Cambridge Mass., 1964; p. 144.

41. *Op. cit.* p. 48.

42. I. D. S. Weerawardena: *Ceylon General Election 1956;* Colombo, 1960; pp. 95–6.

43. Proportions based on Singer; *op. cit.* and later details from the *Ceylon Daily News Parliaments of Ceylon*.

44. Denzil Pieris: *1956 and After*; Colombo, 1958; p. 5.

45. *Ceylon Daily News* 16/3/1968.

46. Brief details in L. G. Weeramantry: *Assassination of a Prime Minister*; Geneva, 1969; p. 4 and D. B. Dhanapala: *Madam Premier*; Colombo, 1960.

47. *Ceylon Observer* 11/10/1966.

48. Sir John Kotelawala: *An Asian Prime Minister's Story*; London, 1956; p. 24.

49. *Daily Mirror* (Colombo) 23/12/1963.

50. *Ceylon Daily News* 8/7/1960.

51. S. W. R. D. Bandaranaike: *Speeches and Writings*; Colombo, 1963; p. 82.

52. *Ceylon Observer* 10/2/1965.

53. All major political events, including the date of elections, are fixed on astrological advice. This applies equally to the launching of the Marxist United Left Front in 1963, the announcing of the Coalition in 1964 and the declaration of the Republic in 1972. Leading members of the JVP consulted a fortune teller about the leadership of the movement (see the evidence of "Loku Athula" to the Criminal Justice Commission) and launched their attack at the Sinhala New Year, although tactics may have determined this decision.

54. Bryce Ryan: *Sinhalese Village*; p. 194.

CHAPTER 3

Sinhalese Party Politics

While there are no major parties which have not contained members of more than one community, it makes sense to talk of the Sinhalese parties when referring to parties drawing most of their support from Sinhalese voters. Such parties are normally led by Goyigama Buddhists. Their M.P.s are aware that their major support comes from Sinhala peasants and that electoral success is granted within constraints formed by their electors' national and religious prejudices. Over the years of independence the Sinhalese parties have steadily come to resemble each other in accepting these constraints. The United National Party, which governed for the larger part of this period, reflects this acceptance in the adoption of Sinhala Only at its Kelaniya conference in 1956, in the formulation of a democratic socialist programme, in selecting some local candidates who cannot speak English and in building a mass party whose membership is socially similar to that of the others. The UNP has its Youth Leagues and trade unions, its coloured shirts and party songs. The change in the past fifteen years is particularly remarkable. "Since its defeat in 1956 the UNP has been wooing the indigenous élite in an attempt to strike the SLFP at its roots . . . Its membership is fast becoming similar to that of the SLFP although it does contain representatives of its bygone character. The typical UNP member of parliament is no longer exclusively Western educated, Western attired, English speaking, a-cultural and 'alienated' but like the SLFP counterpart, national dressed, Sinhalese speaking and revivalist."[1]

Despite these changes it should not be overlooked that from their earliest days in the Ceylon National Congress, the men who were to found and lead the United National Party were mostly Sinhala Buddhists. D. S. Senanayake and D. B.

Jayatillaka became national heroes after their imprisonment by the British following the 1915 communal riots. These two were to dominate the Congress for the next twenty years. After the Tamil leaders, the Ponnambalam brothers, had left the Congress in 1921 it became increasingly identified with the interests of Low Country Goyigama planters and businessmen and particularly with the two close and partly related families of the Senanayakes and Wijewardenas. When the "all-Sinhalese" Board of Ministers was formed in 1936, two of its seven members, D. S. Senanayake, and John Kotelawala, were relatives. Another relative, J. R. Jayawardena, became secretary of the Ceylon National Congress in 1940 and its organiser in 1943, holding both posts until it merged with the United National Party.

The general orientation of the Ceylon National Congress was cautiously constitutional to the point of conservatism. It was never reformed along the lines adopted in India after 1921 and was opposed to the extension of the franchise proposed by the Donoughmore commissioners. However a mildly radical trend grew during the war, associated mainly with Dudley Senanayake and J. R. Jayawardena. In 1942 at Kelaniya the Congress voted for complete independence, forcing D. S. Senanayake to resign from its Executive. In the following year the Communists were admitted to membership and the older Senanayake left in disgust, not to return until the Congress was submerged into the UNP. In 1944 Jayawardena, who had just been elected to the State Council, successfully introduced a resolution favouring Sinhalese (amended to Sinhalese and Tamil) as "the official language of Ceylon within a reasonable number of years." Thus by the time the UNP came to be set up there was already a mildly radical and nationalist element in conservative politics.

The United National Party

The United National Party was established at meetings in June and September 1946 out of the Ceylon National Congress, the Sinhala Mahasabha, the All-Ceylon Muslim League and the All-Ceylon Moors Association. Its president was D. S. Senanayake and its vice-presidents S. W. R. D. Bandaranaike, John Kotelawala, G. E. de Silva, T. B. Jayah (a Muslim) and

A. Mahadeva (a Tamil and son of Sir Ponnambalam Arunachalam). Jayawardena became the treasurer and Kotelawala
was made chairman of the propaganda committee and fund
raiser. In the elections of 1947 the new party got the support of
most prominent families, doing particularly well in the Low
Country between Colombo and Dodangaslanda where members
of the Senanayake and Bandaranaike families won five seats.
The UNP also won all seats in the North Central province and
did well around Kandy. After the death of D. S. Senanayake in
1952 it did even better, eating into the Marxist position south of
Colombo. By then it had attracted most of the independent
M.P.s from the more remote rural areas. By 1950 UNP members
had been elected as Mayors of Colombo, Galle and Kandy.

The strength of the UNP seemed to lie in the relative social
cohesion of its leadership and its control over rural "voting
banks" in an electoral system biassed in favour of the country
areas. These soon came to be a liability as struggles for leadership broke out in the narrow circle at the top, firstly between
Bandaranaike and Kotelawala and then between Dudley
Senanayake and Kotelawala. The voters in the rural areas felt
remote from the Colombo leadership, and their local dignitaries
were affronted by their lack of opportunities. As a Ceylon
journalist said of the 1956 elections: "Fairly often the Rightwing opponent of the UNP campaigned as an SLFP man
because he could not get UNP nomination. The UNP overlooked his claim in favour of a big landowner from Colombo
whose property was located in the constituency he was contesting."[2]

Thus at all levels the party began to lose what had been its
original strength, the recruitment of nearly all politically active
notables. Within the leadership there was considerable resentment among the conservatives surrounding Sir John Kotelawala
when Dudley Senanayake succeeded to his father's leadership.
Kotelawala hesitated to continue in the Cabinet but eventually
re-accepted his original post of Minister of Transport.[3] He
records that he felt cheated out of the leadership and used his
control of the machine to increase the agony of waiting for his
decision. He "could not help feeling that there must have been
a certain amount of panic among the party stalwarts when they
contemplated the prospect of having to do without the UNP

Fund of over a million rupees of which only I could draw as Propaganda Chief and Treasurer."[4]

Naturally, in such an atmosphere, Dudley Senanayake did not have an altogether easy time, particularly as his previous record in the party had been as a liberal nationalist rather than a conservative cosmopolitan. When the *hartal* of 1953 broke out over the Budget "Mr. Dudley Senanayake had to face these troubles without a loyal Cabinet since Sir John Kotelawala had not forgotten or forgiven Mr. Senanayake for his being appointed Prime Minister over his own claims."[5] Kotelawala became Prime Minister and Dudley withdrew from active politics to the point of refusing to stand in the 1956 elections, leaving the UNP altogether shortly beforehand.

While the UNP has never split, preserving a remarkable formal solidarity, Kotelawala's accession hastened the process of decay which began with the defection of S. W. R. D. Bandaranaike in 1951 and ended in the election debacle of 1956. Kotelawala, although a landed gentleman and nominally a Buddhist, was quite unsuitable to the mood of Ceylon politics. His close association with the West, while it made him the darling of the United States and Britain, antagonised those large segments of the Ceylon élite who had been influenced by neutralist or Leftwing attitudes since their university days. His public flouting of many Buddhist practices relating to hunting, racing and drinking upset that section of his party, including most of the Senanayakes, who were active Buddhists or even prohibitionists.[6] Sir Lalita Rajapakse, president of the All-Ceylon Buddhist Congress, left the government in 1953. Dudley's retirement from active politics encouraged many monks of the Ramanya sect to join the nationalist revivalist movement being started by L. H. Mettananda and sympathisers with Bandaranaike.[7]

The melting away of support was marked by the resignation of Maithripala Senanayake in 1953 and of R. G. Senanayake in 1956. The rapid spread of the *swabasha* and Buddhist revivalist movement in 1955 led to continued defections by the nationalist intelligentsia and rural middle-classes. The Ven. Henpitagedera Gnanaseeha, a leading Ramanya sect monk, confirmed in 1962 that this decay had spread so far that Dudley Senanayake himself was approached to lead a new party. Although in-

F

terested, and even promised leadership by S. W. R. D.
Bandaranaike, he felt that he could not work against the UNP
because it had been "formed by his father".[8] Changing his
course too late, in the face of this gathering crisis, Kotelawala
got the UNP committed to Sinhala Only at its Kelaniya
sessions in February, 1956. In his election manifesto he claimed
that he had gone to the polls early because of this policy and
"to enable me to form a government which will, as its first item
of business seek, by amending the constitution at once by
legislative and administrative measures, to implement the resolution that Sinhalese alone should be made the State language."[9]
However not only did this not win the election, but it lost the
UNP the support of all its Tamil M.P.s. It was returned with
eight M.P.s, two of whom, L. B. S. Jinasena and Sir Razik
Fareed, promptly defected to the SLFP.

This was the lowest point in UNP fortunes. The events during
Kotelawala's leadership had the effect of reducing its following,
permanently losing many important local leaders and driving
from politics many of the former State Councillors, including
Kotelawala himself who retired to live in England. The only
important UNP member still left in a position of political
strength was Sir Oliver Goonetilleke who, as Governor-General,
was prevented from taking a partisan role. The recreation of the
UNP, which still had substantial funds and a large vote, was
left largely in the hands of J. R. Jayawardena. It was during the
four year period of recovery which culminated in the very brief
victory under Dudley Senanayake in March, 1960, that the
UNP "nationalised" itself, throwing off its cosmopolitan image
and working actively for the support of the clergy. This process
began with Jayawardena's march on Kandy on October 4,
1957, to ask for the blessing of the *devales* in the campaign
against Bandaranaike's pact with the Federal Party leader,
S. J. V. Chelvanayakam.

The party had already swept the board at the Colombo
municipal elections in 1956, and held most of its gains in 1959.
It joined with all other Opposition parties in forcing the resignation of Dahanayake and found itself in a strong position in
March 1960 because of the fragmentation of votes by the many
splinter parties contesting. Thus although its own government
was immediately defeated it was able to maintain an effective

parliamentary party again under Dudley Senanayake. It won back Catholic support in 1960 by its opposition to the schools takeover and tightened its grip on the Muslim business community as a result of Mrs. Bandaranaike's restrictions on trade. The Coalition between Mrs. Bandaranaike and the LSSP in 1964 won it the general support of the leading monks. The press control measures earned it the fanatical loyalty of the newspapers. Finally the defections from the SLFP in December 1964 brought into its ranks many whose characteristics were those of the other major party. Throughout the whole period of Mrs. Bandaranaike's government the UNP built up its machine on the basis of financial donations and of mass recruitment into Youth Leagues.

The history of the party since the early 1960's is one of cohesion and success, until the landslide defeat in 1970. There was continuing movement into its ranks of those who had previously been with the SLFP or even the Marxists. Remarkably it suffered no serious defections. It took up many of the characteristic positions of its opponents, adopting a democratic socialist objective in March, 1958 which it reiterated at its Kalutara sessions in 1963, adding its backing for a republican constitution.[1] The range of UNP support among traditionalists and even former Leftists may be measured by the rally of six thousand *bhikkhus* organised by it in opposition to the Press Bill at Colombo Town Hall in November, 1964.[11] This was addressed by Dudley Senanayake and J. R. Jayawardena, by I. M. R. A. Iriyagolle, formerly of the Basha Peramuna and the MEP, K. M. P. Rajaratna of the radical communalist Jathika Vimukhthi Peramuna and Philip Gunawardena, the "father of Ceylon Marxism" but now in alliance with the Jathika V.P. All three had been founders of Bandaranaike's MEP in 1956. Thus when the National Government was formed after the election victory of 1965 nearly one-third of it consisted of men who had previously sat on the MEP benches. Of these all but Philip Gunawardena were members of the United National Party by 1969. The Sri Lanka Freedom Socialist Party of C. P. de Silva and the Lanka Prajathantrawadi Pakshaya of W. Dahanayake, became organisationally merged with the UNP at the same time. Throughout the period of its government the UNP enjoyed the support of the Ceylon Workers Congress and of the

Tamil Congress, and was able to work with the Federal Party until 1968.

The UNP has been remarkably stable, except for the period of Kotelawala's leadership. It has built up a solid electoral following, which apart from 1956, has varied between one-third and two-fifths of the total. Even in 1970 it gained more total votes than the SLFP by contesting Tamil and Muslim seats. To some extent its electoral fortunes have been blighted by the very measure designed to advance them, the biassing of electorates towards rural areas. For the UNP has consistently gained high support in urban and Low Country areas which are under-represented. Its original Kandyan basis was never fully recovered after 1956 nor was it able to hold its Catholic support in 1970. Yet the party still enjoys the loyalty of most of the upper-middle classes and this means considerable advantages in access to funds. Despite its democratic socialist and nationalist programme the UNP is still the most effective conservative party in Sri Lanka as it was at its foundation. It is simply pre-serving a *status quo* much further to the Left and more in accord with the views of Dudley Senanayake and J. R. Jayawardena than with those of D. S. Senanayake or Sir John Kotelawala. The death of Dudley Senanayake in 1973 and the election of J. R. Jayawardena as his successor, probably strengthened the element in the party which saw its role as a 'loyal Opposition' in the crisis conditions produced by the 1971 rising. The party has become increasingly concerned with protecting legal and property rights while otherwise appearing to conform to the consensus created by the SLFP.

The Sri Lanka Freedom Party

The Sri Lanka Freedom Party owes its foundation to the insight of S. W. R. D. Bandaranaike in realising that the Sinhala Buddhist majority would eventually sweep to power. It owes its continued existence to the equal acumen of Mrs. Sirimavo Bandaranaike, who found the SLFP in total chaos and rebuilt it as the governing and natural majority party once again. The SLFP had given to the ordinary workers and peasants of Ceylon the feeling that the government belonged to them, which they first showed in 1956 by occupying Parliament

House in the jubilation surrounding Bandaranaike's victory.
Yet it is not a peasant party in any real sense. Nor is it only a
Sinhala Buddhist party. It is a democratic socialist party whose
leaders include Kandyan feudal aristocrats. Its propaganda is
almost exclusively in Sinhala but its Cabinet meetings were
conducted in English. For all of these reasons the SLFP has
been something of a mystery to foreign students. It has attracted
almost no scholarly attention and although recognised by the
Socialist International, is extremely parochial. Its leaders are
unknown outside Ceylon with the exception of Mrs. Bandaranaike. Of all the parties it is the most affected by Kandyan
attitudes, the least influential in the towns. This despite the fact
that its founder went to Oxford and his widow was educated at
St. Bridget's convent, both of them having to relearn Sinhala.

The SLFP can trace its origins back to the Sinhala Maha
Sabha, established by Bandaranaike in 1937 or, indirectly, to
the Buddhist revivalists of the early twentieth century like
Anagarika Dharmapala or Piyadasa Sirisena. In this ancestry
it shares a great deal with the leadership of the Ceylon National
Congress, of which Bandaranaike was secretary for some
years. However, after the creation of the Sinhala Maha Sabha
Bandaranaike drew away from the dominant Senanayake-
Jayatilleke group. As Minister for Local Administration his
work brought him into close contact with village life and allowed
him to build up a network of followers many of whom were to
become active in the SLFP. While leadership of the SMS was
not incompatible with remaining in the Ceylon National
Congress, Bandaranaike's programme already contained many
points which were later to typify the SLFP, in particular his
support for socialism, his opposition to Indian commercial
penetration and immigration, his belief that the majority
community should have majority representation and his
support for the national languages as against English. By 1945,
in regretting the Soulbury commission's refusal to grant
immediate Dominion status, he was claiming that the
Mahasabha was "the largest party in this House today."[12]

The Sinhala Maha Sabha, like all parties at the time, was a
somewhat ephemeral body. Yet it held regular annual sessions
which were at least consulted on matters like the Soulbury
reforms or the formation of the United National Party. In

August 1945 the Kandy sessions authorised "the President, in consultation with the Executive Committee, to try and secure a united front by co-operating with other parties and other sections of the people of the country, with regard not only to elections but also to the formation of a Government after the election."[13] Out of this arose the negotiations which created the United National Party in the following year. Bandaranaike, as president of the SMS, became a vice-president of the new party and the Mahasabha remained within it as a distinct entity, whose membership continued as before to be confined to Sinhalese. He stressed, at the SMS sessions at Galle in July, 1946 that "the work of the Sabha, far from being relaxed, must be carried on with greater vigour than ever".[14] In D. S. Senanayake's first Cabinet there were four SMS members, including Bandaranaike. However his wish to keep the Mahasabha going led to increasing tension with the old Ceylon National Congress leaders and particularly with Sir John Kotelawala.

The whole position of the Mahasabha was anomalous in that it was not an affiliate nor a branch and had no rights in relationship to the UNP. In 1949 Bandaranaike had to answer charges of criticising the party through the SMS. By 1951 he had become completely frustrated. The SMS made one final attempt to put its viewpoint to the UNP only to be told that it had no rights within the party constitution to do so.[15] Bandaranaike resigned as Minister of Health and Local Government on July 12, 1951 taking five other M.P.s with him. He set up the Sri Lanka Freedom Party early in September. As president he stressed the continuity with the SMS. "Its members are all prepared to join the new party", he told the inaugural sessions.[16] However the Sinhala Maha Sabha had always been a rather tenuous body and when Bandaranaike went into the 1952 elections he had no effective organisation. The nine seats he won were those of himself and his cousin, S. D. Bandaranaike, C. P. de Silva's peasant colony at Minneriya, four Kandyan and two Southern Province electorates. All were overwhelmingly Buddhist except at Kadugannawa where the Muslim, E. A. S. Marikkar, was returned in a two-member seat. This was a very scattered base for what Bandaranaike specifically intended to be a major party. He only became leader of the Opposition because the M.P.s following Philip Gunawardena and the Communists preferred him to N. M. Perera.

The successes of the party four years later reflect the degeneration of the UNP as much as any massive development of the SLFP. It began to acquire support from local notables with grievances against the government. Maithripala Senanayake resigned from the government and eventually brought over his network of supporters and relatives in the North Central province. The Rajapakse family brought support in the South. The alliance of Ven. Mapitigama Buddharakkitha, R. G. Senanayake and Mrs. W. Wijewardena started working in the Low Country electorates around Kelaniya and Mirigama.[17] The greatest advantages came from the organisation of *bhikkhus* and the accession of strength from the Left and from rural independents. There were no important defections from the leadership of the United National Party other than Maithripala Senanayake and R. G. Senanayake. Instead a whole range of people who were discontented with the UNP, including some who had failed to get party endorsement in 1952, moved naturally to the new party.

When the Mahajana Eksath Peramuna was formed in February, 1956 it "was an assorted collection of sundry social and economic groups. It was a coalition of resentments against the UNP".[18] The components were the SLFP, the Viplavakari LSSP of Philip Gunawardena and the Samastha Lanka Sinhala Basha Peramuna, led by W. Dahanayake. Both were former Samasamajists, Gunawardena having left in 1950 and Dahanayake being expelled in 1952. Politically they had little in common, the one emerging as a leader of the Left within the MEP Cabinet and the other as a Rightwinger. However their common emphasis on the language issue brought them into natural alliance with the SLFP which had adopted the policy of Sinhala Only in 1955. Gunawardena brought with him a radical reputation, a militant trade union movement based on the Colombo harbour and a political machine in the Kelani valley. Dahanayake's Peramuna, like his personal following, came mainly from the Southern province, the stronghold of Sinhala Buddhism. The MEP was also able to attract a coalition of independents who were mainly committed to it on the language issue. The most important were I. M. R. A. Iriyagolle, a Sinhala

writer, Hugh Fernando, a Catholic Karawa, and R. G. Senanayake, who had resigned from the UNP Cabinet over the
granting of citizenship to some Indians and was resolutely
pursuing a vendetta against his kinsman J. R. Jayawardena.
These locally based notables gave the MEP a strong network
throughout the Low Country, in Catholic coastal areas and
among Philip's working class following. This was to prove a
great strength in winning the election, but a great weakness in
maintaining the party's cohesion afterwards. With so many
leaders who had already established their local bases before
joining with the SLFP, neither the party nor the MEP could
exert effective discipline.[19]

The first rift occurred between the Left and Right wings,
surrounding the policies pursued by the two former Samasamajist Ministers, Philip Gunawardena and P. H. William de Silva,
who controlled Agriculture and Industries respectively. While
the government had been faced with the national emergencies
surrounding the introduction of Sinhala Only, it had held
together well, though leaving considerable initiative to the
Governor-General and the armed forces. Once it moved on to
the social aspects of Bandaranaike's programme its fundamental
lack of agreement soon appeared. The Buddhist clergy, who had
done most of the party's footwork in 1956, began to turn away
from Bandaranaike over his agreement with the Federal leader
Chelvanayakam and the growing influence of the Marxist
socialist element in the government. Gunawardena and
Buddharakkitha, secretary of the Eksath Bhikkhu Peramuna,
were bitter enemies, with Philip calling the *bhikkhu* "Buddy
Racketeer" and the affronted monk replying that he was like a
"frenzied toothless cat".[20] The EBP, like most of the SLFP
Rightwing, were hostile not only to Philip's programme but also
to his support for crippling dock strikes which the two Marxist
parties outside the government were making the most of.

The Left was finally defeated by the so-called "Cabinet
strike" in which ten Cabinet Ministers advised Bandaranaike
that they would not function in their offices until Philip had
been got rid of. In a letter of November 28, 1958 they had
charged that he was generally incompetent, had exercised
massive patronage in the Co-operative Wholesale Establishment, was irresponsibly supporting the portworkers' strikes,

had offended by his attacks on private enterprise and, as a Marxist, subscribed to doctrines incompatible with SLFP membership. It was signed by C. P. de Silva, A. P. Jayasuriya, Maithripala Senanayake, R. G. Senanayake, J. Kuruppu, Mrs. W. Wijewardena, Stanley de Zoysa, C. A. S. Marikkar, S. Wijesinghe and W. Dahanayake.[21] This was a cross section of most of the important people in the party and Bandaranaike had to surrender. Despite this there is some evidence that Dahanayake and Buddharakkitha were working against the Prime Minister's continuing party presidency at the March, 1959 SLFP sessions at Kurunegala.

Thus at the time Bandaranaike was assassinated he had suffered several political defeats at the hands of the party's Rightwing, had seen little but civil disorder for the past two years, and faced an organised bloc in the Cabinet which could dictate policy to him. Not surprisingly the party began to fall apart as soon as he had died. Dahanayake, who had been chosen unanimously to succeed by the parliamentary party, could barely hold on to a parliamentary majority only three years after the MEP landslide. It was now the turn of Ministers to make demands on Dahanayake. In November, 1959, A. P. Jayasuriya, T. B. Ilangaratne, Maithripala Senanayake, P. B. G. Kalugalle, M. P. de Zoysa Siriwardene and S. Wijesinghe demanded that the Finance Minister Stanley de Zoysa be asked to resign because of his brother's implication in the assassination. The entire opposition made a similar demand, following it a fortnight later with a call for Dahanayake's resignation as well. Dahanayake dissolved parliament without telling his Ministers and left the SLFP saying "I have resigned from the SLFP because I do not want my throat cut in broad daylight".[22] He promptly sacked half his Ministers, daring the SLFP to expel the rest. In mid-December Dahanayake formed a new party, the Lanka Prajathantrawadi Pakshaya, and Dudley Senanayake proclaimed prematurely but understandably that "the SLFP is no more".[23]

The SLFP had lost its leader, its Leftwing allies, most of its Catholic and Muslim support, the EBP machine and its cohesion. However it had not lost its voters and, despite the multi-party chaos of the March 1960 election, it miraculously survived under C. P. de Silva's leadership with forty-six seats and nearly a quarter of the total vote. Parties led by Dahanayake and Iriyagolle were decimated although attempting to appeal to the same electors as the SLFP. It became clear that the landslide of 1956 was not an isolated phenomenon and that the SLFP had taken permanently from the Marxists the role of principal opponent of the UNP. In the elections of July, under Mrs. Bandaranaike, and with Marxist support, the SLFP won over one million votes and seventy-five seats. While this was partly a tribute to Bandaranaike's widow, it also underlined the permanence of a party based on Sinhala Buddhist nationalism, socialist economics and a populist appeal.

Mrs. Bandaranaike's victory in July 1960 brought back a purely SLFP government, though one which had the tacit approval of the two Marxist parties. Half her Cabinet had served under her husband, despite the massive split caused by Dahanayake's defection and the implication of Mrs. Wijewardena and Stanley de Zoysa in the assassination. She balanced the previous Rightwing of C. P. de Silva and Maithripala Senanayake with the Left, associated with T. B. Ilangaratne. Mahanama Samaraweera, a former Communist, was the only ex-Marxist and he was far more moderate than Philip Gunawardena.[24] The party was now led by a more coherent group than previously. It was not a particularly powerful combination, lacking any appreciable trade union or Marxist support and with more interest in issues like language and religion than with the growing economic and labour problems of the country. Despite her resolution to carry through her husband's programme, which led her immediately to take over the Catholic schools and implement Sinhala Only, Mrs. Bandaranaike was to find the SLFP still a heterogenous and not notably competent party. The Opposition included many who were bitterly against the SLFP, particularly those like Philip Gunawardena and Dahanayake who had previously worked with it. The LSSP, which had signed a no contest pact with the SLFP in May, 1960 and changed its policy to Sinhala Only, also grew increasingly restive with what it still regarded as a "capitalist party". Within the SLFP there were still repercussions from the split. R. G. Senanayake had opposed the electoral agreement with the LSSP and been left out of the Cabinet. While several independent M.P.s came over to the

SLFP in its first year of office, others started leaving its ranks from 1961 onwards. The party secretary, Jim Munasingha, had been expelled in 1960 and in August, 1961, the SLFP also expelled Dr. W. D. de Silva M.P., the head of its trade union organisation.[25]

These crises began to come to a head in 1962. The LSSP conference in July voted for an "all-out struggle to replace the SLFP government" under the slogan "Forward to a genuine socialist government".[26] This was a complete reversal of the majority decision in 1960 that the party would be prepared to join an SLFP government under certain conditions.[27] The disturbances in the Tamil areas, the attempted coup of January, 1962 and a growing sense of chaos and impending dictatorship all placed stresses upon the SLFP. Felix Dias Bandaranaike, who was suspected by the Left of planning such a dictatorship with N. Q. Dias, Permanent Secretary for Defence, was forced out of office in August, though returning to the Cabinet in the following month. An attempt by the UNP to introduce legislation on bribery which was said to be rampant among some SLFP leaders, brought further disagreement within the party and alienated the Left even more. The Left was also concerned with what it regarded as a "fascist" Bill to control the Press. It began moving for an alliance with Mrs. Bandaranaike's old enemy Philip Gunawardena who had already called for Left-wing unity in December, 1961 on the grounds that "the SLFP is a Radala clan, inefficient and devoid of progressive ideas."[28]

The charge of incompetence against the SLFP became increasingly popular. At Polgahawela in April, 1963 N. M. Perera claimed that "the majority of the government party are blockheads."[29] Two months later J. R. Jayawardena said "the people of Ceylon wondered whether there was a government in the country at all and whether it was necessary to have a government of the type where there was chaos everywhere."[30] Claims were also advanced that the party was controlled by a highcaste, Kandyan clique. These were heightened by the defection of a Junior Minister, Ashoka Karunaratne in April and by the attempt of Lakshman Rajapakse M.P. to form a Low Country movement in November.[31] R. G. Senanayake had already left the party, S. D. Bandaranaike was moving rapidly Leftwards and towards Maoism and one of S. W. R. D.

Bandaranaike's protegés, the traditionalist Mudiyanse Tenna-koon M.P., was expelled in December 1963. Thus by 1964 the SLFP was again showing the fissiparousness and lack of direction which had afflicted it five years before. It was losing support at local and by-elections. By March, 1964 there was a marked economic recession and a growing fear of dictatorship.

Mrs. Bandaranaike skilfully solved the problem by creating the Coalition with the LSSP in June, 1964. This was at last to give the party protection from Leftwing and trade unionist attacks and to establish it firmly as a radical socialist party with a fairly clear cut ideology. Naturally this could not be achieved without a further, and to date, final split. At the first rumours of approaches to the Left, C. P. de Silva, Minister for Lands, began to resist. At the SLFP Executive meeting in May, which voted 209 to 4 in favour of the coalition, he spoke against the resolution but did not vote.[32] L. Weerasinghe M.P., a former independent, resigned from the party in June while M. Samaraweera resigned as Minister for Posts in the same week.[33] P. P. Wickremasooriya, an opponent of the Coalition, was removed as Parliamentary Secretary to the Minister for Justice. Two more M.P.s resigned in November, 1964. The whole crisis was completed by the Press legislation. In the vote on the Address of Thanks on December 3, C. P. de Silva led thirteen M.P.s over to the Opposition side, defeating the Government by one vote. Mrs. Bandaranaike told the SLFP Kandy sessions that this represented a "plot promoted by those very same forces that engineered from behind the scenes the abortive Coup d'état of January 1962."[34]

While this defection meant the defeat of the Coalition and five years in Opposition, it also marked the consolidation of the SLFP as a distinctive, coherently organised party. In the splits of 1959-60, and again in 1964, the major opponents of Marxism removed themselves. For the most part they turned eventually towards the United National Party. Without actually joining the SLFP, the Marxist parties became loyal supporters. Thus the history of the party has been marked by three trends, all moving it towards the Left. The first was the adhesion of many Marxists to the MEP, the second the defection of many anti-Marxists and the third the forging of a permanent coalition which grew from an electoral agreement to regular liaison. The arrangement had effectively stabilised a previously volatile party. Being based entirely on rural seats, on local loyalties and family networks, the original SLFP had great difficulty in holding together. In finally shedding R. G. Senanayake and S. D. Bandaranaike, the SLFP further reasserted itself as a disciplined party rather than a coterie of notables, a development which it underlined by defeating them heavily in 1970 in their "family seats". Since these two left the party in 1968 there have been remarkably few schisms. Mrs. Bandaranaike's Cabinet of 1970 contained some Ministers previously regarded as on the Right, like Felix Dias Bandaranaike, Maithripala Senanayake and T. B. Tennekoon, and some from the Left, such as T. B. Ilangaratne, T. B. Subasinghe and P. B. G. Kalugalle. With the addition of four Marxists, and Mrs. Bandaranaike's own marked move to the Left since 1960, this distinguished the SLFP not only from the UNP, but from its former self.

The party also changed, in the extent to which it appealed to the minority groups. The high point of its communalism, as of the Left in general, was probably marked by the agitations against the Reasonable Use of Tamil regulations in January, 1966. It then raised the cry that the UNP had been elected by the minorities, while the SLFP was based on the Sinhala Buddhists. The natural corollary of this in an electoral situation, was to start appealing to these very same minorities. A report submitted to the parliamentary party in January, 1969, argued that there was a need to capture the votes of Muslims, Catholics and the minor castes.[35] Local election results from Wennapuwa, Madampe and Kochchikade, were submitted to establish that the SLFP, as previously in 1956, could win Catholic votes. The agitation of the Islamic Socialist Front was directed to arguing that Muslims, too, could be reached. Thus by becoming more ideologically distinctive, more coherently disciplined and less dependent on one community, the SLFP had moved most of the way by 1970 to becoming a national party in a basically two-party system. After gaining power it went even further by including a Ceylon Tamil in the government, in gaining the temporary support of the three Tamil Congress M.P.s, in securing the accession of A. T. Durayappah, an important Jaffna politician, and in successfully setting up SLFP branches in the Jaffna peninsula for the first time.

The Marxists

The Sri Lankan Marxist movement has received more foreign attention than the rest of the party system.[36] As the only mass, successful, Trotskyist party in the world, the Lanka Samasamaja Party would be of interest for that fact alone. The LSSP is also regarded as the first modern party in Ceylon, was the fountain-head for all other Marxist organisations and had produced some of Ceylon's leading politicians. Moreover its domination by a highly educated English-speaking élite with strong international connections and interests has made it more accessible to foreign researchers than the two major Sinhalese parties. Thus it is possible to overestimate the relative importance of Ceylon Marxism or to see the LSSP as something unique and totally different from the other parties. In reality the Marxists have played an important but limited role and until the Coalition of 1964 seemed to be declining in strength from the height of their impact in the late 1940's. The Parliamentary vote of clearly Marxist groups (the LSSP, the Communist Party, the Bolshevik-Leninists and Philip Gunawardena's VLSSP) has never recovered to its 1947 level of 23.4% of the total, which returned ten Samasamajists, five Bolshevik-Leninists and three Communists. By 1952 this had dropped to 19% returning thirteen members, in 1956 to 14.7% returning seventeen, in March 1960 it was 17.3% returning thirteen, in July 1960 10.4% returning sixteen, in 1965 only 10.5% returning fourteen and in 1970 12.1% returning twenty-five. Despite the bonus of seats gained by running as Coalitionists in 1970, this is not a story of advance towards the millenium. The Left was stable to the point of stagnation, with its electorates all in the Western, Southern and Sabaragamuwa provinces.

Marxists can take consolation from the fact that in the years since independence their influence has spread. All Sinhala parties now declare themselves to be socialist and most Cabinets since 1956 have contained members who were Samasamajists or ex-Samasamajists. This however, is only one side of the picture. Just as the two major parties have moved towards the Marxists, so they in turn have moved towards the centre, losing many active militants on the way. The Communist Party, which has always been opportunistic in its alliances and policies, has probably suffered less than the LSSP in this regard. In 1970 it finally achieved Cabinet office after twenty-seven years. In the meantime the whole relationship of Ceylon with the Communist world had changed radically. By 1970 Mrs. Bandaranaike was in a position to recognise the German Democratic Republic and the provisional government in South Vietnam. Trade and aid from Communist states was a major element in the country's economy. Many Ministers, including the Samasamajist "Trotskyists", had been honoured guests of the Soviet and other Communist governments. None of this altered the local political fact that the Marxist parties owed their continued importance to a large degree to their co-operation with Mrs. Bandaranaike on programmes which involved abandoning many of the stances of the past.

The Marxist movement in Ceylon had its origins in a group of Low Country Sinhala students and intellectuals whose motives were nationalist as much as socialist. The Colombo working class movement led by A. E. Goonesinha was already weakening and communalist by the 1930's. It never subsequently collaborated with the Marxists.[37] Dr. S. A. Wickremasinghe had been elected to the State Council in 1931 for the Southern province area which he still represented in 1970 and in which his family hold estates. He and a group of returned students including N. M. Perera, Colvin de Silva, Philip Gunawardena and Leslie Goonewardena, took an active part in the nationalist Suriya Mal movement formed in 1933 and in relief work organised by the movement in the malaria epidemic of 1934. This work was mainly concentrated in the Kelani valley area stretching into Sabaragumawa province. Arising from these campaigns and the Wellawatte Mills strike of 1933, the Lanka Samasamaja Party was founded on December 18, 1935. In the State Council elections of 1936 N. M. Perera and Philip Gunawardena were elected in the areas where a base had been built up through the anti-malaria movement. Two districts, around Wickremasinghe's home near Matara and in the Kelani valley, still provide a core of Communist and Samasamajist representation respectively. From its very beginnings the socialist movement was based on middle-class professionals with a rural political following and a Sinhalese nationalist orientation. With the creation of the LSSP, the aims and membership began to broaden. The party's first manifesto called for "the achievement of complete national independence, the nationalisation of the means of production, distribution and exchange and the abolition of inequalities arising from differences of race, caste, creed or sex."[38] Agitation among estate workers, beginning with the attempt to deport the Australian, M. A. L. Bracegirdle in 1937 and culminating with the strikes at Mool Oya and elsewhere in the hills in 1940, gave the Samasamajists a following among Indian Tamils.

The claims of the LSSP to be revolutionary rest mainly on its work on the tea estates and, to a greater extent, on its opposition to the war. The latter led to the imprisonment or exile of most of its leaders in June, 1940. By this time the majority of the party had shed its Stalinist segment, led by S. A. Wickremasinghe and M. G. Mendis. A small "T Group" had functioned since 1938, supporting the views of Trotsky, and this was able to dominate the Executive Committee on the outbreak of war.[39] As well as expelling the Stalinist minority the party also adopted an openly revolutionary, officially Trotskyist programme. Those expelled formed a United Socialist Party in 1940, which was declared illegal in 1942 and converted into the Ceylon Communist Party in July 1943. During these years the Communists were able to establish what still remains their second base, the Colombo harbourside trade unionists, organised by Pieter Keuneman the Party General-Secretary, in the Ceylon Trade Union Federation set up by the USP in December, 1940.[40]

Most of the Samasamajist leaders escaped to India. There they founded the Bolshevik Leninist Party of India in 1942 and gathered to it most of the Ceylonese Trotskyists. By now the party had acquired a Tamil following. It was this Indian connection which was to be used against the LSSP for many years and particularly against those, like Colvin de Silva, who maintained the Bolshevik-Leninists as a separate party after returning to Ceylon. The Communist Party, in contrast, followed the quite different tactic of joining the Ceylon National Congress, to which they were officially admitted by the Ambalangoda sessions of 1943 with the support of J. R. Jayawardena and Dudley Senanayake and against the strong resistance of D. S. Senanayake Keuneman, Wickremasinghe and A. Vaidialingam were elected to the Congress Working

Committee at a time when the Trotskyists were in hiding or in prison for their opposition to the war. They did not leave the Congress again until the end of 1945. This not unnaturally increased bitterness between the two groups which is still remembered. In their period of respectability the Communists were able to build up their trade union strength while it was not until 1946 that the Samasamajists were able to establish their control of the Ceylon Federation of Labour and the Government Workers' Trade Union Federation. At the same time they were splitting into a Sinhala nationalist group and the Bolshevik-Leninists, led by Colvin de Silva, Leslie Goonewardena, Doric de Souza, Bernard Soysa and Edmund Samarakkody. These latter expelled N. M. Perera and the brothers Philip and Robert Gunawardena in October, 1945. Thus the Marxist movement was in three major fragments. The Communists and Samasamajists did not come together again effectively until the United Left Front agreement of 1963. The LSSP and Bolshevik-Leninists were reunited in 1950. However this unification lost them the support of Philip Gunawardena. Even as late as the decision to enter the Coalition in 1964, there was still a legacy from the Bolshevik-Leninist schism, with many original BLP members being opposed to agreement with the SLFP.

These divisions are important, as most of the movement's leaders then are still the leaders today. The unending feud between Philip Gunawardena and N. M. Perera dated from the reunification of 1950 to which Philip was strongly opposed. Communist-Samasamajist hostility, quite apart from the now rather passé Stalin-Trotsky controversy, is sustained by the contrast between Samasamajist imprisonment and exile and Communist acceptance into the very centre of Ceylon bourgeois politics, the Ceylon National Congress. Despite its schisms the Marxist movement as a whole was at its peak in the early days of independence. The bulk of militant unions were under Communist or Samasamajist control and were ready to strike for political issues. In the 1947 election support was the highest ever recorded. The two Samasamajist parties strengthened their hold on the Kelani valley and in the coastal belt between Colombo and Kalutara. The Communists built upon Wickremasinghe's family seat near Matara and Keuneman won

Colombo Central. In general these districts have remained the Marxist base, a largely rural Sinhala one, despite the trade union strength and inter-communal character of the Marxist movement in the late 1940's.

Since these formative years the Marxists have reshuffled and reorganised around the same basis. Their tactics have become markedly less revolutionary and their appeal to the Indian and Ceylon Tamils much more muted. Philip Gunawardena remained lost to the movement which he had helped to found. He fought the 1952 elections in alliance with the Communists, joined the MEP in 1956, was forced out of Cabinet office in 1959, allied with communalists in 1960, joined the United Left Front in 1963, gave his support to the United National Party in 1965, became a Minister in Dudley Senanayake's government and eventually suffered defeat in 1970 in the seat he had held under many labels since 1936.[41] His trade union group remained significant but his part in the Marxist movement can be effectively declared closed by 1960.

The Communists and the Samasamajists began to follow rather similar paths after 1956 although relations between them flared up spasmodically, as in a dispute over the Soviet invasion of Czechoslovakia in 1968.[42] The Trotskyism of the LSSP is still maintained, although the party itself was expelled from the Trotskyist Fourth International in 1964. Once the MEP had swept the board in 1956 the position of the Left became that of a permanent minority. The revolutionary and not totally unrealistic prospect of power in the late 1940's faded away, leaving only the question of how to regard the SLFP and what sort of relationship to establish with it. Generally the LSSP has had more trouble in deciding its position than the Communists. Electoral pacts were arranged with the SLFP in 1956 but these were not completely effective and at least two seats[43] went to the UNP on a split Marxist/SLFP vote. The appointment of N. M. Perera as Leader of the Opposition made it difficult for the LSSP not to oppose the Bandaranaike government and in May, 1957 it moved into open conflict. On the deposing of Philip Gunawardena from the government in May, 1959 the Communists, too, withdrew their support and in July N. M. Perera moved a vote of no confidence in the Bandaranaike government. The support of the two Marxist parties for the

MEP depended on the continuation within it of Philip's group. As the Communist Party Central Committee said, on May 31st, 1959: "Now that the Right-wing has taken command of the Government and set a course that can only lead to an increasing repudiation of the progressive policies of 1956, the Communist Party will not extend to such a Government the critical support which it gave the MEP government in the past."[44]

In the chaos after the assassination of Bandaranaike, the LSSP returned temporarily to the belief that it could recapture the dominant position on the Left lost to the SLFP in 1956. In March, 1960, it put forward one hundred candidates, claiming that it could form a government. This was proved absurd by the results and in July it entered once more into a no-contest agreement with the SLFP. On Mrs. Bandaranaike's victory it took up a position of critical support, similar to that adopted towards her husband in 1956. "The Lanka Sama Samaja Party, while functioning as an independent group bound neither to the Government Party nor the Opposition Party, today adopts a position of general support of the Government, holding itself free to criticise the Government as well as vote against it where it disagrees" wrote the party secretary in 1960.[45] This was not to last for long. The growing economic crisis, culminating in Felix Dias Bandaranaike's budget of July, 1962, persuaded the Marxist parties that yet another attempt at Leftwing unity was needed. For the first time since independence a united Marxist May Day was held on Galle Face Green in 1963. It was the occasion for announcing the United Left Front which temporarily drew together the major segments into which the original LSSP had divided.

The United Left Front once again raised the question of whether the Marxists could maintain an effective independent force in politics and once again the answer was in the negative. By including Philip Gunawardena's MEP, which had become increasingly communalist, the Front immediately presaged its own dissolution. It made it almost impossible to retain the support of the Ceylon Workers Congress and Democratic Workers Congress, which the LSSP Central Committee had originally wanted. Nevertheless the MEP was prepared to accept Tamil as a regional language and that satisfied both the Communists and the LSSP. N. M. Perera proclaimed at the

joint May Day that "if the three Left parties march together in
the manner they had done for the rally it would be possible to
overthrow the Government and establish a socialist state."[46]
Despite objections within the LSSP from Edmund Samarakkody
M.P., and the beginnings of the Sino-Soviet split in the
Communist Party, the ULF agreement was signed on Hartal
Day (at the astrologically auspicious hour of 7.42) by N. M.
Perera, S. A. Wickremasinghe and Philip Gunawardena.[47] The
twenty-one Left M.P.s were to work together and a co-ordinating
committee had already been set up to plan municipal election
contests.

The ULF platform was a compromise but even so was only
adopted by the LSSP Central Committee by 27 votes to 11. Its
short term programme called for full political rights for local
government and public corporation employees, full implementation of the Paddy Lands Act, a government import monopoly
and toddy tapping without a permit. Its long term aims
included a republic, a new constitution, regional councils,
democratisation of the forces and administration, land tenure
reform, the legal protection of basic rights and nationalisation
of all banking and insurance. This was a fairly complete guide
to objectives which were to be pressed later upon the SLFP
through the Coalition. At the time, as Leslie Goonawardena
said: "The Left parties would never again extend their co-
operation to the SLFP government."[48] The ULF went ahead to
win the Borella by-election in January, 1964 and the winning
candidate, Vivienne Goonawardena of the LSSP, argued that
only the ULF and the UNP were effective political forces.

At this point Mrs. Bandaranaike prorogued parliament and
made overtures to Philip Gunawardena and N. M. Perera for
the parliamentary support of the ULF. T. B. Ilangaratne acted
as intermediary and was said to favour admitting the two
leaders to the Cabinet. This started the process which was to
split both the ULF and the LSSP and drive Philip finally into
an alliance with Dudley Senanayake only a year after he had
said "I will not die until I have rid the country of the UNP."[49]
After three months of contorted manoeuvres and plots,
designed mainly to exclude Philip and the Communists from the
government, N. M. Perera, Anil Moonesinghe and Cholmondley
Goonewardene entered Mrs. Bandaranaike's Cabinet. The

ULF was officially disbanded in July. Within the LSSP three factions emerged, one of which left the party altogether. They might be termed the pragmatic (led by N. M. Perera), the dogmatic (Leslie Goonawardena and Colvin de Silva) and the intractable (Bala Tampoe, V. Karalasingham and Meryl Fernando).[50] The first, backed by 507 members at the June 7th LSSP aggregate conference, supported the coalition, the second, supported by 75, wished to retain the ULF, while the third, which walked out to form a Revolutionary LSSP, had 159 supporters who were opposed to parliamentary tactics in any case. Seven M.P.s were 'pragmatic', five 'dogmatic' and two 'intractable'.

The LSSP suffered a considerable split as a result of its decision, which had to be pushed through against major divisions on the Politburo and Central Committee as well as at the special conference where a new Central Committee was elected. The Communist Party, which had naturally wanted to enter the government itself, was annoyed but forgiving. The MEP moved far away to the Right. The immediate results of the Coalition were short lived and Mrs. Bandaranaike lost the 1965 election. In a long term perspective there is little doubt that the 'pragmatic' group were correct. Even with twenty-one M.P.s and most of the militant unions, there was no guarantee that the ULF would make electoral progress. It was highly unlikely to form an alternative government to Mrs. Bandaranaike who would have dissolved parliament if defeated in the House. Philip Gunawardena and N. M. Perera had been enemies for years and fell out violently during the coalition negotiations. The Communists were embroiled with the Maoists and the LSSP with their own Left, neither of them accepting the parliamentary approach of the ULF. In the long run the SLFP, the LSSP and the Communists were able to work out an arrangement which lasted well at national and local level. It was the logical outcome of the pacts and agreements which had started to be made as early as 1955, before the SLFP was victorious. Marxists in 1970 held office in a newly elected government with a huge majority. Recognition of the benefits of the coalition was made by the LSSP 'dogmatists', two of whom joined the 1970 government having refused to serve in 1964. It was even accepted by Karalasingham and other 'intractables', who came back to the LSSP from the weird and faction ridden atmosphere of the small 'revolutionary' groups recognised by various claimants to be the Fourth International.[51] Indeed the very expulsion of the Samasamajists from the world Trotskyist movement was advantageous in making them acceptable to Mrs. Bandaranaike and the SLFP as a truly national party.

The majority of organised Marxists came to agree with the Coalition tactic. Only tiny groups of Maoists and revolutionary Trotskyists remained outside the consensus. Some union officials were critical of an arrangement which limited their freedom to call political or general strikes against an SLFP-dominated government.[52] After thirty years in the wilderness, Ceylon Marxism had come home, tarnished, battered, moderate, but at least in office. Yet precisely at the point of gaining power the Marxist movement began to be challenged by its younger members and by new forces which had not previously been enrolled within any of the older Marxist groups. In 1970 the leaders of the various Marxist parties, N. M. Perera, Leslie Goonewardena and Colvin de Silva for the LSSP, Pieter Keuneman, S. A. Wickremasinghe and M. G. Mendis for the Communists, Bala Tampoe and Edmund Samarakkody for the "revolutionary" Trotskyists and N. Shanmugathasan for the Maoists, had all spent a lifetime in politics and could trace their membership of Marxist organisations back to the days before independence. All their groups seemed to have reached relative stability in the years between 1964 and 1970. However the JVP rising was to produce new rifts in the Left and to provide a new focus for loyalty.

The majority of the JVP leadership had come from Shanmugathasan's Ceylon Communist Party, though a minority had been in the pro-Moscow party of the same name.[53] Disillusionment with Shanmugathasan's leadership had driven away his earlier supporters like Premalal Kumarasiri and S. D. Bandaranaike as well as the much younger group around Rohan Wijeweera.[54] Eventually it was to split the Maoist party altogether, with Shanmugathasan and Watson Fernando mutually expelling each other from a party which had virtually ceased to exist after the 1971 rising.[55] Tensions created by the rising threatened to split the much larger and politically more important pro-Soviet Communist Party. Pieter Keuneman was moving towards the creation of a separate party, with S. A. Wickremasinghe identified with the group supporting the party daily *Aththa* in its attacks on the Coalition government.[56] Wickremasinghe's stronghold in Southern Province had been severely affected by JVP occupation and the Communists faced the prospect of permanently losing their younger supporters if they were too closely identified with the government. The LSSP, in contrast, had no such problems, having lost most of its revolutionary members in 1964. There was, however, a marked increase in support for the party's Left, represented by V. Karalasingham and V. Nanayakkara, in elections to its Central Committee.[57] By 1972 there was a rich variety of factions on the Marxist Left again, with varyingly defined attitudes to the JVP rising, to China, the Soviet bloc, the Coalition and the leaders of the 'old Left'.

Minor Groups

In a system which was fluid, undisciplined and based on rural notables, it is hardly surprising that a variety of parties arose. In the March 1960 elections, twenty-three parties were officially recognised by the Electoral Commissioner. They ranged from the Bosath Bandaranaike Pakshaya of S. D. Bandaranaike, which believed that the late Prime Minister was a *boddhisatva*, to the Jathika Vimukhti Peramuna, one of whose founders, Mrs. K. M. P. Rajaratna, claimed that "the Yugoslav ambassador here was the secret agent of the Catholic Church and was also forwarding the interests of American imperialism."[58] These two parties, in common with most small Sinhalese groups then and subsequently, had similar programmes. All were spawned on the nationalist fringes of the SLFP, were led by local notables, appealed to rural voters in extravagant language and were eventually wiped out by the electors in favour of the SLFP. By 1970 there were no Sinhala M.P.s left who were not in one of the four major parties, except for Mudiyanse Tennakoon of Nikaweratiya who was presumably protected by the Aikanayake *devale* of which he had always been a devoted servant.[59]

The non-Marxist Sinhala fragments must be understood

against their rural background and in terms of the forces which created the SLFP. This applies even to Philip Gunawardena's MEP which emerged from the original MEP in 1959 and rapidly became communalist rather than Marxist. Of the significant new parties which contested in March, 1960 all were led by M.P.s who had co-operated with the MEP in 1956. Most of these had come to Bandaranaike in 1956 bringing a local machine with them, which they took away again after his death. The Ven. Henpitagedera Gnanaseeha and N. Q. Dias met with Bandaranaike, R. G. Senanayake, I. M. R. A. Iriyagolle and others in 1956 with the intention of forming a new front. Iriyagolle, R. G. Senanayake and W. Dahanayake of the Basha Peramuna, like Philip Gunawardena, were all to lead new parties by 1960. All had in common a concern with the language question, with the Buddhist revival and the Indian problem. In this they agreed with L. H. Mettananda, who was to work actively with several of the fragments for years to come.

After Bandaranaike's death and the expulsion of Dahanayake from the SLFP, these segments all re-emerged. Mettananda was instrumental in the creation of a Dharma Samajaya Party, which criticised Dahanayake for his opposition to the Sasana Commission report on clerical and monastic reform, supported neutralism in foreign policy and called for Buddhist Poya days to be made public holidays. In December 1959, Dahanayake announced the programme of his Lanka Prajathantrawadi Pakshaya, which opposed the Sasana Commission and the nationalisation of schools and plantations, and called for the repatriation of Indians. The day before, S. D. Bandaranaike announced that his new Bosath Bandaranaike Pakshaya was for the Sasana Commission, against corrupting Western influences, in favour of repatriating Indians and for the nationalisation of foreign assets. A fortnight later the MEP and the Dharma Samajaya Party issued a joint statement supporting the Sasana Commission and strongly urging Sinhala Only. Iriyagolle had already formed a Samajawadi Mahajana Peramuna which was also strongly committed to Sinhala Only. K. M. P. Rajaratna had been sustaining his own Jathika Vimukhthi Peramuna since he left the SLFP in 1956 as a radical, communalist movement. There were thus six parties concerned mainly with religious and nationalist issues, but differing on

their attitudes towards socialism and reform of the clergy. All
were trying to leap into the gap left by the schism in the SLFP.

The parties were far from modest in their aims. Dahanayake
believed that he would be returned as Prime Minister at the
head of the LPP. Iriyagolle said that he "would be able to form
a stable government if at least forty SMP candidates were
returned." Mettananda told the MEP opening rally that he
"had full confidence in Mr. Philip Gunawardena as the next
Prime Minister." Mettananda's own proposed election broadcast for the MEP was rejected by the Minister for Posts because
"from beginning to end it breathes anti-Catholic venom."[60]
Philip Gunawardena, not to be outdone, promised to distribute
the lands of the Catholic Church and the Malwatte and Asgiriya
monasteries and to "expel all foreign fascist Catholics."[61]
Adding her small piece, Mrs. Rajaratna of the Jathika Vimukhthi
Peramuna said that "the LSSP was a Tamil political organisation
whose leader Dr. N. M. Perera was a traitor."[62] All this was
very alarming, appealing as it did to communalism and
obscurantism in an electorate which might have been thought
very susceptible. But the voters returned only ten MEP members, four LPP, two Jathika V.P. one SMP and one BBP. For
the most part these were the notables who had set up the
organisations.

This was the high point for the minor communal parties. The
MEP began to break up in April 1960 just after Mettananda's
DSP amalgamated with it. In the vote of confidence which
overthrew Dudley Senanayake's government, three MEP
Members voted against the resolution and seven abstained. The
LPP was split even more. Obviously neither had any real
viability and several of their M.P.s defected almost at once.
They faded rapidly after the July election returned the SLFP.
Mettananda, who formed the Bauddha Jathika Balavegaya in
1963 on a strongly anti-Catholic platform, pressed Mrs.
Bandaranaike to include Philip Gunawardena in her Coalition
Cabinet of 1964, but without success. Eventually, in 1965 most
of the former leaders of minor parties, Iriyagolle, Mrs.
Rajaratna, Philip Gunawardena, Dahanayake and C. P. de
Silva (whose Sri Lanka Freedom Socialist Party fought the
1965 election in alliance with the LPP), took office in Dudley
Senanayake's "National Government". Mettananda, though

wanting "to ensure that the BJB adheres to its constitution to protect the Buddha Sasana without entering into party politics"[63] ended the election campaign with increasingly hostile criticisms of Mrs. Bandaranaike and the Coalition.

The tactic of forming an extreme communalist party around a single leader was almost exhausted by 1965. The Jathika V.P. and MEP fought the elections in harness for a "Buddhist government" but won only two seats. One last effort was made by R. G. Senanayake, who had held office under the UNP and the SLFP and had nowhere else to go. As a member of the Senanayake family and the holder of a "family seat" since before independence, he was in a strong position. In November, 1965, while a vice-president of the SLFP, he founded the We Sinhala Movement (Api Sinhale) with Senator A. Dassanayake. This had a strongly anti-Indian and anti-Tamil bias which was acceptable to the SLFP in the bitterness after their electoral defeat. He was also opposed to the coalition with the LSSP and this brought him into conflict with Mrs. Bandaranaike. In 1967 he brought together many of the former Basha Peramuna leaders in opposition to the Indo-Ceylon Agreement Bill.[64] This group blossomed into a Sinhala Peramuna in which Senanayake combined with the veteran Buddhist Congress leader Hema Basnayake.[65] After supporting a movement by Mudiyanse Tennakoon, Somaraweera Chandrasiri and other M.P.s, against the continuing use of English in politics, particularly by the Left, he was expelled from the SLFP in June, 1968. His new party, the Sinhala Mahajana Pakshaya promised to run one hundred candidates at the next election. Senanayake handed his programme to the Sangha at a religious ceremony on July 8, 1968. It was a predictable attack on the Indians, on the District Council Bill and on the Reasonable Use of Tamil regulations. The SMP went on to build up a party office and press and seemed to be getting support from some Sinhala businessmen and newspapers. It ran fifty-one candidates in 1970. All lost their deposits except Senanayake, who lost his seat.

The total fiasco of the SMP and the defeats of the Jathika V.P. and MEP leaders at the same election, probably mark the end of these attempts by local notables to build parties on Sinhala Buddhist extremism. The voters seem more sophisticated than their communalist betters, most of whom have been university graduates rather than backwoods obscurantists. As C. P. de Silva said, on merging his SLFSP with the United National Party, "the people vote either for the Elephant or the Hand and those who wish to remain in active politics should seek election through one of them."[66]

NOTES

1. H. L. Seneviratne: "Affairs of a New Nation"; *Ceylon Journal of Historical and Social Studies* 18: 1 & 2, January–December 1965.
2. Denzil Pieris: *1956 and After*; Colombo, 1958; p. 11.
3. *Ceylon Daily News* 28/3/1952.
4. Sir John Kotelawala: *An Asian Prime Minister's Story*; London, 1956; p. 81.
5. I. D. S. Weerawardena: *Ceylon General Election 1956*; Colombo, 1959; p. 47.
6. Despite resolutions passed at the UNP Annual Sessions. See UNP: *Annual Conference Agenda and Commemorative Number*; Colombo, 1955 calling for the restriction or outlawing of all of these. Kotelawala particularly injured Buddhist susceptibilities by going hunting with the King of Nepal near Buddhist shrines.
7. The Senanayakes were patrons of the Ramanya sect which drew support largely from the Karawa, Salagama and Durawa Low Country castes.
8. See a letter from Ven. Gnanaseeha in *Dinamina* 23/8/1962 commenting on Dudley Senanayake's partial confirmation of this story in the *Ceylon Daily News* 20/8/1962.
9. UNP: *Election Manifesto*; Colombo, 1956.
10. *Ceylon Observer* 22/9/1963.
11. Information subsequently available as a result of currency offences charged against directors of Associated Newspapers of Ceylon, revealed that the company had financed this meeting and had "bought over" some of the M.P.s bringing down Mrs. Bandaranaike's government on this issue. See Anon.: *Why Lake House seeks to destroy the Coalition*; Colombo, 1970 and the speech by Leslie Goonewardena in Parliament on 10/1/1970 in *Hansard* vol. 89, no. 2, cols. 300–337, together with information previously supplied to the author by Mr. A. Nugara.
12. S. W. R. D. Bandaranaike: *Towards a New Era*; Colombo, 1961; p. 118.
13. S. W. R. D. Bandaranaike: *Speeches and Writings*; Colombo, 1963; p. 102.
14. *Ibid.*; p. 116.
15. However the Sinhala Maha Sabha was permitted to submit resolutions to the UNP sessions in 1949. See UNP: *Second Annual Conference Agenda*; Wellawatta, 1949.

16. S. W. R. D. Bandaranaike: *Speeches and Writings*; p. 150.
17. See D. E. Smith: *South Asian Politics and Religion*; Princeton, 1966; pp. 490–499.
18. Denzil Pieris: *1956 and After*; Colombo, 1958; p. 10.
19. For an account of the creation of the MEP see I. D. S. Weerawardena: *Ceylon General Election 1956*; Colombo, 1960 especially pp. 21–26 and 55–59.
20. D. E. Smith: *op. cit*; pp. 496–7.
21. This letter was released by Stanley de Zoysa during the negotiations between Mrs. Bandaranaike and the Marxist parties in March, 1964. *Times of Ceylon* 18/3/1964.
22. *Ceylon Daily News* 8/12/1959.
23. *Ceylon Daily News* 14/12/1959.
24. Samaraweera defected over the press control issue in December, 1964, joined C. P. de Silva's Sri Lanka Freedom Socialist Party and was defeated by a Communist at Matara by less than one thousand votes in March, 1965.
25. *Times of Ceylon* 19/8/1961.
26. *Ceylon Daily News* 24/7/1962.
27. *Ceylon Observer* 1/6/1960.
28. *Ceylon Daily News* 25/12/1961.
29. *Times of Ceylon* 13/4/1963.
30. *Daily Mirror* (Colombo) 18/6/1963.
31. The Ruhunu Rata Balavegaya, which was heavily publicised by the press for about two weeks, seems also largely to have been invented by them. Its founder Lakshman Rajapakse was quoted as saying that "we cannot be blind to the active discrimination now practised by this government against the Low Country Sinhalese." *Ceylon Observer* 19/11/1963. He returned to Philip Gunawardena's MEP and lost his seat under that banner in 1965 by 236 votes, failing to regain it as an independent in 1970. The R. R. B. was never heard of again and neither it nor an earlier Kandyan party was able to create regional loyalties among the Sinhalese.
32. *Ceylon Observer* 10/5/1964.
33. *Ceylon Observer* 12/6/1964 and *Ceylon Daily News* 15/6/1964.
34. *Ceylon Observer* 13/12/1964.
35. *Ceylon Observer* 7/1/1969.
36. See particularly G. J. Lerski: *Origins of Trotskyism in Ceylon*; Stanford, 1968 (from 1935 to 1943); Leslie Goonewardena: *A Short History of the Lanka Sama Samaja Party*; Colombo, 1960; Anon: *Twenty Five Years of the Ceylon Communist Party*; Colombo, 1968; and R. N. Kearney: "The Marxist Parties of Ceylon" in Paul R. Brass and M. F. Franda: *Radical Politics in South Asia*; Cambridge, Mass., 1973.
37. See Kumari Jayawardene: *The Rise of the Labour Movement in Ceylon*; Durham, N.C., 1972.
38. Leslie Goonewardena: *op. cit.*; p. 4.
39. Lanka Sama Samaja Pakshaya: *Visipas Vasarak*; Colombo, 1960.

40. The Ceylon Trade Union Federation split in 1963 when the Maoist Watson Fernando replaced the pro-Soviet M. G. Mendis as president: *Sunday Times* (Colombo) 22/12/1963. A new, pro-Soviet Ceylon Federation of Trade Unions was then set up, with Pieter Keuneman as its president and Mendis as its secretary: *Ceylon Observer* 7/3/1964.

41. Philip was unable to fight his seat of Avissawella in 1952 as he was unseated for offences connected with a strike. However his wife, Kusumasiri Gunawardena, held it for him until his landslide return in 1956.

42. See the Statement of the Central Committee of the LSSP, calling for "the end of bureaucratic regimes and the pernicious influence of Stalinism over the working class of the world" and issued on August 26, 1968: V. Karalasingham: *Czechoslovakia*; Colombo, 1968; pp. 76–81.

43. Hakmana and Horowupotana.

44. *Twenty Five Years of the Ceylon Communist Party*; p. 74.

45. Leslie Goonewardena: *op. cit.*; p. 65.

46. *Times of Ceylon* 2/5/1963.

47. *Ceylon Daily News* 13/8/1963.

48. *Daily Mirror* (Colombo) 12/8/1963.

49. *Daily Mirror* (Colombo) 24/3/1964.

50. For the three resolutions see the LSSP: *Special Conference Agenda and Resolutions*; Colombo, June 6–7, 1964; G. Healy: *Ceylon—the Great Betrayal*; London, 1964 and *Fourth International* (London) 1: 2 Summer 1964 pp. 88–91.

51. The LSSP, before its expulsion, was affiliated to the United Secretariat of the Fourth International in Paris. This accepted the LSSP (Revolutionary), led by Bala Tampoe, into affiliation shortly before the "revolutionary" group split between Tampoe and the two ex-parliamentarians, Samarakkody and Meryl Fernando. The London International Committee of the 4th International, a bitter rival of the Paris bureau, maintained links with a youth and student group, the Revolutionary Communist League led by Kirthi Balasuriya. Karalasingham, who returned to the LSSP in 1966, was associated with a small group within the British Labour Party led by Ted Grant. The JVP, when exploring international contacts in 1970 had discussions with the Paris bureau but decided that nothing would be gained from regular association with any group outside Ceylon. It had links with Ceylonese in London.

52. I. J. Wickrema was removed from his important position as president of the Government Clerical Service Union for criticising N. M. Perera's 1970 Budget and thus losing the endorsement of the LSSP machine in the union.

53. Wijeweera was vice-president of the Maoist party's youth wing in 1965 and already had a faction within the party which included D. A. Gunasekera, Siripala Abeygunawardena, W. D. N. Jayasinghe ("Loku Athula") and about a dozen others. U. Dharmasekera and J. A. G. Jayakoddy came into the group later from the pro-Soviet Communists and Dharmasekera then left to form his own group.

Thus the core of the JVP leadership came from the Maoist youth leagues, though subsequent younger recruits probably had not been in any organisation.

54. Premalal Kumarasiri, a former Communist M.P., was expelled from the pro-Soviet party in January, 1964 (*Ceylon Observer* 5/1/1964) and was already in disagreement with Shanmugathasan by the end of the year. (*Daily Mirror* (Colombo) 7/9/1964). He worked as a translator for the North Korean and Cuban embassies and was active in the North Korean Friendship League, though never in the JVP with which he disagreed. S. D. Bandaranaike was expelled from the Maoist party for standing in the 1970 general election, associated with the JVP from that time and was placed on trial with the other 40 defendants in 1972. See Chapter 10.

55. *Ceylon News* 20/7/1972.

56. *Ceylon News* 12/7/1973 reported the expulsion of M. G. Mendis M.P., together with four other supporters of Keuneman for holding a separate 30th anniversary rally. Keuneman and Mendis set up a Communist Party of Sri Lanka in October 1973 which excluded S. A. Wickremasinghe but the party was eventually reunited.

57. Karalasingham came third in the Central Committee elections of 1971 and V. Nanayakkara, who was arrested in 1971 on suspicion of being an associate of Dharmasekera, did equally well in 1972. However the Left was, in general, kept off the LSSP Politburo which was dominated by supporters of the Coalition. *Ceylon News* 16/11/1972.

58. *Ceylon Daily News* 26/11/1959.

59. Mudiyanse Tennakoon was the youngest M.P. elected to the 1956 parliament and was on the "traditionalist" wing of the SLFP. He left the party in 1964 and was returned as an independent in 1965 and 1970. He is a lay guardian of the Aikanayake *devale* in his remote and backward constituency and frequently appeals to it for help.

60. *Ceylon Observer* 31/3/1960. The full text of the intended broadcast was printed in the *Ceylon Daily News* 9/2/1960.

61. *Ceylon Daily News* 7/3/1960.

62. *Times of Ceylon* 13/3/1960.

63. *Ceylon Daily News* 20/3/1965.

64. *Daily Mirror* (Colombo) 6/4/1967.

65. *Times of Ceylon* 10/6/1967.

66. *Times of Ceylon* 28/2/1969. The Elephant symbolises the UNP and the hand the SLFP.

CHAPTER 4

Party Organisation

The major function of Ceylon parties, apart from structuring representation, has been to ease the transition from a deferential and notable-led system within a colonial administrative framework, to one in which mass parties and pressure groups became effective channels for policy articulation and the promotion of those outside the existing narrow élite. This process, which began in 1920, is still continuing. The vital change has been that under colonialism the election of the older generation was largely on an ascriptive, individual basis, while by 1970 the established parties monopolised representation to as great a degree as in any European country. All but two of the M.P.s returned in 1970 were nominated by six parties, while nearly four-fifths were members of two, the Sri Lanka Freedom Party and the LSSP. Moreover these parties were relatively long established and stable. The LSSP was thirty-five years old, the Communists twenty-seven, the Tamil Congress twenty-six, the United National Party twenty-four, the Federal Party twenty-one and the SLFP nineteen. With this stabilisation of the party system, the organisational model favoured by parties has changed from the classic 'party of notables' described by Duverger to something much closer to the British pattern of a disciplined national structure based on enrolled mass membership.[1] Pre-independence parties, most importantly the Ceylon National Congress, the Sinhala Mahasabha, the Ceylon Labour Party and the Tamil Mahasabha, had little real need of a mass rank and file, despite the Labour Party's attempts to copy British example. Before 1931 less than five percent of the population had the franchise and voters and representatives were thus limited to the wealthy and educated, many of whom knew each other personally or were related. In that environment a mass party would have been functionless. Even after 1931, entry to the State Council was legally restricted to the Anglicised minority, a group which has never exceeded ten per cent of the population. It was primarily the same group of politicians who were returned, even if their appeals had to be retailored for rural and illiterate voters. Parties were largely irrelevant when politicians presented themselves in districts in which their families owned large estates and served in the aristocracy of *mudaliyars* and *dissawes* sustained by the British for local administration. The candidates were assisted by friends, relatives and retainers.[2]

By 1970 the textbook proposition that the British type of electoral and parliamentary system forces a two-party confrontation was largely true outside the Tamil areas. It was even becoming true among the Muslims of the East Coast, who had mostly returned independents in the past, and the Catholics north of Colombo who had previously been treated as in the pocket of the UNP. As the party system has come to resemble the British model, so the parties have adopted an appropriate organisation and structure. The central committees have increasingly intervened in local selections and disputes, limiting but by no means eliminating the power of local notables. Because Ceylon is so small and so well served by transport and because much of the landowning and professional classes have a stake both in Colombo and in the countryside, it has proved possible thus to interfere with local power bases. Not only have parliamentary candidatures become subject to central selection, which means in effect to ratification by the parliamentary leaders, but municipal affairs too are very much the concern of the central party officers. This is particularly so within the SLFP and the LSSP, where local conflicts have sometimes disturbed the unity of the Coalition.[3] The process of endorsement and selection from the centre had become so effective by 1970 that the great bulk of local contests outside the Northern and Eastern Provinces were on strict party lines even for Village Councils. Candidates disobeying party instructions or forming unapproved alliances were liable to expulsion. Of course, as in Western societies, there was considerably more 'floor-crossing' locally than nationally. This was most marked in the choice of council chairmen, where defections were a major tactic in councils which rarely have more than fifteen, and often only nine, members.

Controlling the Party

Virtually all elected representatives in Ceylon outside the Tamil areas, owed their endorsement and increasingly their election, to the party label.[4] Active leaders of the organisation are drawn from these elected representatives. Party and even union officials frequently hold parliamentary office, with the Senate formerly providing a useful lodging place for those defeated at the polls. There is normally little serious conflict between the parliamentary and organisational wings, even in the 'Leninist' parties. Neither the LSSP nor the Communist Party effectively direct their M.P.s from outside parliament, though within their ideology and rules they have greater incentive and capacity for doing so than do the other major parties.[5] While N. M. Perera and his group had great difficulty in winning support for the Coalitionist tactic between 1962 and 1964, they were in no sense forcing the issue upon a reluctant rank and file against the wishes of the extra-parliamentary machine. The three conflicting groups at the LSSP 1964 Special Conference which debated the Coalition with Mrs. Bandaranaike, were equally composed of M.P.s, candidates, union officials and rank and file. While in general the university youth have been on the Left of the party, the rural Youth Leagues provided major support for Perera's parliamentary and coalitionist approach. Within the Communist Party the hold of Pieter Keuneman and S. A. Wickremasinghe, both M.P.s, remained unbroken between the brief "Leftward turn" of 1948 to 1950, which was also led by an M.P., and the divisions in the Party in 1972 which found Keuneman and Wickremasinghe on opposite sides.

To say that the parties are controlled by and in turn control, almost all the elected representatives in the country at national and local level, is not to say that they have totally eliminated the original notable basis nor the possibility of splits and indiscipline based on personal idiosyncrasies. The very act of centralising selections in the hands of the party leaders means that many representatives are beholden to the two dynasties which have divided power between them since independence, the Senanay-

akes and the Bandaranaikes. Mrs. Bandaranaike's use of this
power to promote her own Bandaranaike and Ratwatte
relatives has been commented on frequently by her opponents.[6]
The leading core of the parliamentary parties who constitute
the effective decision-making and élite selection agencies are
still made up of those who came into politics at or before
independence. The three Samasamajist Ministers in Mrs.
Bandaranaike's 1970 Cabinet were all founder-members of the
LSSP in 1935. On his electoral defeat in the same year Dudley
Senanayake handed over leadership of the parliamentary UNP
to J. R. Jayawardena who had worked with him in the Ceylon
National Congress in the early 1940's.[7] Even in the relatively
new SLFP a large part of the Cabinet representation came from
those who had worked with S. W. R. D. Bandaranaike in the
Sinhala Mahasabha, or were related to him or his widow. All
six of the parties in parliament were still led in 1976 by politicians who had taken a leading role in their foundation.

This continued reliance on the old established political élite
reflects the deferential and caste basis of traditional attitudes to
power. Although Ceylon had a highly developed, if very
fragmented, trade union movement, few of its authentic
products have secured parliamentary office. Many of its officials
are middle-class professionals and parliamentarians, with the
legal and language training necessary to deal with government
and employers. Equally, the peasant masses have looked to
their betters to speak for them in parliament and local government. Very few genuine sons of the soil have been returned, and
these have mostly been in the SLFP rather than the Marxist
parties.[8] Where the parties have favoured the lower classes has
been in the growth of the patronage system. In an economy
with over 10% unemployment as a regular feature and with
one-quarter of non-agricultural jobs in the public sector, it
became inevitable even before independence that M.P.s should
show a strong interest in appointments and transfers. In recent
years their concern has spread outside the public service and it
has become conventional for Members to supply lists of
deserving unemployed to Ministers in charge of public undertakings, a practice institutionalised in 1971 by the provision
that each applicant for employment in the public sector must
secure a reference from his local M.P. Seekers after such

endorsement naturally tend to be drawn from party loyalists. This had become such a major part of the work of UNP Youth Leagues between 1965 and 1970 that their officials issued an identity card to ensure that seekers after patronage were genuine party adherents.[9] The various trade unions attached to each party also play a major part in securing employment through partisan patronage and their enrollment tends to oscillate with changes of government. Thus the relatively large enrolled membership of the parties and their Youth Leagues is based on expectation of preferment as much as on ideological commitment. It is concrete enough to ensure that each party which is liable to be successful has a large and active band of workers for national and local elections.

The established élite controls the parties and chooses the parliamentarians, who in their turn try to get preference for their constituents and party workers. Within the structure of modern parliamentary mass parties something superficially similar to the feudal obligation and deference found in the former Kandyan kingdom is reproduced. The resemblance is sustained by the role which Buddhist monks play in the central bodies of all Sinhalese parties, including the LSSP and the Communists since their foundation. Each party also has its astrologers who advise on suitable dates and times for holding elections or signing manifestoes and agreements. Each party leader receives petitioners on his verandah, as do the aristocracy, who are also frequently politicians, to this day.[10] But the parallel with traditional modes of politics soon starts to wear thin. Authority is only enjoyed by individuals while they and their parties satisfy the voters. The elections of 1956 and 1970 show that there were very few safe seats. Members of the élite compete amongst themselves for a deference which attaches more and more to them as 'friends of the people' and less and less as self-selecting patricians. Finally, in 1971, the youthful JVP called the whole tradition of competing élites into question by launching a rebellion which had as its primary objective the smashing of the established party system and the replacement of elected leaders of Left and Right.

Because the parties are run by politicians who in most cases can no longer guarantee their own election, the machines have begun to develop to the point where they could be meaningfully compared with those in industrial societies. The enrolled membership of the parties compares well with European proportions in terms of member-voter ratios.[11] The UNP claimed about 120,000 members with a vote of 1,880,100 (1:16), the SLFP about 60,000 to a vote of 1,806,914 (1:30) and the LSSP 25,000 to a vote of 433,179 (1:17) in 1970.[12] All these totals include Youth Leagues which are normally larger than the party proper, and in the 'Leninist' LSSP are eight to ten times larger. However they exclude members of trade unions ancillary to the various parties. The LSSP, the Communists and the SLFP all control federations with over 100,000 members each, which were moving towards closer co-operation by 1970. The UNP which was a late entry into union organisation controlled about 40,000 unionists by 1970. The above figures relate only to the basic core of partisan federations and do not include separate unions which may be under the control of members of a party but have effective independence and occasional changes of leadership.[13] Nor do they include the two largest unions of all, the Ceylon Workers' Congress and the Democratic Workers' Congress, with nearly six hundred thousand plantation workers enrolled in them. These are pseudo-parties, speaking politically and industrially for their still largely disfranchised members. Membership in the Tamil parties is vaguer, with little more than 2,000 in the Tamil Congress and with the Federal Party still a fairly loose federation of notables and retainers, despite a clear-cut policy-making machine and impressive parliamentary discipline.[14] Discounting the estate workers unions and minor parties, at least 600,000 were enrolled into the major parties, youth leagues and partisan union groups by 1970, or over 10% of the electorate.

While much of this enrolled membership may be dismissed as nominal and transient (which is true for democratic parties everywhere), loyalty to party symbols is highly developed and to some extent has replaced loyalty to the local M.P. The Member retains a vested interest in ensuring a high local enrollment both to boost his campaign machine and to enhance his standing in the national party. Such local membership does not necessarily play a decision-making role in the party, nor is it always entitled to the rights of full party membership. Most of the nominal support is joined up into Youth Leagues, women's groups or trade unions, which are peripheral to the party proper. Patronage systems are based on this membership in such a way that a patron-client relationship exists between the M.P. and his partisans. Control over him, such as it is, comes from the party leadership in Colombo, while his local machine must be understood much more in terms of reciprocal service. There is never any real question of local organisations controlling or being able to displace their Member. Indeed, should he change parties he will normally take a large part of his following with him as they remain dependent upon him for continuing patronage. However the voters are becoming increasingly difficult to detach from party loyalty and it is consequently becoming true that some UNP and SLFP local branches have approximated to the stability and collective loyalty long characteristic of the Marxist parties. While mass defections and large-scale collapse of branches is very common, it is also true that in safe party seats there exist continuing parties to which voters give their loyalty even if the M.P. changes his allegiance.[15] The voters respond to symbols which have become nationally valid since they were specifically allocated to parties rather than to individuals in 1956. These include the Hand (SLFP), the Elephant (UNP), the Key (LSSP), the Star (CP) and the House (FP). A mythology has grown around the most widespread symbols of the Hand, which is associated with the Buddha, and the Elephant, which is associated with the ancient national hero Dutugemunu.[16] Party colours, too, became standardised, with the Blue (SLFP) allied with the Red (Marxists) in every aspect from the flags at meetings to the colour of Mrs. Bandaranaike's *sari* at her inauguration. Most activists in Sinhalese areas wear party shirts of red, blue or green on public occasions. The JVP began adopting a uniform early in 1971, which, in contrast to Marxist tradition, was blue rather than red. In the absence of full mass media penetration, the symbols and colours are vital in spreading the notion of party adherence into rural areas where ascriptive loyalty was the norm until recently. Thus, while there are still important 'family areas' and 'ethnic seats', there are hardly any districts in which a candidate presenting himself under strange colours or symbols is likely to be returned. As a large part of the electorate is between 18 and 30, it has been totally socialised into a situation where these symbols are both established and nationally known. The much older politicians themselves still behave like feudal barons from time to time, changing sides and demanding concessions, but their retainers are increasingly unwilling to follow them into new camps under strange flags.

The major parties are thus bound together by patronage, symbolism, group loyalty and the exigencies of the single-member electoral system. The bonds of discipline and of ideological commitment occasionally weaken even for the Marxists. All the parties face defections by M.P.s and councillors and by their local supporters, if these feel they can gain some immediate benefit. To a large extent this relative lack of loyalty reflects a continuing element of localism and personalism in what is still an overwhelmingly rural society with important caste, class, language and religious divisions. The partisan thus always has centres of loyalty other than the party, however rapidly the latter may have grown as a focus. Family loyalty remains extremely important in the ruling circles of the UNP and SLFP, while Goyigama caste membership is also vital. A politician who is not related to either the Senanayake-Kotelawala-Jayawardena family or the Bandaranaike-Ratwatte family, or is not a Goyigama Buddhist, may find himself inadequately served by the two major parties. Many "outsiders", most notably C. P. de Silva and Ashoka Karunaratne, have in the past changed parties to improve their position. This tactic has been almost *de rigueur* for Muslims. Equally, many important Marxists, including Colvin de Silva, Bernard Soysa, Leslie Goonewardena and Pieter Keuneman, have been outside the Goyigama Buddhist community, as were the leaders of the Labour Party before them. Tamil politicians have normally functioned through the two Tamil parties. Even here defections from the Federal Party have been marked among Muslims, with members of the Vellalla caste (both Hindu and Christian) almost monopolizing power among Federalists and the Tamil Congress.

Apart from loose discipline caused by social pressures like localism and particularism, the vagueness of the ideological dividing lines prior to 1970 allowed individuals to change parties for personal advantage without having to undergo any serious psychological adjustment. Where such adjustment was necessary, as with Philip Gunawardena, the 'father of Ceylon Marxism' who ended up as a UNP Minister, it is eased by the relative cosiness of the social environment within which politicians operate. Even the two 'alienated' Tamil parties are dominated by university educated lawyers who mix socially and intellectually with their Sinhalese counterparts while passively resisting their laws. For a university-trained, landowning Marxist to transfer to the SLFP or even the UNP, does not involve real 'class betrayal'. Many careers have been founded precisely on such a movement to the Right.[17] Indeed one of the major functions of the Marxist parties, and especially of the LSSP, has been to feed graduate material into the two major parties, through a steady erosion by defection which produces instant rewards. Without endorsing the proposition that Ceylon parties were simply groups of ambitious men,[18] this suggests that the rigid loyalties of the 'British' system are more difficult to sustain where most leading politicians have been so socially close. The intensity of adherence to any ideology is likely to be modified by this fluidity of discipline, despite the fierce polemical verbalising that characterizes political debate. However defections have increasingly taken the form of consolidating the two major parties as compared to the relatively directionless trend of defections in the period before 1964. Defectors normally gravitate either to the UNP or the SLFP, if only because those two parties can offer much better prospects of election and promotion than anyone else.

The Structure of Party Organisation

Transformation from the personal followings of socially established individuals into structured mass parties has meant the steady adoption of the forms and practices of European organisations. There is no familiarity with American party structure and no desire to adopt it. The indiscipline, localism and ideological vagueness of American parties is unattractive precisely because it is so reminiscent of earlier experiences in the State Council. With no local selection or primary ballotting and with parliamentary discipline to maintain, the parties of Ceylon could hardly be expected to adopt many American practices except the patronage basis which sprang naturally from local traditions.[19] In their expectation of material award Ceylonese party members differed from those in Britain. In many other respects Ceylon followed faithfully British models of organisation. Several full-time party organisers in the UNP, the SLFP and the LSSP had experience of British methods, while few if any knew anything about other systems. Even the democratic centralism of the Marxists bore little resemblance to that practised in the Soviet Union. The LSSP leaders, brought up on Trotsky's denunciation of Stalinist bureaucracy, were intellectually committed to free discussion and the permission of more factionalism than was normal in Leninist parties after 1917. The LSSP drew far more of its ethos from the Leftwing of the British Labour Party than from the British Communists, let alone from the Soviet Union. This ethos encouraged debate by thesis and manifesto, rather than the imposition of iron discipline or forced consensus. Even the Communist Party was less rigorously disciplined than was normal in Europe. Its leaders and members were middle-class professionals, trained in the academic liberalism of British universities and the law, rather than trade unionists trained in an atmosphere of solidarity.

This predominantly British inheritance of the established parties encouraged the development of practices common to all of them. As in other parliamentary systems the parties came to resemble each other to a greater extent than their ideological differences might suggest. Only on the far Left, and particularly in the JVP, were models derived from anywhere other than Britain or India. Despite the influence of the major British parties, there has not been a mechanical transfer of all practices. While each party has an annual conference and a regularly convened executive, these do not necessarily have the same functions as in Britain. Only in the LSSP could the annual sessions be described as genuinely engaged in policy discussion. Indeed their deliberations are more genuinely concerned with such a function than those of the British Labour Party let alone the Conservatives.[20] In the major parties the sessions are much more in the nature of reunions at which the parliamentary leaders present themselves to the more prestigious rank and file leaders. Most important, there is little local power over the choice of candidates and the constituency organisations thus do not have anything like the power to choose who will represent them which is still significant in Britain.[21] In respect of the fairly ritualistic annual sessions and in the retention of parliamentary selection in the hands of the national leaders, the model is rather that of India. Indeed the Federal Party formal structure is fairly consciously copied from the Indian National Congress. What is retained from British experience, is the basing of the organisation on electoral units, its orientation towards electoral contests, its tendency to become dormant between elections but to provide some continuing activities for its militants, its basis in a relatively large enrolled membership, the exclusion of ordinary voters from any functions within the party structure, the appearance of policy-making and discussion within the structures enrolling the paid-up membership, the creation of ancillaries under party control and the retention of powers of expulsion or other penalties for breach of discipline. The notion that the party is a brotherhood, whose rights and duties are exclusive to its membership, is varyingly subscribed to and practised. As in Britain and elsewhere, this idea is most firmly held on the Left where it begins to verge on Leninist concepts of a disciplined group of professional revolutionaries.[22] It is least relevant on the Right, where deferential attitudes towards the leadership cancel out any notion that the leaders are in any real way the servants of the members. Yet it is remarkable that the UNP, in its various reorganisations, has adopted more and more of the practices of the structured Leftwing parties. Like the British Conservatives, it has combined a very effective organisation in terms of vote-gathering and fund-raising with a high degree of internal unity based on loyalty rather than enforced discipline.[23]

The major parties, despite differences of terminology and ideological tradition, have built up a pyramidal structure in which the most powerful inner body is dominated by Members of Parliament.[24] This group, whether called a Politburo or a Working Committee, is drawn from a larger and less regularly convened national executive. This is answerable to, and to some extent elected from, an annual convention. The annual sessions are composed of delegates from local branches. These are grouped on a constituency basis and, where possible, are presided over by the local Member of Parliament. All party nominees for national and local office, as for delegation to the next higher level, must be paid-up members of these branches. Below this level, and without the same rights to nomination or delegation, are the ancillaries, the youth leagues, women's organisations or trade unions which are normally led by enrolled party members. In contrast to the British Labour Party structure, these ancillaries are not affiliated directly and do not, therefore, have a strong direct voice in party affairs, the determination of policy or the selection of leaders and representatives. Concentric circles reach outwards from the parliamentary leadership and parliamentary party, neither of which are effectively controlled from the mass party, through a series of bodies based on delegated election and away to the ancillary membership and the voters, neither of whom are normally regarded as party members proper. At the centre sits the party leader who, in the two major parties, tends to 'emerge' rather than be elected, in the previous manner of the British Conservative leader.[25] The most important members of the party, who are usually but not always, also in parliament, have in the UNP and the SLFP, chosen this dominant figure with no reference to the lesser elements in the party at all.[26] Even in the smaller parties, the leader has not been created by the party. S. A. Wickremasinghe for the Communists, N. M. Perera for the LSSP, S. J. V. Chelvanayakam for the Federal Party and G. G. Ponnambalam for the Tamil Congress, have all been leaders since the founding of their parties. Only with their passing will the organisations be required to evolve practices for choosing the most important individual in the structure. None of the parties are seen by their leaders, or see themselves, as democratic collectivities in the sense of determining who will lead them.

In general the selection of parliamentarians and the determination of party policy, takes place within a small group of long-standing party members, which always includes the party leader and the most important Members of Parliament. This group is usually formalised as a Working Committee or a Politburo or Executive Committee.[27] Divisions within the party take place as factional disputes within these inner groups, rather than as battles between the members and leaders. Individuals within the inner circle recruit support from the next circle of participation, which is normally the broader national executive or the delegates to annual sessions. These followings, again, are responding

much more directly to a patron-client relationship with the
party leaders, than to pressures from below. Party members
tend to be grouped in terms of their loyalty to prominent
individuals, rather than ideologically. These loyalties may have
a social basis, for example in the Salagama caste following
which C. P. de Silva was able to take with him from the SLFP
to the UNP in 1964. Even within the JVP there were well
substantiated rumours that the split between Wijeweera and
Dharmasekera in 1970 had, as one dimension, tension between
Karava and Goyigama. There may be personal loyalties, as
between the rival followings for "N.M." and "Philip" which
split the LSSP in 1950 and made unity of the Left virtually
impossible thereafter. After 1971 it seemed as though the UNP
would also split along such lines between the followers of
Dudley Senanayake and J. R. Jayawardena, differences between
whom had been rumoured for some years and came into the
open after electoral defeat. There had, equally, been an individual basis to the split in the Tamil Congress between Ponnambalam and Chelvanayakam, from which the Federal Party
emerged in 1949. This division made Tamil unity virtually
impossible until the creation of the Tamil United Front in 1972.
Even then Ponnambalam did not directly participate in the
reunion. On inspection virtually every significant division within
a party reveals the existence of personal, family or caste
followings which can be traced back for some years. Ideological
divisions are only really apparent in the Communist Party and
the LSSP, although these too, sometimes have a personal or
communal dimension. All inner-party strife involves divisions
within the central élite of the party which are reflected in, but
are not initiated by, the mass membership.

Party Unity

The basic characteristic of the mass party is that its members
stand in a disciplined relationship to each other and towards
members of alternative parties. In contrast both to the party of
notables and to the loosely structured American party, the party
following British practices requires devices for controlling and
disciplining its members. This was a particularly acute problem
in Ceylon, as in India. Neither the institutions of colonial rule,

which were based on the committee system, nor the traditions of
society, which made allegiance to family, caste and community
a primary value, made it easy to build disciplined parties. The
Marxists were pioneers. They inherited an ideology which
emphasised discipline. Trotsky himself for the last few years of
his life had serious problems in giving coherence and discipline
to the badly assorted groups which made up the world
Trotskyist movement. The formative years of the LSSP coincided with Trotsky's struggle to instil Bolshevik notions into the
American Socialist Workers Party, while the formative years of
the Communist leaders coincided with the final victory of
Stalinism over world Communism.[28] The Trotskyist majority in
the LSSP expelled the Stalinist minority in 1940, thus asserting
the practice of removing unassimilable groups. Expulsion continued to be used on the Left as the last weapon in faction
fighting although organised defection was just as common. The
Bolshevik-Leninists were able to expel both N. M. Perera and
Philip Gunawardena in 1945, while Philip led his supporters out
of the party in 1951 in protest against the readmission of the
Bolshevik-Leninists. In 1953 another faction left to join the
Communists. The history of Ceylonese Marxism is punctuated
with expulsion and defection until the major divisions of 1964,
after which relative calm descended until the aftermath of the
JVP rising in 1971. There was thus a strand to the tradition of
party discipline which did not derive from British experience
and the need to remain united behind a parliamentary party.
Among Marxists the ideological basis of indiscipline was
frequently stressed. The quest for an ideologically correct party
was a prime consideration until well into the 1960s.

The preoccupation with ideological unity was seen by
Marxists as an essential element in uniting theory and practice.
Such a large part of the inner leadership was drawn from
University-educated theorists that pragmatic considerations
were often positively despised. Trade Union leaders, who provided a reformist base for European Marxist parties, tended to
be drawn from the same highly educated circles in Ceylon.
Some, like Bala Tampoe in the Ceylon Mercantile Union, or the
various leaders of the Government Clerical Service Union, were
periodically accused of temporising in order to maintain the
cohesion of their unions behind their leadership. Others, like

Shanmugathasan of the Ceylon Trade Union Federation, seemed prepared to watch their organisation withering away as the price of maintaining ideological purity. For nearly six years the LSSP leaders resisted the Sinhala Only tide, facing abuse, violence and defection in the process. The final loss of Philip Gunawardena in 1951, while probably inevitable at some stage, equally reflected a clash between the pan-communal Marxist orientation of the LSSP and the growing Sinhala nationalism of Philip and his supporters. Refusal to contemplate an alliance with the Communist Party in 1952, which Philip had been able to cement, led to one of the most damaging defections from the LSSP which went to strengthen the rather weak Communist Party. Within the largest of the Marxist parties there was a constant disciplinary problem created by the tension between adhering to a demanding ideological position and functioning within a society which was making that position electorally untenable. Even with the final victory of pragmatism in 1964, the disciplinary problem was not altogether solved. Not only did two M.P.s willingly sacrifice themselves for 'revolutionary' principles, but large sections of previous support both in the Lanka Estate Workers Union and amongst Ceylon Tamils were abandoned by LSSP participation in the January 1966 demonstrations against the Reasonable Use of Tamil regulations.[29]

It is easy to dismiss these continuing tensions within the LSSP as merely reflecting personal rivalries. Certainly the struggle between N. M. Perera and Philip Gunawardena was between two equally pragmatic politicians who had been in parliament since the party's foundation, who represented rather similar and neighbouring constituencies and who were both to hold Cabinet office. Within the LSSP, as within the other parties, there was only room for one leader who, like both Perera and Gunawardena, should be a Goyigama Buddhist representing a rural electorate. It is perhaps possible to treat the rift between them as based purely on rivalry between two powerful figures for the one available position. Significantly N. M. Perera who stayed within the organised LSSP was ultimately more successful and more faithful to the Marxist cause, than Philip Gunawardena. This reinforced the powerful myth, found in all Marxist parties, that those who go outside the organisation end up as agents of the enemy. For the Marxists believed not merely that unity of theory and practice was essential but that this unity was best achieved through a well organised and disciplined party, that the Marxist in isolation was a contradiction in terms. The LSSP was thus riddled with dissension, which to a large extent prevented it from expanding into the areas so easily captured by the SLFP in 1956. Its constant concern with theory limited its active membership to those educationally capable of assimilating notions which were expressed not merely in English but in a form requiring some knowledge of European history and philosophy.[30] Among this membership ideological dispute was endemic and irreconcilable positions led naturally to defections or expulsions. The 'walkout' became a standard feature of LSSP conferences between 1950 and 1965. At the same time as this small band of ideologues were arguing among themselves, they were confronted with certain hard political realities. The most obvious was the growth of an alternative Left which appealed on nationalist and populist grounds to an ever growing electoral following. The setback for the LSSP in the 1952 elections and the splitting of the party between 1951 and 1953 raised inescapably the whole question of orientation towards the masses. From then on the party was torn not merely between different interpretations of the Marxist truth, but between pragmatists and dogmatists.

The final victory of the pragmatists in 1964 meant that only a rearguard action could be fought by those Trotskyists remaining in the LSSP or returning to it. The price for party unity had been expulsion from the Fourth International, which had a psychological but no political impact, the subsidiary character which the LSSP had to adopt in its relationship with the SLFP and the disaffection of educated youth who had previously been attracted by the very Marxist dogmatism which the party had abandoned. The effective alliance between N. M. Perera, the Youth Leagues, the LSSP unions and the more specifically Marxist and previously Bolshevik-Leninist groups, proved viable. The LSSP still suffered from some of the weaknesses of the major parliamentary parties which it was coming to resemble. Some of its M.P.s and elected councillors had only a loose attachment to the party and were ready to leave it for immediate advantage. Pragmatic behaviour does not necessarily strengthen the junior partner in a coalition and there was a steady seepage away towards the SLFP. Equally the party found its membership becoming intellectually diluted as it grew to provide an electoral machine. The strict distinction between the small and highly educated membership and the large, rural Youth Leagues began to break down.[31] LSSP supporters came to expect patronage in the same way as those who worked for the UNP or SLFP. While the party was rightly able to claim that its leadership was not corrupt, it was less able to appeal to idealistic youth as untouched by power. Within the universities its political control of student societies, which had previously been contested by the Communists, was challenged by the SLFP and eventually the JVP, who were able to appeal to the rural and Sinhala-educated students of the 1970's. While party unity was very effectively maintained after 1964, the LSSP still tended to fall between two stools. It was too ideologically oriented to appeal to the rural masses whose support was preempted by the SLFP, but too pragmatic to be able easily to dominate the Marxist Left. In 1975, when the LSSP was driven out of the Coalition, many of its leaders found difficulty in adjusting to opposition politics, while within the youth leagues there were differing approaches from those committed to parliamentary methods and those younger members attracted to the tactics of the JVP.

LSSP unity was finally achieved not by the imposition of more discipline but by the alliance of its remaining leaders behind the pragmatism of N. M. Perera when that had proved itself in electoral struggle. Samasamajism lost the characteristic factionalism of a sectarian Marxist group, precisely because it merged itself into that section of the masses which was left to it under the Coalition arrangements. Ideological disputes within the party became polemical rather than fundamental.[32] Virtually all its important leaders held parliamentary and official positions after 1970, giving them a further reason for not splitting the organisation. Communist and SLFP leaders had looked with tolerant amusement on the dissensions of the LSSP, who in turn had looked with scorn on the ideological vagueness of Bandaranaike socialism and Stalinism. After 1964 it was the less important of the Marxist parties, the Communists, who began to lose their cohesion and who, by 1973 were showing all the schismatic tendencies which once characterised the LSSP.

The Communist Party had remained curiously immune to the
splits which affected counterparts elsewhere. The major events
of 1956, Khruschev's speech and the Hungarian revolution, had
little impact in Ceylon, where Bandaranaike's victory over-
shadowed foreign crises. European politics had little significance
in Ceylon, as the party's equal indifference to the Soviet invasion
of Czechoslovakia was to underline in 1968. Unity within the
Communist Party was preserved by an alliance between its three
leading members, Dr. S. A. Wickremasinghe, Pieter Keuneman
and M. G. Mendis, all of whom had been involved with the
party since its foundation. Each had his own sphere and no
significant clash of interests occurred until after the Coalition
victory of 1970. Wickremasinghe's electoral base in Southern
Province had been created by him and his relatives since his
first election to the State Council in 1931. Keuneman's electoral,
trade union and municipal base in central Colombo was quite
distinct from Wickremasinghe's in being urban and built up by
conventional organisational methods under Keuneman's personal leadership as Party Secretary.[33] Thus Wickremasinghe
functioned like other Sinhalese notables, while Keuneman was
a modern political organiser. M. G. Mendis, through his
leadership of the Ceylon Trade Union Federation, ran the third
arm of the party. The leaders of the rural base, the urban base
and the trade union base were in substantial alliance. They were
all in good standing with the Soviet Party. Keuneman and
Wickremasinghe regularly visited Moscow, Peking and other
Communist capitals while Mendis was on the executive committee of the World Federation of Trade Unions.

With such an effective alliance the unity of the party could
only be affected by schisms in the international communist
movement, by defections of individuals or by new pressures
growing up within the younger membership. The only international event of importance to Ceylon proved to be the Sino-
Soviet split, from which no Communist Party in Asia could
remain immune. Yet the impact on the Ceylon Party was not
great. The Ceylon Trade Union Federation was captured for
Maoism by its secretary, Shanmugathasan. This proved a hollow
victory, with Mendis able to reassemble the organisation under
the new name of the Ceylon Federation of Trade Unions and
with most of its membership returning to the "Moscow"-led

unions. Shanmugathasan's influence was small among Sinhalese, although the CTUF was led by a Sinhalese, Watson Fernando, who eventually quarrelled with Shanmugathasan in 1971. The Maoist Party was an unhappy group, rent with dissension and although well financed, having more of the character of a sect than of a nation-wide organisation. Most of the young Sinhalese who joined it soon left to form the JVP. Its continuing impact on the larger Communist Party was marginal and there were probably more sympathisers with China in the SLFP than in the whole Marxist movement. The Maoists had no electoral support, their trade union base was largely confined to their plantation workers' union and their recruitment of youth soon dropped off. The whole party was withered and shattered by 1971, when it was able to play no part in the revolutionary situation of April except to lose any official Chinese support which it had previously enjoyed. Apart from the rather farcical Maoist split, the Ceylon Communist Party was not deeply affected by any of the explosions going on in the world Marxist movement. It produced no New Left, as the elements making up such a tendency elsewhere were locally grouped around the LSSP journal *Young Socialist*.

Apart from the defection of two M.P.'s, Stanley Tillekaratne in 1965, and Percy Wickremasinghe in 1970, the Communist leadership remained united until after the Coalition victory in 1970. The Coalition tactic did not produce the public rifts witnessed in the LSSP in 1964, as most of its opponents had already left with Shanmugathasan. The only significant breach of discipline was in 1965, when Sarath Muttetuwegama contested Ratnapura as an Independent, breaking the electoral agreement with the SLFP and causing the UNP candidate to be returned. His candidature was a manoeuvre to establish the Communists' right to a greater allocation of seats. Not only was Muttetuwegama not expelled but he was returned as an M.P. in 1970 and became president of the party's Youth Leagues. However the events of 1971 shattered Communist unity. Their Southern Province stronghold was the centre of major JVP occupation and there was growing opposition to party membership of a government which had been so strongly opposed by many potential Communist voters. The rural Sinhala Youth Leagues of the South allied with the supporters of Wickre-

masinghe against the party's General Secretary, Pieter
Keuneman, who was also a Minister. For the first time
Keuneman and Mendis were found on one side and Wickremasinghe on the other. While it would be facile to see this purely
as a split between the rural Sinhala Buddhists and the urban
cosmopolitans and trade unionists, there were certainly aspects
of this. As previously in the LSSP, there were elements of
dogmatism against pragmatism, or perhaps more charitably, of
placing the integrity of the party above that of the government.
Wickremasinghe assumed the post of General Secretary in
1972, giving him access to the international Communist movement, the parliamentary party of six was split between those
supporting and opposing the government and Mendis was
finally expelled in 1973.[34] The split was not healed for another
two years, when the Communists decided to continue their
alliance with Mrs. Bandaranaike.

Both Marxist parties have thus shown divisions between
pragmatists and dogmatists, although the form of the conflict
has varied and was much more apparent in the larger, more
democratic and more broadly based LSSP. These divisions cannot be dismissed simply as personal or particularistic, if only
because they have occurred in all Marxist parties operating in a
competitive political system. Relatively loose party control over
M.P.s and their tendency to defect are characteristic of all
Ceylon parties. Fundamental disagreements over the methods to
be used and the goals to be sought have been confined to the
Marxists. An analysis which lumps all the parties together only
does them justice on one dimension. As parliamentary organisations functioning largely in the Sinhalese rural community, all
parties have contained a 'notable' element with its accompany-
ing indiscipline and tendency towards patronage. The respective
personal followings for N. M. Perera and Philip Gunawardena
could not be contained within the framework of a disciplined
Marxist party, if only because they did not need such a framework to ensure their election. Equally, S. A. Wickremasinghe
had shown as early as 1931 that he did not need a Communist
Party in order to be returned. Many other local notables, such
as T. B. Subasinghe, P. H. William de Silva or Jack Kotelawala,
were similarly placed with regard to the LSSP. With the
creation of a secure base of safe seats in the Southwest, both of

the Marxist parties were able to free themselves to some extent from the vagaries of independently minded M.P.s. At the core of both parties were lifelong loyalists, who had lived through several schisms and were determined to remain within the organisation rather than suffer the isolation of defectors like Shanmugathasan or Bala Tampoe.

The two major parties did not suffer from ideological divisions of this nature but they equally had passed from a period of fluidity to one of cohesion and solidarity by 1970. Both the UNP and the SLFP were geared to mobilisation of the electorate, while the Marxist structure had derived initially from the needs of revolutionary mobilisation. Their trade union ancillaries played a small part in party affairs and the distinction made by the Marxists between full members with policy-making rights and peripheral members was not effectively made. Those who had control of policy and organisation in the two major parties were invariably politicians, whose followers were loyal retainers rather than potential critics. Factions within the parties were almost exclusively grouped around dissident M.P.s who unlike the Marxists felt no obligation to use the party rank and file as a sounding board or as a final court of appeal. The distinction between pragmatists and dogmatists was irrelevant as there was insufficient clarity of ideology to produce such a division. Both parties were quite unequivocally committed to parliamentary power and neither needed to worry about this commitment clashing with a revolutionary mythology. If there was a division between broad attitude groups it was between loyalists and opportunists, between those who stayed with the party in all conditions and those who left it when a better opening appeared somewhere else. By 1970 the loyalists had clearly emerged in command of both camps. The core of the party around Mrs. Bandaranaike were those who had resisted Dahanayake in the Cabinet at the end of 1959. The core of UNP leadership had equally been with the party for over ten years, with defectors from other parties like C. P. de Silva largely going down to defeat in their electorates.

Parties which are so firmly committed to electoral struggle and are thus led by parliamentarians, need unity in their leading group if they are not to dissolve into factionalism. Such unity was built up by common experiences and steady co-operation

between 1960 and 1970 under the leadership of Mrs. Bandaranaike and Dudley Senanayake. Both were able to command and
to organise a loyalty which their predecessors had failed to
create. Both had popular charisma which bolstered their
position within the party in the absence of a highly organised
and self-disciplined rank and file. Both had a network of
relatives who were able to sustain informal links which reinforced the often tenuous framework of the official party
structure. Each party rested on nearly two million voters, a
foundation which, while different from that of the Marxists
was, at the same time very much more widespread and representative. Although much poorer than the UNP, the SLFP
was able to catch up organisationally once it had won power.
By 1972 it could open a new office which for the first time bore
favourable comparison with those of the other Sinhalese
parties.[35] With the beginnings of bureaucratism it could start
relying, like the other parties, on those who had a vested
interest in the party as such rather than in their personal careers.
Thus imposed discipline became less important and voluntary
dedication to the party and its leaders more significant. The
frantic expulsions which characterised the SLFP in 1960 were a
temporary phenomenon in times of chaos. The droves of
defectors between 1959 and 1964 declined to a mere trickle of
disaffected individuals. Equally in the UNP the open disagreements between Dudley Senanayake, J. R. Jayawardena and R.
Premadasa which followed the defeat of 1970, took place within
the context of a well-organised mass party rather than as the
disruptive quarrel of notables which tore the party into pieces
between 1953 and 1956. Both parties had become well organised
vested interests, to which millions of people looked and for
which thousands of people worked.

Mass Mobilisation

Parties and trade unions are the major agencies bringing the
people into the political process. That they do so very effectively
is suggested by the extremely high voter turnout at national and
local elections and by the level of unionisation. They mobilise
people on a voluntary and spasmodic basis and for specific
objectives. Mobilisation takes place competitively rather than

through orchestration from a single centre. It is thus not mass mobilisation in the totalitarian sense of organising the people as a whole for certain tasks, but rather mobilisation behind competing leaders as a form of exerting pressure and determining representation. The Sri Lanka masses are not formed into labour brigades on the Chinese or Cuban pattern and attempts to organise them for productive tasks as with the Land Army are shortlived and relatively unsuccessful. If the situation has nothing in common with that in totalitarian systems, neither is it strictly comparable with that in most industrial democracies. The parties and unions provide a continous link between government and people. With limited mass media penetration it becomes increasingly important to organise and propagandise through personal contact and through the physical presentation of elected leaders at mass rallies and on all occasions when large numbers are gathered together. The gap between electors and elected which is increasingly bridged by remote electronic media in industrial societies must be closed in Sri Lanka by physical organisation of masses of people. Given that most of those in rural areas still maintain a very deferential and respectful attitude towards their political representatives, it is nevertheless true that the parties must be more than simple election committees. They must penetrate organisationally into the most remote corners of rural electorates, if only because the more remote districts are precisely those where mass media penetration is slightest.[36]

The political process thus differs from that in most Western systems in so far as the parties bring electors into direct contact with their representatives. In many Western countries the mass rally has almost died out. In Ceylon it is a common occurrence. New programmes are launched at such rallies, all elections involve them and a major function of party organisations is to ensure the largest possible turnout for them. Groups will be mobilised to express support for particular individuals and each politician moves around with a bevy of retainers who are more beholden to him than to the party as a whole. These retainers collectively go to make up most of the party membership. They form the bulk of Youth League membership and act as support groups during election campaigns. The mobilisation process takes place in two dimensions, those of personal following and of party loyalty. A politician of any standing can rely on his retainers to look after his interests in a locality, even if he cannot be sure of the methods they might use. Too many personally loyal groups engage in violent conflict with the supporters of others to make them an altogether desirable component of the party machines. The use of hand-bombs, kidnapping and even murder can be traced to the enthusiasm of such followings. Within the fairly strict confines of the electoral laws they may often put at risk the career of their sponsor who is sometimes engaged in a struggle to restrain the coercive enthusiasm of his men. The 'party machine' is made up of many loyal but often embarrassing personal machines who can only be controlled by their patron. They are vital to the assembling of rallies, the provision of drivers, stewards and body-guards and the dissemination of posters and banners. They make up the core of the uniformed marches which normally precede rallies. Without them the mass parties would not be able to reach the electorate as none are sufficiently well-financed to be able to employ many professional organisers and propagandists. Yet the very need for such personally loyal groups helps to maintain the "notable" basis of the major parties in rural areas.[37]

The mass organisations began as confederations of politicians' followings. As most politicians now tend to remain loyal to a single party these followings consolidate into continuing branches of a national organisation. The essential element in party discipline and effectiveness is unity within the parliamentary party and behind the national leader. None of the parties has a sufficiently powerful organisational frame to discipline its local branches without the intermediary power enjoyed by the Member of Parliament. He has the prime responsibility for building up membership and for reaching his voters. Hence even within the Marxist parties the loyalty of Youth Leagues is predominantly to their M.P. Decisions are taken within the hard core of active party members but they are helpless to get these carried out without the local support of the Youth Leagues. The major distinction between the Marxists and other parties is largely that their Youth Leagues have built up a loyalty to the organisation over the years which makes it possible to recruit them against party defectors. In the other major parties such loyalty is still primarily to individuals.

Thus the mobilisation of party followers is not yet done by professional organisers. These are much more likely to be found in trade union work. The parties do not need field workers as long as they have parliamentarians and candidates to do the work for them and to finance it out of their own pocket. Party funds at the centre are spent primarily on the party press, which is usually unprofitable, on the national headquarters staff, on cars and on national election propaganda. Subsidies to trade unions, which need rather larger professional staffs, are frequently made by the national party.[38] Even the national staff tends to be drawn from those with parliamentary positions or with sufficient private income not to need a salary. Although the parties with their ancillaries are quite large, they are not managed by bureaucrats who live 'off' politics but by those who live 'for' politics. There is a marked contrast with totalitarian organisations which can mobilise much more effectively and permanently because they employ huge staffs at considerable expense. The iron discipline and central direction which this makes possible must necessarily be lacking in any system run by amateurs. Party management in Sri Lanka consists largely of retaining the enthusiasm of such amateurs. This is best done by constantly sustaining an atmosphere of excitement and tension based on fierce competition. The amateur has to feel that the victory of his party, which he often equates with the victory of his patron, is more important to him personally than anything else.

Regular mass mobilising campaigns have a dual function of legitimising the leadership by presenting it in person to the following and of enthusing the following so that it will sustain the local organisation. In a rural society politics takes the place held by mass entertainment and mass sport in urbanised systems. The political rally always has features both of entertainment, of education and of religious inspiration. Songs and poems are always performed, speakers impart information and monks attend in large numbers and are usually involved in the speeches. The notion that one party is in lifelong competition with another produces the sort of enthusiastic interest attached to sporting teams elsewhere. Resentments which otherwise focus on family quarrels, land disputes or caste issues can all be sublimated in resentment against the other party. Hopes which

are otherwise realised through astrologers or pilgrimages, may
be transferred to manifestos or speeches by national leaders.
This means that the party must constantly be seen to exist.
Even if its local committees cease to function between elections
the outward symbols of meetings, shirts and banners must
accompany the local Member of Parliament around his
electorate.

The political party, through the intermediary of its local
activists, thus becomes an essential feature of rural life. No
significant contest is without a partisan dimension. In contrast
to many European states, local village elections are just as
partisan as the national contests. The traditional attitude that
villagers should speak with a single voice through their social
superiors, which is still found even in industrialised European
countries, has died out through most of Ceylon. After forty
years of competitive elections the villager came to realise that
such benefits as he derived from the political system were the
price of his support. As the electoral system operated fairly and
without governmental interference his confidence in it did not
become misplaced. Members representing apparently safe seats
nevertheless spent much time keeping in touch with their constituents and with local elected officials who were members of
their party.[39] Frequently an M.P. was elected as chairman of a
Village Council or had served as a councillor. Partisan politics
at the local level was not divorced from the national contest.
Voters expected benefits to come to them, especially if they
were represented by a Minister. To make their demands effective
in between elections they needed local points of contact with
national government. These were largely supplied by party
activists. The bureaucracy was made responsive to local demands
largely through intervention by such activists. The party
member thus became not merely the eyes and ears of the M.P.
in his constituency but a channel through which petitioners
could approach authority. Ministers spoke of their electors as
"their masters".[40] With the weakness of effective local progress
associations, parent-teacher committees or other Western
institutions, the local party became the major instrument for
aggregating and articulating demands. In contrast to the
Marxist-Leninist notion of the party member as a skilled
organiser and leader of the masses, the major parties created

the idea of the member as a bearer of messages between rulers and ruled.

Parties as the Guardians of Democracy

As every kind of activity began to assume a partisan character there were some protests against the divisiveness which this brought. To some extent these came from the Anglicised professionals who found the autonomy of the bureaucracy and judiciary being threatened by politicisation. Their complaints largely focussed on the dangers of patronage, corruption and loss of integrity. There was another strong element which found party strife disconcerting. This was the Buddhist leaders, both modernising and traditional, who feared for the division of the Sinhala Buddhist community in the face of threats from the minorities.[41] The All-Ceylon Buddhist Congress and the Mahanayake Theros repeatedly advised against clerical involvement in politics as disruptive of the unity of the *Sangha*. As a well-educated and well-informed segment to whom villagers looked for guidance and news of the outside world, monks were as unable to remain aloof from politics as were school teachers. Nor could the Buddhist villager be expected to object to partisan divisions. To have united behind a single political leadership would have greatly reduced his bargaining power and given authority into the hands of monastic and upper class Buddhist Sinhala leaders with very little real interest in social welfare or the material improvement of village life.

Far from the party system being abolished, or submerged within a single dominant party, it was flourishing by 1970. Institutional changes made it likely that party members would play an even greater role in politics in future. Not only did they monopolise parliamentary power but about four thousand members of local authorities were also activists in the major national parties and needed party endorsement to secure their election. The planned extension of Peoples' (Janata) Committees through central nomination made it extremely likely that most of the 90,000 places on them would also be held by party activists although these would owe their position to the local Member of Parliament and not to the voters. A quarter or more of all those nominally enrolled in parties or Youth Leagues would thus have some official powers, however limited. It was widely believed by the Opposition that Peoples' Committees would become synonymous with local branches of the governing party. From being merely assistants and messengers for national politicians, the party members would be built into the political system to a greater degree than in most other parliamentary systems. The proposed extension of workers' committees in government establishments and industry would also open up possibilities for party members within the trade unions to take a small part in running economic enterprises and supervising the bureaucracy. While most of the Peoples' Committee members might be expected to be in the SLFP, many of the workers' committeemen would inevitably come from the Marxist parties who controlled most of the industrial and government workers' unions. Right the way through the system, from the factory, office and village to parliament and government, membership of a party could become a passport to political influence. It might equally become a necessary qualification for the job in the growing public sector of employment in which the patronage of M.P.s, Ministers and trade unions was considerable.

The parties would thus extend their functions from being election machines to being an essential component in linking the people with the administration. They would not therefore correspond to the totalitarian party which operates by placing its trained members in all positions of importance. As long as the system remained competitive no party could have a monopoly of power. Even within the ruling Coalition, members of the SLFP, the LSSP and the Communist Party frequently competed for union and local government office and their leaders fought hard for the most favourable allocation of seats under electoral agreements. In Tamil areas it was almost inevitable that Federal Party members would secure office. It was equally likely that activists of the UNP would not be totally excluded from influence in districts with UNP Members. The parties were designed to compete, not to rule, and the changes made after 1970 were unlikely immediately to alter that. Because of their electoral character the parties did not have devices for training skilled members in any case. "Cadres work" in the Marxist parties was very half-hearted and designed to produce good propagandists rather than administrators. In the UNP and SLFP such training as existed within the Youth Leagues was equally designed to produce public speakers, local councillors and branch secretaries. The organisational hold which the national machine had over local councillors was very weak, although the LSSP had a continuing Municipal Committee which arranged training schools from time to time.[42] Within some of the more efficient unions, for example in the GCSU, there were also training schools of a rudimentary sort. These too aimed to produce good agitators and organisers and the existence of Workers' Committees had not led to any effective training for management. Even within the unions themselves a large part of the leadership was recruited from outside and had only a limited faith in the ability of the members to produce competent officials.

The extended responsibilities of the parties would not greatly alter their primary function of mobilising the electors behind their representatives and keeping those representatives informed about local problems. This function did not require substantial administrative skills, except from the representative himself, upon whom fell the main responsibility for keeping his machine efficient. It did require constant confrontation with the other major alternative party in the locality. The parties were essential to the preservation of competitive democracy. They enrolled and influenced most of those who had an active interest in politics. They gave power to the elector provided this power was expressed electorally. They organised the voters to the polls in massive numbers on the basis of party identification. They influenced and permeated most institutions, including the *Sangha*, the teachers, the unions and the professions. There was thus no major area in which some commitment to the democratic partisan process was not commonplace. The most noticeable trend in party politics was the extension of the functions and influence of the parties as collective agencies for policy articulation, leadership selection and the expression of popular interests and demands.

These vital democratising functions were not, of course, carried out in an atmosphere of equality between leaders and led. Party members participated in politics and were occasionally consulted about their views. There was no developed sense of mass control, even in the Marxist parties. While back-bench

Members of Parliament may have risen up through the party by holding local office, the great majority of Ministers and national leaders were at the top of the political ladder because they were also at the top of the social ladder. It was not inconceivable that national leaders and even members of the dominant families could be broken politically by the parties. R. G. Senanayake, S. D. Bandaranaike, Philip Gunawardena and other powerful and well-connected politicians were all so broken by 1970. They had changed parties once too often. The SLFP set itself to destroy C. P. de Silva for his desertion in 1964 and they succeeded. In all these defeats the people had the final say by throwing the defecting notables out of |their once safe constituencies. They had little say in the process by which alternative candidates were produced. R. G. Senanayake and Philip Gunawardena were both defeated by candidates who had only recently defected from the UNP and were thus able to capture some of the party's traditional vote. C. P. de Silva was defeated by a lawyer who had just returned from Peking. In general the party leaders simply place people in those constituences where, for a variety of reasons, they seem likely to win.[43] The local partisans either accept this or defect in disgust to the other side. They have virtually no sanctions which they can apply against the national party which does not need their money nor rely on their conference votes. So long as the candidate can put together a new set of retainers they become the party for that locality, give him their support and enjoy his patronage.

Where, as in Sri Lanka, it is essential to preserve a parliamentary majority, parties need to be well disciplined and relatively few in number. If the electors are not to be alienated from the system the party must reach them on a relatively permanent basis. Where there is very little money for professional organisation then contact must be maintained by enthusiastic volunteers. The system breaks down if party unity disintegrates, if the volunteers lose their enthusiasm or if the voters feel the parties no longer care about them. Only among that section of youth which supported the JVP in 1971 can the latter be said to have happened. In every other respect Ceylon was highly successful in transforming the followings of important individuals into effective nation-wide parties. In the process the entire rural population was politicised and mobilised behind alternative leaders and policies.

Parties as Organised Opinion

The political parties had their origins in loose groups of notables who found it necessary to organise local support, particularly after 1931. Their relative fluidity and lack of discipline reflects these origins as late as the middle 1960's. Yet there was also a long tradition in Ceylon of mass organisation around basic principles and objectives. The Buddhist revival and temperance movements in Ruhunu[44] and the labour movement around Colombo[45], predated the existing parties. Thus there was an important strand of collective discipline behind programmes and objectives which had an influence far outside the narrow circle of élitist politicians who dominated the colonial legislatures. Even they were organised around platforms and attitudes to a limited extent, as the divisions between "constitutionalists" and "radicals" suggested in the inter-war years[46]. The revivalist and temperance movements bequeathed their legacy to Bandaranaike's Sinhala Maha Sabha and to an important extent to the younger element in the Ceylon National Congress around Dudley Senanayake and J. R. Jayawardena. The labour movement of A. E. Goonesinha, which was consciously copied from the British Labour Party and the Trades Union Congress, was replaced by the more radical movements organised by Philip Gunawardena and Pieter Keuneman. At independence the tradition of mass organisation, while submerged by the elitist and noble-led parties represented in the parliament, was by no means dead.

Mass political parties have several dimensions. In Ceylon they undoubtedly served as instruments whereby the political élite maintained and rationalised its rule under mass suffrage. They increasingly came to perform the patronage functions already outlined. They provided identifiable symbols for the electors and gave disciplined coherence to parliamentary majorities. Yet they also gave organised form to attitudes and ideologies and came to dominate the national debate on issues almost to the exclusion of other groups and influences. The newspapers increasingly presented their political news in terms of party behaviour. The discussion of issues turned from the formal debating and learned societies of the colonial period to the party committees and attached ancillaries. Academics, teachers, journalists and monks all became influenced by or even immersed in partisan debate as the parties themselves came to realise how vital it was to recruit opinion leaders from outside the narrow ranks of professional politicians. As electoral ratification came to replace deferential acceptance, so the debates around issues spread outwards into the community.

The major ideological positions which came to structure national debate and to be given organisational form by the parties, centred around the national revival and socialism. The Tamil parties reacted to the ideologies of the majority community by protectively asserting their faith in liberal democracy rather than by developing extreme ideologies of their own. The Marxists came to accept the spirit of democratic compromise within which they were forced to work by the refusal of the masses to be detached from the electoral process. Thus some ideologies, and more particularly revolutionary socialism and national fascism, were rendered invalid by the realities of the party struggle, just as some, such as the national revival, came to be accepted by all parties appealing to the majority. The character of political debate changed over decades as the parties found some aspect of their ideology becoming exhausted or less appealing to the electors. Over a period of fifty years parties are formed around positions, but positions which the more success- ful politicians are prepared to abandon when they no longer seem to appeal. Ceylon parties were not ideologically rigid, responding pragmatically to changing situations. Yet at the same time they became distinctive in the sense of appealing to voters on the basis of programmes and ideas, which they further needed to retain the enthusiasm of their active supporters.

The major debate of the inter-war years was around the pace of development towards national independence. Loosely structured parties formed around more or less radical positions. The dominant Jayatilaka-D.S. Senanayake group in the Ceylon National Congress created a conservative tradition which bound the United National Party together until the debacle of 1956. Senanayake's close allies Sir John Kotelawala, Sir Oliver Goonetilleke and D. R. Wijewardena, provided a consistently

conservative core to the new party as to its predecessor the
National Congress. Senanayake and his supporters were able to
bring independence to Ceylon without mobilising popular
support behind radical anti-colonial sentiments. "In his
personal conversations D. S. Senanayake spoke freely of his
wish that Ceylon, a small dot in the map of Asia, should always
retain and promote her friendship with Great Britain and the
Commonwealth"[47]. Kotelawala and Goonetilleke had similar
attitudes and, despite its origins in the Sinhala revivalist movement, Wijewardena's Lake House press was fully prepared to
join with the traditionally pro-British *Times of Ceylon* in
promulgating these views amongst the literate opinion-formers.
Thus pro-British conservatism became the basis of political
consensus in the otherwise loosely constructed United National
Party and gave direction to the policies of its governments.

The pro-British conservatism which was given organisational
form by the United National Party had only a limited utility
once independence was gained. There was no particular
advantage to supporting the colonial power once it had withdrawn its occupation. The segments of society which had most
to gain from the British connection, the English-speaking
minority, whether Sinhalese, Burgher or Tamil, and the
Protestant Christians, carried little electoral weight even if they
dominated most positions of power and influence. The national
revival and trade-union based socialism, were existing forces
which, despite the political hegemony of the UNP, increasingly
demanded and eventually had created, effective political parties
of their own. The 1947 elections had returned a large bloc of
labour and socialist inspired M.P.s, even if these were to be
found in four different parties[48]. Encased within the United
National Party, principally as members of the Sinhala Maha
Sabha, were supporters of the national revival who had substantial support among rural notables who were not part of the
Anglicised élite. Within the pro-Government Tamil Congress
there was a growing sentiment for Tamil assertion, which was to
break through in 1949 with the formation of the Federal Party.
While the various socialist, nationalist and separatist movements
were all identified with prominent notables such as S.W.R.D.
Bandaranaike, Philip Gunawardena or S. J. V. Chelvanayakam,
they represented forces which would have broken out in some

form or another from the unnatural consensus enforced through the electorally dominant UNP. Even within the ruling circles of the UNP itself, the revivalist sentiment was appealing to those like Dudley Senanayake and J. R. Jayawardena who were not politically sympathetic to Bandaranaike.

Ideological positions and allegiances thus already existed with fairly long traditions of their own, alternative and inimical to the conservatism of the dominant party. The breakdown of the UNP may be attributed to various factors, of which the political insensitivity of Sir John Kotelawala is the most obvious. Yet it is hard to see how party discipline could have been indefinitely imposed against the rise of nationalist and socialist sentiments. New parties were needed not simply because various notables were disaffected, but also because sentiments and ideas which had widespread currency among the masses were not being given scope for effective political expression. The rise of Samasamajism from a tiny group of Westernised intellectuals, to a major influence in the trade union movement and amongst voters in the Southwest, had already provided evidence of the potential strength of ideology as a unifying and driving force. It is doubtful whether the Trotskyism of the LSSP leaders ever appealed to, or even reached, most of their electors. The nationalist and populist sentiment mobilised by N. M. Perera and Philip Gunawardena doubtless had much more appeal, especially in those areas of Southern Province and the Kalutara District which had been swept by the temperance and revivalist movements thirty years before. Yet Marxism, rather than ascriptive loyalty to notables, bound the party leadership together despite factional disagreement and personal jealousies. Notables certainly defected throughout the party's history, from Dahanayake and T. B. Subasinghe to Philip Gunawardena and Jack Kotelawala. The movement continued to maintain its cohesion and to promulgate Marxist socialist ideas, albeit in a less radical form than in its early days. The Trotskyism and Stalinism of the founders naturally broadened in appeal as they secured a mass base. Had this not happened the Marxist movement would have been dissipated in sterile factionalism rather than growing to become a significant and permanent feature of political life.

The Marxist parties were bound together by a set of ideas

which were able to appeal across class, caste and communal divisions, even if the power base of the formal parties rested firmly among Sinhalese Buddhists. These ideas changed their form in the light of political experience. Eventually, by 1971, they had become so moderate as to lose the allegiance of educated rural youth, who turned in their thousands to the Janata Vimukthi Peramuna, a guerilla group also bound together by what it claimed to be Marxist ideas. Whether all or any of the parties claiming to be Marxist were 'truly' so is a 'theological' question which it would be fruitless to explore for the purposes of this discussion. All attached great importance to the ideological element in their appeal, and to the reconciliation of their world view with their specific programmes. They were 'ideological parties' in the sense of making their unity and effectiveness dependent on a set of ideas. Without notables such as S. A. Wickremasinghe, N. M. Perera or Philip Gunawardena, drawn from the politically dominant Sinhala Buddhist Goyigama community, the Marxist parties might have made less headway. It is equally arguable that without ideologues such as Pieter Keuneman or Leslie Goonewardena, who were not from that community, they might well have submerged without trace within the broader socialist populism of the Sri Lanka Freedom Party. The LSSP and the Communists thus avoided the twin pitfalls of 'ideological parties' in liberal democracies, submersion and loss of identity on the one hand or futile sectarianism on the other.

Socialists in Ceylon could not fail to be influenced by the Marxism originating in the Samasamajist movement. In recent years they could not avoid being affected by the well-financed and resolutely advocated ideologies of Russia, China and lesser socialist states such as North Korea, North Vietnam or Cuba. Because Marxism had been a major influence in local intellectual life for many years as well as upon mass electoral and union organisations, some public debate centred around the experiences of societies which were ruled by Marxist socialists. Yet the most electorally attractive and thus politically successful, socialist ideas emanated from the Sri Lanka Freedom Party and from a tradition of national revival which was not only not Marxist but, in some respects, antithetical to Marxisms. S. W. R. D. Bandaranaike, at the first annual conference of the SLFP in

December, 1952, stressed that his new party was to be democratic and socialist. The latter he defined in broad social
welfare terms. "In short, it seems that the resources of our
country should be utilised more fully and effectively for the
benefit of the people. In our country still the large majority of
the people are living below the poverty line, and if they are to
be given a proper standard of living and be provided with the
necessary social services, e.g. education, health, etc., this cannot
be achieved effectively or satisfactorily except on socialist
lines."[49]

Bandaranaike continuously stressed in the formative years of
the SLFP that it was to be a party resting on the three pillars of
democracy, socialism and national culture. In his address to the
first conference he dened that the party was simply a 'Label'.
"We have a positive, concrete policy and programme that differ
from those of all other parties and are more likely to solve our
problems to the satisfaction of our people than those of any
others.[50]" At this early stage Bandaranaike was expressing a
hope, as the divisions in the MEP Cabinet after 1956 were to
underline. There was very little in common between MEP
Ministers such as Philip Gunawardena on the one hand or
R. G. Senanayake on the other. Between 1958 and 1964
defectors as distinguished and well established in the party as
C. P. de Silva, Stanley de Zoysa and Hugh Fernando were to
leave the SLFP and to join the UNP. Yet there remained a
hard core of leaders who held together through all vicissitudes
and were still at the heart of SLFP politics after 1970. They
were not bound solely by family ties to Bandaranaike and his
widow, although these were very important in retaining in the
party many who ideologically might have been more at home in
the UNP. The populist slogans which Bandaranaike had worked
out in his years in the Sinhala Maha Sabha, while ideologically
vague by the standards of the Marxists, seem nevertheless to
have been sufficiently appealing to hold together the varied
elements in the party.

'Bandaranaike socialism' came to form the basis of consensus between the major Sinhalese parliamentary parties.[51] As
Bandaranaike, like most working politicians, was never able to
find the lesiure to spell out exactly what his ideology was, it has
been argued that his approach was purely expedient and

eclectic. For several years the Marxists poured scorn on his claims to socialism, and were to be even more caustic about Mrs. Bandaranaike, whose family had for long been identified with Kandyan conservatism. Yet over the years the SLFP worked out a democratic socialist programme which is no more vague than that of other social-democratic parties and which equally serves as a rallying point for party members of divergent interests and attitudes. After the Coalition agreement of 1964 and through the presentation of common platforms in the 1965 and 1970 elections, the SLFP can be described as a party bound together by an ideology to at least the same degree as the other major parties. As in the other parties the consistency of the ideology relies to a large extent on the party leaders retaining control over the discussion and implementation of economic policy and foreign affairs and the shaping of the election manifesto. Nevertheless it would be a mistake to overlook the ideological impact of the working arrangements which the party has made at all levels with its Marxist partners and, in particular, the role taken by the Socialist Study Circle as a forum for policy debate within the Coalition. Many leading members of the SLFP, including T. B. Ilangaratne, T. B. Subasinghe, Badiuddin Mahmud, R. D. Senanayake, P. G. B. Kalugalle and Mrs. Bandaranaike's own daughter, Sunethra Rupasinghe, have publicly and repeatedly identified themselves with socialist positions which are often indistinguishable from those held within the LSSP or the Communist Party.

It has already been argued[52] that each successive split and realignment within the SLFP served to consolidate the socialist element at the expense of conservatism and simple communalism. Those opposed to Marxism either moved to the UNP or, like Felix Dias Bandaranaike or Maithripala Senanayake, themselves took up socialist policy positions without necessarily lessening their suspicion of the Marxist parties. The communalist element moved away into the smaller parties led by K. M. P. Rajaratne, Philip Gunawardena or R. G. Senanayake, which the voters rejected. By 1970 the common manifesto of the United Front was able to define socialism in a more fundamental way than Bandaranaike had chosen nearly twenty years before. "We shall put an end to these policies of economic dependence and neo-colonialism which have characterised the UNP's regime.

Instead, we shall seek to develop all branches of the economy at a rapid rate and according to a National Plan in order to lay the foundation for a further advance towards a socialist society."[53] This was to be achieved by the nationalisation of the banking system, state handling of the import of essential commodities and their distribution through the co-operative system, state guidance and direction of the plantation industries, state ownership of the heavy and capital-goods industries, state acquisition of shares in locally and foreign-owned firms and a foreign policy based on non-alignment and opposition to 'imperialism and colonialism, both old and new'. These and other policies were aimed at 'the progressive advance towards the establishment of a socialist democracy that was begun in 1956 under the leadership of Mr. S. W. R. D. Bandaranaike.' This was defined in terms of national sovereignty, the elimination of social and economic privilege, organisation of the masses to raise production, raising the moral and cultural standards, allowing the free exercise of all rights and resisting all attempts at authoritarianism[54].

By 1970 the major parties in Ceylon had gathered support to themselves on the basis of general ideologies and specific platforms to as great a degree as in any competitive democracy. The major conservative party, the UNP was clearly defined as such by its opponents and, despite its adoption of a Democratic Socialist programme at Kalutara in 1963, continued to gain support from those conservative ethnic and commercial interests who had supported it under the less equivocal leadership of D. S. Senanayake and Sir John Kotelawala. The SLFP had lost most of its overtly conservative and much of its specifically communalist leadership, yet rested on an electoral base already established by Bandaranaike in 1956. The Marxist parties were visibly less revolutionary but continued to appeal for membership on the same basis as before. In so far as it is possible to describe a political spectrum on one dimension alone, the positions of the parties ran from 'revolution' to 'conservatism'. While this is not a conventional European scale from Left to Right (the value of which was consistently denied by American political scientists throughout the 1960's)[55], it comes reasonably close to the pictures of ideologies to which many practising Ceylonese politicians refer.

The 'revolutionary' position is almost invariably identified with extreme Marxist socialism. There has been no tradition of Fascism or militant conservatism in Ceylon, except briefly under Sir John Kotelawala, when it was repudiated by all major elements in the political system including the voters. To be a 'revolutionary' has always meant to be a 'radical socialist' and it was in that tradition that the JVP rising of 1971 followed, despite the muddled and eclectic ideology of the movement's leaders. In their own eyes they were Marxist-Leninists, as are the Maoists, the Trotskyists and even the Samasamajists and Communists. Thus some commitment to a revolution characterised the Marxist socialist movement and distinguished it from the SLFP, which thought in terms of socialism through the ballot box. Just as there was an identity between being revolutionary and being a Marxist, so there was between being 'pro-Western' and conservative. The term 'reactionary' must here be reserved for those who looked towards an authoritarian regime based on the hierarchical practices of the Kandyan kingdom and, particularly, upon Sinhala Buddhist domination by force over the ethnic minorities. The term 'nationalist' has, correctly, to be reserved for those who wanted Sinhala hegemony to be exercised through the ballot box and through legislation which preserved the rights of minorities as long as they accepted that they *were* minorities. The mainstream of the nationalist revival, from Anagarika Dharmapala, through F. R. Senanayake and A. E. Goonesinha, the Sinhala Maha Sabha, S. W. R. D. Bandaranaike, the Mahajana Eksath Peramuna and the SLFP, is closer to the socialist than the conservative tradition though seen (in Buddhist as much as in secular terms) as the Middle Way. Thus the very claim that 'Bandaranaike socialism' marks the Middle Way, reinforces the notion of a scale of actions and attitudes which lies between the extremes of revolutionary socialism and authoritarian reaction.

There are of course other dimensions to political attitudes than the one schematically represented here. But increasingly the language of politics came to be couched in terms of such a scale. Party identification at least for activists, was increasingly shaped by the manifesto and by an image in which ideological elements were important. While the ideological boundaries between the parties were necessarily shadowy, as in all parlia-

mentary democracies, the parties became agents for the
promulgation of ideologies in the sense of alternative views of
the present and future world. By capturing powerful sentiments
for nationalism, cultural revival, social welfare provision and
trade unionism, the SLFP was able to transform itself from a
loose amalgam of notables into the guardian of the Middle
Way. Other Sinhalese parties were drawn to it, organisationally
or programmatically. Without taking this mobilisation of long-
standing sentiments into account it is impossible to explain the
success of the party or the course which Ceylon has taken
nationally and internationally since 1956.

NOTES

1. See M. Duverger: *Political Parties*; London, 1954 and R. T.
   MacKenzie: *British Political Parties*; London, 1955.
2. For an interesting fictionalised account of a pre-independence
   election see the short story "The Mystery of the Missing Candidate"
   in S. W. R. D. Bandaranaike: *Speeches and Writings*; Colombo, 1963;
   pp. 467–490.
3. See for example the intervention of Mrs. Bandaranaike in the
   Dehiwela-Mount Lavinia municipal elections of 1968 where there was
   a dispute between the LSSP and the SLFP.
4. For the historical development of this process see Calvin B. Woodward:
   The Growth of a Party System in Ceylon; Providence, R. I.; 1969.
5. In 1971 the Communist Party did not expel or even discipline two of
   their M.P.s, Pieter Keuneman and B. Y. Tudawe for voting with the
   government on the Criminal Justice Bill, to which the Party Central
   Committee was opposed. Similarly, in 1969, the LSSP did not formally
   expel an M.P., P. B. Wijesundera, who advocated an alliance with
   the UNP, although his party membership eventually lapsed.
6. See, e.g., *Ceylon News* 28/5/1970; "The Radala Revolution", listing
   relatives of Mrs. Bandaranaike who were standing for the SLFP at
   the general elections.
7. On the death of Dudley Senanayake in April, 1973, J. R. Jayawardena
   was unanimously elected President of the UNP by its Working
   Committee. (*Ceylon News* 3/5/1973).
8. The only politicians in recent years with self-proclaimed humble
   origins have been T. B. Tennakoon (M.P. for Dambulla, SLFP) a
   former labourer, D. G. H. Sirisena (M.P. for Akurana, SLFP) a
   former servant, hawker and self-made businessman, and P. M. K.
   Tennakoon (M.P. for Mihintale, SLFP) a farmer. All represent
   Kandyan seats. In the Senate D. G. William (LSSP) was a former
   waiter, while R. Jesudason (CWC) was an estate worker.

9. Information supplied by Senator J. Niyathapala, president of the UNP Youth Leagues, in August 1969.

10. It was while interviewing on his porch in this way that Bandaranaike was assassinated.

11. For member-voter ratios in European parties see M. Duverger: *op. cit.* pp. 92–98.

12. Voting figures for the 1970 election are from Department of Elections: *Results of Parliamentary Elections 1947–1970*; Colombo, 1971. Party membership figures were supplied to me in interviews in August, 1969 with A. J. Niyathapala (UNP), Herbert Wickremasinghe (SLFP) and Leslie Goonewardena (LSSP).

13. See R. N. Kearney: *Trade Unions and Politics in Ceylon*; Berkeley, 1971, Chapters V and VI.

14. Based on interviews with V. Dharmalingam M.P., and the local secretary of the Tamil Congress in Jaffna in August, 1969.

15. This was already true for the LSSP by the early 1960s and became true for the SLFP by 1970. There have been no defections of UNP Members in recent years.

16. Shortly after the 1970 election Mrs. Bandaranaike was reported as criticising alleged hostility against elephants taking part in the Kandy *perahera*. She said: "the mere fact that the elephant has been chosen as a symbol of a political party should not be held against this innocent animal. I shall be sending my own elephant to participate in this great religious and national festival this year." *Times Weekender* 1/8/1970.

17. For example those of the LSSP defectors T. B. Subasinghe (secretary of the SLFP and Minister of Industries after 1970) and Stanley Tillekeratne (speaker of the National State Assembly).

18. Calvin B. Woodward: *op. cit.* p. 20 where he defines a party as "a group of ambitious men who have chosen politics as a vocation."

19. This is not to argue that Ceylon parties might not behave like American parties, but simply that they do not seem to have adopted any American practices consciously.

20. Until the late 1960s all LSSP members were entitled to attend conference. For the 1964 Special Conference on joining the Coalition "those who were members of the Party on May 10th are eligible to participate" (LSSP Special Conference 6th and 7th June 1964; *Agenda and Resolutions*).

21. The major parties have Nomination Boards elected from their Working Committees and their decision is final on all selections. In 1960 Dudley Senanayake constituted himself a one-man board.

22. LSSP members are expected to engage in regular activity and attendance at party meetings but the original 'Bolshevik' definition of membership obligation is now 'modified' (interview with Leslie Goonewardena in August, 1969).

23. Calvin Woodward: *op. cit.* holds that "the organizational reconstruction of the UNP after 1956 transformed it into the most effectively organised party in Ceylon" (p. 189).

24. See Charts pp. 132–5.
25. For the completely informal manner in which Dudley Senanayake became UNP leader in 1952 and Sir John Kotelawala in 1953, see J. L. Fernando: *Three Prime Ministers of Ceylon*; Colombo, 1963.
26. In 1960 Mrs. Bandaranaike initially became 'patron' of the SLFP which was led in parliament by C. P. de Silva but she was appointed President for the election of July without either being a Member of Parliament or a candidate.
27. Normally the officers (president, secretaries, vice-presidents) meet for organisational discussion as well. (Based on interviews with Herbert Wickremasinghe and Leslie Goonewardena.)
28. See G. F. Lerski: *Origins of Trotskyism in Ceylon* ; Stanford, 1968.
29. For an account of the development of the LSSP see R. N. Kearney: "The Marxist Parties of Ceylon" in Paul Brass and M. F. Franda: *Radical Politics in South Asia*; Cambridge, Mass; 1963.
30. Gananath Obeyesekere has argued that "traditional Marxism was expressed in a high-faluting idiom, which was useful for doctrinal discussions among the intellectual elite, but inadequate for mobilising support among a larger sector of the population." ("Sinhala Nationalism and Culture in Relation to the April 1971 Insurgency in Sri Lanka"; unpublished paper, 1973.)
31. Leslie Goonewardena, contrasting the attitude of new members and his own generation in 1969, said: "I may be old-fashioned but I still believe in Marx" (interview of August, 1969).
32. After the defections of 1964 the LSSP was more affected by movements towards the Right, such as the loss of P. B. Wijesundera M.P. in 1969 and of Dhanapala Weerasekera M.P. in 1971.
33. See Basil Perera: *Pieter Keuneman—a Profile;* Colombo, 1967.
34. *Ceylon News* 12/7/1973.
35. My visits to party headquarters in 1969 suggested that the UNP had the largest, the LSSP the most efficient, the Communists the most modern and the SLFP the most ramshackle.
36. The SLFP secretary, Herbert Wickremasinghe, told me that party branches were regularly activated for ceremonial commemorations, "otherwise you can't keep them lively" (interview of August, 1969).
37. In the SLFP, according to Woodward: *op. cit.,* "the informal personal-influence structure . . . has been so effective that the growth of a formal organization has not been seen to be of critical importance" (p. 206).
38. Both Herbert Wickremasinghe and Leslie Goonewardena confirmed in 1969 that their parties were more likely to give money to unions than *vice versa*. This does not bear out Woodward: *op. cit.,* p. 223 who believes that the LSSP relied partly on its unions' political funds.
39. Based on an interview with T. B. Ilangaratne in August, 1969, who pointed out to me that even Mrs. Bandaranaike, with the safest seat in the country, spent most weekends in her constituency.
40. C. P. de Silva, in an interview in August, 1969, while he was Minister of Lands.

41. At its 1963 annual sessions at Kandy the All-Ceylon Buddhist Congress voted almost unanimously that party politics was a hindrance to further national progress (*Ceylon Observer* 30/12/1963). As the Congress secretary, Professor Hewage, explained to me six years later, "villages are so divided that even the monks cannot unite them" (in an interview at the Congress headquarters in August, 1969). During the 1970 elections the Mahanayake Theros of Malwatte and Asgiriya called for a 'national coalition' if no party were able to form a government. (*Times of Ceylon* 18/5/1970).
42. Information supplied by Leslie Goonewardena in 1969.
43. In 1970 there was much hesitation about opposing S. D. Bandaranaike in his "family seat" of Gampaha but at the last moment the SLFP nominated a local Youth League organiser who won easily.
44. See K. M. de Silva: "The Reform and Nationalist Movements in the Early Twentieth Century" in K. M. de Silva (ed): *History of Ceylon, vol. 3*; Colombo Apothecaries for the University of Ceylon, Colombo; 1973.
45. See Kumari Jayawardena: *The Rise of the Labor Movement in Ceylon*; Duke University Press, Durham NC; 1972.
46. See K. M. de Silva: "The History and Politics of the Transfer of Power" in K. M. de Silva (ed): *op. cit.*
47. J. L. Fernando: *Three Prime Ministers of Ceylon*; Gunasena, Colombo; 1963; p. 36.
48. The Lanka Samasamaja Party, the Bolshevik Leninist Party, the Communist Party and the Ceylon Indian Congress.
49. S. W. R. D. Bandaranaike: *Speeches and Writings*; Department of Broadcasting and Information, Colombo; 1963, p. 155.
50. *Op. cit.* p. 160.
51. See below pp. 332–39.
52. See above pp. 70–71.
53. Ceylon Daily News: *Seventh Parliament of Ceylon 1970*; Associated Newspapers of Ceylon, Colombo; 1970 p. 175.
54. *Op. cit.* p. 182.
55. See for example Chaim Waxman: *The End of Ideology Debate*; Funk and Wagnalls, New York 1968.

UNP Formal and Informal Structure c. 1972

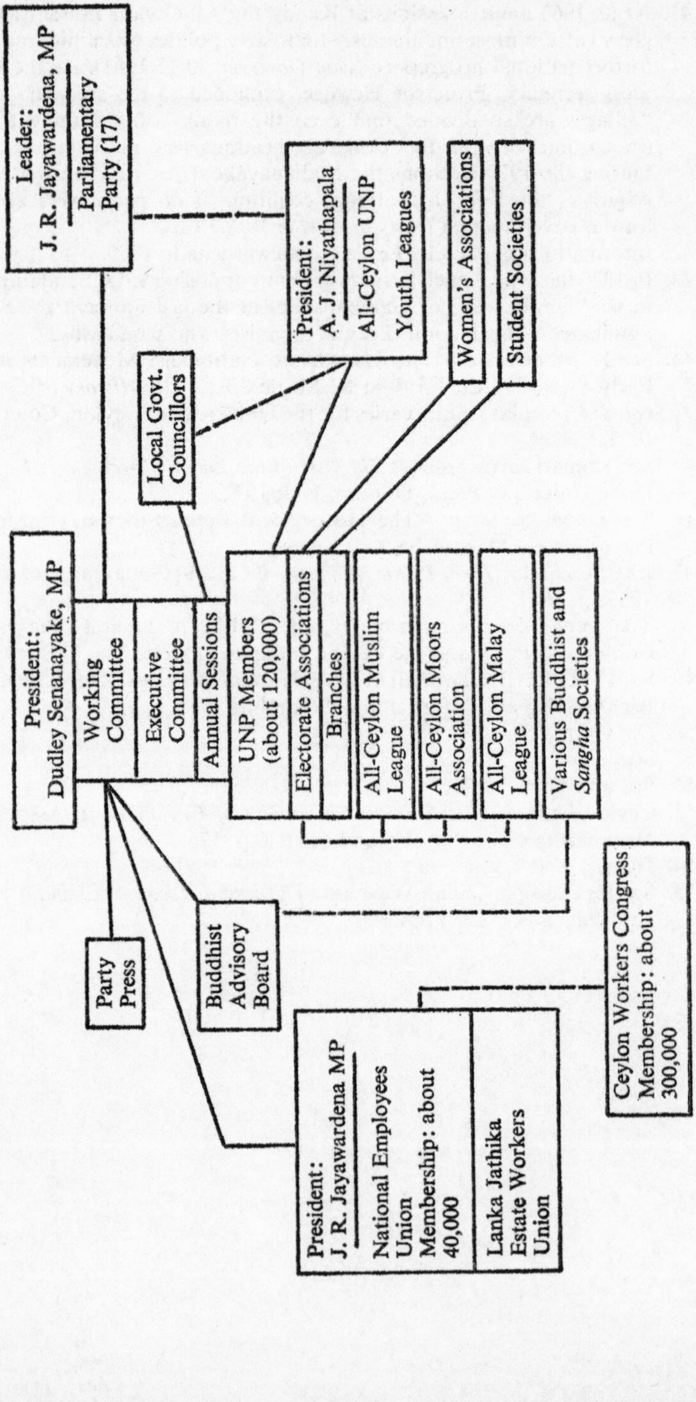

SLFP Formal and Informal Structure c. 1972

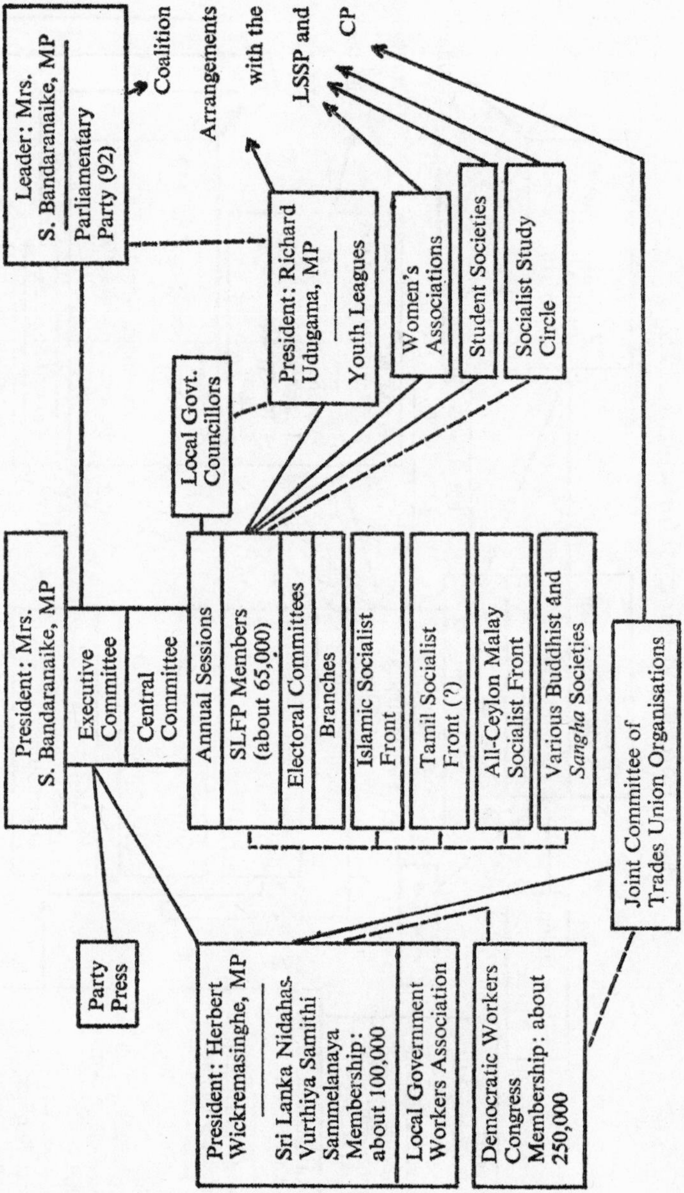

LSSP Formal and Informal Structure c. 1972

Coalition Arrangements with the SLFP and CP

Leader: N. M. Perera, MP
Parliamentary Party (18)

Local Govt. Councillors

President: V. Nanayakkara, MP
Youth Leagues (membership 20,000)

President: Vivienne Goonewardene, MP
Samasamaja Kantha Peramuna (Women's Front)

Student Societies

Socialist Study Circle

President: N. M. Perera, MP
Politburo and Orgburo
Central Committee
Conference
LSSP Members (about 4000)
Locals

Government Workers Trade Union Federation

Government Clerical Service Union. Membership: 20,000

Joint Committee of Trade Union Organisations

Trade Union Bureau

Janadina

President: N. M. Perera, MP
Ceylon Federation of Labour Membership: 120,000

Lanka Estate Workers Union

United Commercial & Mercantile Union

United Motor Workers Union

United Port Workers Union

About 20 other Unions

Communist Party Formal and Informal Structure c. 1972

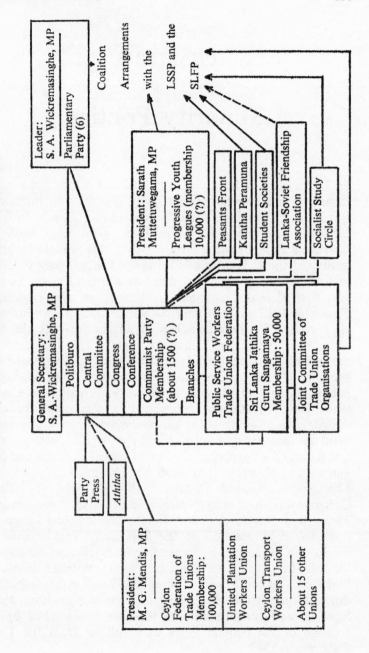

CHAPTER 5

Minority Politics

Sri Lanka does not have a uniform political culture but a major Sinhalese and a minor Tamil party system, and three subsystems for Christians, Muslims and Indian Tamils. Political behaviour and party allegiance differ within each, with the Christians approximating most closely to the Sinhala Buddhist norm and the Indian Tamils being the furthest removed. The longest politically organised minority are the Ceylon Tamils. The first elected "educated Ceylonese" in the Legislative Council in 1912 was the Tamil, Sir Ponnambalam Ramanathan. His brother Sir Ponnambalam Arunachalam was the first president of the Ceylon National Congress. This acceptance by the majority community did not last beyond 1921 when the two brothers left the Congress and founded the Tamil Mahajana Sabha. At the very beginning of party formation in Ceylon there was immediately established a dichotomy between Sinhalese and Tamils which has continued for over fifty years. With the coming of universal suffrage in 1931, many Tamil leaders urged a boycott of the State Council elections and four seats were left vacant. In 1936 an 'all-Sinhalese" Board of Ministers was formed. Finally, in 1944 the All-Ceylon Tamil Congress was founded by its present leader G. G. Ponnambalam. Throughout this development Tamil politicians had fought for protected representation in the legislature. This reached its height with the agitation surrounding the Soulbury Commission for "fifty-fifty", the equal division of representation between the Sinhalese and the other communities. Tamil political leaders, drawn largely from the professional classes, continue to be legalistic and constitutional, a tendency undisturbed by the creation of the Federal Party as a splinter from the Tamil Congress in 1949.

The Ceylon and Indian Tamils

Prior to independence Ceylon Tamils enjoyed considerable political influence. They tended to enrol in the professions and public service to a greater degree than the Sinhalese Buddhists, included a high proportion of Christians and had a good, English-based education system in the Jaffna area. Despite the growing division between Sinhalese and Tamil politicians the Tamil Congress maintained a fairly friendly attitude towards the UNP, a major factor in the breakaway of the Federal Party. Ponnambalam was in the Senanayake Cabinets from 1949 until 1953. Two Tamils were returned for the UNP in the 1952 election and there was no suggestion either then, or previously in 1947, that the party should not contest Tamil seats. In 1947 the bulk of Tamil seats were won by the Tamil Congress by very substantial majorities. Its support slipped in 1952, when it lost to the Federal Party, the UNP and independents. The real catastrophe, from which the party has never recovered, came in 1956 when only Ponnambalam was elected and ten Federalists were returned. The two Tamil leaders, Ponnambalam and Chelvanayakam, have been bitter rivals ever since. Thus the Tamils, like the Sinhalese, were divided between two parties, with similar leadership but different programmes and irreconcilable personal rivalries.

Since 1956 the Tamil Congress has become increasingly the more conservative party, although it refused to take office in UNP governments and its M.P.s allied with Mrs. Bandaranaike after 1970.[1] Its support has been largely confined to Jaffna and Colombo, where there is a large concentration of Tamil middle-class residents in Wellawatte and other southern suburbs. In contrast the Federal Party has adopted the radical tactic of civil disobedience and demanded a federal system to which the Tamil Congress is rigorously opposed.[2] In many other respects the Federal Party's radicalism is very patchy. It temporarily allied with Mrs. Bandaranaike in 1960 and, for a longer period, with Dudley Senanayake after 1965. Its very existence, however, stems from the electors' rejection of the Tamil Congress for close association with the Sinhala majority in the past. It is at best an unwelcome partner for either Sinhala party and, as the 1970 election suggested, could lose support in the Northern and Eastern Provinces too if it did not manoeuvre carefully. Moreover the Federal Party is led almost exclusively by landowning and professional politicians from the Vellalla caste. It is officially opposed to untouchability and its leader and deputy leader were both Christians. Nevertheless its approach to untouchability as to other social issues has been cautious and little less conservative than that of the Tamil Congress. It faces a potential, if weak, challenge from the Left which has become marginally more important since the middle 1960's.

The Tamil political system is quite strictly enclosed and distinct from that in the rest of the country. No electorate in which Tamils form a majority ever returns a non-Tamil, except for the two-member electorate of Batticaloa which normally elects one Muslim and one Tamil. Moreover no Ceylon Tamil has ever been nominated as a parliamentary candidate outside the Northern and Eastern Provinces except in Colombo, where they are never elected. This communal exclusiveness is also reflected in partisan exclusiveness. In Tamil majority seats the vote for "non-Tamil" parties was 25.1% in 1952, 14.3% in 1956, 14% in March 1960, 15.2% in June 1960, 15.4% in 1965 and 17.2% in 1970. This vote is divided largely between Tamil Marxists standing in the Jaffna peninsula and the UNP running in Eastern Province seats with Muslim and Sinhalese minorities. Otherwise the struggle is between Tamil Congress and Federalists with a substantial but diminishing independent vote often for Tamil separatists like C. Sunther-alingam or V. Navaratnam.[3] In all elections since 1956 the Federalists have won nearly all Tamil majority seats, but only in June 1960 did they win an absolute majority of votes.

This segregation of the Tamil political system has meant that Tamils are neither over nor under-represented in parliament. In 1965 11% of the Representatives were Ceylon Tamils, which was exactly their proportion in the general population. In 1970, with the addition of two Nominated Members by Mrs. Bandaranaike, the proportion rose to 13.7%. Ceylon Tamils have nothing to complain about in the electoral system. They benefit from area weighting to the Northern and Eastern Provinces to the extent that Federal M.P.s in 1970 needed only 18,903 votes each to return them, the lowest for any party.[4] Where Tamils have been disadvantaged is in their access to Cabinet office.

There were no Tamil Cabinet Ministers between 1956 and 1965 when Senator M. Tiruchelvam, a Federal Party supporter, became Minister for Local Government. He resigned in 1969 over the government's failure to implement the District Councils Bill. In 1970, however, Mrs. Bandaranaike rather surprisingly made C. Kumarasuriar both a Senator and Minister of Posts and Telecommunications.[5] The operating principle of Ceylon democracy, that no minority must be permanently ostracised, was accepted by the SLFP which had appeared to Tamils in the past as their main enemy.

The two Tamil parties have followed quite different tactics. The Tamil Congress suffered in 1956 and 1970 for its open sympathy with the UNP. A party representing mainly the Jaffna-originating Colombo public servants, it saw co-operation within a unitary system as the best method of preserving the employment and general interests of its supporters. This tactic became less attractive after the UNP had adopted "Sinhala Only" at Kelaniya in 1956. The Federal Party, on the other hand, accepted the notion that Ceylon was inhabited by two nations and wished to give this constitutional form. In so doing it put itself into direct confrontation with all the Sinhala parties. The UNP and SLFP wished to continue the situation created by the Ceylon National Congress before independence, whereby the majority ruled the whole island but made concessions to the minority. The Marxists continued to argue into the middle 1960's that Sinhalese and Tamil were brothers who should not be misled by UNP or Federal Party conservatives. The Sinhalese extremists were totally opposed to any constitutional change which would give the Tamils their own state and hasten what they saw as the threatened annexation of the north by India. For much of the time after its victory in 1956 the Federal Party thus had to operate outside a consensual system. It naturally resorted to the appropriate extra-parliamentary tactics, abandoning them when, in 1957 and 1965, it seemed to have wrung concessions from the majority Sinhala party. As Chelvanayakam said in 1961, at the height of the civil disobedience campaign, "it is when negotiations and debate in Parliament failed that we resorted to the weapon of *satyagraha*."[6]

The Federal Party for many years has pursued tactics designed to secure concessions within the political system rather than to disrupt the system altogether. In 1957, in 1960 and again in 1965 they contracted agreements with the major force in Sinhala politics designed primarily to protect the use of the Tamil language, to secure regional councils which would have substantial administrative powers and to prevent the spread of Sinhalese into 'historic' Tamil lands through extensions of government colonisation schemes. The two arrangements with the SLFP proved very short lived, as the forces behind that party were precisely those most hostile to the Tamil claims. The 1965 arrangement with the UNP proved more fruitful by giving the Federal Party a supporter in the Cabinet for the first time. Yet by then the UNP had changed its character and was also subject to the same pressures as the SLFP. Having moved some of the way towards setting up regional councils the UNP was forced to withdraw and the Federal Party was driven out of its coalition by a combination of forces which included UNP backbenchers, the Opposition Coalition, communalists surrounding R. G. Senanayake and the openly expressed hostility of the Buddhist *sangha*. There were thus proved to be, as on previous occasions, no major groups within the Sinhalese community which wished to concede the demands of the Federal Party. This was not to say that Tamils as a whole were necessarily forced to remain forever outside the political system. The Coalition was already beginning by 1969 to create a Tamil Socialist Front in Jaffna which, it was hoped, might eventually restore Leftwing political fortunes.[7] The tactic of the SLFP and its Marxist allies was to isolate the Federalists and to show that their methods had worked against the interests of the Tamil majority who still persisted in voting for them. At the same time the SLFP began to make inroads among the Muslims, who also spoke Tamil but were very uncertain allies of the Federal Party.

The continuing cycle through which Federalist tactics passed thus included attempts to ally with the currently dominant Sinhala party which had become difficult to achieve with the UNP by 1968 and impossible to achieve with the SLFP as early as 1961. The next step was to boycott parliament and to call a *satyagraha*, which would then be suppressed by varying degrees of force, which consolidated the Tamils of the Northern and Eastern Provinces behind the Federalists in reaction against the intervention of Sinhalese soldiers and police. This tactic in 1958 was a major element in provoking racial riots, in 1961 led to an escalation of military intervention in politics which probably inspired the abortive coup of 1962,[8] was less effective in 1963, but was still being advocated in 1973. By then the battle for federalism was over, as the new constitution of Sri Lanka made it virtually impossible to achieve. The entrenching of the Sinhala language and the Buddhist religion also made the prospect of legally defending Tamil interests much more complex. It was at this stage, as previously in 1961, that the third tactic, of openly advocating secession was called into play.[9] Potentially this was the most dangerous tactic of all. It was the one method guaranteed to revive Sinhalese fears both against the Tamils and against India. It threatened the whole basis of the unitary state by its calls for disobedience, its transformation of the national day into a day of mourning and its calls to the still numerous Tamil element in the public service not to obey their Sinhalese masters. It was also politically dangerous in that it required massive Tamil support in the Northern and Eastern provinces if it were not to be ineffectual. In 1961 this was forthcoming. Although the major Tamil parties had come together in a Tamil United Front by 1973, there was growing disillusionment with Federal tactics as evidenced by their reduced vote in 1970 and by the open collaboration of several prominent Jaffna politicians with Mrs. Bandaranaike's government. As economic issues became dominant so the legalistic concerns of Federal Party leaders were seen by many to be irrelevant.

In none of these tactical postures, even the secessionist, could the Federal Party be said to be revolutionary or to pose a serious threat to the established order. Its ideal was the Swiss federal system which hardly supplies a revolutionary rallying point. During the JVP rising, when Tamil separatism might have been decisive, the Federalists stood loyally by the government and the Jaffna area was so safe from disturbance that the JVP leader, Rohan Wijeweera, was imprisoned there. The Federal Party has been unable and unwilling to tap any radical potential among Indian Tamil estate workers, although it was in defence of their citizenship that Chelvanayakam initially left the Tamil Congress. Federal Party unions set up on the tea estates were bitterly resented by Ceylon Workers' Congress leader, Thondaman, who broke off a tentative arrangement which he had formed with the Federalists in 1960. He did not significantly co-operate with them again until the formation of the Tamil United Front in 1972. Nor has the Federal Party any proven links with the various small groups claiming to stand for the principles of the Dravida Munnetra Kazhagham of South India.[10] The Ceylon Tamils have no general desire to secede or to join India or even a separate Tamilnadu. That is the basic weakness of all attempts to threaten the established Sinhalese parties. For although there are certain threats which the Federal Party can effectively utter in a narrowly divided parliament, nothing would unite the Sinhalese more quickly than any serious, revolutionary attempt to create a separate Tamil state, particularly if it involved joint operations with the DMK and the estate workers. The Federal Party, which still provided the core of Tamil politics even after 1970, prefers to operate legalistically and constitutionally, knowing that it has neither the inclination nor the backing for anything more lastingly disruptive than a *satyagraha*. That is not, of course, to say that younger Tamils, like younger Sinhalese, might not react against the caution of their elders. Indeed the formation of the Tamil United Front suggested that there had already arisen considerable pressure from more radical elements which might have swept away the Federal Party as quickly as it decimated the Tamil Congress in 1956.[11]

Tamil political life is self-contained, embraces other forms of politics than the Federal-Tamil Congress clash and is by no means totally dominated by the Federalists. Apart from containing a large Christian community, Ceylon Tamils are also divided between Jaffna and East Coast Tamils and contain two important caste elements, the Karaiyars and the so-called Minority Tamils (harijans or untouchables). All these divisions have some importance. Since 1956 the parliamentary Federal Party has always contained within itself a Christian segment, which includes its leader. Until 1965 it also included a Muslim element although that was lost by defections to the UNP and SLFP, underlining the difficulty of maintaining discipline over the East Coast representatives. There is no evidence that the Christian Federalists behaved differently in any way from their

Hindu colleagues. Only two of them, C. X. Martyn, who defeated Ponnambalam at Jaffna in 1970[12], and V. A. Alegacone, sat for seats with substantial Christian populations. The only respect in which Christian Federalists might behave differently is in regard to caste issues, which centre around the right of Minority Tamils to enter Hindu temples. Both Chelvanayakam, in whose constituency one of the major temple entry campaigns took place, and G. Nalliah, who was nominated to the Senate to represent Minority Tamils and is also a Christian, have felt inhibited from taking part in this vital issue because it affected another religion.[13]

Temple entry and the rights of Minority Tamils represent one area in which the Left has been able to appeal to the otherwise conservative Jaffna Tamils. The other is among the Karaiyar concentration in Point Pedro. In both cases various Marxist groups have penetrated the Tamil community at its weakest point. Point Pedro elected the Communist, V. Kandiah, to parliament in 1956, the only occasion on which a Marxist has ever been returned for a Tamil seat. Even in 1969, when the Marxist parties were discredited for their pro-Sinhala orientation, two Communists and two Samasamajists were elected to Point Pedro Urban Council out of nine councillors. The electoral consequences of the Minority Tamil agitation is less clear.[14] Two major influences in the struggle, the Maoist Communist Party and the Revolutionary Samasamajists, were opposed to parliamentarianism in any case. There is a considerable gap between them and the All-Ceylon Minority Tamil Mahasabha, whose main objective is the amendment of the Prevention of Social Disabilities Act and whose tactics are those of a pressure group in a parliamentary system.

The extent to which Maoists were involved in the temple entry campaigns of 1967 to 1969 is debatable. The Mass Movement for the Eradication of Social Disabilities was undoubtedly controlled by Shanmugathasan's Communist Party and got the support of S. D. Bandaranaike, the Maoist Sinhala M.P. for Gampaha. They were joined in the occupation of Maviddapuram temple in July 1968 by pro-Moscow Communists, members of the Minority Tamils Mahasabha and Revolutionary Samasamajists led by Edmund Samarakkody. There was considerable factional squabbling between the groups before the police cleared the *satyagrahis* from the temple.[15] The traditionalist opposition led by the veteran Tamil politician C. Suntheralingam, made much of these Marxist connections. The All-Ceylon Saiva (Hindu) Practices and Observances Protection Society had previously attacked the temple entry leaders as "mostly Communists or DMK party followers, assisted by some Christians and Federalists."[16] Certainly the Maoists gained some prestige from their campaign. They were able to influence the inaugural meeting of the Tamil Socialist Front in Jaffna in August, 1969 and probably became the strongest Marxist group on the Jaffna peninsula, if one unwilling to put its following to the electoral test.

Marxists in general, and Maoists in particular, represent one challenge to Tamil conservatism. Tamil separatists represent another. Sinhalese politicians have claimed that the Dravida Munnetra Kazhagham had been organising in Ceylon for some years and Mrs. Bandaranaike's government banned it in 1962 and pressed the UNP to ban it again during 1968. The two strongholds of the DMK were said to be in Jaffna and on the tea estates.[17] Separatism was not widely favoured among Ceylon Tamils until the formation of the Tamil United Front. Both Suntheralingam and V. Navaratnam, who stood for separatist policies, and were former M.P.s, were badly beaten by conventional Federalists in 1970. What does exist in Jaffna is a strong cultural link with Tamil Nadu, based mainly on the film industry. When the DMK Chief Minister of Tamil Nadu, Annadurai, a former film director, died in 1968, there were massive demonstrations of sympathy in Jaffna. The major social centre in many Tamil villages is the "MGR Club", named after M. G. Ramachandram, the film star and DMK activist. These clubs use the red and black colours of the DMK, but do not seem to have any real political importance.[18]

If the Maoists and the DMK are weak among Ceylon Tamils, they are probably little stronger among Indian Tamils. Recognising the rival creeds, the Maoist leader Shanmugathasan wrote that "today in the homes of the plantation workers there are more pictures of Chairman Mao Tsetung than those of Annadurai or MGR."[19] Like most Maoist propaganda in Ceylon this seems a pardonable exaggeration, meant to be read in Peking. One estate workers union, the Red Flag Plantation

Workers Union, is affiliated to the Ceylon Trade Union Federation and the plantations would undoubtedly be the most sensible place for a Maoist party to function. Despite the theoretical possibilities, the high degree of unionisation by the Ceylon Workers Congress and the Democratic Workers Congress, whose leaders Thondaman and Aziz, are committed to the parliamentary system, makes any kind of Marxist success unlikely. Even in 1947 the Marxist vote in Indian Tamil majority seats was only 16% as against 58.7% for the Ceylon Indian Congress, although some CIC M.P.s were generally on the Left. That was many years ago and since then Samasamajist support for Sinhala Only and its connivance in repatriation have lost a great deal of support for the Lanka Estate Workers Union which is its arm on the plantations.

The Indian Tamils are 'silent people' electorally and little can therefore be said about their views. With the highest level of illiteracy and greatest geographical isolation of any community they give allegiance only to their own leaders. "Mr. Thondaman rules the hill country today" is a belief quite widespread among Kandyan Sinhalese.[20] Perhaps the only issue upon which he agrees with his rival Aziz and the DWC, is that other groups should be kept out of the estates. After a brief flirtation with the Federal Party, Thondaman broke with them decisively when they tried to form a party-controlled estate workers union in 1961.[21] Any possibility of a united front of Tamils is thus remote. The Indian Tamils maintain an effective "two party system" between the more or less equally balanced CWC and DWC. Rivalry is for members rather than votes, but nonetheless provides most of the political life which the estate workers now have. Minor intrusions may be made by Maoists, Samasamajists or the DMK. So far they are relatively ineffectual.[22]

The two Tamil communities seem ripest for the "politics of alienation." It is very hard for a Tamil to make his way in Ceylon politics outside the Northern and Eastern Provinces or the tea estates. Perhaps this helps explain why three of the leading Sri Lanka revolutionaries, Bala Tampoe, secretary of the Ceylon Mercantile Union and Revolutionary Samasamajist, Shanmugathasan the Maoist, and V. Karalasingham a leader of the LSSP Left, are all Tamils. Each has found his way barred in the overwhelmingly Sinhala Marxist movement, particularly after the policy changes surrounding the alliance with the SLFP. Equally Maoism and separatism, in so far as they appeal at all, probably find their best echo in the minority castes of Jaffna and on the tea estates. None of this is saying very much except to point to potential revolutionary recruiting grounds. The Ceylon Tamils remain overwhelmingly under conservative and constitutionalist leaders and cling to their traditional social practices. On the whole they are ready to compromise with the Sinhala majority in return for fairly limited concessions. The Indian Tamils remain engrossed in trade union struggles and in the determination of their citizenship.

The Christians

Christians are not normally regarded as a 'community' in Sri Lanka, but in many ways they have political characteristics which distinguish them from the other groups in society. Electorally they are, at first sight, not very significant. They are divided between Catholics (the great majority) and Protestants, and between Sinhalese, Tamils and Burghers. Caste divisions exist as strongly as among Buddhists. The minority contains within it several other minorities, of which the largest is the Karawa Sinhalese Catholic community living between North Colombo and Chilaw. The small numbers and fragmentation of Christians are not a sufficient guide to their importance. Protestants still enjoy a considerable following in the political élite, such that they are always over-represented in parliament. Catholics alone of any religion have a disciplined hierarchy with international connections and a strong interest in political, social and moral issues. Until the coup of 1962 Catholics also enjoyed strong support in the army, navy and police. The fear of Catholic Action, held strongly by L. H. Mettananda and other militant Buddhists for many years, became temporarily influential on the S.L.F.P. between 1960 and 1964.

Christians tended to be feared and envied despite their limited numbers. Bandaranaike's own family were Anglicans and so was the Governor-General Sir Oliver Goonetilleke. Many other important families were wholly or partly Christian.

In contrast to Hindus and Muslims it remains quite possible for Christians to secure election for seats in which co-religionists are a tiny minority. At the 1970 dissolution 14% of the Representatives (including two Nominated Members) were Christians compared with only 8.5% of the population. Even after the Coalition landslide and the disappearance of European and Burgher Nominated Members, the proportion still stood at 10.4%. Although Christians and particularly Catholics have tended to be conservative like other minorities, they are by no means committed in such a way as to lose influence with a change of government. Indeed Christians were better represented in Mrs. Bandaranaike's 1970 Cabinet than in those of her predecessors.[23]

Because Christians are fragmented it is necessary to consider their political role in several different aspects. The fact that a man is a Christian is not necessarily important in his election to parliament and he may well be able to function without much reference to his nominal community obligations. Neither Felix Dias Bandaranaike, nor S. J. V. Chelvanayakam, nor Pieter Keuneman, nor Leslie Goonewardena, owe their political position to their religion.[24] They all sit for electorates in which Christians form a very small minority and have risen to prominence in their parties not because of their religion but often in spite of it. To say that a politician is a Christian is often merely to acknowledge a post-colonial situation in which many members of the élite adhere to the religion of their previous Protestant masters. This is true for half the Christian M.P.s. It is quite unsafe to assume that they are subject to any effective organised religious pressure and certainly three or four of them are not actively practising in any case. On the other hand there are Members, invariably Catholic, who are elected by co-religionists and must be assumed to be susceptible to organised pressure. These have nearly all been UNP, except in the landslides of 1956 and 1970 when the Catholic Sinhalese area was largely won by the SLFP. Thus one must consider cautiously the extent to which Christian voters and leaders act politically through the democratic process.

Although fear of Christianity was used in the 1956 election, coupled with the charge that the UNP was a Christian agent, the persistence of Christian representation throughout the period of independence is a remarkable tribute to the political irrelevance of religion among high status Protestants. S. W. R. D. Bandaranaike's own relatives in the Bandaranaike and Obeyesekere families were able to win as stunning victories as himself in totally Buddhist seats. His Cabinets included several Catholics. But in the breakup of the SLFP after Bandaranaike's assassination a large number of Christians defected, including party leaders like Jim Munasinghe, Stanley de Zoysa, P. B. Weerakoon and Hugh Fernando. Much of the bitterness which typified SLFP—Christian relations in the early 1960's was undoubtedly related to these defections, to Catholic influence in the 1962 coup and to the suspicion of Catholic involvement even in Bandaranaike's assassination itself.[25] The major political issue of school nationalisation was, of course, publicly apparent. Privately there was a feeling of Christian unreliability. Certainly in the next few years Christian voters and Catholic politicians adhered mainly to the United National Party.

In the struggle between Mrs. Bandaranaike and the Catholics there is no doubt that Christian influence declined markedly. The Christian Governor-General, Sir Oliver Goonetilleke, was replaced by a Buddhist. Catholics in the armed forces and police were weeded out. Despite passive resistance, Catholic schools were deprived of the right to charge fees or to teach their religion to those of other faiths. Cardinal Gracias of Bombay had to intervene on the Vatican's behalf to restrain Archbishop Cooray and the local hierarchy from persisting in policies which might have damaged the Church still further. Initially, at least, the result of all this was to drive Catholics into an embattled position where their only hope seemed to lie with the UNP. Protestant politicians had no commitment to a specific position but in the 1965 election eight out of the eleven Catholic Members elected sat for the UNP. They were not, however, rewarded with Cabinet positions. By becoming a captive group the Catholics limited their influence even further. Sundays were abolished as public holidays and replaced by the Buddhist Poya Days. It seemed by the late 1960's as though Catholics would get nothing much from the UNP either, although Christians held the posts of Speaker, Deputy Speaker and Chairman of Committees and Hugh Fernando was made Minister of Commerce in 1968.

For a minority to exert influence within the Sri Lanka political system it must not get itself into such a captive and powerless position. Whether by conscious Church guidance, or by local reaction, Catholics began to reassert their independence of the UNP. While attempts to form separate parties never materialised, electoral switching did. In seats in which Christians formed the largest single group, the UNP vote had nearly doubled since 1956. In that year it was only 30%, in March 1960 40.4%, in June 1960 52% and in 1965 56.8%, when it won seven out of the eight seats. But in 1970 it held only Negombo,[26] Colombo North and Ja-ela and its vote dropped to 48.5%. This had been presaged in council and by-elections in the preceding two years. Although it kept its six Catholic wards in north Colombo in 1969 it lost three at Negombo. "The UNP should not take the Catholics for granted", warned the *Times Weekender*.[27] An even greater shock was felt at the Nattandiya by-election in 1968 when the UNP barely held a seat in which 47.4% of the population are Christians.

Christians do not necessarily act together although in the crises of 1959–1960 many Catholics deserted the SLFP to the Right. Otherwise there is little real evidence of a Catholic bloc in parliament except when, as for most of the 1960s, most Catholic M.P.s happen to be in the same party. Catholic voters, although normally conservative, shook themselves free in 1956 and 1970 by voting for coreligionists from the Left. The Catholics appear well disciplined and have authoritative religious spokesmen in a way which is untrue for any other community. It does not close the enquiry into the Christian's political role merely to speak in terms of his representative or even his vote. The suspicion that attached to Catholics from the early 1950's was that they could wield their organisational hold to a much greater degree than anyone else, thus maximising their statistically limited potential influence.

The Catholic Church has, in the past, clearly attempted to do this in Ceylon as elsewhere. In the Cold War atmosphere of the early 1950's it felt obliged to struggle against Marxism and thus, by default, to support the UNP with its predominantly Buddhist leadership. In 1952 two months before the election, Archbishop Cooray said that the Samasamajists "are a body of Godless people whom we consider as enemies of all forms of religion".[28]

Shortly before the election the Vicar-General, the Rev. Father G. Fortin, stated officially: "No Catholic with even an atom of Christian conscience can vote for a candidate who belongs to a political creed banned by the Church—let it be Communism or any other—or has pledged himself directly or indirectly to an electoral programme inimical to God and to the Church, or who is in sympathy with those who are hostile to the Church. No Catholic must vote for a candidate mainly because they are Catholics."[29] This was the high point of direct Catholic support for the UNP and by 1956 more moderation was shown. The Church instructed that pulpits should not be used for political propaganda, that clergy should not take part in meetings and that Catholic property should not be used for political purposes.[30] How far this instruction was followed may be doubted.

By the late 1960's the whole atmosphere had changed. While Catholic opposition to Communism continued, the Samasamajists were seen as far less dangerous than in the past. In February 1969 pamphlets were issued in Wattala claiming that "Catholic voters have lost a considerable amount of confidence in the United National Party due to its inability to fulfil certain assurances given to them before and after the schools takeover".[31] How representative these were is very doubtful, but the *Daily Mirror*, said to be influential among lower middle-class Catholic clerks, pursued its campaign, claiming that Christians were to form a Human Rights Party.[32] This never materialised effectively. By June a United Catholic Election Front was said to be agitating in the Catholic Karawa belt. Its statements claimed that "a victory gained by the SLFP or UNP nominees in Catholic areas are (*sic*) a victory to the Buddhist community only and a loss to other religious groups in Ceylon."[33] This was going too far in a dangerous direction and the official *Messenger* denounced the idea in the same week.

While some Catholics may have been organising for a separate party, the Church, with a vision wider than that of a small belt of villages along the Coast, seems to have withdrawn from any overt intrusion into party politics. It will neither form Catholic parties nor trade unions, though Catholics have been important in the Ceylon Mercantile Union and through the Young Christian Workers. It is busily "nationalising" itself with the Mass held in Sinhalese and Tamil and the remaining

Catholic schools teaching in those languages. While the bulk of the clergy would probably prefer the UNP to win elections they realise that even their own voters are not immune to Sinhalese nationalist appeals. As both major parties normally put up Catholics in Catholic seats, voting tends to be either on caste or party lines. Even within the clergy itself there are small minorities who are no longer politically conservative.[34] As Father Houtart of Louvain University concluded after an exhaustive survey in 1969: "in Ceylon Catholics cannot any more be considered as one political group but are as diversified as the Ceylonese society itself."[35]

This was strongly borne out by the 1970 elections. There were massive swings against the UNP in Catholic seats, with the exception of Colombo North where the UNP Member was a Buddhist. The SLFP won four of the predominantly Christian seats and the UNP only three, with its support dropping by 19.8% in Negombo and 11.5% in Ja-ela. Apart from Colombo North the average swing against the UNP in Catholic areas was very much higher than in the country as a whole. Possibly as a reward Mrs. Bandaranaike's government immediately restored the seven-day, Sunday based week, the abolition of which had caused much resentment amongst Christians. In breaking loose from the UNP the Catholic Sinhalese rural areas were conforming, however temporarily, to the norm established by the Buddhist Sinhalese.

The Muslims

While the Tamils have naturally taken up a militant role in defence of their position, forming specifically communal parties to wage the struggle, the major religious minorities have been reluctant to follow the same road.[36] Christians enjoyed advantages under the British, which have not yet vanished entirely. They have been forced into a defensive role but one in which the Catholic Church has acted very circumspectly since the school nationalisation of 1960. No Catholic party was formed, the Hierarchy strongly opposing such a tactic on very reasonable grounds. The Christians were fully committed to the existing party system. What distinguishes the Muslims is their almost entirely instrumentalist approach to politics, their repeated party changing, support for independents and refusal, in the main, to be the captive of either of the major parties. The majority of Muslim politicians and the largest Muslim groups have normally been conservative, but they have tempered their conservatism when the Left has been in the ascendant. Muslims have been elected as national or local representatives by all the important parties and there have been Muslims in all Cabinets.

It is often argued in Sri Lanka that Muslims quite consciously adopt the role of serving anyone in defence of their own position. This is to ascribe perhaps too subtle an understanding to an electorate which is the most scattered and illiterate of any. It may be true of their leaders, who change parties with far more agility than those from any other group. The Muslims are neither socially, geographically nor even racially homogeneous. They are normally regarded as distinct from the Malays, who under Senator Kitchilan's leadership were fairly strongly committed to the United National Party.[37] Even so there are several sub-groups within the Muslims whose interests are not necessarily held in common. The majority of Muslims speak Tamil but they have important clashes of interest on the East Coast with the Vellalla Tamil landowners who dominate the local Federal Party. While the Federalists have had Muslim M.P.s and have won East Coast seats, they have never effectively integrated the bulk of Tamil-speaking Muslims into their camp. The majority of business leaders in Colombo are beholden through the All-Ceylon Muslim League to the United National Party of which it was a founding member. Yet there is also a Muslim working-class vote which, in Wekanda, Maligawatte and Kuppiyawatta, can be captured by Coalition candidates.

Muslims form the largest single group only in Colombo Central, Puttalam, Mutur, Kalmunai, Nintavur and Pottuvil. These seats are always represented by Muslims. Normally these have been Independents or in the UNP though Federalists won two East Coast seats in 1956 and the SLFP captured Puttalam[38] and Kalmunai in 1970 and have held one Mutur seat since 1960. Muslim representation is by no means confined to these areas alone. Before the dissolution of 1970 there were twelve Muslims in the House and there were still ten after the massive swing to the Left in 1970. Of those sitting at the dissolution, half represented seats in which Muslims formed less than half the electorate and M. H. Mohamed, the Minister for Labour, sat for Borella which had only a 7.8% Muslim population. In general the rule followed is that any area with a fairly large Muslim population normally elects a Muslim. Thus Beruwela, where Muslims are only 21.4%, nearly always has a Muslim M.P., although only the town itself is predominantly of that religion and controlled by a Muslim council.

The party allegiance of Muslims is fairly fluid. In 1969 eight of the M.P.s were in the UNP, two were in the SLFP, one was an Independent and one was a nominated UNP supporter. After the election the position was reversed with four left in the UNP, four in the SLFP and two nominated of whom one was an SLFP official. The most remarkable feature of such politicians is their record of party changing. Sir Razik Fareed, for example, who was a Nominated Member in the 1965 parliament, left the UNP to become an Independent in 1952, rejoined the UNP in 1956, leaving it in the same year, joined the SLFP in 1956, left it with C. P. de Silva in 1964 and eventually returned to the UNP. His record is matched by M. S. Kariapper who was elected for Kalmunai as UNP (1947), defeated as an Independent (1952), elected for the Federal Party (1956), for the LPP (March 1960) (and defeated for it in July 1960) and elected as an Independent again (1965) being eventually disqualified from sitting. He, like Fareed and another Muslim, held office briefly in the ten man Cabinet of W. Dahanayake, of whom it could be said that they were *all* party changers.

Party changing among Muslims is most marked on the East Coast, one of the most backward Sri Lanka areas and the only Province in which party loyalty remains secondary to individual importance. It stems largely from a search for immediate advantage and from the knowledge that the individual concerned will be endorsed by almost any party because of his relative certainty of being elected. Even the most successful SLFP invasion of the East Coast was on the basis of party defection. The Kalmunai by-election of 1968 was won by M. C. Ahmed for the SLFP although he had run at the previous election as an Independent and had held the seat for the Federal Party in July 1960. While all but one East Coast seat was held for a major party in 1970, as were all other Muslim seats, it is too early to declare the classic Muslim tactic quite dead.

Because of this regular confusion it is more difficult to discuss voting trends among Muslims than among other groups. The Muslim areas are scattered, with sizeable communities from Galle to Jaffna and with little in common between the urban voters of Colombo Central and the tenant ricefarmers of the East Coast. It is even difficult to define a "Muslim constituency" as Muslims may be politically powerful with little more than one-fifth of the total vote and there are only three seats[39] in which they form an absolute majority. Taking all seats in which Muslims form the *largest* single community, the voting trends underline their general conservatism, despite the continuously high Communist vote in Colombo Central. In 1947, 1952, and March 1960 Independents and small parties gained more votes than anyone else with about one third of the total. By 1965 this had fallen to 12.6% (returning two Members) and by 1970 to 11% (returning none). The shredding away of minority support was largely, however, a transfer over to the UNP. Its vote rose from under 30% before 1960 to a high point of 49.6% in 1965 and 45.9% in 1970. At the latter election nearly one quarter of the parliamentary UNP were Muslims and the party was deriving one eighth of its vote from these nine contests alone.

Apart from their parliamentary position, which is proportionately little greater than that to which Muslims are "entitled", they are also important in local government. With a very large shopkeeping and commercial class they are naturally drawn into a field which has attracted such a class in all countries. Apart from East Coast areas with clear Muslim majorities, Muslims play a part in Colombo, Galle, Jaffna, Kandy, Badulla, Beruwela, Puttalam, Negombo and Trincomalee, in all of which there are wards which have Muslim majorities returning Muslim councillors. There is not an important commercial centre in which Muslim interests are not well looked after. The most important role goes of course, to the Colombo Muslims who, by their wealth and prestige form what there is of a recognised Muslim political élite. Normally a quarter of the Colombo council are Muslims and they have provided several mayors. In 1966 the Muslim City Councillors were divided between 10 for the UNP, two for the SLFP, and one for the LSSP. This affection for the UNP was sustained in

1969 although Muslim representation was reduced by two. Of the twentyone wards with over 10% Muslim population, sixteen returned UNP councillors although they were generally in the poorest and oldest parts of the city.

The pattern of Muslim loyalty seems confused because party allegiance as such has only a limited appeal outside Colombo. The whole political structure of the Muslim community is, itself, almost equally vague. As with all religions in Sri Lanka other than Christianity, there is no distinct hierarchical structure, and certainly not one from which coherent political guidance is likely to emerge. By convention political views are not discussed within the mosque although any member of the laity may lead prayers and give a sermon. Mullahs do not join political parties. The entire religious structure makes it unlikely that the sort of intervention common among the Buddhists could arise. The mosque officials, the *khateev* and the *muezzin*, are paid small stipends and are often only part-time officials. The theologians, the *ulema*, have great authority on matters like the determination of fast days and associated practices. This is not extended into the area of political guidance.[40] Muslim leadership is very largely secular and stems from positions in commerce and the national and local office which goes with these. Not surprisingly, as what there is of a Muslim upper class is almost exclusively commercial, these leaders tend towards the United National Party. Their conservatism is modern, and instrumentalist, based on hard cash. It is not necessarily sustained at or between elections by the religious traditionalists.

There are two major centres for Muslim political leadership. These are in Muslim organisations and in Muslim elected representatives. Until 1967 the loyalty of the former towards the UNP was unchallenged. The All-Ceylon Muslim League was always a constituent of the UNP and the All-Ceylon Moors Association was similarly sympathetic. Officials of the two, like M. C. Kaleel, T. B. Jayah, Falil Cafoor and M. H. Macan Markar, were regularly returned to parliament for the UNP, also representing it on the Colombo council. The loyalty of the All-Ceylon Malay Association was equally secure. This united conservative front was broken with the formation of the Islamic Socialist Front under Al-Haj Badiuddin Mahmud, a

vice-president of the SLFP. Associated with Muslim politics
since 1927, a teacher and principal of Zahira College, Mahmud
was somewhat outside the Colombo Muslim political élite
through his lack of commercial background and his sympathies
with the Left which led him to become a founding official of the
SLFP and close associate of the Bandaranaikes. His political
philosophy was an Islamic Socialist one, designed to appeal to a
community almost untouched by Marxism.[41]

The Islamic Socialist Front functioned under the shadow of
the SLFP but despite repeated newspaper stories of clashes
between it and the party, the relationship seems to have worked
as satisfactorily as that between the UNP and the Muslim
League.[42] With 6,000 members in over one hundred branches
the ISF became a natural pole of attraction for aspiring Muslim
politicians who were dissatisfied with the traditional Muslim-
UNP alliance. While gaining some support from businessmen
it appealed to the small but growing Muslim intelligentsia who
tended to look outward towards the Middle East for political
rather than religious reasons. The Islamic Socialism of the ISF
remained more conservative than that of Egypt despite some
verbal resemblances. The Front is concerned with largely
electoral objectives, preferring to leave the traditionalist habits
of the East Coast alone. Although it has a women's branch it
takes no stand on matters like polygamy or other issues raised
by the radicals in the Arab world. Rather the appeal is for the
recognition of the Muslim community as not bound hand and
foot to the UNP, as needing to be bargained for in the same
way as other minorities. The election of four Muslim SLFP
Members in 1970 and the nomination of Badiuddin Mahmud
to the Representatives and his inclusion in the Cabinet, are
signs of at least a modest success in these objectives.

If the ISF was accepted within the largely Buddhist SLFP, it
was resisted most strongly by the established Muslim leaders,
with most of whom Mahmud had been at variance for some
years. The UNP Minister for Labour, M. I. Mohamed, felt
strongly enough to found an Anti-Marxist Muslim United
Front which was not, however, greeted with much enthusiasm
by other Muslim groups. As Mahmud's Front prospered,
particularly after the Kalmunai by-election of 1968, tension
with the established Muslim élite grew. Open disagreement

broke out after the burning of the El Aqsa mosque in Jerusalem in August, 1969. Mohamed and Mahmud appeared together at a mass rally at Maradana mosque which was marked by disunity rather than harmony. Dr. M. C. M. Kaleel, president of the All-Ceylon Muslim League, attacked Mahmud for introducing political controversy and the gathering of 5,000 broke up in haste and with some bitterness. Thus although all platform speakers had agreed that "they must all unite because the cause of Islam was in danger" and that "differences must be sunk now in the cause of Islam", domestic political rivalry proved too strong.[43]

The importance of the rise of the ISF is underlined by this incident. For the first time the Muslim élite has been successfully challenged. Middle Eastern politics became an issue to the point where Mrs. Bandaranaike immediately broke off relations with Israel on her election in 1970. In both respects the Sri Lanka Muslim community is being eased out of its provincial conservatism into a radical and internationalist posture to which it was previously quite unused. Like the other communities the Muslims are now well on the way to absorption into the Left-Right party struggle.

Conclusion

Each minority in Sri Lanka is further subdivided, lessening its cohesion and political effectiveness. Tamil Christians vote for the Tamil parties and Sinhalese Christians for the Sinhalese parties. Muslims are led by secular leaders whose loyalty is normally to the UNP, but they still remain outside the formal party system to a large extent. Some of them identify with the Tamils, others with the Sinhalese. Within the Tamil and Christian minorities differences of caste are as important as among Buddhists and, arguably, even more so. Tamil Karaiyars at Point Pedro do not behave politically like Tamil Vellalas, while Tamil minority castes seem susceptible to extreme Leftwing appeals. The Indian Tamils stand almost entirely outside the political system. Through their unions they can participate in pressure group politics but most of them are barred from electoral action. Even they are divided between the two great organisational empires of Thondaman and Aziz, with Maoists, Samasamajists and Federalists making ineffectual pleas on the fringes. There is no Sri Lanka community likely to act unitedly and very little chance of all the minorities coming together to resist Sinhala Buddhist domination.

The enfranchised minorities do, however, have some common features. They are generally more conservative than the Sinhalese Buddhists in conventional partisan terms. They are also reluctant to become completely committed to one of the two camps into which the Sinhalese Buddhists are divided. Minority voters and representatives are a barrier both to the further development of a strict two-party system, and to the permanent majority of one party over all others. The mechanics by which the minorities act as a kind of pendulum vary. They are probably not consciously understood by any except their own tiny political élites. These are very adept at swinging from one camp to another, trading votes and seats in return for concessions and promising and withholding promises. Nor, indeed, is there much else they could do. Nothing would unite the Sinhalese Buddhist majority more quickly than a serious threat from the minorities. It is arguable that in both 1956 and 1970 a feeling that the UNP had become too committed to the minorities contributed in a major way to its stunning defeats.

Having found that total commitment to one party produced limited benefits, some minority leaders promptly moved over to support for the Left. The Cabinets of the Bandaranaikes have included as many Muslims and more Christians than those of the UNP. Small groups like the Tamil Socialist Front or the Islamic Socialist Front have actually recruited among the normally conservative minority voters. Eventually, in 1970, the SLFP even ran candidates in Tamil electorates and included a Tamil Nominated Member in the Cabinet. They successfully weaned the Tamil Congress M.P.s away from their UNP orientation. The Samasamajists, Communists and Maoists continued, with limited success, to work among the Tamils and even on the tea estates. Aziz replaced Thondaman as spokesman for the estate labourers in parliament. By 1970 both major Sinhalese parties had acknowledged that the minorities must be catered for. The minorities, in their turn, peeped cautiously out of the political ghettoes into which events between 1956 and 1965 had thrust them.

NOTES

1. One M.P., V. Ananthasangare, had been active in the LSSP from 1959 to 1965. The Tamil Congress leader, G. G. Ponnambalam, who lost his seat in 1970, did not support the adherence of the three new Tamil Congress M.P.s to the government party, which did not prove permanent.

2. See A. J. Wilson: "The Tamil Federal Party in Ceylon Politics"; *Journal of Commonwealth Political Studies* 4: 2, July 1966; and R. N. Kearney: *Communalism and Language in the Politics of Ceylon*; Durham N.C., 1967; Chap. 5.

3. In 1970 C. Suntheralingam gained 19% of the vote at Kankesanturai and V. Navaratnam got 19% at Kayts. Both were former M.P.s standing for a separate Tamil state. They subsequently supported the Tamil United Front formed in 1972.

4. Weighting of electorates by area was originally recommended as assisting minority representation. See the Explanatory Memorandum dated 11th September, 1944, on the constitutional scheme formulated by the Ministers (S.P. XIV—1944; pt. 6).

5. Chelliah Kumarasuriar was a chartered engineer and secretary of the Socialist Study Circle.

6. *Ceylon Daily News* 27/3/1961.

7. Based on discussions with Jaffna politicians, including V. Dharmalingam M.P., A. Visvanathan and G. Nalliah in August 1969.

8. See S. Ponniah: *Satyagraha and the Freedom Movement of the Tamils in Ceylon*; Jaffna, 1963.

9. In May, 1973 a Tamil United Front Action Committee, presided over by S. J. V. Chelvanayakam, adopted a Rising Sun flag, urged a boycott of the celebration of Republic Day and decided to draft a constitution for a separate state. *Ceylon News* 24/6/1973.

10. The Dravida Munnetra Kazhagham of Tamilnadu (Madras) had originally advocated secession of South India from the Indian Union, but dropped this in 1962. The DMK has ruled Tamilnadu since 1967. See below for DMK groups in Ceylon.

11. There were reports in 1973 of the formation of a Ceylon Tamil militant youth group similar to the JVP. *Ceylon News* 17/5/1973.

12. C. X. Martyn was expelled from the Federal Party in July, 1971 for refusing to boycott the Constituent Assembly and continued to represent Jaffna as an Independent.

13. Based on an interview with former Senator G. Nalliah, president of the All-Ceylon Minority Tamil Mahasabha, in Jaffna in August, 1969.

14. M. C. Subramaniam was made an Appointed Member in 1970. He was a founder member of the Ceylon Communist Party and of the All-Ceylon Minority Tamil Mahasabha. Minority Tamils have not, however, succeeded in being elected to parliament.

15. See G. de Fontgalland: *Barricades at the Temple*; (Colombo, 1968).

16. All-Ceylon Saiva (Hindu) Practices and Observances Protection Society: *Temple Entry Movement in the North*; Chunnakam, 1968; p. 5.

17. Several groups claiming to represent the DMK have been rumoured since the early 1960s but they seem to have little substance and have never run for office. The Tamilnadu DMK consistently claims to have no branches in Ceylon, nor any interest in forming them.
18. In 1972 the South Indian DMK split and a party led by M. G. Ramachandram took the name Anna DMK in memory of Annadurai. This party also denied any interest in or connections with, Ceylon. *Ceylon News* 11/1/1973.
19. *Ceylon Daily News* 18/2/1969.
20. For details of the CWC and DWC see R. N. Kearney: *Trade Unions and Politics in Ceylon*; Berkeley, 1971; pp. 120–131.
21. The Ilankai Thollilalar Kazham.
22. The Ceylon DMK split in 1957 and the militant section came under the control of Ilanchelian (see feature: "DMK—the Man and the Movement" in *Ceylon Observer* 7/9/1963). By 1970 Ilanchelian was running a group in the tea estates called the Young Socialist Front and held a joint rally with Rohan Wijeweera and the JVP at Norwood (*Times of Ceylon* 19/11/1970). Ilanchelian was later said to have offered his assistance on the tea estates for the rising of April 5, 1971 but, in fact, nothing happened.
23. The term "Christian" as used here does not imply active Church going or belief but simply acknowledges that everyone in Sri Lanka is assumed to belong to one religious community or another. Colloquially a distinction is often made between Christians (Protestants) and Catholics.
24. All are nominally Protestants.
25. This centred around Ossie Corea, a Catholic, who originally supplied the gun which killed Bandaranaike.
26. For the politics of Negombo, which is 74% Christian, see K. P. Misra: "Political Behaviour of the Little Rome"; *South Asian Studies* 3 January 1968, pp. 20–32.
27. *Times Weekender* 16/12/1969.
28. *Ceylon Daily News* 28/3/1952.
29. *Ceylon Daily News* 17/5/1952.
30. I. D. S. Weerawardena: *Ceylon General Election 1956*; Colombo, 1959; p. 136.
31. *Daily Mirror* (Colombo) 14/2/1969.
32. *Daily Mirror* (Colombo) 4/3/1969.
33. *Sun* (Colombo) 11/6/1969.
34. This estimate of Catholic opinion is based on an interview with Father Tissa Balasuriya, Principal of Aquinas College, in July 1959.
35. *Nation* 13/8/1971. See also *Quest* (Colombo), April 1971 for a summary of Houtart's findings.
36. I have not here considered the Hindus as a religious minority as they exert no organised political influence except as Tamils.
37. A Sri Lanka Malay Socialist Front was formed in 1972 to support the SLFP. *Times Weekender* 30/7/1972.

38. The SLFP winner at Puttalam, who had previously been in the UNP, died in 1971 and the seat was regained by the UNP at the resulting by-election. Otherwise it has never been held by the SLFP.
39. Nintavur, Kalmunai and Pottuvil—all on the East coast.
40. This account of the Muslim community is based on an interview with Al-haj Badiuddin Mahmud in August, 1969.
41. See *Badiudin Mahmud—a Brief Life Sketch*; Islamic Socialist Front, Colombo; 1969.
42. For its organisation see *Constitution of the Islamic Socialist Front*; Maradana, 1969. Membership is confined to Muslims under s.3 (a).
43. *Ceylon Daily News* 25/8/1969.

CHAPTER 6

Opinion and Pressure

A participatory democracy functions best when its citizens are well informed, actively interested in politics and have an effective network of secondary institutions which can act as pressures upon government in defence of their interests. In these respects Sri Lanka is well served. Outside the tea estates the great majority of adults are literate and have attended schools where they have received at least an adequate education. Newspapers do not sell widely but circulate to most people through being seen at village shops or in reading rooms.[1] Radio is available throughout the Island though television has not been introduced.[2] The relatively modest penetration of the mass media does not seem to have limited political knowledge or interest. Mass sports or entertainments are unknown in the villages and politics remains a consuming passion. National leaders are well known and electoral participation is among the highest in the world.[3] It may have been true twenty years ago that villagers "are not what might be called 'easy joiners'".[4] Since 1956, however, there has been a positive explosion in formal membership of trade unions, co-operative societies, political parties, youth leagues and many other groups. As all these are divided on community, partisan, occupational or caste lines the variety is enormous and operating efficiency consequently limited. There remains a wide variety of potential pressure groups from the powerful and prestigious Low Country Products Association and the Ceylon Planters' Association to the countless figments of individual imagination on the bizarre fringes of politics.

Public Opinion and the Media

Sri Lanka has no opinion poll organisations and only a handful of market research or anthropological surveys has been carried out. Thus the formation of public opinion remains something of a mystery. How the nationwide landslide swings from UNP to SLFP in 1956 and 1970 were achieved is still unexplained.[5] The great bulk of the press favoured the UNP and the state radio was controlled by their government. In 1956 the Sinhala-wide agitation of the monks might explain the result, but this could not be said of 1970. Yet the same sort of swing occurred time and time again across the country. Bryce Ryan argued for a relatively advanced Low Country Sinhalese Buddhist village that in 1953 "the newspaper is the village's most important source of contact with world events."[6] This probably remains true. In the past twenty years, however, party organisation has reached into the further corners of most constituencies. Politicians, none of whom can be sure of the safety of their seats since 1956, spend a great deal of time cultivating their electors. The joint effects of the mass media, the parties and the politicians keep the villager interested, while his local *bhikkhu*, ayurvedic doctor, teacher and shop keeper are all likely to be politically involved. They are most likely to receive their basic information through the newspaper and the radio, with a fair amount of rumour and gossip being spread in more remote areas by bus and truck drivers, travelling salesmen and returning relatives.[7]

That opinion leaders are so reliant on the press helps to explain the virulent hatred which many politicians express towards the newspapers and their owners. Both in 1965, when Mrs Bandaranaike was defeated, and after her victory in 1970, supporting demonstrators made straight for Lake House, the headquarters of Associated Newspapers of Ceylon, determined to smash up the offices. Mrs. Bandaranaike was herself overthrown in 1964 because of her attempt to nationalise Lake House while they, in their turn, are said to have had over two dozen M.P.s "on their payroll" at the time. If freedom of the press is a necessary feature of democracy, it must be asked why so many Ceylon politicians of otherwise democratic beliefs hate the local press. Even the United National Party leaders were critical of the papers on many occasions during their tenure of office.

Criticism of the press reached its height during Mrs. Bandaranaike's first government. In the Throne Speech of 1960 the Government promised to transfer Lake House and the *Times* group to a public corporation. An official commission was appointed in September, 1963 to investigate a whole series of aspects including "the extent to which and the manner in which newspapers owned or published by the Associated Newspapers of Ceylon Ltd., the Times of Ceylon Ltd., or the Virakesari Ltd., sought to exercise undue influence on voters in the exercise of the franchise at the Parliamentary Elections held in 1956 and 1960."[8] One member of the commission, Mrs. Theja Gunawardene, was forced to resign when the newspaper companies represented that she had conducted a virulent campaign against them for some years.[9] Nevertheless the final report of the commission was still a shrill compendium of motley complaints. Part of its charges endorsed representations made to it by L. H. Mettanada's militant Buddhist pressure group, the Bauddha Jatika Balavegaya. The BJB had been concerned for some years with proving Catholic plots and easily found one in the press despite the fact that Associated Newspapers was established by the devoutly Buddhist Wijewardena family with whom the Senanayakes had been closely connected.

The gist of the Commission charges was that the press had "been lacking in patriotism",[10] that it was "recklessly scattering seeds of indiscipline all around",[11] that an excessive number of Tamil publications were coming in from India and that "the interests of this small group of owners are diametrically opposed to the interests of the people at large."[12] For several pages it wandered off into a general condemnation of Catholic Action which it accused of planning the 1962 coup. It recommended a powerful Press Council, the transfer of the Lake House Group to a public company and the creation of a state news agency. Coming after such a diatribe these recommendations were fairly moderate and sensible and might well have eliminated some of the real weaknesses in the Ceylon press of which the distortion and invention of political news items was the most blatant. The Commission was ineffectual as the overthrow of Mrs. Bandaranaike's government in December 1964 with the active approval of the press, suspended any further action.

The Commission was heavily influenced by one element which is hostile to the press, the extreme Sinhala Buddhist nationalists.

The Marxist parties, despite their equal hostility to Lake House, were very suspicious of the whole enterprise. They had much to fear from a press controlled by the sort of forces represented by Mettananda and were worried about possible interference in their own extensive publications. There is no doubt, however, that the entire Left-nationalist alliance wanted to see Lake House control broken up. The objection to Associated Newspapers was, in their eyes, primarily political, stemming from the life-long association between the Wijewardenas and the Senanayakes, the consistent partisanship shown by Lake House for the United National Party and its opposition to trade unions among its employees. All the major newspaper companies tend towards the Right in varying degrees. A principal shareholder in the *Times of Ceylon* was the veteran UNP official H. W. Amarasuriya, while Ceylon Newpapers, Eelanadu and Virakesari are all Tamil companies of Federalist or Tamil Congress leanings. The only company which periodically gave support to Mrs. Bandaranaike is Independent Newspapers, publisher of the Sinhalese dailies *Dawasa* and *Sawasa* and the English-language *Sun*. They, too, are a family company, owned by the book publishers M. D. Gunasena. Initially they favoured Mrs. Bandaranaike but, as the Press Commission notes, they turned against her when school textbook publishing was made a monopoly of the Government Printer, depriving Gunasena of a very profitable contract. Eventually, in April 1974, the offices of *Dawasa* were closed down by the government acting under emergency powers.

The conservatism of a privately owned press is worldwide. It attracts attention in Sri Lanka largely because the press is almost unchallenged as a partisan influence. While patronage appointments have been made in the Ceylon Broadcasting Corporation it has seldom been as blatantly committed as the major newspapers. The fact that nearly one-third of daily papers sold are still in English arouses the suspicion of Sinhala nationalists. The press, through its syndicated features from abroad, is seen as a corrupting influence on Sinhalese youth and the English-language journalists were specifically condemned by the Commission as anti-national. The English papers are read by most of the political élite and the Colombo middle-classes and give them at least a limited insight into what is happening elsewhere. For the besetting sin of the local press is its appalling provincialism. Only the *Times of Ceylon* gave more than 10% of its space to foreign political news in 1964.[13] As a large part of the domestic news consists of murders, politicians' speeches and rumours, the press as a whole does little to raise the level of political debate. The Commission said that a publicly managed newspaper "could not be worse than the newspapers run by the Lake House and the Times Group".[14] Perhaps the best and most far-ranging papers are the weeklies published by the Communists and the Catholic Church. Certainly the great rash of new dailies published by political groups since 1964 has not done much to raise the level or effectively to challenge the private corporations.[15]

The bitterness surrounding the defeat of Mrs. Bandaranaike's government in December, 1964, ensured that national control over the press, and particularly over the Lake House newspapers, would become a major issue after her return in 1970. In the intervening years the Lake House group had given its full support to the United National Party. The UNP government had moved against the increasingly popular Communist paper, *Aththa* and the LSSP daily *Janadina*, seizing copies and closing their presses under the emergency regulations in force in 1966. This did not effectively stop the growth of an alternative Leftwing press and the bitterness against the major commercial newspaper chain simply grew more acute. The breaking point came in late 1969, when N. M. Perera revealed in parliament that directors of Lake House had been engaged in largescale illegal currency movements to bank accounts in London and Switzerland. This shifted the discussion on press control away from the dubious ground taken up in 1964 which had worried the Marxist parties with their own growing interest in newspapers. The issue became far more attractive when couched in terms of punishing a major company for undermining the country's economy and enriching its principal shareholders, who were largely relatives of the Lake House founder, D. R. Wijewardena. N. M. Perera, in his speech of September 1 1969, estimated that sums of Rs. 20 million were involved, that the Tax Department had raided the homes of Lake House managing directors, and that a leading director, G. B. S. Gomes, had resigned as chairman of the official Development Finance Corporation. The LSSP, in particular, made out a strong political case that the UNP government was protecting Lake House by refusing to appoint a commission of enquiry. In asking for such a commission N. M. Perera claimed that "this matter is too important and the party assumes too large a place in the public life of this country to be ignored, to be brushed aside or set aside . . . they wield a tremendous political influence and they have played a major part in the political life of this country. Should not the public therefore know what this institution has been up to during the last few years?"[16]

The intimate family connections between the Lake House directors and the leaders of the UNP, and their close political alliance over a period of forty years, made Lake House particularly vulnerable upon a change of government especially if it could be established that the company was being used as a major loophole in exchange control. The LSSP leaders had been supplied with ample photostat and other evidence to make their charges effective, although the UNP government was able to defeat the motion for an enquiry.[17] This merely made it all the more certain that such an enquiry would be instituted by the victorious Coalition. There was now a new dimension to the case against Lake House. Attacks on the *Times* and *Dawasa* groups were now muted and the legislation eventually passed in 1973 dealt with Associated Newspapers of Ceylon only. The Associated Newspapers of Ceylon (Special Provisions) Act, which was declared valid by the Constitutional Court and passed through the National State Assembly in July, 1973, reduced the holdings of the existing shareholders to not more than 25% of the total, vesting the remainder in the Public Trustee, under the control of a Minister until their eventual sale to the general public. No individual shareholder was to control more than two percent of the total of shares and, in the event, the existing shareholders were left with 17% of the total. Thus the company was not strictly nationalised, but converted from a private to a public company in which it would be impossible for the previous owners to exercise control, but quite possible for the government to appoint new management and to retain the 'public' element of shares in the hands of the Public Trustee for as long as they thought fit. The control of existing managers was further limited by barring from the Board any person against whom a finding was reached by any commission enquiring into contraventions of exchange, revenue and import regulations.[18]

Sixty per cent of all newspapers sold in Sri Lanka were to pass out of the hands of the descendants of D. R. Aijewardena and were to be controlled by managers appointed by the Public Trustee. As Mrs. Bandaranaike said, the Bill was "designed to broadbase the ownership of the Company. The era when press barons decided the destinies of the people was over."[19] The attitude of the UNP was, of course, quite otherwise, J. R. Jayawardena announced a campaign of passive resistance and boycott of Lake House newspapers, a policy once favoured by the Marxist parties but found to be relatively ineffective. Where the new government was now to direct advertisements towards Lake House papers, the UNP was to direct them away. Where the government would encourage readership, the UNP was to launch a national campaign to reduce the number of readers. The UNP would boycott all newspapers published by the new management. The entire relationship between the major parties and the largest newspaper chain were reversed overnight. While the new board of directors included a working journalist within the organisation, and was said to be legally protected against government interference, there could never be the close family relationship which had previously existed. The Lake House newspapers, while often critical of some aspects of UNP policy, had normally given full support to Dudley Senanayake and J. R. Jayawardena and been hostile to those they saw as their main enemies in the LSSP. Whatever the development of Associated Newspapers of Ceylon after 1973, whether as the voice of the government or as a relatively autonomous corporation, it would be unable to help the UNP in future elections as it had helped them on all previous occasions.

The breaking of family ownership at Lake House was the logical outcome of a generation of hostility between their newspapers and all the forces going to make up the government of Mrs. Bandaranaike. The Press Commission of 1964 had broader aims and some of these were still influential nearly ten years later. Its support for a powerful Press Council was fully endorsed by Mrs. Bandaranaike's government. Although criticised by the All-Ceylon Buddhist Congress and the newly formed Civil Rights Movement and forced to submit the proposed legislation to the Constitutional Court, the government was ultimately successful in creating a Press Council with considerably greater powers than those enjoyed by its British or Indian counterparts. The Sri Lanka Press Council Act finally became law in February 1973.[20] The new Council had a dozen declared objectives which included: to ensure the freedom of the press, to prevent the abuse of the freedom of the press, to safeguard the character of the press in accordance with the highest professional standards, to improve the organisation of the press and of the journalistic profession, to promote common news services, to remedy concentration and monopoly and to advise the government on any matter concerning the regulation and conduct of newspapers. The Council would also have the power to "report offences under this law to the Inspector-General of Police for appropriate action."[21] It was empowered to order corrections of news items, to censure editors and proprietors and to order apologies, to declare a code of ethics for journalists, hold necessary enquiries and register the proprietors of newspapers. Within these very broad powers there were certain specific limitations placed upon the press which aroused considerable criticism. Indecent, profane or blasphemous matter was forbidden, whether in articles or advertisements, an echo of the Press Commission's concern with Western pornographic influences and belittling of religion. More controversially the Council was to reinforce existing provisions of the Official Secrets Act relating to military arrangements. The section which aroused most opposition, and which was drastically redrafted, would have made it almost impossible to discuss any departure in policy or matter of public interest which was under consideration by the Cabinet or by individual Ministers. This would have inhibited any political debate which was not approved by Ministers or by the Secretary to the Cabinet and any discussions or proposed measures which might give financial advantage to individuals made aware of them through the press.

Despite challenges in the Constitutional Court the government of Sri Lanka had, by mid-1973, created a powerful agency of press control and brought under its control the publishers of sixty percent of all newspapers. The government also enjoyed, through its monopoly of broadcasting, a news medium which was more readily accessible to most villagers than were the daily newspapers published in Colombo. Moreover, under the emergency regulations which operated from March, 1971, the government had full potential powers of censorship, although these were not used after the end of 1971. The degree to which news could cease to be spread if the government chose to use its powers was very clear during 1971. Reports likely to cause despondency about the JVP rising simply did not appear. Critical comments on police or army atrocities were impossible. All official government business was made available through the Department of Information or not at all. Throughout the insurgency the radio remained the principal source of information and one which was quite consciously used by the government to counter the pathetic attempts by the JVP to issue local news-sheets. Critical foreign press reports had either to be filed through Madras or not at all. Almost alone among major dailies, the Communist *Aththa* attempted to criticise the government, thus precipitating the crisis within the Communist Party which eventually led to the expulsion of its Managing Editor, Arnolis Appuhamy. This absence of news did not noticeably change established political loyalties. The UNP was able to win three by-elections in 1972 while the Federal Party built up its campaign against the new constitution through the Tamil United Front. The creation of the Press Council, the Lake House legislation and, perhaps most potently, the reserve emergency powers held by the government, all made it possible to limit access to information within the island to a degree previously unknown. News management through government intervention became a concrete reality which Ceylon had not previously experienced except briefly during the crisis of 1958. With very little external supply of news and with most opinion leaders totally dependent on the newspapers and radio, the informational basis for a flourishing democracy in Sri Lanka suddenly seemed rather narrow.

Religious Pressures

In a rural and deeply religious nation, politicians are always liable to pressures from organised religion and from the faithful. In modern industrial societies such pressure may be expressed through official spokesmen for denominations on a national

level. In Ceylon this is impossible except for the Christians.
Muslim religious pressure is almost totally absent. Hindu
pressure is confined almost exclusively to the protection of
temple practices. Naturally enough the great bulk of pressure
comes from Buddhists. Unfortunately no-one can speak for
local Buddhism. The two leading abbots, the Mahanayake
Theros of the Malwatte and Asgiriya chapters, sometimes seem
to be taking the role of national spokesmen. They have been
manipulated by the press in the past and have been far from
wise or consistent in the support they have given to various
causes. In any case they have no authority over any other
Buddhist clergy, let alone laymen. The principal lay organisation, the All-Ceylon Buddhist Congress, is very close in
structure and status to a modern pressure group. It is often at
variance with Malwatte and Asgiriya who fear its meddling in
monastic affairs. As any member of the clergy is entitled to hold
any view he likes, the game of religious pressure is often played
out by getting ever more prestigious figures to speak out for
opposite causes and parties.

The experienced Sinhalese politician is usually much more
adept at this game than the clergy. No political platform is
complete without a monk. The Central Committees of the
Communist and Samasamajist parties have included monks
from their earliest days, as have the two major parties. Men like
Ven. Henpitegedara Gnanaseeha or the late Ven. Udakendawela
Siri Saranankara, were deeply involved in SLFP and Communist
politics respectively.[22] So enmeshed in the SLFP was Ven.
Mapitigama Buddharakkitha that the whole party organisation
in Kelaniya centred around him and was dedicated to the
defeat of J. R. Jayawardena who had opposed his election as
incumbent at Kelaniya temple. In the end his involvement with
the party extended to plotting the successful assassination of
its leader. None of these men, active in politics in their various
ways, were primarily exercising *religious* pressure. They were
simply acting as individuals, though with a following which
owed much to their religious status. The major forms of action
which can be truly termed religious pressure are campaigns by
the All-Ceylon Buddhist Congress, campaigns by mass organisations of *bhikkhus* and campaigns initiated by the two
Mahanayake Theros.

The All-Ceylon Buddhist Congress aims generally at re-structuring the religion so that it may approximate to the Christian model, with clear lines of command, legally regulated relationships with the state and effective unity both for political pressure and theological discipline.[23] In the early years of independence most of its efforts were in this direction. It was formally accepted as a legitimate pressure group by the All-Ceylon Buddhist Congress Act of 1955 which empowered it "to represent the Buddhists and act on their behalf in public matters affecting their interests." The Congress was founded and led by prominent members of the political élite, including F. R. Senanayake, D. B. Jayatillake, Sir Lalita Rajapakse, H. W. Amarasuriya and Dr. G. P. Malalasekera. It was both legally and actually in a dominant political position to influence any government. Its Commission of Inquiry, set up in April 1954, was designed as a high-powered form of pressure. Its report, coming in the Buddha Jayanti year, was a vital factor in making the Sinhala Buddhist revival a major issue in the 1956 general election.

Despite its absolutely central position at the heart of Ceylon politics, the Congress was limited by its secular and modernising character. This made it less of a force in the villages than among the Colombo bourgeoisie. Although the Bandaranaike government went a long way in implementing the Commission of Inquiry recommendations, it was reluctant to do so where these were opposed by the monastic orders. There was no objection to the setting up of a Ministry of Cultural Affairs, to the creation of Buddhist universities or the nationalisation of schools. Two measures were resolutely opposed by the leaders of the Siam *nikaya*. They would not tolerate the meddling of the Buddha Sasana Commission, which Bandaranaike set up officially in March 1957.[24] Nor would they accept the inclusion of temple lands in the provisions of Philip Gunawardena's Paddy Lands Act of 1958. The first was designed to give a formalised structure to the religion, which would have weakened the political power of the Malwatte and Asgiriya chapters in the Kandyan high-lands. The second would have attacked the economic basis of the monastic orders who owned directly at least 376,000 acres of agricultural land.

In these battles between the reforming and monastic pressures the latter came off the winner. The Sasana Commission recommended the creation of a bicameral council which would have supervisory powers similar to those found in the Anglican structure. Nothing has come of this, nor of further recommendations for ecclesiastical courts, for a Commissioner of Temple Lands or for the registration of *Bhikkhus*.[25] The Buddhist Congress fought hard for implementation and seemed to be in a strong position in the anti-clerical atmosphere surrounding Bandaranaike's assassination. But Mrs. Bandaranaike understood the Kandyan situation very well. Her family were closely linked to the administration of the Temple of the Tooth and thus to the Malwatte chapter. Unlike the Senanayakes, whose links were with the Ramanya sect, or the Bandaranaikes, who were Anglicans, the Ratwattes were part of the conservative monastic-feudal structure.[26] Nothing more was heard of the reforms. Another victim of monastic resistance was Philip Gunawardena who was pushed out of Bandaranaike's Cabinet in 1959 by conservative elements who were partly responding to clerical pressure against the Paddy Lands Act. The Buddhist Congress, which was the author of a very large part of the programme which the Bandaranaikes carried out in the cultural, religious and educational fields, was defeated just at the point where its lifework seemed near completion.

Since then the Congress, subsidised and supported by governments of both major parties, has continued to apply pressure on less dangerous topics. Being forbidden by convention to support any particular party, it strives for a consensus within the limits of supporting Sinhala Buddhist interests. Indeed the general viewpoint within the Congress seems to be against the two-party system among Sinhalese, as dividing them against the other minorities. While the Congress does not yet regard the ecclesiastical reform campaign as dead, in the interests of harmony with the monks, who are represented on an advisory council, it has played the issue down. The most successful pressure was against the 1947 Soulbury Constitution, which was inspected and found wanting after the ACBC Kandy Congress of 1963 had appointed a committee to study it. There is nothing specifically Buddhist about the Congress's ideas, which were influenced by Western notions such as a collegiate Cabinet and referendum on the Swiss model, or an Ombudsman on the

Scandinavian. Apart from this major campaign, the Congress has fought against the District Councils Bill of 1968, raised the issue of the Vietnam war, fought for reforms in education, in language policy, the legal system and the administration of charities. It sees itself as "giving a lead on national problems, not just on Buddhist ones."[27]

The All-Ceylon Buddhist Congress is immediately recognisable as a modern pressure group. It deals directly with Ministers and particularly with the Ministry of Cultural Affairs which was largely its own creation. It operates through a formal structure, regular publications and congresses. A lay organisation of middle-class professionals, it would fit easily into any secularised Western political system. Where religion permeates all political activities and the clergy represent a major force in the countryside, more traditional pressures may be even more effective. Where there have been clashes between the Congress and the clergy, the clergy usually won. As W. Dahanayake said in 1959, while Prime Minister, "nobody in this country can thrust down the throats of the Malwatte and Asgiriya chapters anything they do not like."[28]

No government comes to office without its leaders making the round of obeisance at the main shrines and receiving the blessing of the Mahanayake Theros. Nor is this the formality which it might be in a secular polity. While many monks have withdrawn from active politics, the clergy showed in 1956 that when mobilised no other force could stand against it. After the UNP had been denounced by L. H. Mettananda in 1955, the Eksath Bhikkhu Peramuna came into being, organised a mighty force of monks behind the SLFP, and was able to defy the Mahanayake Theros themselves.[29] Their injunction to monks of the Siam sect not to take part in electioneering, which the Prime Minister, Sir John Kotelawala induced them to make, was ignored.[30]

Having got the SLFP into power the EBP naturally expected considerable advantages, and none more so than its secretary, Buddharakkitha. However the SLFP was not a specifically Buddhist party and in any case Bandaranaike was too experienced a politician to be dominated by a newly formed and probably ephemeral campaign group. By June 1959 the Peramuna was openly considering forming a new party. In

September Bandaranaike was assassinated in a plot conceived by Buddharakkitha. This single action did much to discredit clerical intervention in politics. There was strong popular feeling against monks, with violence directed against them in Colombo and other towns. While all Sinhalese parties have continued to use the services of *ad hoc* clerical fronts these have become increasingly discredited and probably enroll only a fraction of the strength active in 1956. The All-Ceylon Buddhist Congress and the Mahanayakes have repeatedly attacked clerical participation in party politics. Nevertheless the Mahanayakes also continued to denounce Marxism from time to time, though occasionally veering towards Mrs. Bandaranaike when she takes a strong stand against Tamil political leaders.

The clergy is still the most important veto group in local society. It defends its interests rigorously, though being more reluctant to make positive new proposals. No politician dare affront the Sangha. In 1969 the UNP Minister for Education, I. M. R. A. Iriyagolle, was forced to apologise for critical remarks of a sort frequently made about the clergy before. He wrote to the acting Mahanayake Thero of Malwatte that "if he had caused any embarrassment to the Maha 'Sangha' he was deeply sorry for the incident."[31] Meetings had been held particularly in the Southern Province, trying to implicate the entire Cabinet and demanding that Iriyagolle worship at the feet of the Mahanayake. Whether for this or other reasons Iriyagolle lost his relatively safe seat at the 1970 election.[32]

Because the *Sangha* acts so effectively as a veto group it is essential that no Singhalese party leader should omit to worship in public or to give thanks after election campaigns. At the week long celebrations in 1969 surrounding the placing of a gold rail around the Bo tree at Anuradhapura, both Mrs. Bandaranaike and the Prime Minister took an active part. Dudley Senanayake even went so far as to pledge "that he and Mrs. Sirima Bandaranaike would work together without any differences and party prejudices in all religious matters for the greater glory and welfare of the Buddha Sasana."[33] Part of the consensus established between the major parties is that religious observance has a legitimate part in politics. While not accepted officially it is a natural corollary of this that monks should take part in politics both as individuals and in organised groups. Above all it institutionalises as surely as in ancient Ceylon, the principle that the Sangha advises the state. The golden age when this was so is regularly referred to by most militant Buddhists. They disagree on whether Buddhism should become a state religion. Because the same sort of interference might arise as was threatened by the Sasana Commission, there is remarkably little pressure for such a policy.

The general consequence of this religious pressure has been to transform the secular state of 1948 into one in which the government is obliged to give Buddhism the "foremost place."[34] The new constitution committed the state to "endeavour to create the necessary economic and social environment to enable people of all religious faiths to make a living reality of their religious principles."[35] It specifically granted the right to freedom of thought, conscience and religion, including "the freedom to have or adopt a religion or belief of his choice, and the freedom, either individually or in community with others and in public or private, to manifest his religion or belief in worship, observance, practice and teaching."[36] These rights and obligations reflect the modern and liberal approach of the Buddhist Congress, rather than of communalists who wanted positions of power strictly limited to Buddhists, who would also, of course, be Sinhalese. The effect of years of religious pressure has been to create a permanent possibility of veto. Measures such as the District Councils Bill of 1968, the Tamil Language (Special Provisions) Act of 1966, the state licensing of toddy tappers in the Budget of 1964 or the Bandaranaike-Chelvanayakam pact of 1958, have all been frustrated by organised clerical opposition. After 1956 Buddhism had become sufficiently well-organised to exert constant pressure, even if it had no ideological consistency.

The Unions[37]

Religious leaders and groups are able to exert effective pressure because the majority of electors are peasants with deep religious commitments. Employees' influence arises because labour is highly unionised. At 45%, the unionised proportion of the labour force is higher than in all but a handful of industrial nations. A large part of the workforce is engaged in peasant agriculture which is not susceptible to unionisation and, the figures suggest that over two thirds of the workers in the plantation, commercial, public and industrial sectors are in unions. Even with inflation of figures, which is controlled to some extent by official registration, this means that the worker is brought into organised contact with politics.[38] The great bulk of workers are in politically active unions. Even within the public service, where overt partisanship among employees is discouraged, some of the most active unions are known to be aligned with a party.[39] The two largest unions are on the tea estates where union enrollment is undertaken by agreement with the employers under a checkoff contributory system. The unions are almost the only political form of pressure open to the estate workers who are disfranchised and geographically isolated, being very unlikely to join the Sinhalese dominated parties in their areas. The whole political life of the largest single proletarian force in Sri Lanka centres on the Ceylon Workers Congress and the Democratic Workers Congress. They, in turn, inherit the mantle of the Ceylon Indian Congress which was driven from electoral politics by the disfranchisement of 1948, but had been registered as a union since 1940.[40]

The estate workers' unions are highly organised and militant, with strikes being held frequently.[41] Because of their overwhelmingly Indian Tamil membership they can only exert political pressure to a limited extent. Since 1960 they have done this by aligning themselves with one or other of the major elements in the Sinhalese party struggle. V. E. K. S. Thondaman, leader of the CWC, after a brief alliance with Mrs. Bandaranaike in 1960, became firmly allied with the United National Party and was nominated to parliament by Dudley Senanayake in 1965. A. Aziz, the rival leader of the DWC, though critical of the communalism of the SLFP, was always identified with the Left and was nominated to parliament by Mrs. Bandaranaike in 1970.[42] With over five hundred thousand members between them, these two men could, potentially, bring the Island to economic standstill.

Because of their rivalry and the lack of civic rights for their membership, their influence is much less than might appear. Their major function as pressure group leaders has been over the repatriation or naturalisation of Indian Tamils. Otherwise, despite their political commitment, they both operate as industrial negotiators rather than as active partisans. With the limited enfranchisement of naturalised Indian Tamils in recent years they have operated electorally by directing their members to support either the UNP or the SLFP.

The largest and most effectively organised part of the local labour movement is, then, largely insulated from the Sinhalese party political system. The plantation unions cannot exert much pressure on local M.P.s who are invariably Sinhalese Buddhists. They are never represented in the government and only marginally in parliament. Thondaman's concessions were gained largely by delivering the small vote of Indian Tamil citizens to the UNP in the 1965 election. It is doubtful if Aziz, who is a Pakistani Muslim by origin, could even do that for the SLFP. Other trade unions are, theoretically, in a stronger position. But the union movement is hopelessly fragmented and is often an adjunct to the parties rather than a major pressure upon them. Unions may be classified into those in the public service, who were fragmented under the Ordinance of 1935 which prohibits members of different grades from joining the same union, those attached to parties, and those functioning relatively independently.[43] The first group are ineffectual because there are over seven hundred of them, the second because there are usually six or seven rivals within each occupation, and the third because there are not many of them at all.

For all their size and coverage trade unions are limited as pressure groups. There is no central body to speak for unionists as a whole. Apart from the CWC and DWC, who control over one-third of all unionists but are bitter rivals, there are several different national federations. The Ceylon Federation of Labour is controlled by the LSSP and has N. M. Perera as its president. The Ceylon Trade Union Federation was captured for Maoism through its secretary N. Shanmugathasan, whereupon most of its adherents left to join the "Moscow" Communist controlled Ceylon Federation of Trade Unions. Neither of these must be confused with the All-Ceylon United Trade Union Federation, which is controlled by the Tamil Congress! The SLFP, UNP and Federal Party all have their own trade union centres while the unions associated with Philip Gunawardena's MEP have theirs and the Ceylon Mercantile Union, controlled by the

Revolutionary Samasamajist Bala Tampoe, also set up its own centre. The Public Service Workers Trade Union Federation is at variance with the Government Clerical Service Union and so on. Indeed a major reason for high recruitment in Ceylon trade unions is that there is constant rivalry and poaching between different unions which, in the absence of a national centre, cannot be avoided.

The tactic of approaching governments on behalf of the trade union movement through a single national centre cannot, then, possibly arise in the present situation. The associated tactic, that of British Labour with which many Ceylonese Marxists are familiar, cannot arise either. There could not possibly be a single Labour Party based on affiliated unions. The beginnings of such a trend, which might have lain in the Samasamajist Federation of Labour in the early 1950s, was completely smothered by the rapid rise in union membership after 1956 precisely on the basis of partisan rivalry. The Coalition unions have worked together through a liaison committee and probably control the majority of unionists outside the plantations.[44] This is not the same as saying that the basis of a labour party has been laid. Unions are ancillary to parties and trade union officials are often drawn from the political élite. Unionists who have risen up through the ranks may not be nearly as important in their respective parties as middle-class M.P.s representing the peasantry.[45]

As the tactics of a national centre and a labour party are not currently feasible, the unions tend to exert political pressure on behalf of their parties, by strikes and demonstrations or by issuing manifestoes. These are likely to be politically embarrassing when the unions' leaders are involved in government. The "Twentyone Demands" drawn up by the United Left Front Joint Council of Trade Unions in 1964, were abandoned when the largest component of the Council, the Ceylon Federation of Labour, was committed by the LSSP to the Coalition with Mrs. Bandaranaike. Subsequent attempts to unite the politically radical unions have been complicated by the political commitments of the party leaders. The United Committee of Ceylon Trade Unions, set up in April, 1966 was a shortlived attempt at uniting the Democratic Workers Congress, the Ceylon Mercantile Union and other unions uncommitted to the major parties.

So well established are the Marxist controlled federations that little effective can be done without their support. At the same time as the UCCTU was being created, they launched the Joint Committee of Trade Union Organisations which gave its support to "Fifteen Demands" and, in 1968, to the Common Programme of the three Coalition parties.[46]

This constant complication of the industrial field by partisan commitment does not necessarily prevent unions of different complexions from co-operating in industrial activity. Rivalry is their more common approach, particularly on purely political issues. Some union officials seem to resent this constant intrusion of partisan considerations into their work. The two major plantation unions have normally been able to hold aloof from the Sinhalese party struggle. Unions dominated by Shanmugathasan and Bala Tampoe have broken away from the Moscow Communists and Samasamajists respectively, forcing those parties to create parallel rivals.[47] Even within the parties, the unions have not necessarily succumbed slavishly to leadership from the politicians. LSSP union officials have sometimes shown the same critical attitude towards the middle-class party leaders which is seen in the labour movements of industrial nations.[48] The unions attached to the United National Party occasionally joined in strikes against the UNP government. These are fairly limited developments as yet, but they point to the possible rise of a genuine, working class labour movement in due course. The union movement had a mushroom growth after 1956 in which the hard core of Marxist unions were completely swamped. A whole new generation of union leaders started to emerge from a rank and file which was not necessarily fully committed to any party. As yet there are few of these who come from the ranks, and virtually none who yet aspire to parliamentary office.[49] It may be that in the future the established political élite will be subject to pressures from the unions which have not, hitherto, been strong enough to disturb or displace them.

Mass Pressure and Agitation

Unions in Sri Lanka, in contrast to those in Britain or America but in common with those in France or Italy, frequently resort to the political strike or mass demonstration. In part this stems from their original foundation by Marxist groups who saw the unions in Leninist terms as weapons in the political struggle rather than as instruments for piecemeal economic reforms. As early as the communal riots of 1915 the railway and other semi-skilled workers were ready to strike and agitate for political ends. The Ceylon Labour Party of A. E. Goonesinha had its origins in such tendencies.[50] The Ceylon Indian Congress was both a party and a trade union. The combination of existing trends with Leninist practice made it inevitable that the unions should see political agitation as a primary function. With the rapid mushrooming of membership after 1956 under party leadership, this tendency was maintained. Part of the folklore of unionism centres around those killed or victimised in political demonstrations, particularly the clerk V. Kandasamy, shot in 1947, the eleven men shot during the *hartal* of 1953 and the Buddhist monk shot in the January, 1966 demonstrations.

It is maintained on the Left that the general strike of 1947 was a major element in the British decision to give Ceylon independence, which was transmitted in June while the strike was in progress. Equally the *hartal* of August 12, 1953 directed against the abolition of the rice ration, is still commemorated as "the most significant direct mass action this country has seen in recent times".[51] A joint statement of the Ceylon Federation of Labour (LSSP), the Ceylon Federation of Trade Unions (CP), the Ceylon Workers Congress and the Ceylon Mercantile Union (LSSP), called upon "the trade unions and all unorganised workers to prepare for a one-day general strike and to form united action committees in all places of work for carrying this into effect".[52] The unions emphasised their role as a veto group, preventing any radical interference with welfare state provisions and causing the rice subsidy to be retained permanently. The threat of similar action forced the resignation of Felix Dias Bandaranaike on his attempt to reduce the rice ration in the Budget of 1962.

At the time of the 1947 General Strike and the 1953 *hartal*, organised unionists numbered less than 300,000 and were mainly in Marxist unions and the Ceylon Workers Congress. More recently, despite the great increase in membership, it has been less easy to produce such effective demonstrations. The increasing commitment of the Marxist parties to the SLFP made it difficult for them to use a tactic of which their senior partner did not fully approve. It is particularly notable that the strike and demonstrations of 8 January, 1966 were on a strictly communal issue rather than an economic one and were not very effective. For those reasons a number of the militant unions under Maoist or Revolutionary LSSP leadership refused to join in. Nevertheless the threat of mass militant action by the unions remains a major potential pressure in Ceylon politics. It has been used, unsuccessfully by the plantation workers' unions in support of Indian Tamil civil rights, by Federal Party unions against the Sinhala Only policy, and by the Sri Lanka Independent Trade Union Federation (SLFP), the CFTU and CFL, to pledge support for Mrs. Bandaranaike in December 1964 in the face of C. P. de Silva's defection. Every May Day the massed unions reassert their organisational power on Galle Face Green as a reminder to any government that up to 100,000 men can be assembled opposite Parliament House at fairly short notice.

Mass action of this kind is mainly confined to the trade unions, who have the numbers, traditions and organisation to make it feasible. Ceylon also follows the Indian tradition in the tendency of its politicians to use civil disobedience or *satyagraha* in support of their objectives. The Federal Party has been most adept in using the *satyagraha* tactic, starting by sitting down on Galle Face Green on 5 June, 1956 in opposition to Sinhala Only. They threatened it against the Official Language Act in 1957 until satisfied with the compromises in the Bandaranaike-Chelvanayakam "pact" of July. The Sinhalese extremists now turned to the same tactic. Defeated by direct action, the Federalists were driven into illegality by the emergency surrounding the riots of May, 1958. The great danger of the *satyagraha* method, as of political strikes, has always been the likelihood of rapidly spreading criminal violence. This was most clearly evidenced in the events of 1956 and 1958.

The Federalists resorted to civil disobedience again in 1961, called on every Tamil public servant not to conduct business in Sinhala and blocked the entrance of the Jaffna district office. Troops were called into the Northern and Eastern Provinces on 1 March and acted with such brutality that an official enquiry was later set up. Protests followed from most of the Marxist trade union groups and support was offered by Thondaman for the Ceylon Workers Congress. Finally on 14 April Chevanaya-kam inaugurated the "Tamil Arasu Postal Service" with its own stamps and post offices on the Jaffna peninsula. This was forcibly suppressed by troops early in April and the Federal Party M.P.s were arrested on 18 April and held in detention for the next six months. During this period Jaffna had been cut off and the whole Tamil area occupied by troops. The movement had very broad support, ranging from the estate workers unions who struck in protest against the arrest of the M.P.s, the Muslim Traders Association of Batticaloa, who closed their shops, most of the Leftwing unions and even the All-Ceylon Brahmin Priests Association. Against the hostility of the great mass of the Sinhalese population and their politicians, the tactic of civil dis-obedience could only be effective in a limited geographical area.

The use of civil disobedience continues for many purposes ranging from strikes, where "sit downs" are very common, to the action of K. M. P. Rajaratna, the Sinhalese communalist leader, in squatting in the parliamentary precincts in 1961 in protest against his sentencing on charges arising from an affray. Catholic parents occupied parochial schools during 1960 to resist their transfer to the state. As a method of exerting pressure the *satyagraha* is probably fairly limited, though it has often been the only weapon that the Ceylon Tamils possessed. For its successful operation it requires a degree of tolerance which was not present on communal issues between 1956 and 1962. While the Federal Party occasionally threatens further civil disobedience it has proved notably reluctant to put this into effect. Indeed the most common use of *satyagraha* in Jaffna in recent years has been in the movement for temple entry. Only with the adoption of the Sri Lanka constitution in 1972 did Tamil politicians turn again to civil disobedience.

The Politics of Pressure

Sri Lanka has a well developed network of pressure groups. Naturally these reflect the communal and partisan divisions within society. The press has both acted as and been seen to be, partisan. Pressure groups tend to operate openly and to resort more quickly to mass action than in most industrialised societies.

A great deal of influence naturally takes place through family networks and it is very much harder to produce evidence for its effects than for those gained by public agitation. Equally, foreign embassies and corporations exert pressure on governments, parties and politicians, sometimes by direct bribery or the offer of free holidays, scholarships or jobs overseas. This, too, cannot be substantiated except from gossip but is obviously important in a country with so many foreign connections.[53] To outline the publicly apparent structure of pressure and influence is not to complete the discussion of influences on politics. As in other systems decisions may be reached to accommodate the interests of partisan supporters and subscribers or relatives. This is particularly noticeable in the field of public appointments. Sri Lanka is not simply a "traditional" system, where most decisions are made on such a personalised basis. On the contrary it has a competent public service whose apparent traditions are wholly "modern". Its government is advised by experts, both Ceylonese and foreign, in constant communication with the World Bank and United Nations agencies and well able to assimilate the most sophisticated analyses and policy recommendations.

The pressures outlined above must be understood more in terms of their function as veto groups than as the originators of economic or social policies. They are most significant in areas of communal tension or in protesting in defence of the status quo for their particular interest. In this they differ only in their readier use of militant tactics from similar pressures in industrial society. The Ceylonese are well integrated into a pattern of secondary associations. Most are actively religious. Most adult males are either in a union or a co-operative society. While much less susceptible to the mass media than citizens of industrial nations, the Ceylonese receive enough political information for most adults to be familiar with national and local leaders, to follow political struggles and to vote at national and local elections. Even the peasant, who had not exerted much organised pressure as such, has tremendous power as a voter and is wooed assiduously because of it.

Where new political threats arise, protective associations are formed very quickly. They too may be fragmented along ideological or communal lines as with the various civil rights movements which sprang up in opposition to the emergency regulations and consequent legal changes of 1971. The Human and Democratic Rights Organisation, led by Prins Gunasekera and Bala Tampoe, was radically to the Left of the Civil Rights Movement, which was dominated by lawyers opposing parts of the new constitution and was actively encouraged by the UNP. The professional and business élite is very highly organised, as in other democratic societies. Each community has its own chamber of commerce, each profession its regulating and defending association. University staffs were quick to form protective groups against the amalgamation of four separate institutions into a single University of Sri Lanka in 1972.[54] Yet these, too, must all be seen as primarily defensive rather than innovatory. Most new legislative proposals arise either in the party struggle, or from the tiny group of economists and professional administrators working closely with international agencies. Budgets are constructed very largely by this element, rather than by pressure groups, who simply oppose measures like reductions in the rice ration or increases in taxation. The masses are mobilised most effectively on communal, religious and trade union issues as in most other systems. Their participation is admittedly manipulated by leaders mostly drawn from the same social circles as leading politicians and civil servants. Nevertheless such participation can be mobilised on a massive and potentially disruptive scale. It is this which gives the major pressure groups their power. What limits that power is the even greater loyalty which the major parties can now command. Where their leaders have stood firm against pressure they have frequently been victorious. They normally stand firm within limits on communal, religious, social and economic innovation set by thirty years or more of effectively organised veto groups.

NOTES

1. Largest daily circulations in each language in 1968 were: *Dinamina* (Sinhalese) 104,372, *Ceylon Daily News* (English) 67,245, and *Thinakaran* (Tamil) 33,608. All were published by Associated Newspapers of Ceylon. (The *Times* (London) Ceylon Supplement 8/1/1969). Total circulation of daily morning and evening papers at the same time was about 500,000. (F. Nyrop: *Area Handbook for Ceylon*; Table 16, pp. 288-9 (which omits the "partisan" press)).

2. A survey by the Information Department in 1973 found that 35·7% of the rural population did not listen to the radio. In the rural sample 18·5% listened at the bazaar against 6·4% in the urban sample. *Ceylon News* 5/7/1973.

3. Voting turnout: 1947—61·3% (55·9%); 1952—74% (70·7%); 1956—71% (69·0%); March 1960—77·6%; July 1960—75·6% (75·9%); 1965—82% (82·1%) 1970—84·9% (85·2%).
   Sources: *Ceylon Daily News Seventh Parliament of Ceylon 1970* and in brackets: Department of Elections: *Results of Parliamentary Elections 1947–70*; Colombo, 1971; p. 6.

4. Bryce Ryan: *Sinhalese Village*; Miami, 1958; p. 150. For the situation in a Kandyan village ten years later see T. von Fellenberg: *The Process of Dynamisation in Rural Ceylon*: Berne, 1966 and M. S. Robinson: *Political Structure in a Changing Sinhalese Village*: Cambridge, 1975.

5. Professor K. M. de Silva of Peradeniya, in a conversation in August, 1971, told me that DRO's and *grama sevakas* had provided him with reliable estimates of local opinion for all elections except 1970, for which no reliable predictions had been possible.

6. Bryce Ryan: *op. cit.,* p. 148.

7. The proximity of most voters to regular bus-services is a major factor in the spread of word-of-mouth information. Ceylon Transport Board fares were said for many years to be the lowest in the world.

8. SP XI—1964: *Final Report of the Press Commission*; Colombo, 1964; p. 6.

9. Mrs. Gunawardena was a vocal supporter of Communist China. See her *China's Cultural Revolution*; Colombo, 1967.

10. S.P. XI; p. 15.

11. *Ibid.*; p. 17.

12. *Ibid.*; p. 12.

13. *Ibid.*; Appendix V.

14. *Ibid.*; p. 15.

15. With the rise of partisan papers in the 1960's Colombo had twenty dailies by 1970, or double the total ten years before.

16. *H. of Reps. Debs.* vol. 87, no. 4, cols. 803-820.

17. The photostat letters are reproduced in Anon.: *Why Lake House seeks to Destroy the Coalition*; Colombo, 1970 pp. 12–25.

18. *Ceylon News* 24/5/1973. See also the broadcast of Colvin de Silva explaining the Act. *Ceylon News* 9/8/1973.

19. *Ceylon News* 26/7/1973.

20. The full text of the Sri Lanka Press Council draft Bill was published in *Ceylon News* 31/8/1973.

21. Sri Lanka Press Council Act s. 8 (11).

22. Ven. Henpitegedera Gnanaseeha was involved in the formation of the Eksath Bhikkhu Peramuna in 1956. He became a critic of party conflict and the parliamentary system and was arrested in connection with the 1966 coup and only released in 1969. In 1970 he was approached for support by some leaders of the JVP but refused to give it. His main influence was in the Ratnapura area. Ven. Udakendawela

Siri Saranankara was a foundation member of the Ceylon Communist Party and was previously in the LSSP.

23. I am indebted to Professor L. Hewage and Mr. H. Caldera, joint secretaries of the All-Ceylon Buddhist Congress, for giving me an interview in August, 1969 upon which much of this assessment of the Congress is based.

24. See S. P. XXV—1957; *Interim Report of the Buddha Sasana Commission* (in Sinhala); Colombo, 1957.

25. An official register of monks was finally completed in 1972, showing there to be 18,000 *bhikkhus. Ceylon News* 31/8/1972.

26. Mrs. Bandaranaike's uncles held official lay positions at the Temple of the Tooth in Kandy.

27. Quoted from Professor Hewage in the interview referred to in fn. 23.

28. *Ceylon Daily News* 9/12/1959.

29. For details of clerical involvement in 1956 see D. E. Smith; *South Asian Politics and Religion;* Princeton, 1966; Part IV and the feature 'Background to Politics' in the *Ceylon Observer* between July 13 and 17, 1962.

30. See I. D. S. Weerawardena: *Ceylon General Election 1956*; Colombo, 1960; pp. 149–50.

31. *Ceylon Daily News* 26/7/1969.

32. Iriyagolle although nominally a Sinhala Buddhist was also a follower of the Hindu reformer Krishnamurthy, a fact which his opponents made known.

33. *Ceylon Daily News* 15/8/1969.

34. Constitution of Sri Lanka s. 6.

35. *Ibid.* 2. 16 (7).

36. *Ibid.* s. 18 (1) (d).

37. For the political involvement of trade unions see R. N. Kearney: *Trade Unions and Politics in Ceylon*; Berkeley, 1971.

38. Trade union membership in 1967 was 1,453,941 (Kearney: *op. cit.* Table 2). The non-peasant workforce was about two million of whom one-third worked on tea and rubber estates. See *Statistical Abstract of Ceylon—1966*; Colombo, 1969; esp. Table 25.

39. See R. N. Kearney: "Militant Public Service Trade Unionism in a New State": *Journal of Asian Studies* 25: 3, May 1966.

40. The Ceylon Workers' Congress took that name in 1950, having previously been the union arm of the Ceylon Indian Congress. It split in 1956 (and finally in 1962) between the CWC, led by V. E. K. S. Thondaman and the DWC led by A. Aziz. The unions have respectively about 300,000 and 200,000 members although there is some movement between them and dispute over their membership. See Kearney: *Trade Unions and Politics in Ceylon*; pp. 121–131.

41. Between 1956 and 1965 over half the man-days lost in strikes were among plantation workers. Kearney: *op. cit.* Table 5 and *Statistical Abstract—1966*; Table 42.

42. My information on the Democratic Workers' Congress derives from an interview with A. Aziz at the union office in August, 1969.

43. *Kearney*: *op. cit.* distinguishes between party-sponsored, party-oriented and uncommitted unions.

44. The United Left Front in 1963 was able to unite all the unions oriented towards the Marxist parties, Philip Gunawardena's unions and the major estate unions, embracing about 75% of all unionists at the time. However the ULF disintegrated upon the entry of the LSSP into Mrs. Bandaranaike's government.

45. The most important trade union official from the ranks was T. B. Ilangaratne, a former president of the Government Clerical Service Union, dismissed for his part in the 1947 strike and a Minister in all SLFP governments since 1959.

46. The JCTUO continued from that date as the unifying force for LSSP, Communist and SLFP unions, embracing about one-third of all unionists.

47. The most important recent example is the United Commercial and Mercantile Union, formed by Anil Moonesinghe of the LSSP specifically as a rival for Bala Tampoe's Ceylon Mercantile Union and having about 60,000 members to his 30,000 by 1972 (based on interviews with Anil Moonesinghe and officials of the UCMU in 1969 and 1971).

48. Based on an interview with I. J. Wickrema, president of the Government Clerical Service Union, in July 1969 and confirmed in a further interview with Leslie Goonewardena, secretary of the LSSP in the same month. Wickrema subsequently lost his position for attacking N. M. Perera's Budget of 1970.

49. See R. N. Kearney: *op. cit.* Chart 1—" 'Outsiders' and 'Insiders' in Leadership Positions of Major Labor Organizations."

50. See Kumari Jayawardena: *The Rise of the Labour Movement in Ceylon*; Durham, N.C., 1972.

51. *Young Socialist* (Colombo) No. 2, 1961, p. 65. Hartal Day is regularly commemorated by LSSP unions.

52. Anon.: *Twenty-five Years of the Ceylon Communist Party*; Colombo, 1968; p. 54.

53. In 1970 Mrs. Bandaranaike expelled the American-financed Asia Foundation and asked for the withdrawal of an American embassy official with Central Intelligence Agency connections. She also expelled the North Korean embassy in 1971 for alleged involvement with the JVP insurgency and with currency offences. Foreign governments continue to encourage overseas trips and jobs through the Lanka-Soviet Friendship Association, the Lanka-China, Lanka-Korean (until 1971 at least), Lanka-German and other Communist oriented associations, the British Council, the Fulbright Programme, Friedrich Ebert Foundation and many other educational and cultural societies. Many embassies, for example the North Korean or Cuban, have very little conventional business but are active in promoting the political system of their country.

54. See for example the *Press Statement on University Reorganisation* by the University of Ceylon Teachers' Association of Peradeniya in August, 1972.

CHAPTER 7

Electoral Politics

Ceylon achieved its greatest political success in institutionalising electoral politics to permit orderly change of government and the consolidation of well disciplined parties. Over the years since independence Ceylon voters became among the most dutiful in the world. Even in 1947 61.3% of the electorate turned out to vote. This had risen to 77.6% in March 1966, to 82% in 1965 and to 84.9% in 1970.[1] This marked a greater participation than in almost any competitive democracy with voluntary voting and exceeded the highest turnout ever recorded in Britain. Nor was participation any less marked in remote rural areas than in the more Westernised seats. By 1970 there were no electorates in which less than three-quarters of the voters recorded their decision. In the great majority of seats between 80% and 90% voted. The only consistently reluctant areas have been among the Tamils, where the status of women and the lower castes and the less effective level of party organisation have been important factors. In the Kandyan areas, in contrast, turnout reaches the maximum found possible in other voluntary systems. Of the ten electorates where over 90% voted in 1970, seven were predominantly inhabited by Kandyans. There is thus no longer the correlation apparent in State Council days between degree of sophistication and level of turnout. East Coast areas show as great a level of participation as anywhere else. Indeed, as is common in industrial societies, voter turnout is lower in some city districts, reflecting inaccurate registration.[2] What is particularly remarkable about Ceylonese voters is that they vote in equally large proportions in municipal contests and at by-elections. They are not simply swept away by the national campaign, as in many Western nations, but take every opportunity to exercise a right which they believe to have meaning for them.

The Electoral System

The electoral system within which this remarkable display of civic duty takes place, is among the strictest in the world. It is modelled very largely on British practice, with suitable modifications for a communally divided society in which a significant number of voters is still illiterate. So satisfactory were the provisions of the Soulbury constitution that they were carried over almost verbatim into the constitution of Sri Lanka.[3] The law provided for electoral districts to be designated by an Electoral Commission on the basis of census returns. This exercised its powers only in 1947, 1959 and 1976. The principle of equalized electorates is breached by s. 41 (2) of the Soulbury Constitution (s. 76 (2) in the Sri Lanka constitution), allowing extra seats to be allocated on the basis of acreage. This biassed seat allocation towards the Northern, Eastern and North Central Provinces particularly. It therefore benefited the Tamils and Muslims to as great an extent as the Kandyans, and discriminated particularly against Low Country Buddhists and Christians in Western Province. Only with the disfranchisement of Indian Tamil estate workers and the consequent Sinhalisation of several hill country electorates, was a bias built in which favoured the Wet Zone Kandyans. In general it was the Dry Zone which gained most because of its relative lack of population. The general effect of this provision has been to distort the principle laid down in s. 41 (3) that "each electoral district of a Province shall have as nearly as may be an equal number of persons." The range in size for single-member electorates in 1970 was thus from 70,236 in Dehiwela-Mount Lavinia to 16,461 in Passara. This was no greater than in Britain at the same time and reflected the tendency found in many systems for suburban areas to grow rapidly beyond the limits laid down in electoral redistributions. In general, electorates are between 35,000 and 45,000 and as the discrepancy cannot be shown to weigh particularly heavily upon one party rather than another, nothing has been done to remedy it in the new constitution.

Apart from this modified attempt to ensure equal electorates, the two constitutions provide for multi-member seats, "where it appears to the Delimitation Commission that there is in any area of a Province a substantial concentration of persons united

by a community of interest whether racial, religious or otherwise, but differing in one or more of these respects from the
majority of the inhabitants of that area, the Commission may
make such division of the Province into electoral districts as
may be necessary to render possible the representation of that
interest."[4] The power to create multi-member electorates has
been used particularly to the benefit of Muslims. Voters are
able to cast two, or in one case, three, ballots for members of
their own community, thus maximising support for minorities
which are too small to be sure of success. Thus there is normally
a Muslim M.P. for the two-member seat of Akurana, although
Muslims are only 17.7% of the electorate. The multi-member
seat can also be used by the parties to secure safe refuges for
some of their leaders. Votes may be 'plumped' for a party as
much as for a community. In 1970 seven out of the eleven
multi-member seats had been safe for one party or another
over four elections, with the UNP, the Federal Party, the LSSP
and the Communists all benefiting. The power to look after
interests has also undoubtedly been used to create caste-based
seats such as Rambukkana and Bentara-Elpitiya, although the
Delimitation Commissioners do not make much reference to
this.[5] In general the net effect of exercising this power has been
to ensure that the communal composition of parliament
scarcely changes at all, and the major communities are all
satisfied.[6]

The law as it stood was designed to ensure fairness to communities, rather than to parties, which had not effectively
emerged by 1947. Subsequent changes have copied British
practice in trying to eliminate advantages accruing to rich
candidates and parties over poor ones. It was clearly to the
benefit of the SLFP to limit the capacity of the richer and
initially better organised UNP to pay for propaganda and
transport on election day. Laws passed in 1964 banned the use
of any transport on polling day to bring voters to the poll. Not
only do Sri Lanka electors turn out, but they must walk to
the polls. Returns of electoral expense are also mandatory, with
legal limits fixed. As in Britain these returns are consistently
falsified. They serve in general to limit the holding of expensive
parties and processions and the giving of gifts, as well as
restricting the amount of printed propaganda and paid can-

vassing help which can be used. In a tightening of the law in 1970, the UNP government banned the holding of processions altogether, thus limiting a favourite device of the Coalition parties. The preservation of public order was further enhanced by barring canvassing, meetings and loudspeakers from the area around polling stations.[7]

These rigid provisions were additional to normal and long-standing prohibitions on bribery and intimidation. As parties came to dominate the electoral process individual bribery and coercion became less common. Offers of jobs as an inducement to vote grew with the party patronage system. This too, was an offence. The provision which existed for unseating a Member of Parliament accused of corrupt and illegal practices was by no means a dead letter, as it had become in Britain over the past fifty years or so. On petition and hearing by an Election Judge an M.P. could not only lose his seat but be prevented from contesting it again for seven years, until the law was modified in 1971. Not only was an offender's election overturned, but his political career could be effectively terminated or frustrated for many years. A number of leading politicians have been so unseated, including Philip Gunawardena, S. A. Wickremasinghe and Anil Moonesinghe. The importance of the offences which may lead to unseating varied enormously. In the 1970 revision, even an unsuccessful candidate could be imprisoned for corrupt practices and deprived of his civil rights for seven years. By 1970 there was a growing feeling that the regular unseating of several M.P.s after elections for offences which may well have been committed by most of their colleagues and opponents, had become too stringent a sanction. In by-elections held in 1972, two unseated M.P.s, one from the SLFP and one from the UNP, were allowed, under the new law, to contest their former seats. Both were returned where, in the past, they would have been barred from politics for seven years.[8]

With all these restrictions and refinements, Ceylonese electoral law can be said to have equalised the chances of the major contestants as effectively as any system in operation anywhere. In practice there has continued to be some intimidation and bribery through patronage, as well as impersonation. There has been no evidence of corruption among electoral officers and the system of appointing poll-watchers would make falsification of results extremely difficult, as party organisation is now strong enough to be able to scrutinise results at every polling booth. Nor is there any compelling evidence of landlord coercion of tenants or of exclusion of poor, low caste or minority groups from voting. The figures for turnout could not be so high were there any effective barriers against substantial groups taking part in the electoral process. The system of registration, which is conducted by local authorities as in Britain, ensures a far more effective enrolment of voters than in many parts of the United States. Despite sometimes wild accusations made at election time by overwrought candidates there can be little doubt that Sri Lanka has built up one of the most successful and fair electoral systems in the world. Through it, the masses have been able to articulate and express demands which are still unformed over much of Asia, let alone given force through a neutral and effective electoral system.

National, Regional and Local Patterns[9]

All electoral systems which have become stabilised show clear patterns of regional concentration in party support. These may correspond to areas of communal concentration, of historic alignments or of class concentration. In Ceylon, as in Canada or Northern Ireland, the minority community voted differently from the majority. It is hardly surprising that the 'Sinhalese' parties won only one Tamil seat between 1960 and 1970 or that no Tamil has ever been returned for a seat in which Tamils are not the largest group. Of the sixteen electorates in which Tamils are the largest group, no less than ten are 'safe' seats for the Federal Party, having remained in its hands over the four elections since the 1959 redistribution.[10] However isolated the party may be, it has always been able to rely on its strongholds in the Northern and Eastern Provinces. For a minority party to continue to exist in a system where all the institutional pressures are towards a two-party division, it needs such a permanent base. The Marxist parties, too, which are vulnerable to being swamped by the SLFP, also had secure areas from which they could not be dislodged. There were seven 'safe' LSSP seats from 1959, including that of the party leader.[11] Equally the Communists had held on to two safe seats, those of the Party

Chairman and Secretary.[12] The stability of all the parties depends upon their leaders being sure of re-election and on them being able to count on a solid basis of 'safe' seats which they can hold in the worst times. Both the leaders of the UNP, Dudley Senanayake and J. R. Jayawardena, held safe seats, as did Mrs. Bandaranaike, Felix Dias Bandaranaike and Maithripala Senanayake in the SLFP, N. M. Perera, Colvin de Silva and Leslie Goonewardena in the LSSP and S. J. V. Chelvanayakam in the Federal Party.

The 'safe' seats form the foundation stone for a working electoral system with stable and continuing parties.[13] Only five parties were able to establish such seats after the 1959 redistribution. With the temporary passage of the Tamil Congress M.P.s into the Coalition in 1972, only those five Parliamentary parties continued to exist. Fifty-two seats may be considered 'safe', in not having changed parties until 1977. This constitutes over one-third of the total, compared with only a quarter of the seats between 1947 and 1959. In the three elections after independence the great majority of seats changed hands, particularly in the landslide of 1956 when the SLFP wiped out the UNP and the Federal Party destroyed the Tamil Congress. Once the system became stabilised there was less likelihood of such landslides. Even with a third of the seats 'safe' over four elections, Ceylon did not approach the British situation, where nearly two-thirds of seats are safe. Since 1945 the possibility of a landslide decimating the ruling party has been remote in Britain. In Sri Lanka it has already happened three times. What has enhanced stability, is the changing character of the safe seat itself. Between 1947 and 1956 the safe seat was, in at least half the cases, the virtual property of the individual who represented it. Of the twenty-five safe seats, only half were safe for parties (and nearly all these for the UNP and the LSSP) while thirteen were safe for individuals who changed their party allegiance but did not lose their seat. These included S. W. R. D. Bandaranaike, who had sat for Veyangoda in the State Council since 1931 and for Attanagalla since 1947, the area later represented by his widow and his nephew. Others who held seats under varying labels included Philip Gunawardena, W. Dahanayake, P. H. William de Silva, T. B. Subasinghe, R. G. Senanayake, I. M. R. A. Iriyagolle, C. Suntheralingam, and Maithripala

Senanayake, to mention only those who became Ministers. These men were so secure in their areas that they could bargain their way into governments, change parties or offer their support to whoever they liked. Some of the most important figures in Ceylon politics had been able for many years to resist the trend towards rigid party discipline and endorsement which is vital to the Cabinet system of government resting on a parliamentary majority.[14]

The 'safe personal or family' seat was naturally found predominantly in rural areas. Only W. Dahanayake in Galle held a personal seat in an urban area. That is not to say that urban contests were always on partisan lines. Nor were the safe seats necessarily in the most remote and backward areas. In the North Central province there had been a long tradition of personal domination. Major Freeman, one of the three Europeans to have been elected to the legislature since 1931, used to tell his voters that "if you vote in the green box I go to the State Council. Vote in the red and I go home to England."[15] As a powerful and admired former government official this was a sufficient threat to ensure his election. The North Central Province was later dominated by Maithripala Senanayake and by C. P. de Silva, both of whom had also been government officials. In the remote Wanni, the Sinhala traditionalist Mudiyanse Tennakoon was able to establish a safe seat which withstood his expulsion from the SLFP and was the only Sinhala seat to return an independent in 1970. On the East Coast the independent was the norm until 1970, particularly in predominantly Muslim electorates. But many of the personal seats were in fairly advanced rubber and coconut plantation areas which were dominated by large Goyigama or Karawa landowners. It was the transfer of most of these to the SLFP by 1956 which was part of the reason for that party's success. While it may be argued that the personal or family seat was found more frequently in remote and backward Dry Zone areas before 1956 and among Muslims and Tamils, this was not so completely true as to sustain the notion that partisan politics spread steadily from the most urbanised and Westernised areas to those least modernised. On the contrary, after 1956, most of these 'traditional' seats became 'safe' for the SLFP. Independents were to be found predominantly among the Muslims. Any other generalisation is difficult to sustain.

The smaller parties and minority communities have a fairly clear electoral pattern. The Tamil Congress has been effectively confined to the Jaffna peninsula, although with the periodic loss of Ponnambalam's seat in Jaffna it cannot be said to have any firm basis in particular electorates. The three seats it won in 1970, when there was a general swing against the Federal Party, had all been safe Federal seats for the previous three elections, while the Federal Party won Udupiddy, which had been safe for the Tamil Congress over the same period. With the exception of the complicated local situation in Jaffna town, the Jaffna peninsula is fought over by the two Tamil parties on personal, caste and local issues. Apart from the Karaiyar concentration at Point Pedro, there are no major distinguishing features between one Jaffna peninsula rural seat and another. They are all overwhelmingly Tamil Hindu electorates, in most of which there are almost no non-Tamil voters at all. Competition is between Vellalla Hindu or Christian Tamil candidates, offering two alternative views of the tactic to be used to protect Tamil interests against Sinhala dominance. Broadly the federalist solution has commanded half the Tamil support or more ever since 1956, in this region. The Tamil Congress solution of collaboration with Sinhalese governments has had more to offer to the Tamil public servants living in the South. Appeals to Tamil separatism, launched by independents and movements associated with C. Suntheralingam and V. Navaratnam have had very little success. The DMK has not even run for office at all. In the second area of Tamil concentration, along the East coast, the picture is complicated by the presence of large, sometimes dominant Muslim communities, and by Sinhalese communities in Trincomalee and in nearby peasant colonisation schemes. In this area the 'personal' candidate has been supreme, veering towards the UNP in most instances, but ready to move towards the SLFP when that party is doing well. In general along the coast the Tamils have been socially dominant over the Muslim peasants, while Muslim traders have dominated the urban centres. Even here party appeal is now supreme and only one Independent M.P. was returned in 1970.

The Dry Zone Kandyan area covers the larger part of the

Island and is predominantly jungle land. Apart from the major colonisation schemes around Polonnaruwa, Anuradhapura and Amparai this is an area of isolated villages where Buddhism is heavily influenced by animism and where the social, educational and transport facilities available to most other Sinhalese are limited. There is little plantation economy in this area and paddy farming, subsistence jungle cultivation and hunting are the major sources of income. Yet there is also a substantial class of teachers, government employees and shopkeepers from whom political activists are drawn. It is these classes which tended to turn towards the SLFP in 1956 and most of the Dry Zone has remained an SLFP stronghold. Of the twenty-two 'safe' SLFP seats held between 1960 and 1970, nine were in the Dry Zone. In 1970 the SLFP won all but two of the eighteen Dry Zone Kandyan electorates. This Dry Zone and irrigation area of eighteen seats is particularly favoured by the rural bias in the distribution of electorates, giving the SLFP a strong vested interest in the continuation of the system. No other party has been able to hold any Dry Zone Kandyan seats for very long. In this sense the SLFP can truly claim to represent the poorest section of the Sinhalese peasant masses. Dry Zone dwellers are also the most 'traditionalist' of the Sinhalese in not being affected either by plantations or by commercial agriculture or industry to the same extent as either the Wet Zone Kandyans or the Low Country Sinhalese. It is here that pre-Buddhist beliefs in magic, astrology and the intercession of the gods are most active.[16] It was also in this area that the historic civilisations were overthrown by the Tamils and where the notion of a 'frontier' between the two races is most meaningful. A solid bloc of SLFP politicians has both to appeal to and be sustained by these attitudes.

The remaining Sinhalese area, which embraces the bulk of the electorates, may be divided between the Wet Zone Kandyans, the Catholic Low Country Sinhalese, the urbanised coastal Low Country Sinhalese and the Southern Province Buddhist Sinhalese. All differ to varying degrees in their political behaviour. While there are no substantial industrial, mining, or suburban groupings of electorates such as are found in Western nations, there are some characteristic differences between electorates even when all of these are rural and inhabited by those speaking the same language. In general the Catholic Sinhalese have supported the UNP and three of its remaining ten safe seats in 1970 had Catholics as the largest community. Because these are also largely rural, Sinhala speaking and caste-influenced, the Catholic seats are not immune to capture by the SLFP in landslide years. They do not provide the same secure reservoir of seats for the UNP that the North Central Province does for the SLFP. This underlines a weakness of the UNP which, since 1956 has found it hard to build up a secure base in any particular area outside Colombo and Kandy. As the party appealing most to the urban voter[17] it has been at a great disadvantage. When neither the Catholics nor the Muslims hold firm, the UNP is forced back upon those rural seats held by the personal appeal of the sitting member. In 1970 this failed completely, as most of the best known UNP Members were Ministers against whom there was a larger than average electoral swing. As in 1956 the wrath of the voters was directed heavily against the best known party leaders, with the exception of Dudley Senanayake himself.

While the few UNP safe seats are predominantly urban and four out of ten of them are dominated by Christians and Muslims, all the SLFP's twenty-two safe seats were rural and Sinhalese Buddhist. The bulk of its safe Low Country seats are in and around the Veyangoda area held by Bandaranaike since 1931. The UNP, again, has been unable to build a similar bloc around the Senanayake or Kotelawala estates. From five adjoining electorates Mrs. Bandaranaike, who represents one of them, drew two other Ministers and two Junior Ministers in 1970. Even the Ratwatte ancestral homeland, which influences the two safe SLFP seats of Balangoda and Pelmadulla, cannot rival the importance of the Bandaranaike heartland for the SLFP. Even today the three pillars of SLFP permanent strength are the Dry Zone Kandyans, and the Bandaranaike and Ratwatte estates. Party support is almost wholly rural, Buddhist and Sinhalese, factors which can only make for permanent strength in a rural, Buddhist Sri Lanka, which is urbanising very slowly and which is extending privileges to the indigenous majority previously enjoyed by Anglicised or non-Sinhala minorities.[18]

In the urbanised and urban influenced belt between Colombo

and Galle, the party contest has been consistently between the
UNP and the LSSP since 1947. While much of the area is rural
and devoted to coconut plantations, the road and rail links
along the coast have attracted commuters into Colombo from
long distances towards the South. Most of the major towns
have some industrial undertakings such as the furniture factories
around Moratuwa or the fairly large industrial district stretching
between Wellawatte and Ratmalana through the constituencies
of Colombo South and Dehiwela-Mount Lavinia. In so far as
there is a genuine urban working-class it is to be found along
this coast and the LSSP has been actively organising amongst
it since before independence. The LSSP had 'safe' seats in
Colombo South, Kalutara and Panadura and in 1970 won over
half its nineteen seats between Colombo and Ambalangoda
and in the electorates adjoining them in the hinterland. These
districts sustain what claims the LSSP has to being a 'working-
class' party. Even they are largely rural, south of Moratuwa.
The LSSP working-class support also includes workers in the
rubber plantations of the interior of Southern and Sabaragumawa Provinces who have been organised for many years by the
party-controlled Lanka Estate Workers Union. Just as there is
a core of truth to the claim that the SLFP represents the
poorest of the Kandyan peasants, so it is partly true that the
LSSP represents what there is of a Sinhala working class, both
in Colombo, along the South Coast and on the plantations. An
even more marked feature of the Marxist vote as a whole is that
it is, with two or three urban exceptions, drawn overwhelmingly
from Sinhala Buddhist electors. Indeed in 1970 two of the three
electorates in which 99% of voters were Buddhists were won by
the Communists. Southern Province and the Kalutara District
are not only Marxist but Buddhist strongholds. Of the twenty-
five LSSP and CP seats won in 1970, eighteen were more than
80% Buddhist and over half were more than 90% Buddhist.
Put another way, while less than three-quarters of the
voters are Buddhist, probably seven-eighths of Marxist voters
are.

Support for the Marxist parties in the most Buddhist districts
of Sri Lanka is related to various factors. Ruhunu, as the
South is known in Sinhalese history, is even more self-conscious
of its role as protector of Buddhism than are the Kandyan

Highlands. Outside of the major towns Christian, Muslim and Tamil influence is virtually unknown. It was from Ruhunu that the leaders of the Buddhist revival, of the prohibition movement, of the Communist Party and of the J.V.P. were disproportionately drawn at various times. It was also in Ruhunu that caste differences assumed political importance in the virtual absence of communal divisions. The important local families of the Hewavitaranas, from which Anagarika Dharmapala came, the Wickremasinghes and the Rajapakses, and prominent individuals such as H. W. Amarasuriya and C. W. W. Kannangara, were all associated with radical, reforming or revivalist movements. For the whole of this century the major political influences upon most of Ruhunu were such as to encourage both militant Buddhism and Marxism, between which many Sinhalese intellectuals see no necessary incompatibility. The reformed Ramanya and Amarapura sects had more support in an area where there were large Karawa, Salagama and Durawa concentrations than in the more conservative Kandyan highlands where the Goyigama Radalas were supreme both over politics and religion. It was the reformed sects which provided most support to the MEP in 1956 and swung Ruhunu away from the UNP.

Ruhunu has been consistently politicised for nearly a century.[19] The Marxist parties have benefited most from this in electoral terms. With twenty-seven seats in Southern province and Kalutara district, this heartland of militant Buddhism is also politically very important in deciding the composition of the government. The inclusion of Marxists in the Coalition with the SLFP after 1964 was a recognition, among other things, of their firmly based support in this region, which was more secure than the following for the SLFP. In 1970 the seats in the area were divided between twelve for the Marxists, fourteen for the SLFP and Dahanayake's solitary outpost for the UNP at Galle. This was in a landslide year. The area also contains six seats which have changed parties at every election since March 1960 and the SLFP has only one safe seat. Thus the importance of gaining Marxist co-operation is undeniable. Much of Ruhunu shares with the Kandyan highlands the character of being politically volatile between the two major Sinhala parties. Election results are largely de-

termined in these two areas. The UNP and the SLFP, in
competing at the margin for support, do so to a major extent
in Southern Province and highland Kandyan electorates. The
party which wins power nationally is invariably the one which
wins a majority in these two areas. The high degree of politicisation of the area is further enhanced by this concentration of
swinging and shifting seats. The need to appeal to Sinhala and
Buddhist revivalist sentiment is thus not simply a result of the
Sinhala Buddhist community being in the majority throughout
the island, but in its concentration in Ruhunu and the Kandyan
highlands. While the UNP, the SLFP and the LSSP all had
some safe seats in the latter region, the typical Wet Zone
Kandyan electorate is narrowly divided between the two main
parties and thus constitutes a major focus of attention for any
political leader hoping to form a government.

The net effect of these regional variations is such as to
encourage the two major blocs to emphasise Sinhala Only and
the granting of Buddhism its rightful place. As Ruhunu and the
Kandyan highlands were not effectively penetrated by Western
influences, appeals to nationalism and against the Anglicised
minority are most potent there. Ruhunu is reformist while the
Kandyans are conservative. Parties must try to cater for both
attitudes, espousing socialism and religion at the same time,
promising land reform which does not affect temple lands,
using Radala influence at Malwatte and Asgiriya monasteries,
while at the same time ensuring Karawa and Salagama representation in parliamentary leadership. In most of this the SLFP,
particularly after the Coalition arrangement, is at an advantage.
The Marxist base in the South and the SLFP base in the Dry
Zone are both in predominantly Buddhist areas. What appeals
to those two areas may be assumed to appeal to Ruhunu and
the highlands respectively. Whether the Coalition base is
expanding or contracting, it rests very firmly among the
indigenous majority. The UNP in contrast, is much more
beholden to Muslim, Catholic and urban minority interests
which are all suspect to the typical Sinhala voter. His popular
culture, whether taught by monks or by state school teachers, is
much more receptive to appeals from the sort of base which the
Coalition parties were able to establish in key areas.

The Urban Vote

Not only is Sri Lanka a predominantly rural country but the electoral system enshrined in the constitution further enhances the power of the rural voter. By weighting provincial representation by area (in s. 41–44) the Soulbury commissioners played into the hands of those who wanted to limit the electoral voice of the towns. Believing quite wrongly that the urban vote would be predominantly Leftwing, some leaders of the State Council deliberately encouraged tendencies to rural bias often found amongst British framers of electoral laws.[20] The second prong of their offensive against the Left, the disfranchisement of Indian Tamil estate workers, had to wait until after independence.[21] Its effect, apart from obliterating the Ceylon Indian Congress as a parliamentary force, was to increase proportionately the number of exclusively rural Sinhala seats in the tea areas. By 1950 Ceylon had a double bias against the towns in its electoral system, the weighting of the Northern, Eastern and, particularly, North Central Provinces, and the *de facto* weighting in Central, Uva and Sabaragamuwa Provinces arising from the Indian disenfranchisement.

Whatever may have been the situation at independence, the urban vote has not been predominantly Leftwing. Marxist theory and conservative fear notwithstanding, the towns became increasingly favourable to the United National Party. At the electoral debacle of 1970 no fewer than seven of its remaining seventeen M.P.s were returned for purely urban seats in Colombo, Kandy and Galle, compared with only five Marxists out of twenty-five. In the twenty years before, the UNP, the Tamil Congress and independent conservatives had normally dominated the urban representation. Indeed until 1970 the conservative position in urban electorates increased regularly from the low point of 1956.

In such an overwhelmingly rural country, an 'urban' seat is a rare phenomenon. While there is no official definition of such a category, it may be described as one in which all, or a clear majority, of the voters live in Municipal, Town or Urban Council areas. On this very generous definition, which allows for a considerable rural or semi-rural element, there are still only seventeen such seats (eight in the Colombo area and nine in the provinces) or only 11% of the total. Because of the rural bias in distribution, they include about 14% of the electorate, with voters in Colombo Central and South being able to cast multiple ballots. Despite the relative generosity of the definition, electorates outside Colombo which can be called 'urban' cover only the towns of Kandy (2), Jaffna (2), Galle, Moratuwa, Negombo and Trincomalee (which has a large rural hinterland as well).

A rigid theoretical model which equates urbanisation with political modernisation tends to break down nearly as quickly as the Marxist model which presupposes the greater radicalism of the urban proletariat. In several urban contests, and particularly in Galle and Jaffna, personal followings for individuals have been as marked as in the most backward rural districts. Even in Colombo independents and party-changers have been returned, and in Kandy the Senanayake-Ratwatte family struggle is carried on as resolutely as on the national scale. While party organisation is well advanced in Colombo and its suburbs, the personal machines of W. Dahanayake in Galle and G. G. Ponnambalam in Jaffna have been engaged for many years in struggles against the respective followings of W. D. S. Abeygunawardena and A. Durayappah which cut across and totally confuse the national party alignments. These fights have centred to a large extent on municipal contests but have naturally overflowed into the national arena. In 1956 W. D. S. Abeygunawardena fought for the UNP against Dahanayake and the MEP, beat him in March 1960, was beaten by him in July 1960 (at both of which elections Dahanayake ran under his new LPP label), was driven out of the UNP in a municipal dispute and turned up as SLFP candidate in 1970 by which time Dahanayake was in the UNP! In the smaller towns the personality based politics found in the countryside, were also the norm.

Even more marked than this phenomenon has been the consistent support which the UNP has gained in the towns and most notably in Colombo, Kandy and Negombo. This has been sustained in municipal politics to as great an extent, with the UNP winning the great majority of Colombo Municipal Council seats even in 1969 when its fate was being determined in far less favourable Village Council contests.[22] Nor is this support in any sense confined to middle-class suburbs. On the contrary the suburban districts of Dehiwela-Mount Lavinia, Kolonnawa and Kotte have been far more consistently Leftwing than the inner slum belt of central Colombo. In Colombo itself the Marxist representation, apart from a bridgehead maintained by Pieter Keuneman and the Communist Party around Kotahena, has likewise been in the outer suburbs along Baseline Road rather than in the historic centre. Apart from the brief period in 1954 when N. M. Perera was made Mayor of Colombo on a casting vote, the conservatives have normally controlled the affairs of the only true city in Sri Lanka.

That this is not simply a product of arbitrary ward boundaries can be seen by a study of the urban vote throughout the island. The Colombo boundaries have been altered three times since 1950 without basically changing the picture of UNP dominance and the general conduct of municipal elections is carefully scrutinised by the Ministry of Home Affairs to avoid local corruption and gerrymandering. Taking the UNP together with its normal allies the Tamil Congress, the Labour Party and the LPP, it has controlled the largest bloc of votes at all general elections in the urban seats, with the exception of 1956 when its support was marginally less than that of the Samasamajist and Communists who were not really in alliance with each other. The support for the 'conservative bloc' expressed as a proportion of the total 'urban' vote was 42.3% in 1947, 45.4% in 1952, 34.9% in 1956, 38.5% in March, 1960, 41.8% in June 1960, 57.1% in 1965 and 51.2% in 1970. This ignores the vote of some minor independents who were generally conservative Muslims. At the Colombo council elections in December 1969 the UNP alone secured 52.5% of the poll compared with 25.3% for the two Marxist parties and only 30% for the three Coalition parties combined.

Even more marked than the UNP predominance is the very late intrusion of the SLFP into urban politics. In the early days of independence the confrontation was between the conservatives and the Marxists. Communist support has been confined to Colombo Central, but the Samasamajists have been important throughout Colombo, in Dehiwela-Mount Lavinia and Moratuwa. Dahanayake first won Galle as a Bolshevik-Leninist while in 1956 even the Catholic stronghold of Negombo fell to a Samasamajist. Only in Jaffna, Kandy and Trincomalee have Marxists failed to make any impact. But the SLFP as a force in urban politics was confined almost exclusively to Kandy until very recently. Even in 1956, MEP candidates got only 14.6% of the vote in urban seats and those were mostly for Philip Gunawardena's disciple M. S. Themis in Colombo Central. This support had scarcely risen at all by 1965 and in the 1970 landslide the SLFP only won a single urban seat. This was despite some consistent work among the Muslims of Colombo and on the semi-rural fringes which raised their Colombo Council representation from three in 1966 to six in 1969. Even Kotte, which they did hold, was first won by the sitting member, Stanley Tillekaratne, as a Communist.

The SLFP still relied upon its Marxist allies to bring in an urban vote while they, in turn, normally trail behind the conservatives. Only in Kandy, with Ratwatte support, does the SLFP command a strong following. This is, of course, fairly readily explained by the communal composition of the towns. Jaffna and Trincomalee, being Tamil, are closed to Sinhalese parties. Even the other towns, and particularly Colombo, are not typical communally. Negombo is predominantly Catholic and thus, normally, UNP. Colombo, Galle, Jaffna and Kandy all have large Muslim minorities while Moratuwa, Colombo and Jaffna have large Christian populations as well. To discuss the 'dilemma' of urban conservatism is simply to repeat what has already been said about the communal basis of politics. Communalism as an electoral base is as marked in urban as in rural voting, nor, with the example of the United States before us, is there any real reason in theory or practice why this should not be so. The only apparent exception to this rule is the powerful local loyalty built up by the Burgher Communist Keuneman in non-Sinhalese areas of Colombo Central. Otherwise it is generally true that Catholic or Muslim wards normally vote for co-religionist candidates, who are usually more successful if nominated by the UNP. This helps to explain why the Marxists are more successful in seats like Borella, containing Colombo's most bourgeois wards, than in Colombo Central, containing its worst slums. In Colombo it is not how 'proletarian' a ward is that normally determines its representation, but how Buddhist. The same must be presumed to be true in the smaller towns, although personal followings are much more important there. Despite a high urban vote, the Marxists are forced back into peasant areas for the election of most of their M.P.s to as great a degree as anyone else. In any case a true, factory-employed proletariat is rarely found even in the older parts of the towns. Militant unionists are more likely to be whitecollar employees, living in lower middle class suburbs. The Sri Lanka town is largely a commercial centre with little industry.

Influences on Electoral Behaviour

The influences on electoral behaviour in Western nations are very fully documented, both through market research and through the correlation of economic and social data with voting records. Unfortunately neither method has proved possible locally. There have been no electoral surveys, in the absence of any commercial or academic opinion polling organisation. Attempts to use Peradeniya university students to gauge opinion in 1970 failed against the opposition of the UNP which claimed, probably correctly, that the students were combining their surveying with canvassing for the Coalition. Attempts to correlate social statistics with voting behaviour are in an early stage of development at the London Institute of Commonwealth Studies and Columbia University.[23] Because of delays in publishing the 1970 Census, and the form in which data is presented, very little has yet emerged from such surveys. What is known about electorates is almost entirely expressed in communal and religious terms in the three Delimitation Commission reports of 1947, 1959 and 1976. Ceylonese newspaper coverage of elections has made much use of this communal data. The general conclusion that election behaviour is largely determined by communal considerations may in part be simply a by-product of the availability of information. The geographical survey above suggests that communal loyalty is most important. Poorer Dry Zone Kandyans do have a predilection towards the SLFP but so do the more prosperous Sinhalese in areas influenced by the Bandaranaike and Ratwatte estates. The backward Muslim peasantry of the East Coast has remained immune to Marxist appeals as have the bulk of overcrowded and even low caste Tamil peasants of the Jaffna peninsula. What little evidence there is from tea estate constituencies like Nuwara Eliya suggests that enfranchised Indian Tamil labourers have been persuaded by the Ceylon Workers' Congress to vote for the conservative UNP. In the cities, as we have seen, communal composition seems more important in determining national and local results than class composition. The Buddhist slum dwellers and workers of Colombo and the South Coast have been susceptible to Marxist and SLFP appeals but Christian and Muslim workers have not. Even if detailed correlations could be established between social class and voting behaviour, it is doubtful whether this would show the clearcut patterns apparent in Europe. Something closer to North American behaviour might emerge, with ethnic, religious and regional factors and the personalities of candidates and opinion leaders being even more important than in the United States or Canada. There are, in any case, no class or occupational figures broken down for constituencies, nor, in most of the rural areas, are there clearcut distinctions between such classes as the professional and landowners, labourers and sharecroppers or peasants and service workers. Even in the cities, prosperous upper-middle class parts of Borella or Colombo South have large servant populations who may vote quite differently from their masters, a factor confusing the general picture of UNP support in such districts.[24]

The parties themselves act, in general, as though communal considerations were the most important. Even the Marxists prefer to appeal to 'the masses' rather than to the working class. The Coalition manifesto of 1970 appealed in turn to the common man, the workers by hand and brain, the mass of peasants and the small Ceylonese industrialists, handicraftsmen and retail traders. This covered the entire population except for 'a small handful of foreign and local capitalists' who were said to be the only class to benefit from UNP rule. Specific categories mentioned in the manifesto included subsistence and 'other' farmers, teachers, public employees, Ceylonese retail traders, landless peasants, irrigation farmers, fishermen, handloom workers, females, swabasha educated clerks, youth, students, Western and ayurvedic doctors, writers and film producers and non-Sinhalese Ceylon citizens by descent.[25]

The particular emphases here are consistent with SLFP policy
since its foundation. There is no acceptance of Marxist notions
that the industrial workers and poor peasants are the spearhead
of progress towards socialism. The SLFP appeal covers everyone likely to vote for the Coalition, with special attention paid
to a variety of middle-class interests from which most SLFP
activists were drawn. The UNP appeal, while naturally based
more on past achievement than future promise, also attempted
to reach a similarly broad sweep of the people. The UNP
manifesto made specific reference to fishermen, hand-loom
workers, paddy farmers, Ceylonese manufacturers, graduates,
'employees of all grades of the public and private sectors',
public servants, Ceylonese traders, Kandyan peasants, and
youth. The party repeated its Kalutara declaration of 1963
that "all our liberties, all our freedoms, rest upon the rights of
the individual to own and dispose freely of his talents and his
lawful possessions. If you have a little property of any kind,
say a small business or a small house, you are by that much,
independent."[26]

Reading around the propaganda appeal, it is fairly clear that
both parties are appealing at the margin to the bulk of small
landholders and property owners who characterise a large part
of peasant society. The SLFP appeals more directly to the
landless and employees, the UNP to businessmen. These are
not the 'floating voters'. Over half Sri Lanka farms are
family-owned, while in every village there is a middle-class of
teachers, shopkeepers, government employees, monks, estate
or land managers, all of them literate and politicised. While it
is generally argued that the SLFP appeals most strongly to the
poor and the UNP to the rich within the villages, both have to
appeal to those with some small investment in property or
position, as they may well be the numerical majority in rural
constituencies, and will normally make up the great bulk of
active workers for both parties. There is thus no substantial,
predictable vote based on class, as in industrialised nations.
Votes float and seats shift in the Sinhala areas for two major
reasons. Firstly, a large part of the electorate has no firm
conception of class interest such as would polarise the parties
between 'workers' and 'owners'. The 'class enemy' to all the
major parties, including the UNP, is confined to 'foreign-

ers', big capitalists and moneylenders, all, significantly, groups in which the Sinhalese are weakly represented. Even indigenous plantation owners are not attacked, as a large part of the leadership of all major parties is drawn from that class. The second major reason for shifting allegiances is that such a large part of the electorate is renewed every five years by the addition of young voters. As these are unemployed to a disproportionate extent, they are liable to be motivated by hostility towards the current government.

Much of the Sinhala Buddhist rural electorate can potentially be appealed to by either major party. In the opinion of T. B. Ilangaratne among others there is no 'captive vote' and the great majority of seats are quite uncertain.[27] In contrast to India and to Ceylon before 1956, there are no longer any major 'vote banks' which can be delivered by notable leaders, unless they can also campaign as party leaders. The feudal, ascriptive basis of loyalty has rapidly disappeared, making necessary an effective party organisation which can conduct house to house canvassing in Low Country seats and public meetings and processions in Kandyan areas. On this analysis, which was borne out by the defeat of many notables in 1970, the electoral process is thoroughly 'modern'. The situation approximates to the model of Downs[28] in which each party has a secure social base and concentrates its attention at the margin, thus tending to identical appeals and programmes. Election results become difficult to prophesy and greater control of wealth or access to the media may be deciding factors. In Sri Lanka some modifications need to be made. Only a part of the electorate, living predominantly in Ruhunu and the Kandyan highlands, is so loosely committed as to make the model work in its pure form. Even so there are certain peculiar features. Every government in Ceylon has been at a disadvantage at election time, whereas in affluent and expansive Western societies the opposite has been true. All governments have to face the wrath of the youth and unemployed, rather than the selfsatisfaction of increasingly prosperous electors. They have insufficient influence over public opinion to be able to manipulate voters through the mass media. A Minister is as likely to bring down the wrath of the dissatisfied as to earn approval for his labours. In 1970 not only did eleven Ministers lose their seats but some did so by larger than average swings. The second modification arises from the continuing existence of blocs of voters, who while they do not form 'vote banks' which can be delivered by individuals,[29] nevertheless introduce variations into the general picture of a swinging, amorphous mass who can be equally reached by either major party.

If voting blocs are not based on class, as in Western societies, they are clearly based on race, religion, caste and local allegiance. In no system containing substantial racial or religious minorities can the 'Downs model' apply to the whole electorate. Almost invariably one of the major parties gains much more support among certain segments than does the other, or certain segments are represented by minority parties. Thus only in the relatively homogenous Buddhist districts, or in Hindu areas for the Tamil parties, can there be 'perfect' two-party competition. As this two-party competition tends to be based on appeals to sentiments which are unacceptable to the various minorities, programmes and appeals must be modified in minority areas. To appeal to the socially and politically dominant caste, all Sinhalese parties must be Goyigama-led and all Tamil parties Vellalla-led. Yet they must also attack caste discrimination, as did the Coalition and the Federal Party in 1970. The smaller castes, and particularly the Karawa and Salagama, must be appealed to as blocs by fellow caste members.

Voting Trends

Stable two-party electoral systems not only show patterns of concentration of regular support, but also tend towards fairly evenly spread nationwide swings between the major parties. The vote becomes equally divided between the major contestants, with both tending to hold about forty per cent of the vote and to be aiming at adding less than ten per cent at the expense of the other party and minor groups. Any party or combination winning half the total vote is assured of landslide victory, provided the distribution of electorates is equitable and proportional representation is not in use. Satisfaction and dissatisfaction with the government combine with traditional loyalties to produce a loose equilibrium in which neither party remains out of office for ever and neither is wiped out. There is no steady progress by one or the other towards a permanent majority, although peculiar features of electoral distribution may keep one party in office for many years. The abstracted two-party electoral situation, on which Downs' model is based, has two equally balanced forces, campaigning at the margin of each other's support, with a gain of one vote for one party meaning its loss by the other. As has been argued above this has tended to be the case over a large part of the Sinhala Buddhist electorate, with qualifications having to be made for Tamil, Christian and Muslim areas and for areas which have been made safe over the years for one or other of the major parties.

In Ceylon the two-party model began to take recognisable form in 1960. In March 1960 there was essentially a five-party result and in July 1960 a four-party result. In the second election of 1960 the results in terms of seats disguised what was happening to the vote. Two-thirds of the vote went either to the UNP or the SLFP and there was a margin between them of 121,000 or less than two per cent. The distribution of seats and the preservation of LSSP and Federalist safe districts distorted the parliamentary representation and disguised the extent to which a two-party bifurcation had occurred in public opinion. The signing of the Coalition agreement in 1964 institutionalised this division by limiting the effective contestants in future to two in all non-Tamil or East Coast constituencies. In 1965 and 1970 three-quarters of all voters supported either the UNP or the Coalition, while in Sinhala electorates the proportion was very much higher.

Underlying and sustaining such a strong trend towards a strict two-party division, other features of electoral behaviour characteristically appear. Nationwide swings in opinion become common, with regional and local variations beginning to disappear. In Britain and the United States the national swing is now an established phenomenon, enhanced by nation-wide mass media presentation and propaganda packaging. These are largely absent in Ceylon, yet there are clear signs that nationwide swings are now occurring, such as to sustain national parties against local indiscipline and resistance. Not only are candidates chosen centrally, but those resisting the

machines are defeated by the electors, often in a most humili-
ating manner. Between 1960 and 1970 the national election for
national party candidates became the norm. The swing of 1956
had been uniform throughout the Sinhalese districts for the
MEP and Marxist parties, and in Tamil areas for the Federal
Party. The UNP was almost demolished and the Tamil Congress
virtually disappeared. In 1960, with the breakup of the MEP
and SLFP there was confusion again, with changes in results
frequently caused by defection or multi-candidacies. In a
simple majority system the splitting of support between more
than two candidates can produce quite unrepresentative and
unpredictable results and that was the case in 1960. The SLFP
returned more than twice the M.P.s of the UNP with a smaller
vote in July, 1960, whereas at all elections before and since the
party or combination gaining the most votes has also won the
most seats and been able to form a government. The bias in the
system towards rural electorates, and the withdrawal of many
candidates who had run in March, 1960, both helped the
SLFP inordinately. Despite the distortion in the result it was
clearly based on a two-party alignment among the Sinhalese.
The SLFP naturally sought allies from the Marxists, and the
UNP from the Federalists and defectors from the SLFP, as
these elements controlled enough seats to be able to decide the
issue in an evenly divided parliament.

Two characteristics of classic two-party systems began to
emerge. These were the settling of support for individual
candidates of the two blocs around the fifty per cent level, and
the nationalising of trends towards one or other of the blocs.
Candidates winning over 65% of the vote, or securing under
45% (other than in multi-member seats) began to disappear,
indicating the rise of effective opposition in 'family seats' on
the one hand, and the decline in the number of effective candidates on the other. Fewer seats became 'hopeless' and fewer
were won on such a small proportion of the vote as to lead to
dissatisfaction with the system. Both reflect the spread of
genuine two-party competition throughout the island, whether
between the UNP and the Coalition or between the Federal
Party and the revived Tamil Congress. By 1970 the vast majority of winning candidates (128 out of 151) were gaining
between 45% and 65% of the votes cast, the 'normal' pro-

portion in such classic two-party systems as those of Britain
and the United States. A relatively small nation-wide swing
between the two blocs of less than 10% is enough to produce a
clearcut change of government. Even in a 'landslide' such as
1970 there were swings of over 15% in only twenty-two
contests of which five were in Tamil electorates.

The 'nationalisation' of this swing after July, 1960 further
indicates two-bloc polarisation. If the electorate behaves
uniformly over most of the country in choosing between two
alternatives, then it can be said to have accepted and internalised
a dichotomous partisan alignment. Local variations become
relatively unimportant, except where there are ethnic or
religious differences which fundamentally influence the voter's
behaviour. In 1965 the general trend was towards the UNP and
its closest allies, the MEP and SLFSP, and away from the
SLFP, the Marxists and the Federal Party. This was remarkably
uniform. Of the seats won by the UNP and its allies, percentage
support dropped only for the Jathika VP and for four others,
or in only one instance in fifteen. The UNP more than doubled
its representation, gaining 43 seats and losing only 5. The
SLFP made only 6 gains, saw the vote for its winning candidate
rise in eight other cases and drop in 29 contests. In general, and
taking into account that a considerable number of SLFP
defectors were running under the protection of the UNP, there
can be no question that in virtually all electorates there was a
swing against the Coalition and the Federalists. In 1970 the
picture was even clearer. The Coalition was no longer a new
phenomenon and two-party division was quite familiar to the
voters. The percentage support for SLFP winners rose in all
cases except Tissamaharama, where the new young candidate
had a very hard fight against two former M.P.s. The UNP
winners' support dropped everywhere except in the four Muslim
and Tamil seats of Akurana, Kalkudah, Padiruppu and
Pottuvil. All LSSP and Communist winners had higher percentage support except Colvin de Silva in Agalawatte where, as
a Salagama he was probably at a disadvantage compared with
the unseated LSSP Member, Anil Moonesinghe, who was a
Goyigama. All Tamil Congress winners had higher support,
while seven Federalists had more support and six had less.
Among those losing support was the party leader S. J. V.

Chelvanayakam. His deputy E. M. V. Naganathan, and the Party Chairman S. M. Rasamanickam lost their seats altogether. Quite apart from the rather distorted result in terms of seats won, there is no doubt that there was a uniform swing from UNP to Coalition amongst Sinhala voters, including Christians, and away from the Federalists among Tamils.

How these swings become uniform is a hard question to answer. The great majority of newspapers were strongly in favour of the UNP both in 1965 and 1970. There was nothing like the partisan support of monks which had been so decisive in 1956 and the leaders of the Siam Nikaya were on record as opposing Marxism. The Catholic Church, while neutral compared to its stance until 1965, was hardly enthusiastic for the SLFP and also on record as opposing Marxism. In 1965 it is possible to explain the UNP victory in terms of the decline in the GNP, the press nationalisation controversy and the split in the SLFP. There was no comparable situation in 1970. In formal terms the economy was expanding very satisfactorily. The UNP was united and its quarrel with the Federal Party could only help it in Sinhala electorates. Yet the voters seemed to single out its Ministers for demolition. There were swings of over 15% against four Ministers. Only the non-Sinhala East Coast, which had never behaved like the rest of Ceylon electorally, resisted the general sweep. Obviously forces were moving the electors fairly uniformly in 1970, much as the better documented forces moved them in 1956. It cannot be overlooked that in 1956 not only was the Sinhala conservative UNP defeated but so was the conservative Tamil Congress. While the upsurge of Sinhala nationalism was a major factor,[30] the collapse of the Korean War commodity price boom may have been significant as well. Similarly in 1970, while there had been five years of internal peace and formal prosperity, the rise in the GNP had been accompanied by a rise in prices and in youthful unemployment. For all its success with the 'Green Revolution', the impact of which had been marked on the East Coast, the UNP had failed to meet the expectations of the *swabasha* educated youth, those between 18 and 25 who had not voted in 1965. During those years the number of unemployed had risen from 500,000 to 750,000, including nearly 10,000 graduates. The cost of living index had risen from 112 in

1965 to over 122 in 1970, which for Ceylon was unprecedented after the years of virtually unchanging prices.[31] It was generally accepted that the young voters were largely hostile to the government. "These 18–21 years groups had organised themselves so well that they left nothing to chance to undo the Senanayake government."[32] Not only had the electorate divided itself between two alternatives, reacting fairly uniformly to them throughout the country. As also in Western democracies it was being moved primarily by economic concerns, where before 1960 it was motivated by nationalistic, religious and communal forces. The SLFP, which had built its support on these latter, was allied with the Marxists who had always emphasised economic problems. The party which relied most heavily on the traditionalist Kandyan vote was allied with those who appealed to the most politicised Low Country Buddhists. The national swing in their favour and against the incumbent government could hardly have failed. Yet it was precisely in those areas which swung most heavily towards the Coalition[33] that the JVP insurgency took its most acute form one year later. The frustrations which created the new government almost destroyed it. A fully effective 'modern', two-party electoral system existed, in which the voters chose fairly rationally on economic grounds between two alternative blocs, neither of which could immediately solve the problems which had led to their respective victories and defeats in 1965 and 1970.[34]

NOTES

1. *Ceylon Daily News Seventh Parliament of Ceylon 1970*; Colombo, 1970.
2. Madan Lal Goel; "Urban-Rural Correlates of Political Participation in India:" *Political Science Review* (Jaipur) vol. 10 nos. 1–2, June 1971 (p. 54) found that rural voter turnout was also higher than urban in India.
3. See Chapter 9.
4. Constitution of Ceylon s.41 (4) and Constitution of Sri Lanka s.76 (4).
5. Report of the Delimitation Commission (S.P. XV—1959); Colombo, 1959; s. 23–25 acknowledged that representatives of "certain castes" had asked for separate representation, which had been refused. The Commissioners added: "The people, we are afraid, have not yet learnt to think sufficiently in terms of principles and policies in preference to race, caste or religion, but they are rapidly developing a political

consciousness which tends to what is called a polarization towards the right, centre or left. Till this tendency is completed we cannot altogether ignore, without doing injustice or creating a sense of frustration, the feelings of caste and religion" (p. 13).

6. Only Indian Tamils are 'underrepresented'.

7. The laws of 1970 are summarised in the *CDN Seventh Parliament of Ceylon 1970* pp. 19–21.

8. Nuwara Eliya was retained by the UNP and Ratnapura by the SLFP.

9. See Appendix I for a summary of national election results between 1947 and 1970.

10. They were: Kayts, Kankesanturai, Uduvil, Kopay, Point Pedro, Chavakachcheri, Mannar, Trincomalee, Mutur and Batticaloa.

11. Colombo South, Panadura, Kalutara, Agalawatta, Baddegama, Yatiyantota and Dehiowita.

12. Colombo Central, Akuressa.

13. The term 'safe seat' is used for those seats held by the same *party* (not necessarily by the same candidate) for three elections before the 1959 redistribution or four elections since 1959.

14. See Chapter 2 for a brief discussion of the 'Family Seat'.

15. *Ceylon Observer* 26/6/1962.

16. See E. R. Leach: *Pul Eliya*; Cambridge, 1961 for an analysis of primitive beliefs in a North Central Province Sinhalese village which lies within an SLFP stronghold.

17. Six out of the UNP's remaining ten 'safe' seats in 1970 were urban.

18. A regional and area study of aggregate voting patterns is contained in D. R. Gamelin: *Ceylon's Political Parties in Three General Elections, 1960 and 1965*; Unpublished Ph.D. Thesis, Duke University, 1968.

19. In 1915 the Government Agent for Matara reported that "it is most significant that the riots in this district occurred where the temperance societies have been most prominent; Akuressa, Kamburupitiya and Weligama" (quoted by K. Jayawardena in "Economic and Political Factors in the 1915 Riots"; *Journal of Asian Studies* XXIX; 2, February 1970). Two of the three areas named are now Communist strongholds.

20. See the formula in the Constitution of Ceylon, s.41 (2) which allows extra representation on the basis of "one additional electoral district for each 1,000 square miles of area calculated to the nearest 1,000." This was carried over into the constitution of Sri Lanka—see Chapter 9.

21. Under the Ceylon Citizenship Act of 1948 as upheld in the cases of Mudanayake v. Sivagnanasunderam (1952) 53 NLR 25 and Kodakan Pillai v. Mudanayake (1953) 54 NLR 433.

22. Colombo Municipal Council election results have been as follows:

	UNP	LSSP	CP	SLFP/MEP	Others
1956	18	3	2	5	3
1959	23	8	1	1	4
1962	40	3	1	1	2
1966	33	6	1	3	4
1969	32	5	2	6	2

The boundaries of the City were extended to the Southeast in 1960 and the additional wards have normally been won by the LSSP and the SLFP.

23. These have been conducted at London University under the supervision of Professor Morris-Jones (See Judith Bara: "An Aggregate Ecological Analysis of Voting Behaviour in four Commonwealth States', London PhD thesis 1975) and by Frank Ceo at Columbia under the supervision of Professor Wriggins. The Ceylon Census provides figures on a Provincial basis which is too large to be used for calculations of constituency correlations.

24. When the United Left Front won the by-election of January, 1964 in Borella, which covers the richest areas of Colombo, the successful candidate, Mrs. Vivienne Goonewardena (LSSP) drew attention to the large number of servants living in the constituency, while the defeated UNP candidate attacked "the lethargy of the Colombo 7 rich." *Ceylon Observer* 19/1/1964.

25. *Ceylon Daily News Parliament of Ceylon 1970*; pp. 171–182.

26. *Ibid.* p. 183.

27. In an interview in August, 1969.

28. Anthony Downs: *An Economic Theory of Democracy:* Harper and Row, New York; 1957.

29. T. B. Ilangaratne told the author that he "would not believe someone who promised to deliver a large number of votes." He held that "vote banks" had disappeared after 1956 in Sinhalese areas and that all M.P.s had to cultivate their entire electorate.

30. See I. D. S. Weerawardena: *Ceylon General Election 1956*; Colombo, 1960.

31. Working from a base of 100 in 1952.

32. *CDN Parliament of Ceylon 1970*; p. 14.

33. See Chapter 10.

34. For a full account of the 1970 election see A. J. Wilson: *Electoral Politics in an Emergent State*; London, 1975.

CHAPTER 8

Transplanted Institutions

In the century-and-a-half of British rule a whole series of practices, attitudes and institutions were transferred from the colonising power and grafted onto existing practices. By the end of the period Ceylon had a large Anglicised middle-class which in most politically relevant respects was more British than Sinhalese or Tamil. Its private life, in the sense of marriage and property arrangements, caste divisions and religious beliefs, was varyingly affected. The public aspects of life were drastically altered. The entire educational system, which created and moulded the political and social élite, was modelled on England, with its hierarchy of elementary, 'public' and university teaching and its orientation towards examinations based purely on academic accomplishment. In local government the Kandyan aristocracy and kingship was replaced by Government Agents and Divisional Revenue Officers, the *Dissawes, Mudaliyars, Ratemahatmayas* and Village Headmen.[1] All but the latter were normally drawn into the Anglicised community. In national affairs a professional bureaucracy was created on British lines, with entrance by competitive examinations which presupposed an Anglicised education, with promotion on merit, which ran counter to traditional practices like nepotism or caste preference, and with an ethos, varyingly accepted, which rejected any form of corruption or inducement. After 1931 parliamentary institutions became fully entrenched. They were dominated by the Anglicised. Even after independence both the Senate and the Nominated M.P.s secured entrenched positions for the European and Burgher minorities, as for the Anglicised professionals. The backbone of parliamentary politics was provided by the legal profession, which, more than any other, was grounded in and perpetuated British attitudes, laws and practices.

Each institution, whether education, the law, parliament, national and local administration, was transplanted from Britain and depended for its entrenchment on the grafting of British culture and traditions upon the aristocracy and the upper-middle classes.[2] The maintenance of law and order, whether through the police, the judiciary or the army, was fully based on British principles. The army and police were to be free from political commitment and patronage and the judiciary held office during good behaviour. Before independence these characteristics were maintained by the British themselves, who held the pinnacles of office. After independence the Burgher community and Anglicised Christians, Buddhists and Hindus quite naturally assumed the same role. While at the lower levels the police, the administration, the politicians and the judiciary were never as free from corruption and patronage as the British model required, the general ethos of political life rejected such practices. Codes and devices were maintained to ensure impartiality, neutrality and incorruptibility.

That all significant political institutions were so transplanted was a source of concern to the Buddhist revivalists and nationalists who provided the main local thrust towards independence. They themselves were sufficiently affected by the educational system, sufficiently enmeshed in the plantation economy and sufficiently modern in outlook, not to harbour romantic delusions about returning to Kandyan ways. Only in stressing the importance of adhering to religious principles and consulting the *sangha* did any important political tendencies in Sri Lanka argue for a return to former practices. None the less, most nationalists and socialists have been concerned to give an indigenous character to British-derived political institutions. The most influential text for Buddhist nationalists, D. C. Wijewardena's *The Revolt in the Temple*, had claimed that the Ceylon Independence Act of 1947 "does not confer national freedom on Ceylon."[3] Wijewardena's argument was similar to Bandaranaike's and to those of the constitution framers of 1971. "Our ultimate goal should not be Dominion status, but Independence," he wrote, "and a constitution, not imported from Whitehall but drafted by a Constituent Assembly."[4] To this end he supported the abolition of the Senate, the ending of the British Commonwealth connection, and the replacement of

R

the British monarchy by a republic. Wijewardena's vision of
the future state was almost identical with that of Bandaranaike.
It was to be democratic, socialist and Buddhist, in the sense of
"a State which is governed according to Buddhist principles."[5]
There was no incompatibility between the emphasis on religious
principles and upon political democracy for "the Buddha himself was a staunch democrat. The Buddhist assemblies were
fully democratic and had elaborate rules of procedure, election
and debate."[6] Unlike some Buddhist thinkers in Ceylon,
Wijewardena did not reject the British heritage of parliamentary
democracy. On the contrary he believed the "priceless boon of
democracy" to be "a gift for which the people must thank the
Donoughmore Commissioners . . . It is the greatest boon conferred on the people of Ceylon since the inception of British
rule."[7] Through the franchise the people were to bring in a
socialist society. "The task remains to convert the State to a
programme of Socialism through the conquest of public
opinion. Specifically the plan is to use three main agencies. A
Socialist political party will organise citizens as voters to elect
sympathetic officials and to sponsor remedial legislation.
Workers are to be organised in strong class-conscious unions:
their function will be to win immediate concessions. Finally
both consumers' and producers' cooperatives will be fostered
to promote the principles of non-profit enterprise and improve
the standard of living."[8]

In most respects this epitomised the aims of nearly all non-
revolutionary reformers in Ceylon. Wijewardena denied the
need for class struggle and sectional divisiveness. "This is the
Buddhist ethic and the last word in nationalism," he wrote,
"the recognition that we are parts of the whole, and that in
politics as in everything else, co-operation must be the keynote
of the future."[9] The political system would be socialist and
co-operative, indigenous rather than neo-colonalist. Yet it is
clear from Wijewardena's advocacy of such alien institutions
as political parties, trade unions, co-operatives, the franchise
and parliamentary democracy, that he, like Bandaranaike, took
a large part of his political inspiration from that aspect of the
British tradition which was radical and social-democratic,
rather than conservative. In the colonial situation it was natural
that the preservation of law and order through a hierarchical

administration based on an equally hierarchical educational
system, should have been the most apparent feature of the
British heritage. Many of the debates about political institutions
and goals which raged over the years between 1931 and 1972,
rested upon a counterposing of one part of the British tradition
against another. The rapidly ascending role of the political
parties and the elected parliament, as against the declining
importance of the professional bureaucracy and judiciary, arose
from the widespread adoption of British radical notions of
popular rule, rather than from American or Soviet concepts,
let alone purely indigenous Sinhalese ones. Attacking both
capitalism and the Soviet State, both the Kremlin and the
Vatican, Wijewardena believed that "the final solution of the
problem . . . will be neither Communism nor Capitalism but
something midway between the two, represented by that new
social and economic order known as Socialism."[10] All these
concepts were, of course, European ones. The belief remained
that Ceylon, by combining its religious inheritance with the
best aspects of foreign ideologies, would once again become a
beacon as it had been in the far-off days of Anuradhapura. "If
Lanka takes the right Path, the rest of the world will follow,"
concludes Wijewardena.[11]

This general orientation towards the future came to be
accepted by all the major parliamentary parties within ten years.
Most criticisms and reforms of political institutions were influenced not merely by the extent to which these were alien, but
by the obstacles they presented to achieving socialism by
democratic means. Bandaranaike's own criticisms of the
Soulbury constitution, which he made in a memorandum to the
Sinhala Mahasabha in 1945, focused on the extent to which
the limited independence then offered would inhibit the power
to control economic affairs. While strongly against the proposed
new Senate, which no one but the British really wanted, he
strangely regarded the adoption of a Cabinet system as "not a
matter of vital importance."[12] His recommendation was, with
reservations over Dominion Status and the Senate, that
Ceylonese politicians should generally approve "the structure of
the Constitution recommended by the Soulbury Report."[13] On
the coming of effective independence Bandaranaike continued
to support, in the strongest terms, the practices of parliamentary

democracy bequeathed by the British, and to warn against the extremes of fascism and communism. After the creation of the Sri Lanka Freedom Party his criticism of the local practice of parliamentary democracy became more open. As he argued in 1953: "In the political sphere, the mere substitution of a set of native rulers for a set of foreign rulers does not necessarily confer freedom on a people; nor does the mere observance of the forms of democracy confer the democratic freedoms on a nation."[14] Once in power, Bandaranaike began the process which, fifteen years later, was to produce a new constitution for Sri Lanka. Even at this stage he found the Soulbury constitution generally satisfactory and rejected an amendment proposed by G. G. Ponnambalam in favour of producing a new constitution through a Constituent Assembly.[15] After ten years of independence the Prime Minister was concerned mainly with four weaknesses in the constitution; the monarchic connection; the absence of guaranteed fundamental rights; the position of the Senate and Appointed Members; and the Public Service Commission and the Judicial Service Commission. The most important institutions transplanted by the British, and particularly responsible parliamentary government based on universal suffrage, remained acceptable to all major parties.

Government and Parliament

The influence of Sir Ivor Jennings on the constitution of Ceylon, and the grounding of all lawyers and most politicians in English constitutional history and law, ensured that there were few initial departures from the formal aspects of British practice. The Governor-General was assumed to have the limited functions of the British monarch, and thus to be effectively answerable to the Prime Minister of the day. In fact the much stronger traditions of the British Colonial Governor were also influential in ensuring that Sir Oliver Goonetilleke on at least two major occasions, took an initiative which was highly controversial. His predecessors, who were both British, also had the responsibility in 1950 of choosing N. M. Perera, as Leader of the Opposition, and in 1952 of choosing Dudley Senanyake as Prime Minister, in the absence of complete agreement among parliamentarians as to who should hold the appropriate office.

As the leaders of the two major parties 'evolve' rather than submit to elections, the relationship between Governor-General and party leader was somewhat similar to that existing in Britain before the Conservative Party began electing its leaders. In 1960, Sir Oliver exercised his constitutional discretion three times: by asking Dudley Senanayake to form a minority government, by granting him a dissolution, and by making Mrs. Bandaranaike both a Senator and Prime Minister.[16] As the most actively partisan of Governor-Generals, Sir Oliver, a former UNP Minister, could not enjoy precisely the relationship with parliamentary leaders which the constitution envisaged. His successor after 1962, William Gopallawa, who became President of Sri Lanka ten years later, was much better able to maintain a neutral posture. He too, in December 1964 and in March 1965, had to exercise some discretion in a confused situation. Like Sir Oliver, he granted the prime minister a dissolution when she could no longer command a majority in the Representatives. He did not exercise substantial powers in any of the emergencies arising during his term of office, including the JVP rising of 1971. The Prime Minister and Cabinet were in full command after 1962, whereas it is clear that in the racial rioting of 1958 Sir Oliver Goonetilleke took control of emergency arrangements.[17]

By the early 1960s the Prime Minister had emerged as the most powerful individual within the system, as the constitution framers clearly intended. The constitution itself obliged the Prime Minister to take on the control of external affairs, not normally an official duty of British premiers but becoming increasingly common in practice. As in India under Nehru, the Prime Minister also took on responsibility for economic planning. Control over the Cabinet, party leadership, national inspiration, overseas representation and economic overlordship became concentrated into the hands of one person. With the exception of S. W. R. D. Bandaranaike no Ceylonese Premier could truly be termed 'charismatic', and thus dictatorial tendencies inherent in the constitution were avoided. They were further modified by the natural inability of one person to carry out all the functions which were assumed. The Premiers have all played a major role in dealing with other heads of state involving their absence from the country, and have been the

main initiators of foreign policy. Sir John Kotelawala kept
Ceylon close to the Western powers, a stance reversed by S. W.
R. D. Bandaranaike. Dudley Senanayake was less engrossed
in foreign affairs and more concerned with economic development. Mrs. Bandaranaike became very actively interested in
foreign relations, especially with China. Much of this was consistent with the tendency in newly independent nations for the
state to be internationally represented by the individual who
held most domestic power and for a professional career diplo-
matic service to develop slowly and to have limited influence.

In the other areas in which the Prime Minister held formal or
de facto control, power has tended to be shared with other
party leaders or officials. Dudley Senanayake left party management to J. R. Jayawardena, R. Premadasa and A. J. Niyathapala
and in economics he relied heavily upon the professional advice
of Gamani Corea, a public servant. Mrs. Bandaranaike took a
more direct role in party management, particularly ensuring
that ultimate control of parliamentary selections remained with
herself. She depended upon N. M. Perera in economic affairs
and upon her nephew Felix Dias Bandaranaike in domestic
affairs. It was a central weakness of the governments of S. W.
R. D. Bandaranaike, W. Dahanayake and Mrs. Bandaranaike
before 1964 that they were unable to rely on loyal and consistent support in areas in which their duties exceeded their
personal competence. Despite the undue burden placed upon
Prime Ministers by the constitution and by the growth of
central economic control, the basic requirement of the British
type of Cabinet government was that, through the party system,
a reliable and permanent team of assistants to the Prime
Minister would be maintained. While the party system was in
a state of flux this was impossible. Even in the early years of
the system, prior to 1953, the front rank of the UNP tended to
see themselves and to act as rivals for power rather than as
colleagues. It was the defection of Bandaranaike and the
struggle between Dudley Senanayake and Sir John Kotelawala
which broke up the apparently invincible UNP government in
less than five years.

The adoption of Cabinet government formalised the notion
of collective leadership, which had already developed rather
hesitantly through the Board of Ministers. Under the old

system each Minister had a vested interest in looking after his own affairs rather than in collaborating under a single acknowledged head. One of the arguments put forward for the 'all-Sinhalese' Board of 1936 was precisely that its unified communal basis would give it solidarity in its dealings with the British administration.[18] This was certainly the case during the negotiations over the Soulbury constitution. Until 1948 Ceylon had an embryo Cabinet which gave a collective leadership to the Sinhalese politicians, without being based on a disciplined party and without being able to bind its individual members either to secrecy or to totally unified action. This continued to be characteristic of Ceylon Cabinets for many years after. As they were normally based on coalitions, their individual members were torn between collective responsibility and the protection of the independence of their own parties. Ceylonese Cabinets gradually became as collectively united as those in Commonwealth countries such as Australia in which coalition was normal. The individually recalcitrant or unco-operative Minister was as common as the party-backed dissident. No Minister of the LSSP or the Communist Party defected from Mrs. Bandaranaike's Cabinets until forced out in 1975 and 1977. Indeed in 1972 the Communist Party was severely split by the refusal of its Minister and Junior Minister, Pieter Keuneman and B. Y. Tudawe, to join with their parliamentary colleagues in condemning the government's Criminal Justice Commission Bill. The Marxist Ministers in S. W. R. D. Bandaranaike's government in 1958 did not resign voluntarily but were driven out by the SLFP majority. The same was true of the LSSP Ministers in September, 1975, who were offered portfolios which they felt unable to accept. The fact that there have nearly always been representatives of minority parties in Cabinet has not led to them breaking up in confusion.

Stable Cabinet rule, with its presuppositions of collective responsibility and majority support in the lower house, survived much more effectively than in many Indian states or in Western Europe. Governments were infrequently replaced and Prime Ministers were not often overthrown. From 1947 until 1974 only six individuals had been Prime Minister of Ceylon, compared with three Prime Ministers of India, seven of Australia, and seven of Britain. It is true that no national

government in these other Commonwealth countries had been
defeated in parliament, whereas this happened in Ceylon in
1960 and 1964. To that extent Ceylon developed a system
of 'parliamentary' government rather than 'Cabinet' government. While the government is rarely overthrown the threat of
overthrow was frequently there. Bandaranaike's government
might have been defeated at any time after 1958, had the rate of
defections continued. Dahanayake's government only saved
itself from total defeat by calling an election, having lost all
semblance of parliamentary support. Dudley Senanayake was
defeated in parliament immediately upon gaining office in 1960
and had to go to the electorate, who defeated him. Mrs.
Bandaranaike's first government was, arguably, only saved by
the Coalition of 1964 and then only until the end of the year
when SLFP defectors overthrew it. Dudley Senanayake had to
spend agonising days in 1965 piecing together a government out
of mutually incompatible elements because the UNP did not
have an overall majority. It was a tribute to his skill that the
government ran its full term of office even after the withdrawal
of Federal Party support in 1968. This periodic instability has
not meant that governments are frequently changed. The UNP
from 1947 to 1952, the SLFP from 1960 to 1965 and the UNP
again from 1965 to 1970 all ran their full term of five years and
had it not been for Bandaranaike's assassination the same might
have been true of his government. The SLFP alone in 1970 won
enough seats to ensure its full term of office even without its
Coalition partners, provided the party did not split. The reality
of a threat of defection made the Ceylon political system
approximate more closely to the model of British responsible
government than does Britain itself. Real power resided in the
lower house, elected by adult franchise and because of the
multi-party situation it resided there to a greater degree than in
Britain.

This has meant that Cabinet Ministers are less insulated from
popular and partisan pressures than has tended to be true in
Britain after the Second World War. Cabinet Ministers are
frequently defeated at the polls and this was particularly
marked in 1970. Both as Ministers and as Members of Parliament, they are obliged to endorse many hundreds of appli-
cations for posts and promotions from their constituents. The

burden of active political involvement at this level makes them less effective either individually in relation to their full-time officials, or collectively as a Cabinet. The ILO mission of 1971 argued in relation to the need for more frequent meetings of the Cabinet Planning Committee, that "one great obstacle here, of course, is the enormous pressure on the time of ministers, strikingly evidenced by the queues always present outside their offices. Ministers need to be protected from such pressures so that they have time to study and discuss the central issues of policy."[19] Ministers are constantly beset by petitioners for preferment and favours as well as by constituents who are prepared to travel to Colombo and, if necessary, camp out until they see their Member of Parliament. Moreover, every Minister, to an even greater extent than the M.P., is expected to be present on ceremonial occasions, to give prizes, make speeches, attend weddings, come forward as godfather and, perhaps most important, take part in funeral rites, for a whole host of individuals who look to the Minister as socially superior but who will, equally, punish him at the polls if he does not fulfil his reciprocal obligations. The burden rests most heavily upon the Prime Minister whose responsibilities extend to the whole nation. The frequent references to Mrs. Bandaranaike as *Amma* or Mother, are not simply figurative. All national religious occasions, national holidays, politically or socially important occasions are opportunities for the masses to see their leaders. In the absence of effective mass media penetration this personal contact, whether face-to-face or simply through the mass rally, is a vital element in binding the voters to the politicians. In the case of Ministers it seriously interferes with their ability to perform executive functions.

The relative slowness and ineffectiveness with which economic policies were pursued in independent Ceylon no doubt owes something to the pre-occupation of Ministers and M.P.'s with their electoral and partisan obligations. A large part of parliamentary debate was taken up with historical reminiscences and party bickering which suggest that many legislators had learned nothing new for many years. The same incidents and grievances were retailed again and again and were repeated through the newspapers and at political rallies and election campaigns. The central characteristic of the parliamentary process thus became party strife rather than legislative or administrative supervision and control. In common with the British parliament, the parliament of Ceylon did not develop effective sub-committees for investigating legislative or administrative areas. As in the rather smaller Australian House of Representatives, the great bulk of legislation was dealt with in committees of the whole house, passing through the conventional succession of first, second and third reading. The budgetary process was equally modelled on Westminster and was possibly even less effective in asserting genuine parliamentary control over expenditure. M.P.s were too busy with electoral problems or party battles to be able to cope effectively with specialised material, particularly if they were unable to understand enough English to read the vast bulk of economic or social analysis in the libraries of parliament, the universities or the Central Bank. The obsession of many rural Sinhala-speaking M.P.s with cultural matters clearly reflects their inability to handle other issues with the same degree of competence as their English-speaking colleagues. Debate on economic affairs, which should have preoccupied parliament more and more, remained dominated by a small group of Anglicised M.P.s, some of them former State Councillors. Even within the Anglicised majority of M.P.s, the greatest expertise was in law and the basic training in British law, history and literature.

Parliament, which might have been a sounding board for public opinion or a specialised agency for controlling and inspecting government, was neither. The masses were not effectively represented in parliament because of its social composition and where they were, often had Sinhala-speaking rural M.P.s who could not take a meaningful part in debates conducted in terminology learned in British universities. Ministers were almost invariably English-speaking and frequently tertiary educated. There was thus a gap between Ministers and M.P.s as between politicians and electors. The Minister remained dependent upon his fellow M.P.s who might turn him out of office, just as the M.P. depended upon his less sophisticated electors who might do the same. Hence the tendency for parliamentary debate to be turned outwards towards the masses rather than inwards towards the specific problems under consideration. To that extent the electorate were better able to follow and take an interest in parliamentary debates, which were seen as gladiatorial combats. At the same time the effective control of national policy remained the prerogative of a relatively small group of Ministers and Permanent Secretaries except where issues like communalism were raised. In this area everyone had an opinion. Debate was sustained by genuine popular involvement in the age-old struggle between Sinhalese and Tamil. Parliamentarians were constantly under pressure to generalise, while the structure of parliament, with its absence of specialist committees or effective agencies for controlling expenditure, further rendered them ineffective in the sense of being unable to formulate and secure the implementation of national economic policy.

Parliament was located at the centre of power, where the constitution of Sri Lanka formally entrenched it. The Member of Parliament gradually came to take over the prestigious position previously enjoyed by Government Agents under the colonial system. Those politicians who did not already come from locally important families were able to build up party machines and patronage systems which established them as important people, at least as long as their constituents did not vote them out. The M.P. was comparable to the Member in Edwardian England rather than to the ineffectual, underpaid and disregarded M.P. of contemporary Britain. His function as a link between people and government became more and more important, while his legislative powers were increasingly limited by party discipline and by his relative inability to cope with sophisticated economic or social policy. One of the major criticisms of the parliamentary and Cabinet system remained that, unlike the State Council, it focused debate on party issues rather than upon administration. It wasted the talents of Opposition and backbench M.P.s in contrast to the State Council practice of attaching every member to a Ministerial Committee. There was of course, nothing constitutionally forbidden in equally attaching every Representative to a specialist committee concerned with the area of responsibility of a particular Ministry except that virtually all constitutional thinking took place within the blinkers provided by Jennings and British example. To have looked to the European or American legislatures or to have demanded a return to State Council methods was to depart from the Westminster model in a direction which British parliamentarians themselves were very reluctant to take until the late 1960s and then took very hesitantly and ineffectively. It would have weakened the powers of Ministers and civil servants as well as loosening the bonds of party discipline which had only painfully been created.

The relationship which had developed between parliament and government was summarised thus by Gamini Dissanayake M.P. in the Constituent Assembly debates:

"We know the distance which exists, though undesirable, between the backbencher and the frontbencher. We know the gap which separates the Opposition and the government. Cabinet government presupposes the continued backing of Members of Parliament, but by the operation of the whip, by the operation of ties of loyalty to party leaders, we know today that government by Cabinet is really a fairly iron-fisted government. It is true that theoretically a Cabinet can be overthrown but in fact we know the rigours which Members of Parliament have to face when confronted with the whip."[20]

In other words, by 1971, the basic relationship between parliament and government appeared very similar to that in Britain, at least to some of those engaged in parliamentary politics. Nothing in the new constitution was to change this. The strongest political figure was to remain the Prime Minister rather than the President and he or she would still be an ordinary Member of Parliament with the same constituency obligations as anyone else. Cabinet government would continue through the Cabinet of Ministers, every one of whom would likewise be an M.P. There was no obligation upon the National State Assembly to organise itself in a form different from the previous House of Representatives. The single house became constitutionally what it had already become in practice, the centre of political power. It seemed highly probable that this power would be exercised by a relatively small group of leaders of the party commanding a majority, in consultation with the professional bureaucracy in the Ceylon Administrative Service. Power had shifted from government to parliament after 1947. The consolidation of the parties made it almost inevitable that it would move back to government again in Sri Lanka, a process hastened by the creation of an executive presidency in 1978.

An Outline of the Structure of Government in 1976

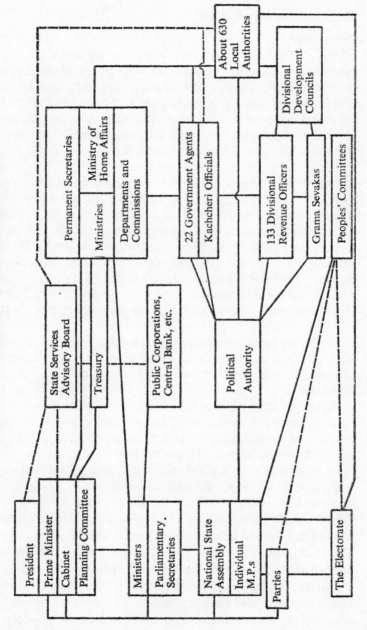

The Administrative System

The administrative system of Ceylon was the most consistently criticised of all the institutions created by the British. Most of this criticism came from politicians, who progressively asserted their own power against that of the professional bureaucracy. The broad administrative structure of Sri Lanka can be depicted as in the Chart. While the basic relationships between Ministers, the Cabinet and the Ministry officials is similar to that in Britain, a number of modifications arose from the colonial situation. In order to protect the former Ceylon Civil Service (which became the Ceylon Administrative Service in 1963) against patronage or partisan interference, all appointments to it and promotions within it were made subject to a Public Service Commission. This was answerable only to the Governor-General and each of the three members was appointed for five years and eligible for reappointment.[21] A Local Government Service Commission had also been created in 1945 to ensure a national career structure for local government officers. Reconstituted in 1968, its essential function remained the protection of local officers from partisan or communal interference and their control and disciplining through the central government. This was seen as particularly important in view of the record of incompetence and corruption in Village Councils and small municipalities.

As well as ensuring a neutral, career service for national and local government, the colonial power needed to rest its local services on something more powerful and competent than the elected local authorities. In contrast to the British situation, local government in Ceylon was weak and poverty stricken. The British operated through a hierarchy of Government Agents, who were members of the Ceylon Civil Service, Divisional Revenue Officers and appointed Village Headmen. This administrative structure paralleled a hierarchy drawn from the local aristocracy and having largely peace-keeping and minor judicial functions. The Village Headman system fell progressively into disrepute because of the conservative allegiances of the headmen and their reputation for arbitrary and corrupt domination of their areas. The LSSP and SLFP campaigned against the system which was altered in 1961. On the Indian model, local village headmen chosen for their standing in the community were replaced by central government officers, the *grama sevakas*, who could be assumed to be better educated, less corrupt, less subject to local relationships and loyalties, and more responsive to the wishes of the Ministry of Home Affairs. The colonial system was retained at the Divisional and District levels. The one-hundred and thirty-three Divisional Revenue Officers worked under the direction of the twenty-two Government Agents, whose function was to co-ordinate the services provided by various Ministries within their Districts. Operating through the *kachcheri* in the District chief town, the Government Agent was in no way answerable to elected bodies within his area of control. His responsibility was to the professional bureaucracy of which he was a career member.

As the functions of central government grew, so the *kachcheri* system became more ponderous and inefficient. Representations over land, complaints against the level of services and group or individual disputes were all handled by the administrative and judicial officers at the *kachcheri*. This involved endless delays, especially as the normal form of pressure was through the presentation of grievances and requests in person. The local resentment against the consequently abolished Village Headmen became transferred to the professional bureaucrats at the *kachcheri*. The locally elected M.P.s and councillors found themselves increasingly in the role of petitioners before an authority over whom they had no direct control and, because of its protected position through the Ministry and the Public Service Commission, very little indirect influence. Partly to alleviate the resulting objections by M.P.s, District Co-ordinating Committees were established on which the M.P.s, local councillors and the Government Agent and Divisional Revenue Officers could meet to discuss the operation of government services. These were largely decorative bodies which met only annually. As more and more of the population participated in the electoral system, so the demand grew for greater influence or even control over the powerful regional bureaucracies. The citizen's involvement in the welfare state, with the police and in land disputes, brought him increasingly into contact with his M.P. as the one locally responsive person with any power at the national level. The *grama sevaka* was not elected, while the local council chairman had insufficient influence and, as a party member, tended to work through the Member of Parliament in any case. The M.P. alone could gain access to officials by direct representation, by parliamentary questions and by approaches to the Minister or his national officials in the Colombo Secretariat. The M.P. thus became the essential, and increasingly overworked, link between the citizen and the Government. This relationship was formalised in 1973 by giving M.P.s some executive power in their own areas through the system known as Political Authority, which permitted them to issue instructions to local officials.

The strengthening of local government, which might have transferred some of the burden to elected councillors, was scarcely feasible. The bulk of voters lived in the areas of over five hundred Village Councils, which had neither resources nor influence. The major towns, with the exception of Colombo, had little more influence and even Colombo was normally controlled by the UNP which made it difficult for the council to receive a friendly hearing from SLFP governments. Two solutions were sought, one by the UNP in 1968 and one by the SLFP in 1970. The former, the creation of District Councils, had its historic origins in a recommendation of the Donoughmore commission, which was never put into effect. This was debated in the State Council between 1937 and 1940, during which time S. W. R. D. Bandaranaike was Minister of Local Administration. Such councils, which Bandaranaike likened to English county councils, would be based on the DRO's divisions and would have co-ordinated local government functions, be indirectly elected from existing authorities and include the Government Agent, whose powers would consequently diminish. The Provincial Councils would, Bandaranaike claimed, "be a new vehicle, a more popular vehicle replacing the Government Agent system."[22] However the war prevented further progress and the preoccupation of post-independence governments with communal problems postponed reforms still further. In 1968 the UNP government attempted a similar reform, with its proposals for District Councils. These, too, were to be based on DRO's divisions and to be indirectly constituted from M.P.s of the district, the Chairmen of local authorities in the district and nominees of the Minister representing special interests.[23]

Acting through the Government Agent as Commissioner, and under the direction of the appropriate Minister, the Councils were to have powers over agriculture and food, animal husbandry, industries and fisheries, rural development, works, housing and regional planning, education, cultural affairs, ayurvedic medicine, social welfare and health services. This would have made them potentially powerful bodies. The fear that they could provide a base for quasi-federalism in Tamil areas and the strong support for them given by the Federal Party, led to a major political crisis and their abandonment by the government in an atmosphere which made it extremely unlikely that such a reform would be adopted in the foreseeable future.

The problems referred to by the Donoughmore Commissioners forty years before and by Bandaranaike thirty years before, had become even more acute by the accession of Mrs. Bandaranaike's second government in 1970. Local Village Councils were still weak and corrupt, the Government Agents' staffs were still remote and increasingly overworked and the decisions were still highly centralised at the *kachcheri* or the Colombo Secretariat. A Government Agent was quoted in 1971 as arguing that "regional development cannot be really effective if it is tied down to the existing framework of government departments working along vertical lines of authority with funds allocated to the heads of departments in Colombo."[24] The system was criticised as thwarting initiative and as inhibiting "the co-ordination of departmental plans at the local level and (preventing) the local establishment of budgetary priorities in expenditure." The ILO team, which made these observations, advocated devolution to a reformed local government system. The problem remained either of devolving to authorities which were incompetent to manage significant affairs, or to create divisional councils on a basis rejected by Sinhalese politicians for fear of giving power to the Tamils of the Northern and Eastern Province.[25] The government was thinking along alternative lines of using local initiative to give citizens a feeling of participation in government without giving them any administrative power. They instituted People's Committees, on the basis of the smallest unit of all, the wards of local authorities. The implemented proposals of 1970[26] specifically rejected the larger divisions as too extensive. The People's

S

Committees were to be advisory and supervisory only. They were to be institutionalised pressure groups, representing local citizens to authority, dealing with the bureaucracy, reporting on abuses by the police or other public officers and inspecting retail or wholesale traders for price excesses.[27] The Minister for Home Affairs, despite criticisms from the LSSP who wanted elected bodies, ensured that the People's Committees would be nominated in such a way as to preserve the power of the local M.P.s, whose functions they supplemented.[28] They were thus not designed, like existing Divisional Development Councils, to administer economic development. The intention was to assist the local politicians, to criticise government servants and to draw prominent villagers into a more active and less deferential relationship to government than either the parliamentary or the administrative system made possible.

At the national level the administration was also increasingly criticised for its ineffectiveness in dealing with the expanded role of government and for its isolation from the general public. The conventional relationship between Ministers and Permanent Secretaries was as fraught with difficulties as in Britain. Ministers had nothing like the experience in departmental affairs possessed by their full-time officials.[29] Every government had a large 'tail' of Ministers included to satisfy minor parties or communities, or to fulfil political or family obligations. While the great bulk of Ministers came from the Anglicised élite and were thus on a social and educational level comparable to their civil servants, the trend towards *swabasha* educated rural politicians raised the question of their competence to deal with men so socially and educationally 'superior' to themselves. On the Left there remained a suspicion that civil servants who had been educated by the British and in many cases recruited by them, were not sufficiently adaptable to the new policies demanded by nationalist and socialist politicians. The large non-Buddhist and non-Sinhalese element in the Ceylon Administrative Service was also suspect to Sinhalese revivalists. The removal of the protection of the Public Service Commission in the new Sri Lanka constitution was the logical outcome of such suspicions. It remained true, as in India, that the professional career bureaucracy provided a highly competent cadre of public servants not only in the Ministries but also in the public corporations, where management talent was severely limited. The main charge against such a cadre was not that it was incompetent and corrupt, but rather that it was socially exclusive, too highly paid and too conservative. Indeed, for all the cries of corruption which went up at election time, there was never any suggestion that this applied to Ceylon Administrative Service members. Rather it was the politicians, local councillors, local policemen and clerical grades who were most frequently found to be corrupt in the rather strict sense in which this crime was defined by colonial statutes.

The social isolation and alien culture of the top bureaucracy was most frequently stressed in partisan argument. There was also a developing feeling that the colonial structure was no longer suitable for the increased functions laid upon it. The independent state inherited basic welfare provisions which involved the creation of a free education system from primary school to university, the rationed and subsidised distribution of food and the maintenance of clinics and hospitals within the free health system. The wartime administration which had dealt with these developments as well as with general rationing and defence, had been bureaucratically co-ordinated by one man, Sir Oliver Goonetilleke, acting under a British Governor and in consultation with the elected State Council. After independence, despite the powers concentrated in the office of Prime Minister, such a highly centralised administration was no longer possible, even if it were desirable. Ministries developed their own identities and interests and, as in Britain, the Minister often became the voice of his officials in the Cabinet, rather than the voice of the Cabinet in his Ministry. Suggestions for administrative reform were made in 1966[30] which would have made the newly created Ministry of Planning and Employment a central agency for controlling the relevant Ministries. These remained supervised through the British practice of 'Treasury control' which made the competent and financially prudent conduct of their affairs a more important priority than innovation. Prime Ministerial control over the Ministry of Planning, and the existence of a Cabinet Planning Committee, helped to give the administrative structure some coherent leadership. However the various plans adopted by governments were not effectively carried out. The ILO team in 1971, argued strongly for more highly trained staff to be recruited into the service and for an economic model to be built for the guidance of future planners.[31] A more searching criticism might have focused on the primitive conditions of most government offices, on the paper-bound formalism bequeathed by the British, on the reluctance of governments to continue the policies of their predecessors and on the parochial and partisan preoccupations of many Cabinet members which forced them to discuss the results of public examinations when unemployment was increasing daily and revolutionary frustrations were building up hourly.

The Patronage System

In the British constitutional tradition patronage had been officially frowned upon since the Civil Service and Army reforms of the nineteenth century. In the colonial service a form of patronage continued to exist. Many positions in the colonies were reserved for United Kingdom nationals both in commerce and the Civil Service. Only after the 'March resolution' of the State Council on 1 March 1933 did public service appointments come completely under the control of Ceylonese, enabling them to replace British policy-making administrators almost completely by independence.[32] The principle of 'communal patronage', that is the filling of vacancies in accordance with *de facto* communal quotas, became central to politics precisely because the British, like the Dutch before them, had given preference to themselves, to Burghers, Christians and Ceylon Tamils in public service appointments. Many of the nationalisation and licensing measures adopted after 1956 owe their origins not simply to socialist theory but also to the need to Ceylonise control of the economy which had fallen largely into European and Indian hands during the colonial period. Parliament, since 1931, has been predominantly Sinhalese and Buddhist, and the principle of communal patronage came to be applied in the public service, the armed forces and police, business and commerce, education and even manual employment.

Three major forms of patronage exist, all of them sanctioned by public attitudes. These are communal patronage, partisan patronage and nepotism. Caste preference, while it exists, is less favoured and even nepotism is seldom acknowledged as desirable though accepted as a natural result of traditional family obligations. The British constitution makers were anxious to avoid all these forms and set up several institutions designed to limit patronage. The most important of these were the Public Service Commission, the Local Government Service Commission and the Judicial Service Commission. Sections 56 and 62 of the Soulbury Constitution specifically protected the Public Service and Judicial Service Commissions from interference with their functions, which included recruitment to the appropriate service. Despite this both services came to mirror the communal composition of the population. Of the ten Puisne Judges in 1968, seven were Sinhalese, one a Tamil and one a Burgher. Of the Permanent Secretaries of Departments sixteen were Sinhalese, three Tamil and one a Muslim.[33]

The principal agents in urging communal patronage in the public services were the militant, modernising Buddhists associated with the All-Ceylon Buddhist Congress, particularly L. H. Mettananda and N. Q. Dias. The former prepared figures of public service membership in association with the campaign for the Buddhist Commission Report. The latter, who was Permanent Secretary of the Ministry of Defence and an active member of the SLFP, was president of the Congress of Government and Local Government Services Buddhist Associations, one of the main aims of which was to increase the number of Buddhists in the public service. That this was necessary was emphasised by the National Education Commission of 1961. Its report showed that of 3,299 Civil List Officers 1,331 (40.5%) were Buddhists, 732 (22.4%) Hindus, 523 (16%) Catholics and 529 (16%) Protestants.[34] This reflected the extent to which Christians had been favoured under colonialism. One of the major incentives behind the Official Language policy was precisely to reverse this bias in favour of English-speaking Christians and Tamils, by making public service entry and continued membership dependent on proficiency in the language of the majority. In contrast to Malaysia, no formal communal quotas were adopted.

Partisan patronage was scarcely an issue before independence in the absence of effective parties. As early as 1942 Sir D. B. Jayatillaka, a founder of the Ceylon National Congress, was

made Ceylon Government Representative in India on his retirement as leader of the State Council. Another State Council
Minister, A. Mahadeva, a founder and vice-president of the
UNP, was similarly made High Commissioner in India after
his electoral defeat in 1947. It was thus early established, as in
many other countries, that ambassadorships were a major
method of rewarding politicians. Among leading parliamentarians so rewarded have been Sir Oliver Goonetilleke, A. E.
Goonesinha, T. B. Subasinghe, Robert Gunawardena, Sir Lalita
Rajapakse, Sam C. P. Fernando, Stanley de Zoysa and J. C. T.
Kotelawala. R. S. Gunawardena, a Minister in D. S. Senanayake's
first Cabinet, became the first permanent representative at the
United Nations when Ceylon was admitted in 1955. A substantial part of Ceylon's overseas representation, including that
in the most important posts, conventionally became an area of
partisan patronage.[35]

A second area for rewarding politicians was opened up by the
growth of public corporations after 1956. With a very limited
entrepreneurial class of Sinhalese it was natural, again as in
many other countries, to fill the leading positions with partisans.
The past master in this art was Philip Gunawardena, both in
the Bandaranaike and Dudley Senanayake governments. In
1967 a member complained at the UNP Youth League sessions
that "Mr. Gunawardena has solved the unemployment problem
of all the defeated candidates of the MEP in nominating public
corporation executives."[36] The UNP had also rewarded its
other small party ally, the Jathika Vimukthi Peramuna, by
appointing its leader K. M. P. Rajaratna as chairman of the
Fisheries Corporation. Another of its appointments, A. W. A.
Abeygoonesekera, chairman of the Port (Cargo) Corporation,
offended against the conventional non-partisan role of public
servants by openly campaigning as a UNP prospective candidate
while retaining his appointment, although he later resigned his
office.

By the 1960s Ceylon was developing something not unlike the
American spoils system, despite the restrictive nature of British-
inherited conventions and forms. In 1970 Mrs. Bandaranaike
immediately made a series of patronage appointments. Two
editors of party journals, Susil Moonesinghe and Hector
Abhayawardhana, became chairmen of the Ceylon Broadcast-

ing Corporation and the Peoples Bank, R. L. Obeyesekera, secretary of the SLFP trade unions, became chairman of the Co-operative Wholesale Establishment, and Anil Moonesinghe, an LSSP Minister in 1964, became chairman of the Ceylon Transport Board. Mrs. Bandaranaike also extended patronage into the public service by appointing two university teachers, Professor H. A. de S. Gunasekera (SLFP) and ex-Senator Doric de Souza (LSSP), as permanent secretaries at the Ministries of Planning and Plantations.[37] Her daughter, Sunethra Rupasinghe, was made her private political secretary and became a major influence on the administration.

Apart from this patronage for political supporters, partisan influence has spread further down the public service and, to a limited degree, into the police and army. The coups of 1962 and 1966 gave the SLFP and UNP governments respectively an opportunity to deal with those in the forces they suspected of plotting against them. The largely Catholic, Burgher and presumably UNP group around the de Mel family in the army and navy and those in the police associated with the de Zoysas were replaced, tried and temporarily imprisoned. In 1966 the UNP, in connection with the events of January, suspended Deputy Inspector-General I. van Twest, whom the SLFP had promoted in 1962, and arrested Mrs. Bandaranaike's relative Major-General Richard Udugama, who had become commander of the army following the 1962 coup. It also rewarded ex-Assistant Superintendent of Police Lionel Goonetilleke, who had been arrested in 1962, by making him an official of the State Petroleum Corporation. These changes in the forces are obviously of great potential importance when serious crises arise. As well as being largely partisan, the changes of 1962 effectively ended Catholic predominance, extending the principle of communal patronages to the last major Christian stronghold.

As one quarter of non-agricultural employment is in government or public agencies, the potential for patronage could extend over four hundred thousand jobs. While some Ministers may have aspired in this direction there are many regulations which make a pure spoils system impossible. It is still possible for many new appointments to be made on a patronage basis, and for transfers and promotions within the service to be affected by partisan or nepotistic considerations. School-

teachers, as the largest single group of State employees, and
one most likely to breach public service regulations by being
active in politics, have suffered the most, to the extent that
"punitive dismissals and transfers for alleged political activity
have broken the back of the profession."[38] I. M. R. A.
Iriyagolle, Minister of Education from 1965 to 1970, made
himself particularly unpopular by his partisan interference in
education and by the creation of the National Council for
Higher Education which showed signs of extending this policy
into the Universities.[39]

This widespread use of patronage, which had already become
marked before independence, is natural in a system where unemployment is rife and government service highly prestigious.
Social and cultural factors come into direct collision with
constitutional provision and public service regulations designed
to preserve the efficiency of government and the security of its
employees. As the parties have built mass machines they have
naturally extended their patronage. Much of the discontent
expressed by UNP Youth Leaguers against Ministers in the
late 1960s was based on their apparent reluctance to give party
supporters a virtual monopoly on new appointments.[40] The
spread of patronage naturally induced those in the service to
work for the party in office. As early as 1954, the SLFP candi-
cate in the Kandy by-election, who had been a Divisional
Revenue Officer, complained that "Ministers brought pressure
on me and the Village Headmen working under me to actively
work for the UNP during previous elections."[41] Active unionists
engaged in political strikes contrary to regulations, have
suffered likewise. Two presidents of the Government Clerical
Service Union, T. B. Ilangaratne and I. J. Wickrema, were
suspended from the service for their respective parts in the
strikes of 1947 and 1966. Pressure, transfers and victimisation
became an almost inevitable result of partisan patronage. As
Mrs. Mallika Ratwatte M.P. was reported as saying: "Some
government servants are hand in glove with the UNP and are
working against others who are not UNPers. Note them well
even if they are transferred from your areas. We know how to
deal with them. Taking revenge is evil but we have to do it as
the UNP has taught us to take revenge."[42] In this atmosphere
the officially desired norm of a neutral public service seems hard

to sustain.[43] Whether it will become even more difficult after the long-awaited extension of political rights to public servants, first promised by Bandaranaike in 1956 and legislated for in 1972, remains to be seen.

"Peace, Order and Good Government"

The Soulbury constitution, in standard British terminology, gave Parliament "power to make laws for the peace, order and good government of the Island."[44] While the concrete content of these terms is never spelled out, it is possible to judge the performance of the Ceylon political system against some common sense concept of their meanings. The system was specifically designed to preserve law and order and to set up standards of fair, rational and responsive government. Before the British departed they promulgated public security and bribery and corruption ordinances and drew up defence agreements with the new government.[45] These latter fell into disuse by mutual agreement with Bandaranaike in 1957, when the British airmen and sailors left Katunayake and Trincomalee never to return. The security and bribery ordinances remained, together with institutional devices and judicial traditions designed to prevent patronage, arbitrary government, the suspension of elected institutions and to ensure the periodic answerability of the government to the people. If peace means the absence of involvement in warfare or freedom from invasion, then there need be no further discussion of the ability of the Ceylon system to achieve such an objective. Ceylon had never engaged in foreign warfare, had never been invaded and, after 1957, had only once had foreign troops on its soil when Indian airmen guarded the international airport during the JVP rising at the request of the Ceylon government. Ceylon's geographical location had protected it from the warfare which has plagued northern India or Southeast Asia. The Ceylonese armed forces were kept at a level necessary to control illegal immigration, fishing rights and smuggling. It had no treaty commitments after 1957 obliging it to send troops anywhere or to join with any other nation in military activity. At the United Nations Ceylon became fully identified with neutralism, with the creation of a nuclear-free Indian Ocean and with all disarmament proposals.

Because it rested in the shadow of the overwhelming but friendly military power of India, Ceylon felt no need to maintain armed forces effective for international warfare. As it had no alliances it was under no pressure to rearm against real or imagined threats. As an island it was not subjected to border intrusions. Indeed, one of the basic weaknesses of the JVP in 1971 was that it had no immune geographical bases to retire to and no military support. Its equipment had to be gathered exclusively within an island in which the major supplies of weapons lay in the hands of the police, the armed forces, farmers and criminals. The general attack on police stations, while it has aspects of ideological mobilisation, was tactically designed to lay hands on the supplies of weapons kept in police armouries. No similar attack was successfully launched against the much better protected military establishments. Raids on individual farmers and relationships with smugglers were equally designed to get hold of weapons. Bank robberies had as an objective the purchase of dynamite and, through smugglers and international connections, to buy from the vast stock of weapons built up in the Middle East but hitherto completely inaccessible from Ceylon. Neither potential revolutionaries, nor the forces against which they fought, had any substantial access to modern weapons of war. Neither side had any experience of guerilla warfare, nor of armed resistance to authority of any kind.

The military forces in Ceylon had, however, built up many years of experience in dealing with civil disorders. Under the public security ordinance designed by the British they were able to take over police functions from an increasingly demoralised and ineffectual police force.[46] Major functions of the Navy, the prevention of illegal immigation and smuggling, were partly related to social control in the domestic field. Navy units were also used in the temporary exchanges of population between Jaffna and Colombo during the race riots of 1958. The very small air force had related functions, particularly where rapid mobility was required. Inevitably the army, as the largest of the three, took the major part in police functions. It was used against narcotics growers in 'Operation Ganja', against race rioters in 1956 and 1958, in occupying the Northern and Eastern Provinces during the Federal Party *satyagraha* of

1961, to control the demonstrations of January 1966 and finally, and most spectacularly, against the JVP in 1971 and in the maintenance of the curfews which lasted in some areas until the end of that year. Army and Navy personnel were deputed to guard the houses and persons of ministers as well as foreign embassies. The operation of emergency regulations was delegated to regional army commanders during 1971, giving them control over marches and demonstrations. This further strengthened their already existing powers of helping the police to control illegal movements of goods under the rice and sugar rationing schemes. In 1971 the army became the professional core of resistance to revolution. The air force had bombed the Thulhiriya textile factory and, with foreign supplied helicopters, was able to make reconnaissance sorties. The navy was able to ensure that smuggled arms did not enter the country, assuming that any had been despatched which seems unlikely. It was the army, particularly under the command of Lt. Col. Cyril Ranatunge in the Kegalle area, which worked steadily through jungle areas, both by shelling and on foot, and was responsible for the isolation of pockets of rebels in remote jungle.

The substantial and growing involvement of the army in civilian and insurgent control did not necessarily mean that Ceylon was moving towards a military dictatorship. Until 1971 all the security forces together, police, army, air force, navy and customs officers, numbered less than 21,000, the police providing the largest element.[47] This force was so inadequately armed that even the hand bombs, old rifles and choppers of the JVP were enough to force evacuation of police stations over large areas of the countryside. The budget of the defence forces had been kept to a minimum which made Ceylon one of the most lightly armed states in the world. Being outside the alliance systems it required and received no significant military aid. There were no special security forces equivalent to the French CRS or the American National Guard. In the British tradition, the ordinary police force supplied, through specially created units like the Insurgency Squad or the Special Branch, all that was thought necessary in the way of controlling or penetrating subversive forces. In the light of general Marxist hosility to the police extending back many years, it was very difficult to gain political acceptance for any police interference in radical

political activities. Under Sir John Kotelawala there had been
growing suspicions of his 'fascist' intent and in the reaction
against this after 1958 the police were discouraged from
developing any para-military or counter-intelligence units. The
police were also ineffective when faced with massive civil disorder
or insurrection, because their prestige in the general community
was very low. Their relationship with the public had been
destroyed by years of bribery, intimidation and arrogance,
particularly in rural areas. Several politically explosive cases of
death while in police captivity had erupted since the early
1960s.[48] Not only were the police poorly armed and equipped
but they did not enjoy sufficient confidence to be able to gain
public co-operation in 1971.

On the occasions of maximum public disorder there was a
vacuum in the preservation of law and order which had to be
filled either by the armed forces or by civilian volunteers. In
1958, in 1966 and in 1971 there were instances of conflict between
the police and the forces, with the army normally emerging
supreme. The army professionals had little confidence in the
efficiency of the police, and there were lower rank rivalries
which occasionally led to pitched battles. Public hostility against
the police in the aftermath of April, 1971 was such that the
military tended to take over normal police functions, including
the arrest of suspects.[49] Nor were attempts to form civilian
brigades any more successful. The Land Army, formed by the
UNP government of 1965 and not specifically engaged in
policing functions, was immediately wound up by Mrs.
Bandaranaike in 1970. There was suspicion that, like the earlier
Pioneering Corps of Sir John Kotelawala, it might become a
para-military wing of the United National Party. The volunteer
squads created to deal with the JVP in 1971 were also very carefully watched by the relevant minister, Felix Dias Bandaranaike,
for fear that they might assume the same role for the Marxist
parties and unions which had been most active in recruiting
them. A particular feature of these brigades was the imposition
of a lower age limit of thirty-five to protect them against JVP
infiltration. The role of the public in assisting authority was
never placed on a permanently organised basis. The parties did
not realise their occasionally declared intent of transforming
their youth leagues into semi-military units.[50] No-one in

authority wanted powerful groups which might challenge the police and even the army. The answer to broadening responsibility for maintaining 'good government' was seen to lie rather in the People's Committees. As Senator Reggie Perera of the SLFP said: "The People's Committees will be given wide powers to deal with smuggling, illicit immigration, corruption and waste, but that does not mean they will be used unless in exceptional circumstances." Even this was going too far for the former UNP Minister of Justice, Senator A. F. Wijemanne. He warned of "grave complications in a situation where about 100,000 untrained and ill-disciplined persons were let loose on the community probing into their every day affairs."[51]

The difficulty of maintaining discipline within the police and the armed forces, and the danger of civilian volunteers behaving in an even worse manner, is a major problem in maintaining order in a political system where the use of passive resistance, mass rallies, marches and strikes had become a routine feature of political life. The Ceylon state, through its police, security forces and courts, normally behaved in a liberal manner. The one 'political execution', of the monk Somarama, was legally for the civil offence of murder. Until 1971 no one who had been charged with conspiring against the state, whether in 1958, 1959, 1961, 1962 or 1966, had suffered more than several years of imprisonment while awaiting trial or, by most standards, relatively short terms on conviction.[52] While the leader of the Janatha VP, Rohan Wijeweera, was sentenced to fifteen years by the Criminal Justice Commission in 1974, most defendants were given relatively light terms, and Wijeweera discharged or was freed in 1977. Deaths arising from *hartals* and demonstrations were so rare that the clerk Kandasamy, the eleven victims of 1953 and the monk Nandasara who was shot during the 8 January, 1966 march, all became heroes of the Left. Yet during the period between 1956 and 1972 several thousands died in civil disorders, their numbers uncounted and the responsibility of the police and army either discounted or overlooked. In race riots in 1956 one hundred and fifty people died, mainly in the colonisation schemes around Gal Oya. In 1958 "the death toll mounted into the hundreds. Thousands of Tamils were evacuated to the North and Sinhalese to the South."[53] Finally, in 1971 the government estimated that 1,200 had been killed, including 60 members of the security forces.[54] A total of 16,000 were interned and there was widespread feeling that at least five thousand had actually died. Although a small number of atrocity cases were tried in the courts, there was a general feeling in 1971 that the army, and more particularly the police, had taken the opportunity to kill many young people against whom no concrete evidence might have been gathered. On all three occasions it was evident that the maintenance of order and discipline had collapsed and that only military rule, censorship, curfew and mass arrest could deal with the problem. Far from being a repressive state, Ceylon was on three major occasions unable to prevent breakdowns. Despite the powers granted to the Governor-General in 1958, the creation of a joint all services Security Council since 1965 and the setting up of the police Insurgency Unit in 1970, riot and revolution reached the stage where the poorly armed and disciplined police were almost swept aside. The centralised discipline of the army, itself small and badly armed, was enough to restore order in a relatively short time.

Ceylon was not, then, a 'broken-backed state' in the manner of Burma or Indonesia.[55] The collapse of social control was not endemic but spasmodic and relatively quickly restrained. During such collapse many hundreds died, often at the hands of other civilians. The primary function of the police remained what it had been during colonial days, the control of theft, riot and murder and the general prevention of crime. It was not equipped to take on the overtly political role of social control. This remained in normal times in the hands of the bureaucracy, who proved quite capable of registering every citizen for voting, of enrolling the great majority of children into school, of checking and distributing rationed rice and other commodities, of registering applicants for work, of issuing licences, supervising land claims, providing medical attention, public transport, roads, lighting and basic municipal services. Not only was the Ceylon state not 'broken-backed' or repressive. It was managed with an efficiency rare in Asia and came into everyday contact with the citizens not as a policing agency but as a provider of goods, services and facilities. As the only effective welfare state in Asia it was particularly important that Ceylon should be run with efficiency, without corruption and with due regard to the wishes and interests of its citizens. The periodic breakdown of order and the need to resort to military control under emergency regulations is the most important single indicator that this sometimes proved to be impossible. The regular but unsubstantiated charges of corruption which were commonplace in politics, the equally regular amnesties for tax evaders, the widespread currency black-market and the prevalence of smuggling all suggest the inability of the state to cope with activities which undermined its general objectives. Without effective collection of taxes and duties, welfare provisions could not be financed. Without control over currency speculation and smuggling the balance of payments and international indebtedness became worse. Without the public exposure of corruption and bribery public faith in civilian institutions became progressively undermined to the point where citizens might be no more ready to defend them than to co-operate with the police.

It is very difficult in Sri Lanka, as everywhere else, to measure and evaluate the extent and the impact of illegal activities.[56] While the suspension of Village Councils and municipalities for corruption and incompetence is quite common and fully recorded, prosecutions for bribery, smuggling or tax evasion were relatively rare and always liable to be frustrated within a legal system which gave advantages to defendants with substantial incomes. Given the widespread family obligations which exist many such cases never come to the public gaze. Whole communities, particularly among the Muslims or Ceylon Tamils, are said to live from smuggling or black-marketing in gems, yet their communal solidarity is such that action can rarely be taken against them. The continued hold of Indian businessmen over trading functions nominally denied to them by law suggests the inefficacy of formal legal regulation directed against tightly-knit, rich minorities. Major acts of parliament, including the Paddy Lands Act of 1958, were rendered partly inoperative by the inability of authority to secure full co-operation from affected interests. The whole weakness of 'socialism through legislation' in Ceylon was precisely that the wealthy and property-owning minority had sufficient political and social power to evade laws which had, in any case, contained escape clauses. Overworked and possibly corrupt Customs clerks, police or taxation inspectors lacked the political power to bring many cases to a successful conclusion. Institutions which were designed for a self-limiting colony with a healthy overseas trade balance and a duty to protect expatriate business interests, transferred uneasily into the service of a nation-state with rapidly mounting foreign debts and with a greatly expanded social and economic role. Legal and political traditions grounded in classic British liberalism tended to inhibit effective state action and to protect the evaders of laws designed to shift the social balance towards the indigenous majority.

There was thus a contradiction between notions of 'good government' based on the protection of individual and property rights, and the democratic socialist ideas which came to form the basis of the political consensus. There was declining acceptance of ideas of individual and group rights which stressed the protection of minorities rather than the assertion of the majority. The concept of 'entrepreneurship', urged on Sri Lanka by the World Bank and international agencies and missions, ran up against the reality that some of the most enterprising businessmen were actively engaged in flouting exchange and taxation controls which the same agencies held to be essential. Most importantly the regular use of charges of corruption as part of the language of politics, reinforced popular experiences in dealing with clerks or policemen. This situation might have continued indefinitely, slowly eroding faith in institutions and ideals, undermining the economy, but not actually destroying the ability of the system to carry out its policing and welfare functions. The system was legitimised more in terms of its responsiveness through elections than its operating efficiency, failings in which were noticeable to the national administrators and to the general public. The events of 1971 showed that smuggling could be used to import arms, that bank robberies were relatively simple in poorly policed villages, that popular discontent allowed thousands of youths to organise and train for months in well-populated rural areas, that poor intelligence allowed plots to flourish, that cynicism at the failure to implement electoral promises was widespread, that the education system was deficient, the economy lagging behind population growth and the informal social control of traditional village life no longer very effective.

The government newly elected in 1970 was already conscious

of the major weaknesses in the system, and the difficulty of effectively using the existing machinery either to control social conflict, or to secure adherence to laws, efficient and honest administration or the creation of new practices which would allow the transfer of property from private individuals to the state. The government continued the policies of its predecessors in limiting private enterprise in retailing and wholesaling by expanding co-operative facilities, by channelling paddy sales through the Paddy Purchasing Board and by setting up a State Gem Corporation which could control one of the major avenues through which illegal foreign exchange deals were made. Through the Business Acquisition Act it was enabled to take over any concern which, in the view of the government, was run inefficiently or dishonestly. One of the first nationalisations was of the graphite mining industry in which the Senanayakes and Kotelawalas had made their fortunes. The government was further empowered to take over plantations on a similar basis, and began acquiring a substantial interest in tea estates for the first time although without attacking the major holdings of expatriate companies until 1975. By nationalising the agency houses in the export trade the government hoped to gain further control over the major element in the foreign exchange balance. From 1 April, 1972 a ceiling of Rs.2,000 a month was placed on disposable incomes, the residue to become compulsory savings, thus forcing the rich to do what they had previously refused, to invest their funds in productive and government-approved industries. Finally, the imposition of a land reform ceiling promised to make possible what had been frustrated under the earlier Paddy Lands Act, the breaking up of large tenanted estates and the extension of ownership to greater numbers of peasants. None of these measures involved outright expropriation, however, not even the enforcing of public company status upon Associated Newspapers in 1973.[57] They were all designed to use the government's massive parliamentary majority to place it legally in a position where it could begin on the reallocation of resources which had so often been frustrated since 1956. It was hoped that, by the next elections of 1977, all such measures would be sufficiently entrenched and so manifestly successful as to make them irreversible even in the event of electoral defeat.

The government was thus concerned with the rapid creation of a new legislative and administrative framework within which its policies could more effectively be carried out. It was also conscious of the collapse of social control, and of the protection which the judicial system had so far extended not merely to subversive and even revolutionary political activity, but also to corrupt and illegal practices. Bandaranaike had argued in the past that the independence of the judiciary was "the last citadel of democracy."[58] It also functioned in an extremely complex, cautious and expensive manner which, in the light of the series of emergencies which began in 1971, made it seem an obstacle to effective government. Felix Dias Bandaranaike, after his experience with the coup trial of 1962, was not alone in believing that few if any of those arrested after the JVP rising were likely to be successfully prosecuted under the law as it stood. The rapid and almost public spread of smuggling and currency speculation raised the question of whether the courts were not protecting the interests of those who were busily undermining the economic system. Hence the highly controversial creation of the Criminal Justice Commission in 1971, which tried not merely the insurgents but also alleged speculators who included one of the country's leading businessmen, Bhagwandhas Hirdaramani.[59] In 1962 the SLFP had similarly tried to legislate through the Criminal Law (Special Provisions) Act No. 1 which altered the rules of evidence, created new crimes and penalties, was retrospective and specific to the 1962 coup, and allowed the Minister for Justice to nominate judges for a trial without jury. It was eventually condemned by the British Privy Council as "a legislative plan *ex post facto* to secure the conviction and enhance the punishment of those particular individuals."[60]

With the total collapse of previous legislation in mind, the new government was faced to an even greater degree with the probability that existing measures would not secure convictions either in the insurgency, the smuggling or any associated cases. With a potential of 5,000 insurgents liable to trial, the likelihood of indefinite delay became a certainty.[61] Even with the creation of the Criminal Justice Commission it took the state almost a full year to deploy its case against the forty-one defendants and final judgement was not made until two-and-a-half years after the trials began. The rules of evidence had been changed substantially along the lines desired in 1962. The members of the commission were appointed by the government and no jury was called, again as desired in 1962. Evidence from defendants who had become state's witnesses was not only called but they were allowed to cross-examine other defendants. The general charge of police intimidation was not held to invalidate statements made in custody. Despite all these changes, which applied equally in the parallel Hirdaramani case, the traditions of the legal profession were still such that professional defence was available, that cross-examination proceeded in public and that minute and time consuming questioning of police officers was a central feature of the early months of the trial. While it was undoubtedly the intention of the government to secure convictions which might not otherwise have resulted, it remains arguable whether the creation of the Criminal Justice Commissions marked the departure from judicial independence and impartiality which national and international critics claimed.[62] Rather the new institutions of law might be seen as complementing the new legislation allowing more effective state intervention. The SLFP had won its two-thirds majority and it took every opportunity not only to change the constitution itself, but to speed up all the rather conservative institutions and practices left behind by the British. These had proved quite viable for preserving the system, but a major obstacle to changing it. By 1971 the economic and social system was itself in such a dangerously volatile state that conservative institutions had become a positive barrier to preventing its erosion and overthrow.

NOTES

1. With the ending of the Village Headman system in 1961 all local officials were drawn from a professional service. The old titles ceased to be used after 1956 for public purposes.
2. See J. Jupp: "Constitutional Developments in Ceylon since Independence"; *Pacific Affairs* XLI: 2, Summer 1968.
3. (D. C. Wijewardena): *The Revolt in the Temple*; Colombo, 1953; p. 155.
4. *Ibid.* p. 150.
5. *Ibid.* p. 631.

6. *Ibid.* p. 595.
7. *Ibid.* p. 222.
8. *Ibid.* p. 629.
9. *Ibid.* p. 453.
10. *Ibid.* p. 434.
11. *Ibid.* p. 676.
12. S. W. R. D. Bandaranaike: *Speeches and Writings*; Colombo, 1963; p. 109.
13. *Ibid.* p. 110.
14. *Ibid.* p. 162.
15. S. W. R. D. Bandaranaike: *Towards a New Era*; Colombo, 1961; p. 138.
16. J. Jupp: *op. cit.* p. 172.
17. Tarzie Vittachi: *Emergency '58*; London, 1958; esp. pp. 68–72 and 75–78.
18. *Ceylon—Report of the Commission on Constitutional Reform*; Colombo, 1969 (reprint); pt. 58.
19. *ILO Report*; Geneva, 1971; p. 153.
20. *Constituent Assembly Official Report*; vol. 1, no. 23; 12/6/1971, col. 1586.
21. Ceylon (Constitution) Order in Council; s. 58.
22. S. W. R. D. Bandaranaike: *Towards a New Era*; Colombo, 1963; p. 251.
23. *Proposals for the Establishment of District Councils under the Direction and Control of the Central Government*; Colombo, 3/6/1968; s. 4.
24. *ILO Report*; p. 158.
25. *Ibid.*; p. 160—but they do not refer to the previous experience with District Councils.
26. *Proposals for the Establishment of People's Committees*; Colombo, 1970 and an interview with W. Lionel Fernando, secretary of the Janata Committees Department, in August, 1971.
27. *Ibid.*; pp. 5–6.
28. Felix Dias Bandaranaike, the Minister responsible, introducing his White Paper on the Janata Committees argued that 90,000 places would be available and would tend to be filled by supporters of the government, on the understanding that the next government would replace them. "People of standing in the village" would naturally tend to be chosen. *Ceylon Daily News* 29/11/1970.
29. Exceptions include C. P. de Silva who was previously an official of the Department of Lands, where he was Minister for thirteen years (Interview of August 24, 1969) and Maithripala Senanayake who spent seven years as a Cultivation Officer under a Ministry which he later headed.
30. See *Report of the Committee Appointed to Report on the Ceylon Administrative Services*: S.P. VI—1966; and *Report of the Committee on Administrative Reforms*; S.P. IX—1966.
31. ILO Report; p. 153.
32. The last British appointment to the Ceylon Civil Service was in 1937.

33. *Commonwealth Year Book*; London, 1970.
34. *Final Report of the National Education Commission*; S.P. VII—1961; p. 35.
35. In 1970 Mrs. Bandaranaike recalled all Ceylon's overseas representatives many of whom were UNP patronage appointments. Those of major importance retained by the new government included Shirley Amerasinghe, ambassador to the United Nations and later President of the General Assembly.
36. *Daily Mirror* (Colombo) 2/12/1967. Previously the World Bank had noted that "public enterprises and corporations are grossly overstaffed as a result of political patronage." IBRD: *The Foreign Exchange Problem of Ceylon*; Colombo, 1966.
37. These two appointments did not interfere directly with the principle of "permanence". Gunasekera replaced Gamini Corea, who returned to the Central Bank from which he was seconded in 1965 and later became Secretary-General of UNCTAD. De Souza's Ministry was a new creation.
38. J. E. Jayasuriya: *Education in Ceylon 1939–1968*; Colombo, 1969; p. 202.
39. Iriyagolle's intrusions into the University caused him to be successfully sued by Professor A. J. Wilson of Peradeniya for wrongful intervention in his promotion procedure. Wilson is the son-in-law of the Federal Party leader, S. J. V. Chelvanayakam.
40. *Times of Ceylon* 25/2/1969.
41. Piyasena Tennakoon; Election Address; Kandy, 1954.
42. *Ceylon Observer* 15/1/1969.
43. In 1964 N. M. Perera told Treasury officials that he was not interested in their politics provided they were loyal to his policies even when disagreeing with them. *Ceylon Daily News* 13/6/1964. However he seems to have changed his mind by 1970. See Chapter 9, fn. 86.
44. Ceylon (Constitution) Order in Council, s. 29 (1).
45. The defence agreements of 1947 were published by the British Government as Cmd. 7257 of 1947. See also the Public Security Ordinance (as amended in 1959) of 1947.
46. Tarzie Vittachi (in *Emergency '58*; pp. 105–117) reproduces a verbatim report of a police officers' meeting of June 13, 1958 to discuss police morale after the 1958 race riots. During the discussion an officer reported that "the men were just dispirited and that they had confidence neither in themselves nor in their officers." Five of the thirty-four present were later arrested in connection with the 1962 coup,
47. During the same period British security forces in Northern Ireland numbered 26,000 to deal with a much smaller area and population.
48. In 1973 a commission enquired into the deaths of L. V. P. Podi Appuhamy ("Dodampe Mudalali") and Corporal Tillekewardena, who died in custody after the 1966 coup attempt.
49. There were widespread rumours of mass executions and burials at some police stations, particularly at Hanwella, during April, 1971. The best publicised Army atrocity, the rape and murder of Premawathie

Manamperi at Kataragama, brought two sentences of sixteen years imprisonment. *Ceylon News* 7/6/1973.

50. Leaders and activists of the Marxist parties took to wearing military-styled uniforms, particularly during the United Left Front period of 1963. One of the major issues between the LSSP and the SLFP in 1975 was over the creation of LSSP para-military youth groups which were outlawed under emergency regulations in December 1974.

51. *Ceylon Daily News* 16/3/1971.

52. The two major conspirators in the 1959 assassination, Buddharakkitha and H. P. Jayawardena were sentenced, on appeal, to life imprisonment and Buddharakkitha died while in prison.

53. R. N. Kearney: *Communalism and Language in the Politics of Ceylon*; Durham, NC., 1967; p. 86.

54. Statement to Parliament by Mrs. Bandaranaike, 20/7/1971. For an extreme estimate of 50,000 dead see Lord Avebury: "An Island behind Bars": *Guardian* (London) 2/10/1971.

55. This phrase, used by Professor Hugh Tinker (in "Broken-backed States": *New Society* No. 70, pp. 6–7) describes a state which cannot effectively control its territory or administer its services, but which, nevertheless is not overthrown.

56. The terms 'bribery' and 'corruption' as used here imply illegal action punishable under the Bribery Act and involving the passage of money for services, appointments or other favours which should legally be provided as of right. This largely excludes patronage, nepotism or personal favouritism which are now so widespread as to constitute normal behaviour. A Bribery Commissioner, with a full-time staff, investigates illegality under the Bribery Act.

57. The nearest to direct expropriation was the imposition of a capital levy in 1973.

58. S. W. R. D. Bandaranaike: *Speeches and Writings*; Colombo, 1963; p. 163.

59. The investigations of the two Commissions were related in that attempts to find the sources of JVP funds led to discovery of major foreign currency offences involving Ceylonese businessmen, Yugoslav engineers and the North Korean embassy. Trials of alleged currency speculators eventually spread to include leading Sinhalese and in February 1976 the former Governor-General, Sir Oliver Goonetilleke, was sentenced to four years in his absence in England.

60. Liyanage v. The Queen (1965) 68 NLR at 284.

61. The average daily prison population in Ceylon was normally 5,500 but between 1971 and 1973 the number interned in special camps averaged between 14,000 and 16,000. The imprisoned proportion thus rose from ·045% (less than the United Kingdom) to ·16% (or approaching the United States).

62. In a debate on the Sri Lanka Republic Bill in the House of Lords on June 13, 1972, a former British Lord Chancellor, Lord Gardiner said that: "the rule of law as we understand it is being infringed in very many directions ... and the standards of justice are being reduced."

(*House of Lords Debs.* vol. 331, col. 777). Lord Avebury claimed that the Criminal Justice Commission Act contravened the United Nations Declaration of Human Rights, (*ibid.* 778) but Lord Brockway (cols. 779–81) believed that the Act was very similar to the Special Powers Act being used in Northern Ireland to intern suspects without trial. Lady Tweedsmuir, replying for the Government, asked Sri Lanka to take note of criticism of the Criminal Justice Commission. The Criminal Justice Commission was abolished by the UNP government in 1977.

CHAPTER 9

Reforming the Political System

One of the first major acts of Mrs. Bandaranaike's government in 1970 was to create a new Ministry of Constitutional Affairs and to declare the House of Representatives a constituent assembly for the purpose of drafting constitutional amendments. While this was not strictly the procedure envisaged by the Soulbury Commissioners, it was accepted unanimously by the House. The Soulbury Constitution stated that "Parliament may amend or repeal any of the provisions of this Order" on condition that "no Bill for the amendment or repeal of any of the provisions of this Order shall be presented for the Royal Assent unless it has endorsed on it a certificate under the hand of the Speaker that the number of votes cast in favour thereof in the House of Representatives amounted to not less than two-thirds of the whole number of members of the House (including those not present)."[1] As Mrs. Bandaranaike's Coalition had well over two-thirds of the seats in the Representatives she would have had little difficulty in making any changes even without the approval of the Opposition. Hers was the first government to be in such a position since Kotelawala's majority allowed him to pass the franchise amendments of 1954.

Nationalist Criticism

That constitutional reform was so important to a government facing major economic problems is a reflection of the legalistic obsessions and professional concerns of many Ceylonese politicians. It could be argued that the constitution had worked very successfully and that its replacement would not put one cent into the hands of a single peasant.[2] However, Bandaranaike himself, as well as the Marxists from a different angle, had been critics of the Soulbury constitution from its inception. He had played a leading role in securing the non-cooperation of the Board of Ministers with the commissioners in 1945. On seconding the resolution of November, 1945 accepting the Soulbury constitution with reservations, Bandaranaike spoke of "acquiescing" in a measure which seemed inadequate. On coming to office Bandaranaike had set up a Joint Select Committee on constitutional revision and outlined the major areas in which he felt amendment was necessary. These were: the establishing of a republic, the guaranteeing of fundamental rights, the position of the Senate and Appointed Members of the House of Representatives, and the Public Service Commission and the Judicial Service Commission.[3] These objectives reflected the experience of India which had both declared itself a republic and institutionalised individual rights in 1950. Bandaranaike had a standard and quite reasonable suspicion of upper houses and a sense of frustration at the safeguards against patronage and partisan influence in the administration and the judiciary. As with much of the discussion of the Constitution, legalistic and ritualistic attitudes were extremely important to Bandaranaike. In 1970 the reformers were still deeply concerned that Ceylon was not a republic, although its formal status as a 'realm beyond the sea' of Queen Elizabeth had made not the slightest difference to its internal politics in the intervening fourteen years, a fact tacitly recognised by governments of all parties when they took no action to implement their republican pledges.[4]

When the motion to reconvene the Select Committee was moved in November 1957, C. Suntheralingam had interrupted Bandaranaike with the claim that "they will labour and deliver a mouse".[5] The prime minister poured scorn on this but it was a very accurate prophecy. None of the objectives set by Bandaranaike was achieved and in the years between 1958 and 1962 constitutional government itself was in such grave danger that the luxury of verbal amendment became less attractive. Throughout its twenty-two years of operation up to the appointment of the Constituent Assembly, the constitution had been amended only rarely and inconsequentially. The three franchise amending Acts of 1954, which aimed at setting up a separate electoral roll for Indians, were never implemented and were subsequently repealed. The only important alteration was one naturally accepted by all parties, the extension of the size of the House of Representatives under the Ceylon Constitution (Amendment) Act of 1959. Even this left alone the rural bias in electorates which had always been contentious to the Left and did nothing to upset the communal balance of representation. The most important political changes in Ceylon, including the Sinhala Only legislation, the nationalisation measures, the Indian citizenship laws and the emergency provisions were all implemented without any constitutional amendments being needed. Parliamentary processes and judicial review were far more important than changing the document bequeathed by the British.

Nevertheless the fact that the document was so bequeathed made it suspect to many elements in local politics.[6] Initially the Marxists, as in other colonial situations, simply refused to believe that the British would genuinely give away their control over the political system, even while retaining their control over the economy. The generally accepted Marxist line today is that the British handed control to their "trusted lackeys" in the UNP. Even this transfer of authority was doubted into the early 1950's, mainly on the basis of the "secret" defence agreements which were found, after 1956, never to have been made. At the Unity Conference of June 4, 1950, which brought together the LSSP and the Bolshevik-Leninists, the party had declared its first transitional demand to be "cancellation of All Agreements made by the Ceylon bourgeoisie with the British Imperialists, which serve to maintain semi-colonial subjection. Withdrawal from the Commonwealth and the setting up of a Republic. Withdrawal of British armed forces."[7] On this analysis, parts of which Bandaranaike was later to accept and, indeed implement, it was the whole relationship with Britain which had to be abandoned and not simply the constitution.

Apart from the Marxists, the other elements criticising the constitution, and influencing the Bandaranaikes' resolve to change it, were Sinhalese Buddhist traditionalists who disliked modern institutions and particularly parties, Ceylon Tamils who saw in unitary government a device to take away their rights and privileges, and lawyers of many persuasions who were attracted by the idea of formalising political and civil rights. Discontent with the structure of government was also marked among those committed to long-term planning, which the creaking, annually accountable and paperbound machine left behind by the British was never meant to encompass. Reformers were concerned to end the village headman system, which was abolished in 1961, and the *kachcheri* system, centred on the district officers and their staff, which continued despite its general unpopularity. Critics of the political system have operated from varying motives and at the two levels of fairly abstract analysis of constitutional principles and more piece-meal administrative adjustments. What all have in common is their desire to "nationalise" alien institutions. Until 1970 at least, they were all equally incapable of doing so in any major respect.

Radical Criticism

The revolutionary movement in Ceylon was almost exclusively confined to those inheriting the Samasamajist tradition. Groups of Maoists and "Guevarists" began to appear among students in the late 1960's, recruiting those who had not previously been in any of the major Marxist parties. Their criticisms of parliamentary democracy do not differ in most respects from those common to such movements. But from its very foundation the LSSP was in a more ambivalent position. It attacked British colonialism but immediately returned two members to the State Council. The anomaly remained that even at the height of revolutionary fervour in the 1940's, the Marxists were led by parliamentarians or those who were to become parliamentarians. The tactic of running for elected office was never abandoned. Even the revolutionary breakaway from the LSSP in 1964 was led by two M.P.s, Edmund Samarakkody and Meryl Fernando, who presented themselves for electoral slaughter in 1965. Since then, it is true, neither the revolutionary Samasamajist splinters, the JVP, nor the Maoists have officially presented candidates. This probably reflects the lessons of 1965 when all such candidates lost their deposits.

The Marxist critique of institutions has operated on two levels. On one, the revolutionary, the whole idea of "bourgeois parliamentarianism" is rejected. On the other, constitutional and administrative adjustments are urged which scarcely differ from those also adopted by the SLFP. Many Marxists are prepared to subscribe to both positions at once, even if on paper they are incompatible. In the discussions leading up to the creation of the Constituent Assembly in 1970, many Samasamajists urged both the creation of a constitutional republic and the setting up of workers' and peasants' councils which would presumably supplement or even replace existing local government institutions.[8] This ambivalence was not, of course, confined to Ceylon and in the earlier days of the movement was justified by ample quotations from Lenin and Trotsky based on attitudes towards the Tsarist Dumas and the Russian Constituent Assembly of 1918.

When the Samasamajists reunited with the Bolshevik-Leninists in 1950, the two groups controlled eighteen M.P.s and could not, therefore, ignore the parliamentary arena. However, their first two "fundamental aims" were: "the overthrow of the Capitalist state maintained in Ceylon through the political alliance of the British Imperialists and the Ceylonese bourgeoisie" and "the seizure of political power by the working class at the head of the toiling masses and the establishment of a democratic Workers' and Peasants' (Soviet) Government— (i.e. the dictatorship of the proletariat supported by the urban and rural poor)."[9] This formulation was strengthened by the note that "the above fundamental aims cannot be realised through bourgeois parliaments. The inevitable resistance of the bourgeoisie to their achievement necessarily calls for mass revolutionary action as the only means of realising the will of the majority." The programme went on to declare that "as the struggle assumes revolutionary proportions the Party will agitate for the formation of SOVIETS, in order to draw the broadest masses of the toilers into the arena in an organised and democratic manner and to organise the proletariat as a class for its revolutionary tasks. Under revolutionary conditions the Party will agitate for the ARMING OF THE PROLETARIAT, the formation of WORKERS MILITIAS etc."[10]

All this followed naturally from Trotsky's theory of permanent revolution and a section of the programme was devoted to drawing a distinction between this position and the slogan of a Democratic Dictatorship of the Proletariat and the Peasantry, then being advanced by the Communist Party. The Communists were rather more willing to accept parliamentary institutions than the Trotskyists, having already deeply committed themselves to the Ceylon National Congress during the war. Apart from their brief lurch to the Left under Harry Abeygunawardena M.P., between 1948 and 1950, the Ceylon Communists have been markedly unrevolutionary by Asian standards. The Party's Fourth Congress, which put the moderate leadership of Keuneman and S. A. Wickremasinghe back into power, stressed that while "the working class is the most reliable force of the revolution and its leader" the "intelligentsia, the white-collar employees, professional men, small businessmen, petty traders, handicraftsmen etc." having also been exploited by imperialism and feudalism "will form part of the forces of the revolution."[11] By 1955, at its Fifth Congress, the Party was defending the democratic rights of the people against the "fascism" of Sir John Kotelawala and urging a united front to defeat him in the elections. In 1956 it recognised that "the electoral victory over the UNP and the formation of the new Government represent a significant shift in the balance of forces in Ceylon."[12] With the adoption of its 1960 Programme the Communist Party became, at least on paper, as deeply committed to parliamentary socialism as the SLFP and has been much more interested in foreign policy issues than in domestic constitutional reforms.

The Samasamajists, on the other hand, being a larger and more democratic party, continued to adhere at least partly to a revolutionary position and to allow such a position to be advocated at conferences even after the split of 1964. On returning to the LSSP in 1966 after a brief sojourn in the LSSP (Revolutionary) breakaway, V. Karalasingham claimed that "the place of all serious revolutionaries today is in the LSSP so that in participating fully in the task ahead they could intervene energetically when the inevitable class differentiation of the mass movement takes place."[13] Karalasingham's position was apparently endorsed by many delegates to the LSSP conference in 1969 when he was elected in third place to the Central Committee. The majority position of the Party by the late 1960's was far from that proclaimed in 1950. The Political Resolution for the 1969 LSSP conference attached primary importance to the forthcoming election campaign. It was still sufficiently radical in its outlook to adopt the "defensist" position once favoured by Kautsky and the German Social-Democrats. It argued that "while radical economic, administrative and political measures taken by the United Front Government will arouse the enthusiastic support of the people, it must not be forgotten on the other hand that those who stand to lose by such changes, both vested interests in the top bureaucracy as well as reactionary forces in the country, are likely to meet such changes with obstruction, sabotage, resistance of various kinds and, after some time, even with reactionary conspiracies aimed at overthrowing the state." The defence against this was to be "the awakened masses and their united strength."[14]

Essentially the LSSP position, for which they gained some support in the drafting of the Common Programme on which the 1970 election was won, combines this notion of "defence" against reaction, to protect a victorious Leftwing government, with a belief that the masses must be more actively engaged in the political process than is possible in an electoral situation alone. In the words of the 1969 resolution this meant "associating the people through committees of various kinds with the running of the administration and the economy."[15] Mrs. Bandaranaike's Speech from the Throne in 1970 endorsed the LSSP position to the extent of promising to "transform the administration thoroughly, make it more democratic and link it close with the people through (i) elected Employees' Councils; (ii) Advisory Committees in Government offices; and (iii) People's Committees on a territorial basis."[16] From the original commitment to a Soviet structure the LSSP had moved in twenty years to forms of popular participation owing more to liberal and social-democratic than to Leninist thinking. The SLFP was able to accept this position, seeming as it did to represent a final break with the authoritarian traditions and aloofness of the colonial administrative system. To some extent even the UNP had accepted this aim by continuing the practice of having workers' representatives on the boards of public corporations although it did not go as far in the direction of workers' control as was planned by the Samasamajist Minister for Communications, Anil Moonesinghe, shortly before the overthrow of Mrs. Bandaranaike in 1964.[17]

These shifts in the LSSP position, from aggressive revolution to defensism, and from a Soviet system to participation within a parliamentary framework, have naturally been rejected by the breakaway Trotskyist and Maoist groups which appeared in 1964. In an "open letter" to LSSP conference delegates in August, 1969, Bala Tampoe argued on behalf of the LSSP (Revolutionary) that "the futility of trying to fight the state bureaucracy within the framework of the capitalist administrative system was proved to the hilt under the Coalition Government.... We believe that even the most well-intentioned ideas of fighting bureaucracy, bribery and corruption, black-marketing etc., or any of the other inherent evils of the decaying capitalist system in Ceylon, will prove to be as completely futile as they proved to be under the Coalition Government of 1964."[18] Tampoe went on to argue that desirable though constitutional amendment through a Constituent Assembly may be, the Common Programme of the three Coalition parties simply aimed at preserving a form of state capitalism. He, too, adopted the standard Ceylon Marxist position of calling upon the masses to make strong demands through mass action but while using the word "revolutionary", his perspective remains that of the early 1950's, with no recourse suggested to guerilla warfare or armed rising.

Even the Maoists seemed very reluctant to urge such tactics. On his expulsion from the Maoist party for insisting on standing in the 1970 election, S. D. Bandaranaike claimed that its leader, Shanmugathasan's "only claim to be a revolutionary according to his own admission is that he has posed for photographs in China." S. D. Bandaranaike, who transferred his allegiance to the Janatha Vimukhthi Peramuna, disagreed with the tactic of total abstention from elections, an issue as old as the Marxist movement. He claimed that, while an M.P. he was "able to make use of Parliament as a platform and show the people of this country that the bourgois parliamentary process was a fraud."[19] S. D. Bandaranaike had always been very ambivalent about the parliamentary system of which he had been a part. In 1964 he publicly supported dictatorship on the grounds that "Ceylon was developed during the reign of the

Sinhalese kings because they governed the country on autocratic lines."[20] It was this general suspicion of democracy,
rather than any genuine conversion to Marxism, which seems
to have motivated his wanderings through several parties in the
previous decade. The JVP believed that "it was a lesson of
history that socialism was not possible *via* institutions set up by
the colonialists." They also claimed to be peaceful and propagandist and to be ready to support the United Front Government if it seemed to be making progress.[21]

Marxist and revolutionary criticism of the constitutional
system was thus either gradualist or marginally effective until
1971. The reforms proposed by Mrs. Bandaranaike were
entrusted to Colvin de Silva, a lifelong Samasamajist and a
critic of proposals to introduce Cabinet government even as
early as 1937.[22] His chief public servant was Doric de Souza,
who had written in 1961 that "if democracy has not hitherto
guided the nation to a basic stability, it is because this is
impossible to attain within the framework of the bourgeois
economy."[23] The electors have repudiated specifically revolutionary candidates since 1960, despite any previous support
they may have had as members of the established parties. It
seemed by 1970 much more likely that constitutional change
would be gradual and legal, if also radical, than that it would
be forced through by overtly revolutionary parties.

The Legal Critics

Marxists, Tamils and Buddhists all criticised the Soulbury
constitution from partisan and ideological positions. One of the
strongest influences had been from the legal profession which, in
Ceylon as elsewhere in democracies, was inordinately influential
upon practising politicians. The strict adherence to constitutional processes itself reflects the legal training of much of the
political élite. While Bandaranaike's approach was inspired to
some extent by radical and socialist ideas, it can be traced much
more directly to debates among lawyers and politicians which
had been going on since the early 1920's. The very origins of the
Ceylon National Congress itself were in a conference on
constitutional reform and, as with subsequent parties, many of
its leaders had legal training. Colvin de Silva, the Minister for

Constitutional Affairs was one of the Island's most distinguished barristers. Among the Marxists, Tamils and even Buddhists it was the legally trained élite which showed most interest in constitutional affairs, with the Federal Party in particular being wholly legalistic in its suggestions for change.

The most succinct and influential statement of the legal critics was the Sir James Peiris Centenary Lecture by J. A. L. Cooray, Lecturer in Constitutional Law in 1957, at the time of Bandaranaike's appointment of the select committee on reform. Cooray argued that the Constitution had arisen from debates in the British Parliament and could not, therefore, command the full respect of a document like the Irish or Indian Constitution, which had been drafted by bodies chosen from the independent nation itself. A locally drafted document approved by the entire people would make it more likely that "government will be carried on with proper regard to the spirit of the limitations or restrictions which have been imposed by the framers of the Constitution upon the powers of the government."[24] This echoes the criticism voiced by Bandaranaike in 1953 that the government had "chosen, in the main to follow the pattern of the previous Colonial regime. It is itself not adequately responsive or sensitive to public opinion; public servants have not yet learned to be servants of the public; pressing problems created by Colonialism, political, economic, social and cultural, far from being solved have worsened, and democracy itself runs a risk of being a label rather than a practice."[25] A major incentive to reform has simply been the very ease of transfer of power, with its concomitant of the survival of colonial practices, forms and words long after the British departure.

Cooray's doubts about the effective sovereignty of the Ceylon parliament were shared by most lawyers. While arguing that Ceylon was fully sovereign as an independentnation functioning in the world community, Professor C. F. Amerasinghe held later that "the Ceylon Parliament is, in fact, not sovereign in the same sense as the United Kingdom Parliament, because of express limitations contained in the Constitution, at any rate in regard to the extent of its powers."[26] These limitations he saw as centring around s.29, in particular those parts of it guaranteeing the rights of religious and racial minorities,[27] and on the separate establishment of the judicial power. While the first provision, although the only basic right guaranteed, seems to have been ineffectual, the principle of judicial separation from the executive and legislature has been much more consistently upheld, most notably by the Privy Council in its rejection of the procedures adopted in trying the 1962 coup conspirators.[28] It is clear from the debates surrounding the Soulbury Constitution and subsequent litigation, that the British intent was that sufficient checks upon the lower house should remain to prevent it from altering either the communal balance or the protected status of the judiciary and the higher bureaucracy. The imposition of the Senate by the British represented a further safeguard. Its membership was expected to be drawn very largely from the professional and most Anglicised classes. Strangely, in view of his general support for SLFP attitudes towards the constitution, J. A. L. Cooray was not ready to urge the total abolition of the Upper House in 1957. Cooray agreed that "there has been far too little of the careful and efficient scrutiny or the mature discussion of legislative measures that one expects of such a revising Chamber."[29] He goes on to subscribe to precisely the same notion of a 'non-party' upper house which the Soulbury commissioners found attractive, despite strong local opposition.[30]

Fears that the Ceylon legislature was not fully sovereign were based either on the proposition that Britain could still exercise final authority having granted the constitution in the first place, or that so many safeguards had been written into the Soulbury constitution that the parliament was unable to function as freely as its British counterpart. The first argument tended to lose its practical meaning after 1956, remaining largely a topic for debate amongst lawyers. The second remained fully valid and was even strengthened as SLFP governments found themselves frustrated in their dealings with the judiciary and the bureaucracy. Cooray was also concerned with the absence of fundamental rights in the constitution which, if justiciable, would have certainly made the parliament even less effectively sovereign than it was. Such rights, if written into the constitution, would only have been removeable by two-thirds of the legislature and could well, as Indian experience showed, prove a serious obstacle to effective government.[31] Cooray, like Bandaranaike, fully committed himself to following the Indian example, as it then stood, of justiciable fundamental rights and non-justiciable Directive Principles of Policy. When the constitution makers came to this issue in 1971 they were faced with a difficulty. Either they could incorporate fundamental rights, which would inhibit parliamentary power, or they could omit them or make them ineffectual, which would implicitly reject the basic case made by Cooray and Bandaranaike in 1957. They took the second course.

Cooray's argument rested largely on the need to protect minorities, which had also motivated the only specifically protective clause in the Soulbury constitution.[32] He believed that "democracy in a country where there are national, religious and other differences does not work quite satisfactorily."[33] The necessary rights must be enshrined in such a way that they "cannot in any event be restricted by any claims of uncontrolled power on the part of governments. Even the exercise of those rights can only be restricted by law, and that also only in the interests of justice or for purposes of public order or morality."[34] It was this proviso which was to allow the escape clause provided by s. 18 (2) of the Sri Lanka constitution.[35] It was obvious that Cooray had a more binding concept of entrenched rights than was subsequently adopted. He believed that such rights would give a new constitution a moral foundation which, with its basis in popular approval, would give it more lasting power than the document bequeathed by the British. He draws heavily upon the Indian constitution here, as also when discussing Directive Principles. The inclusion of these would mean that a new constitution would "command the respect and hence the obedience, of the people as their political covenant, besides being their supreme legal document."[36]

In his support for rights and principles, as with his criticism of the Senate and of the independent character of the Public Service Commission, Cooray drew upon the Indian Constitution and was an accurate predictor of the new constitution which was to be promulgated fifteen years later. To that extent he can share with Bandaranaike the title of "Father of the Constitution", a fact recognised to some extent by his appointment to the new Constitutional Court in 1972.[37] In some other respects his approach, as that of most established lawyers, was also more conservative than practising politicians found acceptable by 1972. He does not question the separation of powers in so far as it preserved the independence of the judiciary. Professor Amerasinghe, at a later date believed that "interference by the legislature with the judicial power would also be prohibited under the Constitution as a result of the presumption in favour of the separation of judicial power" which he held to have been fully established by case law.[38] The constitution of Sri Lanka was specifically to reject this view in holding that "the National State Assembly exercises (c) the judicial power of the People through courts and other institutions created by law."[39] In 1957 very few lawyers advocated such a merging of legislative and judicial power. It is particularly hard to see how such an assertion of the former over the latter could be made consistent with the entrenching of justiciable fundamental rights, in the defence of which the judiciary must necessarily stand separate from the executive and legislature. To that extent Cooray represents a legal tradition which was little less conservative than that of the Soulbury Commissioners and was certainly no more radical than the drafters of the Indian Constitution.

Cooray's approach was the dominant one among reforming lawyers, other than Samasamajists like Colvin R. de Silva, in whose hands the eventual framing of the new constitution rested. Even de Silva accepted many of Cooray's arguments and there is much more of Cooray's and Bandaranaike's thinking verbally incorporated in the text of 1972 than there is of LSSP lawyers. The fundamental change between 1957 and 1972 was that the SLFP and LSSP had both had years of government experience. They were not prepared as politicians to tolerate obstacles and institutions for which they might have argued as lawyers. They were not anxious to preserve judicial independence to the point which Privy Council decisions had brought it, a point arguably closer to the American than the British tradition in the sense that acts of government could be overturned in the courts. Nor could they have the same enthusiasm for civil rights couched in individual liberal terminology which many cases in India and the United States had shown to be obstructive to state economic intervention. The document which eventually emerged, though much of it may have been predicted from Cooray's lecture alone, was not going to replace the institutional restrictions of the Soulbury constitution by legalistic barriers. Such concessions as were made to legal opinion were to be the result of hard fought political battles.

The Constitution of Sri Lanka

Despite the labours of the Constituent Assembly and the Ministry for Constitutional Affairs, nearly one-fifth of the Constitution of Sri Lanka was taken verbatim or in substantially similar form, from the Ceylon (Constitution) Order in Council of 1946. Virtually the whole of the provisions relating to electoral delimitation and to the control of finance were copied directly from the British statute.[40] Several major institutions of British origin remained the same or had their powers enhanced. Sri Lanka retained a parliamentary system, governed by a collective executive responsible to an elected house. The head of state was virtually powerless to act save on the advice of the Prime Minister. There was no return to the Donoughmore experiment of Ministerial Committees. Sri Lanka remained a unitary state, although more specifically so than Ceylon. Its judges and public servants were still career, rather than patronage, appointees, although the possibility of direct political interference in the judiciary and bureaucracy was substantially increased. In most significant respects Sri Lanka, like India which inspired parts of the new constitution, was still to be governed more closely in accord with the "Westminster model" than all but a handful of Commonwealth states. Experiments with presidential election, referenda, all-party Cabinets or federalism were rejected in favour of practices which, under different terminology, had characterised Ceylon politics since independence. Nevertheless the abolition of such institutions as the Senate, the Public Service Commission, the Judicial Service Commission and the Nominated M.P., and the entrenchment of the Sinhala language and centralised government, may breed a whole new set of conventions which will take Sri Lanka away from the path set down by the Soulbury Commissioners nearly thirty years before the inauguration of the republic.

The Preamble met the objections of S. W. R. D. Bandaranaike, J. A. L. Cooray and D. C. Wijewardena to the British origins of the old constitution. The process of setting up a Constituent Assembly on the basis of the elected House of Representatives, was designed precisely to breach any implied continuity with the British heritage. Legal critics who doubted whether the old constitution could be repealed[41] may have had some influence in causing this symbolic breach. Basically the object was to be able to present such a Preamble as "we the people of Sri Lanka . . . give to ourselves a constitution which . . . will become the fundamental law of Sri Lanka deriving its power and authority solely from the people" in place of "it is hereby ordered by His Majesty by and with the advice of His Privy Council."[42] The question of "sovereignty" which had worried constitutional lawyers in respect to the amendment or repeal of the Order in Council, or to s. 29 (2) or s. 52–6,[43] was finally resolved, even if it had never been very significant.

The declaration of a Republic simply ratified the declared intention of all Ceylonese parties and particularly of S. W. R. D. Bandaranaike. A more important departure was the description of Sri Lanka in s. 2 as a "Unitary State". This was anathema to the Federal Party and had been a major factor in their boycott of the Constituent Assembly. While Ceylon had also been unitary, there was no constitutional entrenchment of that arrangement.[44] The aborted District Councils of 1968 had, in a substantially similar form, been urged by J. A. L. Cooray,[45] within the context of regional devolution under a central legislature. But s. 45 (1) of the new document stated that "the National State Assembly may not abdicate, delegate or in any manner alienate its legislative power, nor may it set up an authority with any legislative power other than the power to make subordinate laws." This not only ran counter to the Federal Party's proposed constitution[46] but made it much more difficult for future governments to introduce any devolution other than the small amount allowed to local authorities. But s. 6 on Buddhism and Chapter III on Official Language were an even worse rebuff to the Federal Party, whose decentralising aims had become unrealistic with the defeat of District Councils. The Federal Party resolutions for the Constituent Assembly had called for the right to transact all official business in any citizen's mother tongue, and for education to be in the mother tongue as well as examinations for all state employment. Their projected state was to be both federal and secular. Without making Sri Lanka officially Buddhist, the new constitution, unlike the old, made it a duty of the State "to protect and foster Buddhism while assuring to all religions the rights granted by section 18 (1) (d)."[47] This may not have worried the Federalists unduly. The following s. 7 declaring "the Official Language of Sri Lanka shall be Sinhala as provided by the Official Language Act No. 33 of 1956" and s. 8 that "the use of the Tamil language shall be in accordance with the Tamil Language (Special Provisions) Act No. 28 of 1958", meant the entrenching of the disadvantageous position of Tamils outside the Northern and Eastern Provinces, including not only the tea estate workers but also the public employees of Colombo.

The closest the Federal Party had got to protecting the interests of its supporters was between 1966 and 1968. The new constitution, only amendable by two-thirds of the National Assembly, made it highly improbable that the party would ever be so successful again. The sections on official language made no concessions to Tamils outside the Northern and Eastern provinces, in contrast to the regulations of 1966. Participants in court proceedings were entitled to interpreters but the language of the courts outside the Northern and Eastern provinces was to be Sinhala, while even in those provinces a Sinhala translation had to be made available. All new laws were to be in Sinhala with a Tamil translation, while existing laws were to be translated into Sinhala and Tamil "as expeditiously as possible". While it was not specifically stated, knowledge of Sinhala would become essential for all public servants and lawyers who wished to make a career outside the Tamil homeland. The Federal Party, in contrast, were for bi-lingualism throughout the Island. Objection to the Official Language provision was also taken by the Bar Council, many of whose members were much more proficient in English than in either of the indigenous tongues and many of whom were Tamils. The Bar Council wanted all reference to the language of the courts, the language of legislation and the publication of laws to be deleted and dealt with under ordinary legislation as previously.[48] Its objections were that Ministerial regulations were more flexible than constitutional provision in a transitional period, that the sources of Ceylon law were varied and entirely in

English, that technical matters required reference to English
texts, that judges needed discretion on the extent to which
English might be used in cases, that Sinhala amendment of
existing English-language laws was undesirable, and that the
absence of any requirement for an English translation would
cause anomaly and confusion. To avoid this the Council urged
a new Basic Resolution that "the use of the English language in
the courts shall be permitted at the discretion of the judge and
where necessary for the efficient administration of justice."[49]
The Council also wished that "existing arrangements regarding
the language of the courts and the language of legislation shall
be continued, subject to provision to the contrary by the
National Assembly, if it deems expedient for facilitating the
implementation of the provisions of the Constitution relating
to the language of the Courts."[50] All such suggestions ran
counter to the symbolic significance of the new Constitution. It
was designed to consolidate the gains made by the Sinhalese
majority since Bandaranaike's election in 1956 and to entrench
his wishes in a form which would make them immune from
erosion by the Tamil or English-speaking minorities, whatever
their professional status. Whether "a language other than
Sinhala or Tamil" might occasionally be used was left to the
discretion of the Minister and Cabinet.[51]

It had always been Bandaranaike's desire that the Ceylon
constitution should contain statements of rights, freedoms and
objectives. The first two terms of reference of the Select Committee of 1958 had been the establishment of a republic and the
guaranteeing of fundamental rights.[52] J. A. L. Cooray had
argued at the same time that "it is only a Constitution which
embodies what are considered by all sections of the people to be
the principles of good and just government that can command
the necessary loyalty and respect of the people."[53] The Indian
example was most influential upon Ceylonese thinking.
Principles of State policy were incorporated in the Indian
constitution, although it was felt necessary to make them non-
justiciable.[54] The framers of the Sri Lanka constitution made it
clear in s. 17 that the principles of state policy "do not confer
legal rights and are not enforceable in any court of law." The
Ceylon constitution had contained only one entrenched protection, in s. 29 (2). The rights of minorities thus protected

were, in fact, not specifically repeated in the new document, nor indeed had they been very helpful to the Ceylon and Indian Tamils in the past. As Senator Nadesan had pointed out, in arguing for Tamil participation in the Constituent Assembly, s. 29 (2) "in practice has not provided any safeguards for the minorities."[55] Tamil leaders drawn from the Tamil Congress, the Federal Party and independent groups agreed with general Federal Party propositions to the extent of wanting the abolition of caste, parity for the Tamil language and citizenship for all of Ceylon-born parentage or resident since Independence Day.[56] Most of this, too, ran counter to the Sinhalising objectives behind the constitution and all that was incorporated was a ban on caste discrimination in public employment, a provision much more limited, if more operable, than the blanket illegalisation of caste discrimination provided in the Indian constitution. There remained only the non-justiciable commitment to "full realisation of all rights and freedoms of citizens including group rights."[57]

Non-justiciable principles of State policy may be largely decorative. However they give a further guide to the intentions of the constitution framers and there was some controversy about their content.[58] The United National Party was concerned with the socialist emphasis in the principles of State policy, which went beyond the Indian terminology. The party wanted a strengthening of fundamental rights and of references to democracy and in particular "the right to acquire, hold and dispose of property" subject to "reasonable restriction" by law.[59] The UNP also wished to give the Supreme Court power to protect fundamental rights, which, combined with its proposals on property, would have brought the constitution closer to that of the United States. This was not, of course, acceptable to the United Front majority in the Constituent Assembly. In fact the protection of fundamental rights was substantially weaker than in most comparable documents. The Bar Council had asked that these rights "should be secured",[60] but this can hardly be said to have happened. Fundamental rights and freedoms "shall be subject to such restrictions as the law prescribes in the interests of national unity and integrity, national security, national economy, public safety, public order, the protection of public health or morals or the protection of the rights and freedoms of others or giving effect to the Principles of State Policy set out in section 16."[61] As these Principles included "the progressive advancement towards the establishment in Sri Lanka of a socialist democracy" and the elimination of "economic and social privilege, disparity and exploitation", there was no possibility of the fundamental rights being used as a legal safeguard against socialist measures. The outcome was the opposite of that desired by the UNP. In the British tradition there were to be no fundamental rights which could not be overridden by a sovereign parliament. The new constitution solved the dilemma of granting rights while asserting the supremacy of the legislature at the same time. Despite urgings from the Ceylon branch of the International Commission of Jurists there was to be no following the American precedent of entrenched rights.

In general the first six chapters of the constitution represent the entrenching of measures adopted since 1956 and forming the programme of the SLFP at elections during that period. Sri Lanka became a Buddhist, Sinhala, democratic socialist society in which the parliamentary majority was supreme. The principles of State policy were reformist rather than revolutionary and showed very little influence from Soviet or Chinese sources. Minorities were promised protection but were not guaranteed it legally in any meaningful sense. Nowhere did the constitution go as far as desired by Sinhala Buddhist extremists. Hema Basnayake, speaking for a group called the Council of All-Ceylon Sinhala Societies, wanted Buddhism to be the state religion and for the State to be termed "the Buddhist Socialist Republic of Sri Lanka". Laws should be in Sinhala only, the President should be a Buddhist and admission to the public service should be based on communal quotas and require a knowledge of Sinhala in addition.[62] This went well beyond the objective of the All-Ceylon Buddhist Congress which, while also wanting the President to be a Buddhist, required only that the duty of the State towards Buddhism should be more explicitly worded than in the traditional but almost meaningless formula of granting "its rightful place."[63] Just as the Tamils and the UNP were given almost no concessions, so the forces of Sinhala Buddhist extremism were not acceptable to the United Front. Mrs. Bandaranaike had told the opening session of the Constituent Assembly that "our Constitution must be such as helps to strengthen the one-ness of our nation."[64] Neither minorities nor the majority were to be given legal advantages not available to all citizens.

The Institutions of Sri Lanka

Every party wanted Ceylon to become a republic and the Marxists, in the past, had also wanted it to leave the Commonwealth. There had been no urgency to achieve the former and no desire to bring about the latter on the part of the UNP. Dudley Senanayake had announced legislation to create a republic in 1967 but nothing had happened. India had been a republic for fully twenty two years before Ceylon broke the monarchical connection or even abandoned final appeals to the British Privy Council. As for leaving the Commonwealth, this had never been desired by Bandaranaike and was scarcely an issue by 1970.[65] There was, however, some controversy as to the election and powers of the new President. The final draft of the constitution left the situation almost exactly as before, with the president merely the old Governor-General under a new title and no longer formally appointed by the British monarch. His formal powers of declaration, appointment, accreditation and pardon were spelt out, his term of office was limited to four years and he was required to be a citizen. Otherwise the new role was exactly the same as before and the existing Governor-General, William Gopallawa, simply became the new president. There were some who looked to an elected president, possibly as a counter-weight to a prime minister who became even more powerful under the new constitution than before. J. R. Jayawardena had asked for a president elected by the legislature in 1970[66] but by the following year was favouring a strong, popularly elected president who would have taken over many of the powers normally exercised by the prime minister in the British tradition.[67] The UNP official proposals envisaged a president elected by a college of parliamentarians and local councillors, somewhat on the model of the original provisions of the French Fifth Republic. He would have wide discretionary powers in an emergency but would otherwise act under direction from the prime minister.[68] The Federal Party, too, favoured an elected president. [69] All such suggestions would have created a quasi-presidential system under which power would have alternated between president and prime minister, depending on the personality or public backing for each office-holder. This was totally unacceptable to those who had determined not merely that British precedent should be followed as hitherto, but that the majority leader in the National State Assembly should, through a disciplined majority party, be able to exercise unchallengeable authority with no real separation of powers. A presidential system had to wait until 1978.

The new constitution stated unequivocally that "the National State Assembly is the supreme instrument of State power of the Republic." [70] While in Britain, parliamentary sovereignty had become something of a myth, in Ceylon the coalition character of most governments and the laxer degree of party loyalty had meant that real power resided in the lower house to a greater degree than in Britain. In this respect nothing fundamental was changed, although the abolition of the Senate removed the relatively feeble obstruction to the work of the lower house which that institution had provided. Here again, the UNP was at variance with the Basic Resolutions. Its official memorandum wanted not merely to retain a Senate based on government nomination and provincial election but to give the Supreme Court powers of constitutional review. But the Senate had already been abolished by normal legislation under the old constitution and had, in any case, never been wanted by most Sinhalese politicians in the first place. [71] No new arguments for an upper house, other than those canvassed in textbooks for decades, were brought forward. In the old House of Representatives only sixteen votes could be found for the Senate's retention in October, 1970, or less than half the nominal strength of the Opposition at the time. There was very little enthusiasm either for a return to the Donoughmore practice of a house divided into subject committees, chaired by the respective minister. Several legal critics in the past had seemed to favour such a system and their views were lent support by moves in the British parliament for something like the American or European subject committee system. Colvin de Silva himself had argued against Cabinet government when it was first suggested in 1937 on the grounds that "the Executive Commit-

tee system has produced a genuine tendency to make the
Council the arena of political struggle. The cabinet system in
the suggested form will definitely reverse the tendency."[72]
J. R. Jayawardena wanted a committee system to run alongside
Cabinet government, as in Europe, a weakening of prime
ministerial power consistent with his desire for a strong, elected
president.[73] Groups like the All-Ceylon Buddhist Congress,
which had been critical of party politics, also favoured departures from the principle of a strong Cabinet based on a
disciplined majority party. The days of Donoughmore were far
off and virtually unknown to the new intake of M.P.s in 1971
to whom strong majority rule was much more attractive.

The outstanding feature of the constitution, its emphasis on
parliamentary supremacy, not only ran against any lingering
nostalgia for the old State Council but also firmly precluded
any Leftwing hankering after alternative political forms. These
were to be satisfied outside the constitution by workers' and
peoples' committees which could be altered or abolished at
will by a simple legislative majority. Colvin de Silva himself had
continued to believe that "the parliamentary system was an
ineffective instrument for radical change" and had promised
that the United Front "would bring the masses directly into the
process of government."[74] Prins Gunasekera, a radical
Sinhalese nationalist, believed that "the present parliamentary
system of government should be done away with and the
masses be led to form some other suitable form of government
that could reflect the people's wishes."[75] What such a form
might be was never revealed. The earlier LSSP committment to
a Soviet style of government found its expression only in the
creation of people's and worker's committees, which were to be
strictly advisory and supervisory. In essence the "Westminster
model" of a sovereign parliament was not simply retained but
strengthened.

In view of the abolition of the Senate and the ending of Privy
Council appeals, it seemed to most legal and conservative political opinion in Ceylon that the new constitution needed stronger
protection than that afforded by a partisan majority in the
National Assembly, or even by the two-thirds majority required for amendment or repeal. The major alternatives put
forward were those by the UNP and Federal Party favouring

judicial review by the Supreme Court, and those by the All-Ceylon Buddhist Congress and the Ministry for Constitutional Affairs which favoured a Constitutional Court and were eventually adopted. The Bar Council was critical of the proposed new institution and succeeded, along with the UNP, in securing an amendment permitting any citizen to petition the Constitutional Court. The Bar Council had objected to the original suggestion that only the Attorney-General, the Speaker, party leaders or a quorum of the National Assembly could so petition and the Minister acquiesced in this objection at the end of the Constituent Assembly's deliberations. He did not accept the Council's further objection that the Court should be permanent. Its composition remained subject to change on the dissolution of the National Assembly. As the composition of the Court was to be determined by the President, presumably on Cabinet advice, it was feared that such a limited term would ensure its subservience to the party in power. Nevertheless the potential power of the Court remained substantial, particularly where a government had a small or unstable majority. It has the power to advise that any law or part of a law is inconsistent with the constitution and must, therefore, be passed by a two-thirds majority in the Assembly.[77] While the constitution remains flexible enough to obviate much of the obstruction found with judicial review in other systems, there remains more likelihood of such obstruction than under the Soulbury constitution. Of course, the Constitutional Court, like the Senate before it, could still be abolished by a two-thirds majority if it proved consistently recalcitrant.[78]

While the Constitutional Court is a completely new institution, the electoral laws for constituting the National State Assembly remain virtually unaltered as the largest section of the constitution copied verbatim from its predecessor. The Marxists had for many years attacked the bias built into the system by allowing extra representation for area and by counting "persons" rather than "citizens" which gave a further bias in favour of the Kandyan hill areas where large disenfranchised Indian Tamil populations were counted for allocating seats but were unable to vote.[79] Doric de Souza, Permanent Secretary to the Ministry of Constitutional Affairs, had earlier argued that this provision was designed specifically to frustrate the Leftwing parties.[80] Colvin de Silva had likewise maintained that inequality in electorates was a serious fault of the Soulbury constitution.[81] The inbuilt rural bias had proved beneficial to the SLFP since 1956 and there were no protests from its Marxist partners about the retention of a measure which had for long been held to frustrate their own growth. Kandyan voters would continue to hold the balance in Sri Lanka. While minorities were to retain the right to some multi-member seats, they lost the representation through Nominated Members which had lasted since 1931. Over two-thirds of the Sri Lanka National State Assembly are always likely to be Sinhalese Buddhists.

Provisions for a permanent Commissioner of Elections, for the control of finance and for the structure and functions of executive government were also largely identical with the wording, practices or legislation already existing at the time of the declaration of the Republic. The criticism made by the Communist leader, Pieter Keuneman, that the bureaucratic system was "in no way tuned to the needs of rapid economic development",[82] was not met by any changes in the financial procedures. The entire British practice of a Consolidated Fund, an annual budget and control by an Auditor-General remains and there is no mention of specific planning machinery, of the relationship between the executive and public corporations or of the role of the Central Bank. If there were any expectations that the constitution would depart from conventional descriptions of the role and structure of government they were disappointed. The major innovation in Chapter XIII, apart from renaming the Cabinet the Cabinet of Ministers, was to cope with the confusions which had arisen in 1960 and 1965 about the transition process from one Prime Minister to another. This was a concern largely of constitutional lawyers who had found British precedents unhelpful in a multi-party situation.[83] Under s. 99 (1) the Prime Minister would be deemed to have resigned "at the conclusion of a general election" thus departing from formal British precedent but not from actual practice. The short period of uncertainty in March, 1965, when Mrs. Bandaranaike's resignation seemed to hinge on gaining the support of the Federal Party, could thus be avoided in future.

Where the constitution departed radically from its pre-

decessor, and where the most acute controversy and persistent
pressure was aroused, was in its abolition of the Public Service
Commission and the Judicial Service Commission. These had
been created by the British to avoid patronage interference in
the bureaucracy and the judiciary. Their replacement by
advisory boards naturally aroused fears both among politicians
and in the professions concerned. The bureaucracy and the
judiciary, as the most Anglicised sections of Ceylon society,
had long been suspect to the elements who made up Mrs.
Bandaranaike's majority. One of the objects of the Sinhala
policy had been to break down the Anglicised character of the
public service but this had been relatively ineffectual in the
upper levels. The SLFP Manifesto in 1965 had called for the
compulsory retirement of obstructive government officers.[84]
There had been considerable resentment against the public
service in Bandaranaike's government. T. B. Ilangaratne,
himself a former public service trade union leader, argued at
a Socialist Study Circle seminar on Parliament that "the 1956
Government failed because the administration had failed
them."[85] At the same seminar Felix Dias Bandaranaike
stressed the lack of effective contact between parliamentarians
and the bureaucracy and the extent to which public administration was still carried on in English, making it inaccessible
and incomprehensible to the average citizen. After winning
office the Coalition began making the same threats against
public servants that had characterised the 1965 election campaign. N. M. Perera, who had previously been favourably dis-
posed towards his Treasury officials, argued that "most of the
Permanent Secretaries and key officials could not be fully
trusted to implement the programme of the new government.
So many of them will have to be retired."[86] In this atmosphere
the abolition of the Public Service Commission was generally
taken to herald a return to the Donoughmore days, when
Ministers intervened constantly in appointments. In contrast to
the Donoughmore period, such interference in Sri Lanka
would be able to reach the highest policy making levels which,
in colonial days had been in expatriate hands.

The Soulbury constitution provided in s. 60 (1) that "the
appointment, transfer, dismissal and disciplinary control of
public officers is hereby vested in the Public Service Com-

mission" and went on to prescribe penalties for interference in its work. The Sri Lanka constitution is fundamentally different. "The Cabinet of Ministers shall be responsible for the appointment, transfer, dismissal and disciplinary control of state officers and shall be answerable therefore to the National State Assembly", reads s. 106 (1). There was thus nothing to stop public appointments becoming, as in the United States, subject to legislative approval and investigation and to party patronage. Public servants were to hold office "during the pleasure of the President."[87] As such officers included the heads of the Army, Navy, Air Force and Police Force, the power of the legislative majority party, on whose advice the President depended, was greatly enhanced. As argued elsewhere, political patronage had already grown substantially in these services since the coup of 1962. To the Minister for Constitutional Affairs neutral appointment through the Public Service Commission had become a 'pretence'.[88] After growing opposition from the UNP and some public service organisations, the Government instituted a State Services Advisory Board and a separate State Services Disciplinary Appeal Board. Under ss. 111 to 120 some semblance of continuity with the old Public Service Commission was retained. Essentially the new system was to be one based on partisan and possibly communal patronage, subject to parliamentary scrutiny and debate. Examination systems would remain in being but in future it seemed likely that changes of government in Sri Lanka would bring more drastic changes in the administration than had those in Ceylon.

The judiciary, too, had often been accused of partiality, conservatism and undue orientation towards Britain. The Bar Council, which fought hard against almost the whole of the new provisions on justice, felt it necessary to defend the judiciary against such charges, even quoting Colvin de Silva in their defence. It dealt with four major arguments for the new proposals; that they brought the system into line with British practice; that the Judicial Service Commission from 1965 to 1970 appointed a disproportionate number of Tamils; that the judges by background and nature were reactionary and obstructed socialist measures; that it was undemocratic to leave the Prime Minister with sole responsibility for appointments to the Supreme Court and Commissioners of Assizes.[89] Such criticisms had certainly been made. The lawyers' group of the SLFP had argued that the judiciary wished to be above the political system of which it, nevertheless, formed a part.[90] Prins Gunasekera went further and charged the judiciary with being "completely slavish to the British," while in the same Constituent Assembly debate Pieter Keuneman also argued that the legislature, not the judiciary, must be supreme.[91] As constitutional review was not to be a function of the formal judiciary but of the Constitutional Court there was, in any case, only a limited political role for the judiciary in the new Republic. Nor had governments been constantly frustrated in the past except in the overturning of the 1962 coup case convictions, which had been the work of the no longer relevant British Privy Council. The judiciary was, however, the pinnacle of the legal profession in career terms and the desire for patronage was probably as important among many reformers, as the urge for political control.

While objecting to most of the Basic Resolutions relating to the judiciary, the Bar Council fought hardest for the retention of the Judicial Service Commission. Its suggested resolution 21 (6) read: "The mode of selection of judges of the Supreme Courts, their irremovability except on specific grounds, their age of retirement, and payment of salary shall be provided for in the constitution. These provisions shall be such as to secure the independence of the judges from political pressure. Judges of the Superior Courts shall be appointed by the President after consulting the Prime Minister, from amongst persons whose qualifications are specified in the Constitution. The other judges shall be appointed by a body similar to the present Judicial Service Commission, and with identical powers."[92] Some of this requirement was met by copying verbatim from the Soulbury constitution the conditions for appointing, remunerating and retiring judges of the Appellate Court and the Supreme Court. The abolition of the Judicial Service Commission completely altered the situation of lower court judges. These could find their appointment the subject of debate in the National Assembly if the Cabinet of Ministers refused to appoint from the list submitted by the new Judicial Services Advisory Board.[93] The nomination of judges by Ministers had been one of the points at issue in the 1962 coup case.[94] It had

further caused controversy and international comment when
the Criminal Justice Commission had been set up outside the
normal judicial framework to deal with charges arising from
the JVP rising in 1971. Under the new constitution both the
Ministerial appointment of judges and the creation of such
Commissions became normal rather than aberrant or illegal.

The Judicial Services Advisory Board was created during the
process of discussing the constitution, principally as a compromise between the government's desire to retain the appointment
of judges in its own hands and the opposition of much of the
legal profession to this aspiration. The Special Committee of
the Bar Council reported in March, 1971 its "deep anxiety"
over the Basic Resolutions on the Judiciary. Its own proposals
were: "that judges of the Supreme Court and Constitution Court
should be appointed by the President on Prime Ministerial
advice without any involvement of the Council of Ministers; a
judge of a Superior Court may only be removed after an
address by the National Assembly with two-thirds support; the
Judicial Service Commission should be appointed by the
President on prime ministerial advice without involvement of
the Council of Ministers; all appointments and removals of
the minor judiciary should be made by the Judicial Service
Commission."[95] While strengthening the role of the Prime
Minister this would have left things essentially as they were
under the Soulbury constitution. The UNP in general took the
same position as the Bar Council. They wanted no control of
the judiciary by the legislature, judicial power would rest
entirely with judges who could not be removed except by a
judicial body, the Judicial Service Commission would be
retained and Supreme Court judges would be appointed by the
President and not by the Cabinet of Ministers.[96] In May 1971
the Minister accepted the creation of the Advisory and Disciplinary Boards which at least left the legal profession to some
degree in charge of their own affairs.

The provisions relating to the public service and the judiciary
were consistent with the general aspiration of making the
National Assembly truly sovereign. It would now be possible
for it to debate bureaucratic and judicial appointments,
although most would continue to be made within the respective
profession. The isolation from popular influences which the

judiciary in particular had enjoyed was finally ended. Indigenisation had come to two areas from which it had partly been
excluded by the protective Commissions set up under Soulbury.
Patronage had almost certainly come too, although this could
be seen as a move towards democracy rather than away from it.
While there was little reference to American precedent in this
area, the placing of bureaucratic and judicial posts within the
political arena is clearly in that tradition rather than the
British. With a strongly disciplined socialist party in power the
long-awaited transformation of the bureaucracy and judiciary
might be expected to begin. The caste, communal and nepotistic
character of existing patronage practices made it more likely,
as opponents of the system argued, that the methods used to
staff public corporations would spread into the state service,
the courts and the military. Nor was this surprising. The logic
of the move from Ceylon to Sri Lanka was precisely that such
alien notions as an insulated judiciary and public service
should be abandoned and that groups and classes previously
excluded from these areas of government should be free to
enter them. The colonial Platonism which had inspired Soulbury
was replaced by a cruder but more politically realistic assertion
of majority domination. While politicians were to have a much
greater say in these areas there was still constitutional protection
of the administration of justice. The Bar Council had argued
that "one request which is not made of an M.P. is that he should
speak to a magistrate or judge who is hearing a case in which
the constituent is interested. . . . The moment judicial appointments come to savour of political appointments and are
subject to debate in the Cabinet, the National Assembly etc.,
this state of affairs will start to change."[97] However, under
s. 131 (2) a penalty of one year's rigorous imprisonment was
prescribed for any unauthorised interference with judicial
powers and functions.

The final Chapter of the constitution once again emphasises
the continuity with the colonial past. It leaves in being the
Public Security Ordinance "unless the National Assembly
otherwise provides."[98] The Ordinance had been repeatedly
attacked by the Left in the past but the recent experience with
the JVP had muted such criticism. The powers which the Ordinance gave the then Governor-General, Sir Oliver Goonetilleke

in 1958, had been considerable. L. J. M. Cooray argues that "the wide and general law making power conferred by sections of the Public Security Ordinance enables the government of the day to bypass Parliament and create rules of law."[99] The Prime Minister and President, acting together, were in a strong position during any emergency. With this even the UNP agreed. The JVP rising had made it clear that Sri Lanka must be able to act ruthlessly and efficiently in any future emergency. The sovereignty of the National Assembly asserted elsewhere was inoperable where the whole political system was challenged. Under s. 45 (4) the National Assembly was permitted to delegate all significant powers to the President during the emergency although not the power to suspend the constitution itself. A temporary dictatorship would be possible under the Public Security Ordinance. A permanent dictator would have to act unconstitutionally.

NOTES

1. Ceylon (Constitution) Order in Council of 1946; s. 29 (4).
2. See J. Jupp and L. J. M. Cooray: "The Constitutional System in Ceylon"; *Pacific Affairs* XLIII: 1, Spring 1970; pp. 73–83.
3. S. W. R. D. Bandaranaike: *Towards a New Era*; Colombo, 1961; pp. 135–143.
4. Bandaranaike informed the 1956 Commonwealth Prime Ministers' conference that Ceylon intended to become a republic. The Joint Parliamentary Select Committee on Constitutional Reform, set up on November 27, 1957, had the creation of a republic as its first term of reference. In the 1965 and 1970 elections all parties favoured a republic and in 1967 Dudley Senanayake had announced that legislation was being prepared. See also J. Jupp: "Constitutional Developments in Ceylon since Independence"; *Pacific Affairs* XLI: 2, Summer 1968.
5. S. W. R. D. Bandaranaike: *op. cit.* p. 137.
6. As Mrs. Bandaranaike said at Kandy, on obtaining the blessing of the Sacred Tooth relic upon the new constitution: "Today we are in the proud position of owing no allegiance to anyone else, but totally and in every respect, owing allegiance only to our own country." *Ceylon News* 1/6/1972.
7. LSSP: *Programme of Action*; Colombo, 4/6/1950 (Mimeo).
8. Fundamental LSSP opposition to the constitution continued as Leslie Goonewardena made clear in 1970: "The present constitution in Ceylon aims at two ends—one to collect taxes from the people and the other to suppress the people if they try to rise against the Government in power." *Ceylon Observer* 24/6/1970.

9. LSSP: *Programme of Action*, 1950.
10. Speaking in the Budget debate of 1970, R. D. Senanayake, a junior minister, urged that "peoples' militias should be set up in all electorates" to counter capitalist opposition to the United Front government. *Ceylon Daily News* 4/11/1970.
11. Anon.: *Twenty Five Years of the Ceylon Communist Party*; Colombo, 1968; p. 43.
12. *Ibid.*: p. 70.
13. V. Karalasingham: *Senile Leftism*; Colombo, 1966; Introduction.
14. LSSP Conference (1969); *Political Resolution* Part V (Typescript).
15. *ibid.*
16. *Ceylon News* 25/6/1970.
17. See e.g. *Workers Advisory Councils—Draft Regulations and By-Laws*; Ceylon Transport Board, Colombo; 1964.
18. *Open Letter to Members of the LSSP from the LSSP (R)* Colombo, 1969; Mimeo.
19. *Ceylon News* 27/8/1970.
20. *Times of Ceylon* 14/4/1964.
21. See Chapter Ten and *Ceylon News* 1/10/1970.
22. Colvin de Silva: *Towards Dictatorship*; LSSP, Colombo; 1937
23. Doric de Souza: "Parliamentary Democracy in Ceylon"; *Young Socialist* (Colombo), no. 3, October-December 1961; p. 139.
24. J. A. L. Cooray: *The Revision of the Constitution*; Colombo, 1957; p. 4.
25. S. W. R. D. Bandaranaike: *Speeches and Writings*; Colombo, 1963; p. 162.
26. C. F. Amerasinghe: *The Doctrines of Sovereignty and Separation of Powers in the Law of Ceylon*; Colombo, 1970; p. 58. Amerasinghe earlier holds that there was an effective 'legal revolution' in 1948 such as to confer *de facto* independence upon Ceylon (pp. 18–23).
27. S. 29 (2) of the 1948 constitution provided that no law shall—"(a) prohibit or restrict the free exercise of any religion; or (b) make persons of any community or religion liable to disabilities or restrictions to which persons of other communities or religions are not made liable; or (c) confer on persons of any community or religion any privilege or advantage which is not conferred on persons of other communities or religions; or (d) alter the constitution of any religious body." This provision had been tested in respect of the legislation removing citizenship from Indian Tamils and found to be ineffective in Mudanayake v. Sivagnanasunderam (1952) 53 NLR 25 and Kodakan Pillai v. Mudanayake (1953) 54 NLR 433. It was based on an article in the Northern Ireland constitution (which had not been very effective either!).
28. See Amerasinghe; *op. cit.* Chapter VII and Liyanage v. The Queen (1966) in the Privy Council arising out of The Queen v. Liyanage (1962) 64 NLR 409. (Summarised in *Law Quarterly Review* vol. 82 no. 327, July 1966, pp. 289–91).
29. J. A. L. Cooray: *op. cit.* p. 10.
30. *Ceylon-Report of the Commission on Constitutional Reform (Soulbury*

Report); Colombo; 1969 (reprint); Chapter XIV. (Originally published as Cmd. 6677).

31. See M. V. Pylee: *Constitutional Government in India*; Asia Publishing, Bombay; 1968; Part IV (Fundamental Rights and Directive Principles).

32. S. 29 (2) (see fn. 27 above) of which Cooray said that "it is difficult to maintain that the famous Section 29, sub-section 2 provides us with a satisfactory substitute for . . . comprehensive chapters defining and guaranteeing fundamental rights . . ." (*op. cit.* p. 7).

33. J. A. L. Cooray: *op. cit.* p. 5.

34. Cooray: *op. cit.* p. 6.

35. See the *Constitution of Sri Lanka*; Colombo, 1972, s. 18 (2) which reads: "The exercise and operation of the fundamental rights and freedoms provided in this Chapter shall be subject to such restrictions as the law prescribes in the interests of national unity and integrity, national security, national economy, public safety, public order, the protection of public health or morals or the protection of the rights and freedoms of others or giving effect to the Principles of State Policy set out in section 16." Thus the Principles, though not justiciable, might be used to limit the Rights, scarcely an eventuality foreseen by Cooray in 1957.

36. Cooray: *op. cit.* p. 9.

37. Cooray resigned with the rest of the Constitutional Court, Justice T. S. Fernando and Mr. H. Deheragoda, in December 1972 after the Court had not complied with s. 65 of the Sri Lanka constitution requiring them to submit their findings on constitutionality within fourteen days of receipt of a reference to them. The issue in question was the Press Council Bill which was later declared consistent with the constitution by a new court, which included a former SLFP Member of Parliament, Jaya Pathirane.

38. C. F. Amerasinghe: *op. cit.* p. 189.

39. *Constitution of Sri Lanka*, s. 6 (c).

40. *Loc. cit.*, Chapters 11 and 12.

41. For example L. J. M. Cooray: *Essays on the Constitution of Ceylon*; Colombo, 1970; pp. 58–9, 206 and elsewhere.

42. This wording is close to that of the Eire constitution quoted by J. A. L. Cooray; *op. cit.* p. 2.

43. S. 52–6 of the Soulbury constitution deal with the judiciary and the Judicial Service Commission.

44. Amerasinghe; *op. cit.* pp. 59–71 argues that under the Soulbury constitution Ceylon could not set up a "rival law-making authority" but could only delegate its authority. Under this interpretation true federalism would have been impossible, or at least unconstitutional.

45. J. A. L. Cooray: *op. cit.* p. 16.

46. For the Federal Party proposals see *Daily Mirror* (Colombo) 5/2/1971. The Federal Party boycotted the Constituent Assembly after the rejection of its federalist and language parity proposals.

47. *Sri Lanka Constitution*, s. 6.

48. Memorandum by the Bar Council of Ceylon on the Draft Basic

Resolutions—Colombo 9/3/1971, p. 7. I am indebted to Desmond Fernando, secretary of the Bar Council of Ceylon, for sending me their memoranda.

49. *Loc. cit.* Annexure p. 8; New Resolution 25 (b).
50. *Ibid.* New Resolution 26.
51. Under s. 11 (6) which was a concession to the legal profession, added to the Draft Resolutions.
52. *Second Report from the Joint Select Committee to Consider the Revisions of the Constitution*: Parliamentary Series No. 15, 1958–9; p. 2.
53. J. A. L. Cooray: *op. cit.* p. 6.
54. Pylee: *op. cit.* Chapter 23.
55. *Ceylon Observer* 18/7/1970.
56. *Daily Mirror* (Colombo) 10/2/1971.
57. *Sri Lanka Constitution* s. 16 (2) (a).
58. Pylee: *op. cit.* pp. 336–9 draws attention to several Indian cases in which the Directive Principles were referred to in overturning petitions against the unconstitutionality of property redistribution. In his opinion "nothing should be allowed to stand in their way, even the fundamental rights guaranteed to the individual" (p. 339). This was the attitude of the Coalition government of Ceylon and was given constitutional force in s. 18 (2) (see above fn. 35).
59. *Ceylon Daily News* 4/2/1971.
60. Memorandum by the Bar Council of Ceylon on the Draft Basic Resolutions: p. 6.
61. *Sri Lanka Constitution* s. 18 (2). Judgement by the Constitutional Court on the Associated Newspapers of Ceylon Limited (Special Provisions) Act, raised some doubts about the securing of the fundamental rights. The government's submission claimed *inter alia* that "Section 18 (1) in no way limits the sovereign power of the National State Assembly, nor are the fundamental rights and freedoms enumerated in section 18 (1) guaranteed by the State" (*Ceylon News* 28/6/1973). The Court, judging the measure constitutional, also added that "Section 18 (1) of the Constitution of Sri Lanka is not merely declaratory but that the fundamental rights enshrined in this section are secured to the people by the Constitution." (*Ceylon News* 19/7/1973). It did, however, draw attention to the limitations imposed by s. 18 (2). J. A. L. Cooray appeared in this case and argued that the fundamental rights listed could only be changed by an amending majority of two-thirds of the Assembly (*Ceylon News* 28/6/1973).
62. *Sun* (Colombo) 11/2/1971.
63. The final formulation of s. 6 substitutes "foremost" for "rightful", the word used in the original Draft submitted to the Constituent Assembly by Colvin de Silva on December 29, 1972.
64. *Ceylon Daily News* 20/7/1970.
65. W. Dahanayake parted company with the UNP in August, 1970 over his views on the constitution, which included the demand that Ceylon should leave the Commonwealth. *Ceylon Daily News* 2/8/1970 and *Times of Ceylon* 3/8/1970.

66. *Sun* (Colombo) 13/8/1970.
67. *Ceylon Daily News* 1/2/1971 and *Times of Ceylon* 28/2/1971.
68. *Ceylon Daily News* 4/2/1971. See also J. R. Jayawardena's proposed amendments to this effect in the Constituent Assembly. *CA Debs.* vol. 1, no. 32, Friday 2 July, 1971; cols. 2625–2637.
69. *Daily Mirror* (Colombo) 5/2/1971.
70. *Constitution of Sri Lanka* s. 5.
71. See B. C. F. Jayaratne: "Abolition of the Senate of Ceylon"; *Parliamentarian* 53: 2, 1972, pp. 104–112.
72. Colvin R. de Silva: *Towards Dictatorship*; Colombo, (1937?).
73. See his memorandum published in the *Sun* (Colombo) 13/8/1970.
74. At a Socialist Study Circle seminar on Parliament. *Ceylon Daily News* 13/13/1969.
75. *Sun* (Colombo) 4/4/1969.
76. *Daily Mirror* 5/7/1971. See the amendment of Basic Resolution 29 (2) (e) moved by Colvin de Silva in the Constituent Assembly; *CA Debs*, vol. 1, no. 34, Sunday 4 July, 1971; col. 2859. This became s. 54 (2) (e) of the Constitution of Sri Lanka.
77. *Constitution of Sri Lanka* s. 55 (4)
78. For the resignation of the first Constitutional Court see fn. 37 above.
79. In 1958 in the Select Committee on Revision of the Constitution, Colvin de Silva, N. M. Perera, Pieter Keuneman and Senator Nadesan had voted for eliminating the weighting by area and twelve had voted against them (Parlty. Series 1958–9, no. 15 p. 25).
80. Doric de Souza: "Progress and Reaction in Ceylon" in *Organising for Democracy*; Community Institute, Colombo, 1964; pp. 24–26.
81. *Ceylon Observer* 11/9/1970.
82. *Ceylon Daily News* 22/7/1970.
83. See e.g. A. J. Wilson: "The Governor-General and the Two Dissolutions of Parliament"; *Ceylon Journal of Historical and Social Studies* III, 2, July-December 1960; S. A. de Smith: *The New Commonwealth and its Constitutions* (Stevens, London, 1964) pp. 81–5; L. J. M. Cooray: *Essays on the Constitution of Ceylon;* Colombo, 1970, section 16.
84. *Ceylon Daily News* 16/2/1965.
85. *Ceylon Daily News* 13/12/1969.
86. *Ceylon Daily News* 30/6/1970.
87. *Constitution of Sri Lanka* s. 107 (1).
88. Statement by Colvin de Silva to a delegation led by Sir Cyril de Zoysa. *Times of Ceylon* 30/1/1971.
89. Special Committee of the Bar Council: *Statement on the Basic Resolutions relating to the Judiciary*; Colombo, 16/3/1971.
90. See "Independence of the Judiciary or Supremacy of the Judiciary?"; *Nation* 19/11/1970 and 26/11/1970.
91. *Ceylon Daily News* 22/7/1970.
92. Memorandum of the Bar Council of Ceylon on the Draft Basic Resolutions; Annexure p. 6.
93. *Constitution of Sri Lanka* s. 126 (4).

94. Analysed in L. J. M. Cooray: *op. cit.* pp. 187–200 and C. F. Amer-
    asinghe: *op. cit.* pp. 223–7.
95. Special Committee of the Bar Council: *Statement on the Basic Reso-
    lutions Relating to the Judiciary*; pp. 12–13.
96. See the UNP proposals in the *Ceylon Daily News* 4/2/1971.
97. Memorandum of the Bar Council on the Draft Basic Resolutions; p. 5.
98. *Constitution of Sri Lanka* s. 134 (1).
99. L. J. M. Cooray: *op. cit.* p. 223.

CHAPTER 10

The Revolutionary Challenge

With the victory of Mrs. Bandaranaike in May, 1970 the hopes of a generation of Ceylonese radicals seemed to have come to fruition. Through an unchallengeable two-thirds majority the Coalition could not only change the Constitution, which the MEP had failed to do after 1956, but be expected to resist the rapid disintegration, in the face of economic and political challenges, which had almost destroyed Bandaranaike's Cabinet before his assassination. The transition from "Ceylon", a post-colonial society still deeply influenced by British ways, to "Sri Lanka", a fully independent, authentically Sinhalese society based on the traditions of two thousand years, seemed almost complete. To the Left, which remained ambivalent about the extent to which it wanted to "return" rather than "go forward", the victory opened up a variety of possibilities. On defecting from the LSSP to take up an ambassadorship to Russia in 1969, Jack Kotelawala had said: "I waited for the revolution for the last thirty five years. As it has not come I am going to the country where the revolution started."[1] There must have been many more in the LSSP leadership who doubted, after the same period in Leftwing politics, whether socialism would ever come. Bandaranaike's reforms had changed only the outward face of Ceylon. Basically it was still a trading and plantation society. Some economic power had passed from the British and Indians to Sinhalese. Some land distribution had taken place. Some public corporations were functioning in the manufacturing sector. But essentially the Low Country planters, the English-speaking professionals, Indian businessmen and British tea companies still dominated those facets of society which Marxists considered important. The administration of the country remained in the hands of British educated civil servants operating through the colonially bequeathed structure. Where there had been changes away from the colonial political culture, these were not necessarily in a socialist direction. The new "beedi and biscuit bourgeoisie" who had risen up from the Ceylonisation and import-control measures since 1956 were in Marxist eyes a "national bourge-oisie". Their loyalty wavered between the UNP and the SLFP, depending on which was in office at the time. Some features of society, such as the reaffirmation of caste, communal and nepotistic factors in recruitment to jobs, seemed retrograde to all Westernised elements, Marxist or not.

The Coalition victory promised to give power to the Marxists for the first time. As argued elsewhere, the SLFP had consis-tently moved Leftwards. The Mrs. Bandaranaike of 1970 was not the ally of conservative Kandyan paddy-land owners that she had seemed fifteen years before. A substantial part of the SLFP leadership either had a consistent Leftwing record, like T. B. Ilangaratne or T. B. Subasinghe, or like Felix Bandar-anaike or Maithripala Senanayake, were anxious to work with the Left. Most important to the Left was the belief that their superior experience, education and intelligence would allow them to take effective control of economic and social policies. These hopes seemed nearer to being attained when the Cabinet was formed. Now that N. M. Perera was in charge of Finance the main planning powers were under LSSP domination. Colvin de Silva was not only given the new Ministry of Plantations, but was further made Minister for Constitutional Affairs. Thus he controlled the largest sector of the economy and the processes by which "Sri Lanka" was to emerge from "Ceylon". Leslie Goonewardena was to control communications while Pieter Keuneman gained the small but potentially important Housing Ministry. Leftwing appointments did not stop at the formal Cabinet positions given to Marxists, vital though these were. Foreign and internal trade were under the control of Ilangaratne, who had forged the Coalition in its beginnings in 1964. Education was under Badiuddin Mahmud, who was not only very favourable to the Soviet Union but who worked with B. Y. Tudawe, his Communist Parliamentary Secretary and a teachers' trade union leader for many years. T. B. Subasinghe's control over Industries and Scientific Affairs gave that veteran

Marxist and former LSSP leader a post from which he could plan the industrialisation to which all Leftists had been committed since the founding of the Samasamajist movement. As Parliamentary Secretary for Planning and Employment under Mrs. Bandaranaike, Ratne Deshapriya Senanayake, although in the SLFP, could be expected to take a position similar to that of the Marxists, being one of the best known admirers of Communist China in the government.

Administrative appointments further strengthened the position of the Left. Colvin de Silva brought the veteran Samasamajist (and former Bolshevik-Leninist) Doric de Souza into the permanent secretaryship of his new Ministry of Plantations. Leslie Goonewardena appointed Anil Moonesinghe, former LSSP Minister, as Chairman of the Ceylon Transport Board, the largest single employer of labour in the Island. Anil's brother, Susil, an SLFP member, became Chairman of the Ceylon Broadcasting Commission and thus responsible for propaganda through the one element of the mass media completely under government control. H. A. de S. Gunasekera, an academic with an LSSP and SLFP background, was made permanent secretary of the Ministry of Planning which, although nominally controlled by Mrs. Bandaranaike, was actually much closer to the LSSP controlled Ministry of Finance. At all significant levels of government for economic control and planning the long-awaited advent of Marxists to office seemed complete. True, they were still junior partners both in parliament and the Cabinet. But the leading Marxists who had been prepared to go along with the tactic of Coalition were at last in a position to achieve some of the goals they had fought for since the 1930's.

This coming to fruition of a whole generation of waiting helps to explain the bitterness and lack of comprehension with which the established parliamentary Left met the youthful critics and, later, revolutionaries of the JVP. That movement, in turn, can be understood against the background of the social character and political history of the new government. As suggested elsewhere, the Marxist parliamentarians were no more "representative" of the people than anyone else. Because of their derivation from the English-speaking professional classes, they were even less representative than the SLFP and certainly much less so than the predominantly Sinhala-educated youths of the JVP. Of the twenty-five Marxist M.P.s elected in 1970, seven had been to overseas universities and another five to the University of Ceylon or Colombo Law College. At least twelve had been educated at the leading Colombo schools, St. Thomas', Royal and Ananda. They were a world away from the village educated youth of the 1970's. The Left leaders had themselves been the product of a 'generation gap' in the late 1930's, when British colonialism was challenged not simply by the Trotskyists but also by the younger group around J. R. Jayawardena and Dudley Senanayake in the Ceylon National Congress. In that situation there was only a gap in years and experience. By 1970 there was an unbridgeable social chasm as well.

The Leftwing critics who had broken away from the LSSP and Communist Party in 1964 over the Coalition tactic had remained ineffectual precisely because they were so firmly rooted in the traditions and social character of the groups which they had left. Bala Tampoe, Shanmugathasan, Meryl Fernando, Edmund Samarakkody and Karalasingham differed in their political views from the Coalitionists. They were equally from the generation of the 1940's, from the English-speaking professional classes, from the scholastic tradition of Marxist exegesis. Their polemics were conducted in English and their following was among the university students and clerical workers.[2] Attempts by Revolutionary Samasamajists or Maoists to enter parliament showed their complete isolation from the rural masses. Only S. D. Bandaranaike retained some following in his 'family seat' and, in the event, only he identified himself completely with the JVP revolution. With their attention focused on the existing Marxist parties, the dissidents of 1964 overlooked what was happening among the *swabasha* educated, whose grasp of Marxism was limited, whose ability to take part in learned debates was non-existent and whose social origins were rural.[3] The Left radicals were as foreign to them as the established Leftwing politicians, Mrs. Bandaranaike or the UNP.

It is this tremendous social gap which helps to explain the total unpreparedness of Ceylon's political society for the 1971 revolution and its refusal to believe in the spontaneity and indigenous character of the movement. For thirty-five years Leftwing politics had been the exclusive province of the few thousand hard core members of the LSSP and the Communist Party, with peripheral support among Philip Gunawardena's rapidly declining group and on the Left of the SLFP. With its limited and unchanging electoral base and long-established leadership, the Marxist movement had come by 1964 to see its main problem as losing support to the SLFP rather than of gaining it by a reaffirmation of previous revolutionary positions. In 1967 Justus van der Kroef wrote that "both parties clearly fear the political limbo that might follow a break with the SLFP—and the SLFP knows it. The doctrinaire extremism and isolation of the CCP (Peking) and the LSSP (R) serve as an unmistakable warning in this respect."[4] Less than four years later it was the established party leaders who seemed isolated; large sections of their youth leagues defected to the JVP which occupied areas of their constituencies for weeks at a time. What was most remarkable about the whole April, 1971 rising was the failure of politicians with years of grass-roots organising to know what was going on among the youth of their own districts. Just as the UNP had failed to understand the rural attitudes of 1956, so the Marxists failed to comprehend the undercurrents of 1971.

The Character of the JVP

Unlike all previous Leftwing groups in Ceylon, the JVP did not arise from within the LSSP. Its leader, Rohan Wijeweera, came from a Communist Party family in the Party's stronghold near Matara. Some other JVP leaders had similar backgrounds.[5] What little is known about most of the leaders and the great bulk of the rank and file, suggests that they had few links, if any, with the established Marxist movement. Wijeweera had been converted to Maoism not by Shanmugathasan and the local party, but by his experiences at Lumumba University, Moscow. There was no British influence on the JVP at all, in marked contrast to the educational moulding of the LSSP and CP leadership. While the Western-oriented University of Ceylon at Peradeniya provided many JVP supporters, its main student leadership came from the former Buddhist seminaries

of Vidyodaya and Vidyalankara. Despite a student strike at
Thurstan College, Colombo, which was attributed to JVP
influence, the major Colombo schools were relatively impervious. It was the high schools of the country towns, in
which English was an imperfectly taught second language,
which responded through their teachers and pupils. Again,
while some of the children of the political élite were believed to
have JVP sympathies, it was essentially the lower-middle
classes, peasants and labourers of the villages and small towns
which contributed most to JVP strength.[6] While the LSSP and
the Communist Party were led by Goyigamas and Christian
Karawas, the JVP appealed to the Buddhist Karawa, the
Durawa, Batgam, Wahumpura and other lower castes. There
is considerable evidence, both from the Southern Province and
from the Kegalle District, that anti-Goyigama feeling was a
motive behind mass recruitment into the JVP in certain villages.

The geographical distribution of JVP strength, while related
to that for the Marxist parties, was not coterminous with it. Of
course, as the Front did not contest elections it is more difficult
to say exactly where their main support was concentrated. As
a secret group, they did not issue lists of branches, nor hold
open conferences, from whose delegations regional concentration can be estimated. The best indication of JVP support
can only be gained from looking at those areas which they
occupied in April, 1971, in which the fiercest fighting occurred,
and in which police, military and other intelligence reports
claim them to be influential. The original heartland of the JVP
was in the Matara area, from which both Wijeweera and
Mahinda Wijesekera came. This had for long been dominated
by the Communist Party. The LSSP was weaker than either
the SLFP or the UNP in most of the adjoining electorates. It
was an overwhelmingly Low Country Sinhala Buddhist area,
with very little population drawn from any other community.
It was also riven by serious caste conflicts. Both Matara and
Devinuwara electorates contained large Durawa and Karawa
communities, such that a combination of these two castes was
always sought by any party hoping to win the seat. B. Y.
Tudawe, the Communist M.P. for Matara was a Durawa, and
Wijeweera and Wijesekera were Karawas. Caste was important
in rallying the Southern Province electorates to the Left.[7] Of

the nine seats around Matara and eastwards which were largely occupied by, or heavily influenced by the JVP in 1971, five were held by the SLFP, three by the CP and one by the LSSP. Normally up to half these seats returned Karawa or Durawa Members.

The second area of concentration was also in the Southern Province and included the area of Elpitiya occupied by the JVP for three weeks in April, 1971. This, too, was predominantly Buddhist, away from the coast where there were Muslim and Christian communities. It was also an area of considerable caste tension. On the coast, Karawa and Salagama concentrations ensured, as around Matara, that Goyigama candidates were less likely to be elected than elsewhere. In this area the SLFP shared power with the LSSP, and the Communists were unimportant. Of the five seats around and including Bentara-Elpitiya, three were represented by the LSSP and two by the SLFP. While the prosperous Karawa and Salagama shared power with the Goyigama, there were also concentrations of much poorer castes who were particularly favourable to the JVP. Elpitiya town was surrounded by a number of Wahumpura villages.[8] It was this lowly caste, together with the even poorer Padu (Batgam), which provided the backbone of the movement around Kegalle as well. Here the population was mainly Kandyan Buddhist, and caste rather than race or religion provided the main divisions. The Rambukkana electorate had been largely created to cater for smaller castes. Intelligence reports from nearby Warakapola claimed that most of the JVP there were Padu.[9] In this area, as also around Elpitiya, there was considerable co-operation between villagers in low-caste areas and the JVP, which was largely led by their caste-relatives. Around Kegalle however, there was no strong Marxist tradition. It was the original heartland of the SLFP and most seats in the district had been held by that party since 1956.

The Matara, Elpitiya and Kegalle districts, then, provided the most consistent and hard-fighting support for the JVP.[10] The buildup of the organisation in these areas had been noted by the police for over two years. What they have in common is an overwhelming Sinhala Buddhist character, dense population, coconut and rubber cultivation through Sinhalese owned and worked estates, a Leftward but not always Marxist electoral

W

allegiance, and a history of caste tension. Many of these features help to explain the particular local appeal of the JVP. It was precisely such a combination of factors which heightened and gave political expression to the frustrations of unemployed, educated youth. While these were to be found everywhere, they were particularly disadvantaged in areas of low urbanisation, high population density, a concentration of lower castes and weak influence of the English-language culture. Similar factors were important in other areas. On the rice colonisation schemes around Polonnaruwa, there was likewise a high concentration of Sinhalese Buddhists and of lower castes often originating in Southern Province. There was little urbanisation or industry and the population was growing rapidly. The colonisation areas which had seen most activity during the communal rioting of 1958 saw strong, if inadequately sustained, initial support for the JVP. Whether there was similar support in the jungle areas around Anuradhapura is harder to determine as these were natural guerilla areas which seemed to have been used by groups from other districts. In the cities, the only strong support seemed concentrated in Wanathamulla, the Sinhalese slum ward of Colombo where the JVP had its headquarters. Otherwise the cities were relatively untouched, possibly because they were more cosmopolitan and offered more employment than the Sinhala rural districts.

The general character of JVP membership is well established. All reports show it as overwhelmingly Sinhala Buddhist youth between fifteen and twenty-five years of age, drawn largely from the areas described above, and thus both Low Country and Kandyan. In some areas, markedly in Elpitiya and Deniyaya, school children led by their teachers were an important element. University students were less significant. Sepala Attygalle, commander-in-chief of the Ceylon Army, estimated that of 20,000 members of the JVP known to security, 75% were under twenty, 15% were twenty to twenty-five and 10% were over twenty-five.[11] Of these a considerable proportion were recruited from the disbanded Land Army, set up by Dudley Senanayake's government. It was this factor which prompted the arrest of Captain C. P. J. Seneviratne, the former junior Minister in charge of the Army, and Jinadasa Niyathapala, former Senator and leader of the UNP Youth

Leagues.[12] Further recruitment from those beholden to the UNP took place at the Thulhiriya State Textile Mills, where workers appointed under the UNP and dismissed or down-graded by the SLFP, took over the factory, precipitating its bombing by the Ceylon Air Force.[13] In general, recruitment was from Leftwing areas and organisations, in particular the Communist Youth Leagues in Southern Province. The leader-ship of the JVP is hard to classify as no reliable records are available of its Central Committee membership. The whole structure was based on circles of five and only the national leadership were aware of local organisers.[14] Among those arrested or charged very few had previous political significance. Of the forty-one named by the Attorney-General on June 13 1972, only Wijeweera, Wijesekera, the former Maoist M.P., S. D. Bandaranaike, and Susil Siriwardena, the former Director of Agrarian Research in the Ministry of Lands, had been of national importance. All these suspects were Sinhalese.[15]

The extent to which the JVP rested on the unemployed or the labouring classes is, again, very hard to determine. The Front's student leader claimed that the original small groups led by Wijeweera, "studied thoroughly and deeply the difficulties and problems of peasants, workers, students, fishermen and even street-hawkers and unemployed young men and women. . . . Revolutionaries from all other established parties joined us and worked hand in hand in our campaign."[16] This seems a reasonable picture of the social and political basis on which the JVP was built. A less propagandist and more academic analysis also stresses the breadth of appeal of the JVP to the frustrations of those who, because of their youth, rural background and inadequate education, were unable to share in the benefits which urban Marxists had promised them. H. A. I. Goonetilleke, librarian of the University of Ceylon at Peradeniya, writes that "the insurrection embodied in substance the explosive force of an extremely left-oriented militant cross-section of under-privileged rural youth in the upper forms of secondary schools, a minor army of frustrated and largely jobless school-leavers, plus a sprinkling of university graduates and undergraduates from the forgotten back-woods of Ceylon. This millenial style party emerging from the grass-roots level in the middle Sixties, driven by primitive socialist urges, openly professed its disen-

chantment with the prevailing political system with its inherent
inhibitions and built-in weaknesses, and was desperate to alter
the shape of Ceylon's society to their romantic heart's desire.
These young men and women were caught up in a system alien
to their lives and subjected to tremendous pressures to achieve
ends with which they could not identify. The revolting students
were not gangs of incorrigible juvenile delinquents nor
anarchist hordes of 'terrorists'. Their protest was a symptom
of a deeper malady in our society and economy, and a reflection
of the policy of drift in education. Their violent belligerency
betrayed besides a great concern with the quality of education,
the integrity of the educators and the ultimate objectives of the
educational process."[17]

The JVP Critique of Ceylon's Institutions

Because of its youthful, rural and Sinhala-educated character,
the JVP developed its ideology less consistently and with less
learned references to Marxist classics than any previous
Leftwing group since the founding of the LSSP. Its leaders
claimed to be Marxist-Leninists, working in the not necessarily
compatible traditions of Mao and Guevara. They specifically
rejected the title of 'Guevarists' as an invention of the press.[18]
In any case it is not clear what constitutes the ideological core
either of Castroism or of Guevarism, unless it is a rejection of
formal Communist Party tactics based on the urban working
class and its institutions. With this aspect of the Cuban approach
the JVP was fully in agreement. In stressing the role of the
peasantry in the revolution it was neither able, nor probably
willing, to earn the support either of China or of its local
representative Shanmugathasan. While there were sufficient
links between North Korea and local revolutionaries to earn
the disapprobation of Mrs. Bandaranaike, it is certainly not
established or even officially claimed, that the JVP studied with
any care the four-volume Sinhala edition of Kim Il-Sung's
works which were expensively produced during 1970. Had they
done so it is not clear what any of it would have meant in the
Ceylon context. In brief, the ideology of the JVP was totally
eclectic. From the LSSP tradition it drew Trotsky's criticism of
Stalinism and of the Ceylon Communist Party's 'popular

front' approach. From Maoism it drew on the assertion that the peasantry would be the backbone of the revolution, and from Cuba that armed insurrection was the only means of bringing socialism. Many of its beliefs were indigenous and their source was the Leftist interpretation of Bandaranaike socialism and nationalism. The generation which produced the JVP were mostly born after independence and came to political consciousness when Bandaranaike socialism formed the basis of consensus among all non-Tamil parties and when Bandaranaike nationalism inspired education, official culture and campaign rhetoric. While works by Lenin, Mao, Trotsky and Guevara were available in Sinhala by 1971,[19] the cultural environment within which rural youth lived was largely the product of the Buddhist revival and of SLFP political dominance. Apart from rejecting America as an enemy of China and Cuba, the JVP were not so much influenced by Western radical thinking as unaware of it. The small contingent of London-based students apart, they were created by and oriented towards the Third World as seen through Sinhalese eyes.

The JVP attacked on a broad front. Its strongest and most relevant thrust was against neo-colonialism, the parliamentary system and the established Left parties. While there is no totally reliable account of the five lectures which formed the basis of JVP indoctrination it seems clear that these three topics were a major preoccupation.[20] On such matters as Indian expansionism, the reactionary nature of Bandaranaike's thought or the backwardness of religious beliefs, JVP lecturers seem to have trimmed their sails to local winds. Despite the apparent communalism of the attack on "Indian expansionism" Wijeweera was ready to speak with Ilanchelian, reputedly the leader of the DMK on the tea estates, and to share a platform with the Tamil Trotskyist Bala Tampoe.[21] Although some JVP speakers were very critical of religion, the Front, like all other Sinhalese parties, maintained an organisation for *bhikkhus*.[22] Equally the JVP had no specific vision of the type of society which would be founded after the revolution. In those areas which were occupied, methods of administration ranged all the way from *ad hoc* shotgun committees to the appointment of JVP members within the old colonial structure of divisional officers. The extent to which ordinary villagers were drawn into or driven away from the guerilla structure varied immensely. It was in this that the JVP was furthest from Maoism and closest to the romantic improvisations of Cuba and Bolivia.

The concept of neo-colonialism was not, of course, invented by the JVP and they added nothing to its general understanding on a global scale. The dependence of Ceylon on the tea industry, World Bank loans and foreign aid, was well known to everyone active in Ceylon politics. The LSSP had argued twenty years ago that Ceylon's formal independence merely hid its total dependence on Western markets, plantation owners and financial institutions. The Communist Party had equally stressed that the United States had replaced Britain as the centre of world imperialism and maintained that position by military pacts, CIA interventions and the trading policies of multi-national corporations. It would have been hard to find anyone in Mrs. Bandaranaike's government who disagreed with these general propositions. Where the JVP developed its critique was in pointing out that the Coalition government itself was part of, created by, and necessary to, neo-imperialism. The SLFP, they argued, was the party of the national-bourgeois class, having strong affiliations with the imperialists who had created them by replacing the feudal economic system by a neo-colonial capitalist economy. The 'middle path' between capitalism and communism espoused by Bandaranaike was denounced as opportunism and "a perfect example of the weak vacillating nature of this particular class".[23] Thus "anyone who thinks that he can achieve socialism through aligning with the national bourgeois class is either a fool or an agent of the capitalists". This was very similar to the analysis of Karalasingham, Tampoe and Samarakkody on leaving the LSSP in 1964.

The particular features of a neo-capitalist economy were spelled out in the lecture generally called "Economic Chaos", and its political implications were explored in most of the others. While accounts of the lectures vary and they remain unpublished, the general attack on neo-colonialism may be summarised as follows. Ceylon's plantation economy had become incapable of dealing with its population growth. The Island was consuming more than it was producing, particularly as the middle-classes were unready to make sacrifices. The most exploited sections were the Kandyan villagers who had lost their forest lands to plantations, who saw estate methods producing erosion and who had no industry to absorb their sons. The education system produced merely clerks and unemployable Arts graduates. Thus there were three million surplus, educated youth with no future. So far all of this was widely known to economists and politicians. Their solution had lain in a combination of industrialisation and foreign aid. The JVP saw such foreign-induced aid as merely linking Ceylon more firmly to neocolonialism. While there is some doubt as to whether the JVP really wanted complete self-sufficiency on an agricultural basis, its general tenor was in that direction. It believed that tea plantations should cease to expand and that food should be grown on abandoned estates. Land tenure had become so unequal that collectivisation was the only solution. Rice imports would be stopped and the resulting foreign exchange used for capital development. Rivers would be harnessed for hydro-electricity as a basis for industrialisation and water would be redirected into the Dry Zone for irrigation. In general foreign aid was to be rejected unless it led directly, as with much East European aid, to the building of productive enterprises. The outstanding feature of much of this programme was that it derives to a large extent from most of the Marxist and Left-SLFP analyses made over the past twenty years. Where it departs is in the emphasis on cutting foreign economic links and in its tendency to see agriculture as capable of providing most of the future employment. Only in its demand for total collectivisation of land and commerce is it fundamentally different from the analyses and prescriptions made time and time again with little effect. This futility, the JVP argued, arose because the national bourgeois class had no vested interest in breaking with foreign capital or in losing its wealth in land and commerce.

The political consequences of neo-colonialism were traceable to the fact that power had been handed over by the British to those who had worked for them and whose interests lay in preserving their institutions. The established parties rested on the patronage system which parliamentary institutions made possible. Basically the administration and the armed services remained unchanged, following neo-colonialist traditions whether the UNP or the SLFP were in office. The JVP believed that British institutions were not suitable to Ceylon and were only preserved because the classes which dominated the system benefited from it. In particular, the alternation of parties, while it did not change the fundamental nature of the system, interfered with planning for consistent development. The advantage of a one-party system with popular support was that it made such development possible. In so far as the JVP had any coherent outline for the political future, they favoured strong one-party rule, collectivisation of the land and the centralisation of villages so as to improve the provision of common services. This was vague utopian rhetoric. In essence the JVP wished to abolish parliamentary government and the alternation of parties. "The people must realise that parliament is an agency of the bourgeois intended to confuse the people and divert their attention from the real problems of our country."[24] A one-party dictatorship was intended and in this respect too, the JVP moved away from the traditions of Ceylon Marxists among whom multi-partyism and dissent had been advocated for more than twenty years.

In attacking the British connection and traditions of Ceylon, the failure of successive governments to tackle well-known and often discussed economic problems and the parliamentary system, the JVP was attacking the Left parties all of which wished to retain the basic features of the existing system, and all of which had been involved in the governmental process. The lecture generally called "The Left in Ceylon" argued that the Marxist leaders were British-educated, had no revolutionary experience, either in Britain or Ceylon, but had simply graduated from respectable institutions and returned to become established members of the upper-middle classes who talked of revolution while drawing their parliamentary salaries and professional fees. The JVP particularly launched attacks against the Communist Party leader S. A. Wickremasinghe, a Goyigama landowner representing a seat in the heart of Wijeweera's Southern Province. Even the dissident Marxists who appeared to agree with JVP criticisms of the established parties were equally seen as Westernised pseudo-revolutionaries. Wijeweera repeatedly attacked Shanmugathasan and stated that he left the Maoist party because its leader was simply an arm-chair revolutionary. The JVP analysis tried to establish that the class basis of the Marxists made them, like the SLFP, products and agents of the process of neo-colonialism. The new middle-class of "small landowners, small traders, contractors etc." sent their sons to be educated in England. This gave rise to the "so-called Marxist movement" originated by "a few middle-class western-educated young men."[25] In contrast to the Trotskyist and Maoist dissidents, who subscribed to a 'betrayal theory', the JVP held that the Left movement was inadequate from the beginning because of its social origins in satisfied classes. From this standpoint the Coalition agreement of 1964 was not a betrayal at all but a perfectly logical development. The LSSP leadership "never abandoned its class origins". It was thus different from those misled by 'revisionism' to whom the JVP continued to appeal. Revisionism, too, arose from neo-colonialism. But it was Soviet neo-colonialism which had produced this phenomenon. The JVP leaders remained true to Maoism in holding that this practice began after Stalin's death, rather than subscribing to the LSSP tradition that the departure from the truth began with Stalin's defeat of Trotsky in the 1920's. In this, as in many other respects, the JVP was virtually uninfluenced by the sophisticated and cosmopolitan approach of the LSSP. Its ideology was "anti-elitist, anti-bureaucratic, anti-capitalist, anti-imperialist, anti-Indian expansion, and last but not least anti-imperialist trained army and police."[26]

Tactics of Insurrection

Armed with this eclectic but often conventional critique, the JVP launched what the radical Trotskyist Edmund Samarakkody called "the most serious attempt on the part of a section of the exploited masses to overthrow the State power in this country."[27] Several years of simple but effective indoctrination had produced a body of youth ready to take up armed struggle, a phenomenon previously unknown in Ceylon. Just as they rejected the ideology of the established Left, so they rejected its tactics. These had been classically concerned with mass mobilisation through trade unions, strikes, rallies and electoral campaigns. The working class was to be the spearhead, suitably led by trained Marxists. They were to build their institutions, including unions and parties, and defend these against attack. As argued elsewhere the approach was primarily 'defensist', believing that, even with the mobilisation of the voters behind a Left majority, the ruling class would not surrender voluntarily but would have to be forced from office. While the JVP certainly agreed with the last part of the proposition, it rejected the rest of these tactics as reformist, revisionist and, in the last analysis, as diverting the masses from their true tasks. In this respect they were following in the Castro-Guevara tradition as elaborated by Regis Debray. Vasudeva Nanayakkara M.P. who was arrested as a JVP supporter but subsequently released, tried to establish an intermediate position in an article on *Debray, Che and Revolution* written before the insurrection.[28] He argued that: "We in Ceylon with our own experience and that of India surely know that parliament today is not merely a platform for socialism but a point of take-off in that direction. To accept this is not to accept also the absence of any need for armed revolt. The necessity or otherwise of revolutionary violence in the entire process of the transfer of political power into the hands of the workers and peasants is dependent and wholly dependent, on the reactions and counter-revolutionary activities of the capitalists and imperialists who will lose their power and privileges. For the Marxist there is no solution short of the transfer of absolute power from the vested interests to the hands of the workers and peasants." He concluded from the Latin American experience that "revolutionary violence is necessary at some stage in the process of transferring political power to the hands of the people." While this may have earned Nanayakkara his term in detention, it was not precisely what the JVP had in mind.[29] Rather than believing in using parliament as a platform and defending the revolution for which the masses had voted, the JVP rejected parliamentary methods *in toto* and saw a sharp and final blow against the system as the only way of changing it.

The contempt of the JVP for reformist trade unionism made them ignore the major tactic used by the Left in Ceylon, the mobilisation of unionists for strikes or *hartals*. Even a sympathetic critic, Edmund Samarakody, had to admit that "the organised working-class as such did not participate in this armed struggle of the youth."[30] Nor was this surprising in view of the emphasis placed by the JVP on rural agitation. As the party newspaper stated: "The rural population represents a considerable proportion of the entire population. Of this rural population the majority belong to the oppressed classes. Due to the vastness of the number of the rural poor, they are the moving force of the Ceylonese revolution. The socialist revolution would succeed in Ceylon only when the oppressed peasantry become politicised and under the leadership of the working classes begin their class struggle."[31] Quite apart from this Maoist political formulation, the youth of the JVP membership and its high level of unemployment or student status made it very weak in the organised trade union movement.[32] Indeed the Coalition unions formed the backbone of volunteer vigilante squads formed to combat the JVP during the insurrection.

Apart from the theoretical stress on peasant numbers, the JVP also adopted tactics which were closer to those urged by Guevara and Debray than to the mass approach conventional to Ceylon Marxists. Just as the ideology was eclectic, so the tactics were opportunist. In 1970 Wijeweera had split with U. D. Dharmasekera over "showing the party's face to the people." Wijeweera had begun to agitate openly in the conditions surrounding the general election, holding rallies and openly organising classes.[33] He was beginning to act like a conventional Marxist. The conspiratorial group around Dharmasekera which was probably responsible for the attack on the American embassy in March, 1971, continued along the line of secrecy and violence. Yet Wijeweera's open tactic was only part of a strategy which included armed revolt as well. Recruitment was much easier under Mrs. Bandaranaike's government than under the UNP as the JVP had earned the right to open agitation by its support for the Coalition in the general election. Wijeweera took up a variant of the 'defensist' position, arguing that only if harried by the police would he advocate revolutionary resistance. In April, 1970, there were strong rumours of a planned coup. CID investigators claimed that "the plan also included an attack on police stations and raids on villages and large firms where guns were stored. In addition to raiding government institutions where explosives were stored, a part of the plan was to stop all transport in various areas and rob what was in the vehicles."[34] As this bore a startling resemblance to what actually happened a year later it seems highly probable that the JVP was planning to over-throw the UNP should it win the election. Mrs. Bandaranaike was later to claim that police reports on the JVP were missing from the files when her government took office. But there was ample newspaper evidence in early 1970 that the insurrection which broke out exactly a year later was already in train in precisely the same places and using precisely the same methods which were held in abeyance while Mrs. Bandaranaike's government was put on probation. Wijeweera's 'open' tactic was much less of a conversion to conventional Marxist methods than his opponents believed.

The JVP suffered two divisions on tactics, that outlined above and an earlier defection over their participation in the 1970 elections. By late 1970 Wijeweera seems to have gained support for a strategy which was in fact followed even after his imprison-ment. This was to function openly as an agitational group, while at the same time recruiting to a clandestine organisation. When the clandestine activities were attacked by the police and JVP members harried or arrested, this was to be taken as indicative of the failure of gradualist methods within the constitutional framework. The JVP would then arise at every point where it had a following and upon the same day. Infor-mants within the police and army had advised that these forces had insufficient ammunition to resist an Island-wide rising taking place simultaneously at many points. It would thus be possible to overthrow the State "at a single blow" without the long-drawn out guerilla warfare favoured by Mao and Guevara. In so far as Wijeweera made a contribution to revolutionary thought it was in urging the tactic of the 'once and for all' rising. Had the JVP been better co-ordinated and its leaders out of jail it is quite possible that he would have succeeded. Ceylon had one of the weakest armed forces in the world and its police were both poorly armed and very unpopular. The government had dropped most charges against the JVP laid under its predecessor and was reluctant until the March, 1971 attack on the American embassy to take any action against those who looked like the youthful embodiment of the past of so many Cabinet Ministers. Wijeweera himself, presumably trying to counter growing police pressure upon the government, denied the very tactics which his supporters were to use after his arrest. "We have never decided to attack police stations and capture arms and ammunition and will never resort to this type of offensive activities," he said at Anuradhapura in September, 1970. "Our policy is to attack no-one but to explain to the masses how the Government in power is trying to hoodwink them and attain their own personal ends."[35] Less than six weeks before the insurrection Wijeweera was still holding to the 'defensist' line. "We will strike when we are provoked to do so by the armed forces which are now trying to accuse us of conspiracy, but we are not conspirators", he told a rally at Hyde Park, Colombo. "We caution the Government not to send us underground. The revolution will commence on the day that our group is banned as we would have no alternative but to retaliate."[36]

When the insurrection came, it was sufficiently well co-ordinated and so nearly successful as to suggest that Wijeweera was disguising his true intentions. Even before his arrest on March 14, 1971 a bomb explosion had occurred at Esalamulla and there were signs of preparation for a rising at Kegalle and elsewhere. When the insurrection broke out on April 5 ninety-three police stations were attacked in two days over a wide area covering most of the Southeast of Ceylon. Subsequent activity was so widespread and initially successful as to suggest the plausibility of the 'single stroke' tactic in the Ceylon situation. The attack on police stations not merely focused attention on that aspect of the state most unpopular in rural Ceylon, but also gave access to the largest stocks of arms available in rural areas. There was little evidence of follow-up or contingency plans to meet the more resolute opposition of the Army and the intervention of foreign and particularly Indian assistance. The very spontaneity of the attacks on April 5, organised as they seem to have been only three days beforehand[37], meant that the JVP groups had no fall-back positions and only the most elementary plans for withdrawing into jungle and wild-life reserves. The JVP organisation itself had become fragmented and factionalised, with the groups around Badulla which launched the first attacks under the control of the most militant elements. In contrast none of the Universities provided effective bases and few undergraduates seem to have become directly involved. The 'single blow' tactic, having initially failed, became such a liability that no effective long-term guerilla warfare followed the initial defeat of the JVP.

The JVP and its Opponents

The most fervent critics of the JVP were fellow Marxists. To Mrs. Bandaranaike the movement remained one of 'misguided youth' and her analysis of it was typically conservative in stressing the need for parental guidance and a return to religious principles. The older generation of SLFP leaders had no real understanding of what had happened, nor any ideological riposte to positions with many of which they agreed. Equally the UNP had nothing to say about the JVP at all and Dudley Senanayake was reprimanded for refusing either to support the government or attack the insurrectionists.[38] The whole issue had nothing to do with the Tamils who had been completely uninvolved. To the Marxists, in contrast, the JVP represented a real threat to their future base, as well as an affront to their own claims to be leaders of the socialist revolution. Their criticisms may be categorised as simple abuse, ideological differences, tactical differences and grudging sympathy. Of the first type were the oft-repeated claims that the JVP was serving the interests of the CIA and the UNP. At one time it seemed as if Mrs. Bandaranaike herself subscribed to these.[39] Her government had asked for the withdrawal of an American embassy official who was believed to be connected with the CIA, and had expelled the Asia Foundation which was believed likewise to be a front for American intelligence. *Young Socialist*, which had translated Guevara's *Guerilla Warfare* into Sinhalese, made the claim of CIA support as early as April 1970 and many Leftwing intellectuals continued to believe this even after it became manifestly absurd. The pro-Soviet journal *Tribune* made the same claim.[40] In August 1970 the United Front parties jointly attacked the JVP as "an agency of reactionary forces."[41] At the same time N. M. Perera claimed that "the Che Guevara movement in Ceylon is a part of the American secret service."[42] The pro-Moscow Communist Party's own variant linked the reactionaries and the Maoists with the JVP. Its official statement claimed that having lost interest in the "Tampoe and

Shan groups" "the reactionary forces hope to capitalize on the political inexperience of sectors of the youth."[43] By the time of the insurrection Coalition Marxists were linking the JVP with the CIA, the UNP and "the very same people who were responsible for the assassination of the late Mr. S. W. R. D. Bandaranaike, the coup of 1962 and the bringing down of Mrs. Sirimavo Bandaranaike's government in 1964."[44] Even after the revolt, LSSP member Batty Weerakoon was still claiming UNP connections with the JVP through the disbanded Land Army.[45]

The revolt made it improbable that either the UNP or the CIA were really backing the JVP. The Left also had many serious reservations about the Front's tactics and ideology and the failure of the rising was seen as justifying these. From the extreme Left, Shanmugathasan had early distinguished himself from the JVP, though this was not to stop him from being arrested during the emergency. He accused them in May, 1970 of "petit bourgeois romanticism which violates the teachings of Mao Tse-tung Thought by repudiating the necessity for a revolutionary party". In particular he emphasised as the whole Left was to do later, that a revolution "is not a conspiracy or a coup. It is something in which tens of thousands of people are roused and actively participate."[46] After the defection of S. D. Bandaranaike, Shanmugathasan issued a further statement arguing that the former Maoist M.P. had "never either understood nor believed in Mao Tse-tung Thought" as proved by his action of "jumping on the bandwagon of the local Che Guevarites."[47] All this was perfectly in line with the opinion of the Chinese government expressed after the failure of the revolt. Chou En-lai's message to Mrs. Bandaranaike said: "Following Chairman Mao Tse-tung's teachings the Chinese people have all along opposed ultra 'Left' and right opportunism in their protracted revolutionary struggles. We are glad to see that thanks to the efforts of your Excellency and the Ceylonese government, the chaotic situation created by a handful of persons who style themselves 'Guevarists' and into whose ranks foreign spies have sneaked, has been brought under control. We believe that as a result of your Excellency's leadership and the co-operation and support of the Ceylonese people, these acts of rebellion plotted by reactionaries at home and abroad for the purpose of undermining the interests of the Ceylonese people are bound to fail."[48]

On the whole it was only the Maoists and the revolutionary Trotskyist groups which engaged in serious polemic with the JVP before the insurrection. The "CIA-UNP" smear was the usual weapon of the Coalitionists. They believed, in the words of T. B. Ilangaratne at a Ceylon-China friendship rally, that "we need not use guns or any other weapon to usher in the revolution. We have the Government now and it is up to us to develop the country on a truly socialist footing."[49] Only S. D. Bandaranaike and Philip Gunawardena[50] declared open sympathy for the JVP and they had climbed on so many bandwagons that no-one was surprised. To the established Left the most obnoxious feature of the JVP was its eclectic and nationalist ideology. The Coalitionist *Nation* repeated on several occasions that the JVP was 'Fascist'. After the revolt Batty Weerakoon, the editor, wrote that Wijeweera had "built up a political mumbo-jumbo which was the closest Ceylon has so far got to Fascism."[51] The pro-Moscow Communist Party held a similar position. Pieter Keuneman argued, immediately after the outbreak of the revolt, that "all the JVP offers is an infantile form of negative nihilism. It proclaims an absurd so-called 'war between the generations'. It exalts violence for its own sake. It calls for the destruction of what it considers the 'Establishment'. Let us make no mistake about it. In the JVP we are confronted with a potentially fascist and terroristic movement which serves the interest of sinister forces who have not yet declared their hand."[52] This was in line with the statement issued by the constituents of the Joint Committee of Trade Union Organisations in the same week which declared it "the bounden duty of the working-class to defeat these insurgent activities directed at overthrowing the present United Front Government . . . and setting up a Fascist dictatorship."[53]

This was all simple abuse, based on fear and incomprehension. As the revolt died down and the Coalitionists began to realise the breadth of JVP support, some more sophisticated attempts were made to understand this new phenomenon. A special number of *Nation* largely devoted to the JVP in May, 1971 continued the editorial line that the coup had been engineered by the Rightwing using "the entire machinery of the former

Land Army."[54] Another article denounced the ideology of the JVP student wing as "a disorderly mixture of Leftist and revolutionary slogans borrowed at random from Mao, Che, Lenin etc., of appeals to chauvinism and the age of Dutugemunu, of anti-Indian and racial propaganda and of somewhat hair-raising schemes to ensure national economic development and cultural isolation of Ceylon from the rest of the world. The whole thing was cemented together by a wild, fanatical cult of violence." A more sober analysis followed in the same anonymous article. The failure of the Left to conduct political education since 1960, coupled with the spread of Sinhala education which cut students off from the great bulk of Marxist literature, was blamed for the spread of this mindless eclecticism. Students, it was argued, were now largely of rural background with practical experience of peasant life. Thus it was not surprising that the conventional Left had to fight hard to regain its hegemony at Peradeniya.[55] In the same issue T. B. Ilangaratne wrote quite sympathetically of the motivations of the JVP. One important element, he argued, had been the "anti-feudal caste elements who have suffered long from poverty and indignity, and particularly the educated among them (who) might not have seen any impending change in the social structure." Ilangaratne went on to warn that "we have to recognise that iniquities in society will not be tolerated by the have-nots and the so-called depressed any more."[56] Ilangaratne, as a Kandyan, was one of the very few on the Left to draw attention to the caste factor.

The Effects of the Insurrection

Ceylon's first revolution failed. Once the government's ammunition shortage had been overcome by foreign aid, and the collapse of morale stopped by the vigilante squads, the JVP's own organisational failings were enough to ensure its defeat. The Front found its conspiratorial structure excellent for surprise attack, but too fragmented for a long-drawn out struggle. The curfew, censorship and suspension of mail and public transport made it impossible for what was left of a central command after the arrests of March, 1971 to keep in touch with local units. The 'single blow' strategy came close to working in the first three days and could well have done so if Colombo had not been so resistant to JVP organisation. The abortive collapse of the plot to kidnap Mrs. Bandaranaike and other government leaders was probably crucial.[57] The fallacy of rural guerilla operations, that power can be seized without capturing the seat of State power, was fully exemplified in Ceylon. After the first few days the only alternative for the JVP was to wage protracted warfare from established jungle bases. The 'single blow' strategy did not allow for this. While large parts of the country, including most of the Southeast and areas in the North Central Province, were occupied for weeks, they had no way of extending their territory. Once the cities were made immune by military control, it was simply a matter of time before order could be restored in the isolated areas around Kegalle, Elpitiya, Deniyaya and Kataragama. The importance of the revolt was not so much in its success or failure as in the impact it had on Ceylon's institutions and practices. These had been moulded in the tradition of British constitutionalism for three generations. Like the British, the Ceylonese had not witnessed revolutionary violence. The test of institutions is not whether they function in normal conditions but whether they survive abnormal upheaval. The JVP might have lost the immediate battle but it may have shifted the focus of politics from parliamentary to revolutionary struggles.

Even before the revolt there were signs of increasing police intervention in politics. Since the defeat of Sir John Kotelawala and the coup of 1962, the Ceylon police had retired into the background, engaging in normal policing duties only. Early in 1970 the CID began to investigate and report on classes and training camps being held in the jungles. In April, 1970, in expectation of a rising, police leave was cancelled, an all-Island alert was mounted and the Inspector General of police issued a circular describing JVP activities and using the term 'insurgent'.[58] Following a number of arrests a special section of the CID was set up under A. M. Seneviratne, Assistant Superintendent of Police, but its findings were largely ignored or overlooked by Mrs. Bandaranaike's new government when Wijeweera and others were released after the general election. However, after three months a new 'Insurgent Unit' under K. H. de Silva, ASP, was created.[59] By the time of the Esalamulla explosion in March, 1971, elements in the Coalition were openly calling for "a secret political police as an arm of the parties in power,"[60] and arguing that it was "high time the Government set up a secret service to combat political conspiracy".[61]

Once the insurrection was underway, the government had, necessarily, no inhibitions about using all the powers bequeathed by the British through the Public Security Ordinances, including curfew, censorship, arrest and detention on suspicion, military support for the police and state control over essential services. Many of these powers remained in effect for months after the insurrection, the Colombo curfew not being raised until November, 1971 and newspaper censorship remaining for longer. Trials of accused detainees did not begin until June, 1972 and the bulk of those detained were still in camps at the beginning of 1973. Thus the government had at its disposal the entire paraphernalia of a police state. Elections were not resumed until October, 1972 and all organisations and publications named as connected with the JVP remained banned. Emergency regulations of 1971 made it possible to prohibit processions and meetings, control publications through a 'competent authority', impound printing presses, licence the publication of newspapers, permit the burial or cremation of bodies by the police if necessary in secret, extend powers of search, seizure, arrest and detention to any police, military or prison officer, ban the distribution of leaflets, search for subversive literature, prohibit striking in essential services, suspend *habeas corpus* for detainees, and suspend local authorities. These powers were widely interpreted. The 'competent authority', for example, prohibited publication of court proceedings arising out of 'atrocity' cases against the police or military.[62] The most controversial measure was the creation of a Criminal Justice Commission to try those charged with treason from among the detainees. The delays of normal legal process were given as the reason for the creation of the Commission, although the opening of its first trial did not take place until over a year after the insurrection was completely crushed.

The continuing detention of 15,000 young people, without charges being brought against them, caused increasing concern within Ceylon and internationally. Prins Gunasekera M.P. was expelled from the SLFP for his activities on behalf of detainees, including the former Maoist leader, S. D. Bandaranaike. W. Dahanayake, once again an independent M.P., raised as a matter of privilege the detention of V. Nanayakkara M.P. and gained an apology from the government to the Speaker for not officially advising parliament of this, the only detention of a Member. Most government Members were very reluctant to criticise or take any steps which might be seen as questioning the wisdom of long-term internment. The burden of resistance fell upon the UNP, members of the legal profession and the still legal extreme Trotskyist groups led by Bala Tampoe and Edmund Samarakody. These all assisted Lord Avebury's mission on behalf of Amnesty International between September 18th and 28th, 1971 which ended with Avebury's expulsion from Ceylon. The Trotskyists and Maoists also maintained two separate and hostile 'solidarity campaigns' in London whose main objective was to oppose detention.[63] Avebury's report drew attention to a number of objections to continued detention. These were (1) that a monthly schedule should be set for release of all those against whom no legal action was planned; (2) that precise numbers of those to be charged be published; (3) that facilities be made available for legal representation of all detainees; (4) that a date be published for the beginning of legal proceedings; (5) a list be published of places of detention and the number available; (6) an up-to-date list of detainees be published; (7) the regulation permitting unsupervised cremation of corpses be repealed; (8) that those released from detention be assisted to resume employment.[64]

In view of Lord Avebury's expulsion and his continued association with Prins Gunasekera, Tampoe and Samarakody, his report had little immediate effect, apart from embarrassing Ceylon in England. His allies in Ceylon undoubtedly used his visit to make political capital. His report underlines the radical changes which had taken place as a result of the JVP rising. The coup case defendants of 1962 and 1966 had been tried through the normal judicial processes, which had taken several years and resulted only in their imprisonment while awaiting trial. Ceylon had never had concentration camps or mass internment before, nor special commissions for trying criminals outside the normal legal processes, nor a vast expansion in police powers and the size of the armed forces. One factor in the Communist Party's disaffection with the Coalition was the belief that these new powers would prove permanent and could be used against genuine, peaceful agitation within the political system. While the LSSP remained silent, many of its leaders were concerned about the expansion of the army to nearly three times its previous size, fearing the possiblity of a military coup. The widespread belief in police and army atrocities during 1971 gave substance to these fears. Mrs. Bandaranaike's own treatment of these stories was not altogether reassuring. She told parliament on July 20, 1971 that she did not condone excesses committed by the armed forces and had set up two Ministerial committees to investigate and receive complaints. She stressed that the guerillas had also committed atrocities and concluded that "it is also well for us to remember that had not the Security Services measured up to their tasks, we may not have been here today."[65] In view of the fact that the economy of the country was severely strained by added defence expenditure, internment and rehabilitation costs and the repair of damage, and that 15,000 people were in camps, normal civil rights were suspended and the great majority of M.P.s were silent or acquiescent, it might be argued that the JVP had done nearly as much to damage the structure of "Sri Lanka" in its first year as anyone had done to weaken "Ceylon" for the previous twenty-three years of its independent existence. The revolutionary challenge to Ceylon's institutions had been more successful than the organisation which made it.

A Fundamental Shift?

The JVP rebellion was so surprising to nearly everyone active in Ceylon politics that it brought into question the validity of politicians' claims to be in touch with their electors. A basic premise of effective parliamentary democracy is that the periodic appeal to the voters and the associated need to maintain mass organisation in the electorates, makes the parliamentarian highly sensitive to shifts in opinion and responsive to demands arising from the masses. In Ceylon, a small and well-educated nation with citizens actively taking part in the democratic process on all possible occasions, this seemed not to be the case. Almost the only sections of political society apparently aware of the spread of JVP influence were the police, who were ignored, and a few highly unrepresentative individuals on the far Left margin of politics. The JVP functioned within one sub-culture, while the established politicians functioned within another. Communication between the two was either faulty or non-existent. The characterisation of the JVP as "misguided", as "agents of the CIA" or as working for foreign powers or major (and still undiscovered) figures within established politics, are all unconvincing. They are particularly so when made by the same people who failed completely to predict the rising despite years of working in rural electorates and among Left-oriented youth.

The flaws in the political system which the rising revealed may be analysed in terms of lack of communication, of hierarchical relations between young and old, low and high caste and English and *swabasha* educated. A Marxist analysis, such as that of the JVP itself, is less satisfactory. The party organ claimed that "the oppressed classes have created the Janatha Vimukthi Peramuna, which represents the needs of the people".[66] In fact only particular sections of the masses seemed responsive. The trade union movement, on the whole, was remarkably impervious to JVP influence. Plantation workers, even Sinhalese labourerers, were only slightly affected. While some bus workers were involved in the JVP, the Ceylon Transport Board employees voluntarily set up a counter-intelligence service which was more effective than that of the police or army in reporting on JVP units in rural areas. To classify the JVP strictly in class terms does not lead very far. It had remarkable success in bringing poor village youth into active positions, but its leaders' statements of policy still reflected the cosmopolitan concern with Marxist theory which has characterised Ceylonese students for over thirty years.

The eruption of the JVP suggests that 1971 might prove as important a dividing line as 1956. In that year the rural masses saw their instrument in the SLFP. It would be an exaggeration to argue that the following for the JVP was on anything like that scale. Whole areas which had swung behind the SLFP in 1956 remained indifferent to the JVP or positively worked for its destruction. Yet the basis of the appeal was similarly populist and socialist. While the JVP leaders saw themselves as Marxist-Leninists, their followers, like those of Bandaranaike before, were relatively indifferent to such Western notions. They were fundamentally Sinhalese nationalists, despite the tenuous alliance between Wijeweera and Ilanchelian. Just as no Tamil districts responded to the SLFP in 1956, so there was no JVP impact either on the Indian Tamil tea workers or on the Northern and Eastern Provinces. Just as Colombo had proved impervious to the SLFP in the past, so it provided very weak support for the JVP in 1971. The JVP, like the SLFP before it, was a movement of rural Sinhalese, Kandyan as well as Low Country, Catholic as well as Buddhist. In this sense it was a true child of the victors of 1956.

NOTES

1. *Ceylon Observer* 15/11/1969.
2. Although there was some Maoist influence on Ceylon and Indian Tamils (see Chapter 5) it is unlikely that the pro-Peking Communist Party had more than a few hundred members in 1971. The various Trotskyist groups were of a similar size, although Bala Tampoe's control over the Ceylon Mercantile Union gave him some national significance.
3. In March, 1964 Suriya Books began translating Trotskyist works into Sinhalese. The Editorial Board (Meryl Fernando, V. Karalasingham, C. Goonetilleke, W. Andradi and Upali Cooray) aimed at rescuing "Marxism in Ceylon from the paralysing embrace of the old Brahmins." *Young Socialist* 3: 1 March 1964, p. 36.
4. J. van der Kroef: "Ceylon's Political Left"; *Pacific Affairs* 40, 1968.
5. W. D. N. Jayasinghe ('Loku Athula') listed the Politburo of the JVP in evidence as: Rohan Wijeweera (general secretary), W. P. Vittharana ('Sanath'), W. T. Karunaratne, U. M. Jamis ('Oo Mahataya'), B. A. R. Kurukulasuriya, W. M. S. Deshapriya, N. K. M. Senanayake, J. P. P. Dhanapala, S. Kumanayaka, T. D. Silva, L. G. Mahaduwage, W. S. Chandra and himself. Others of the forty-one charged before the Criminal Justice Commission on June 13, 1972, included: W. A. Osmund de Silva, M. D. N. Nimalaratne, N. Premaratne ('Chukki'), W. de S. Kanagaratne, S. V. A. Piyatilleke, Sarath Wijesinghe, S. Wickrama (all alleged members of the Central Committee) and S. D. Bandaranaike, Susil Siriwardena and Mahinda Wijesekera. Eleven of the suspects were not under arrest at the time of the initial hearing and some of these were presumed dead. See *Ceylon News* 22/6/1972 and 27/7/1972 and 'Loku Athula's police deposition,' as presented and cross-examined at the CJC (*Ceylon News* 16/11/1972–8/3/1973) and published in Sinhala in *Dinamina* in November 1972.

6. See G. Obeyesekere: "Some Comments on the Social Backgrounds of the April 1971 Insurgency in Sri Lanka"; *Journal of Asian Studies* 33, 1974, pp. 367–384.
7. The JVP was often called the 'K Guevarists' in reference to its Karawa leadership. Its leadership would not necessarily appeal to the lower castes on caste grounds, as the Karawa regard themselves as superior to the Goyigama, especially along the coast between Colombo and Matara from which a large number of the JVP leaders come.
8. I am indebted to Professor K. M. de Silva of Peradeniya for this information.
9. Ceylon Transport Board Intelligence Report no. 54; 23/4/1971. I am indebted to Anil Moonesinghe, chairman of the CTB, for allowing me to see these reports based on the observations of bus crews during the rising.
10. It was only in these areas that long-term occupation and open fighting with the military took place. The JVP district secretaries for these areas (according to 'Loku Athula'), were Sarath Wijesinghe (Kegalle), 'Jagath' (Galle) and Susil Wickremaratne (Matara).
11. Quoted in U. Phadnis: "Insurgency in Ceylon"; *Economic and Political Weekly* (Bombay) 6: 19, May 18, 1971, pp. 965–8.
12. They were not released until late December, 1971, but no charges were ever brought against them. *Ceylon News* 6/1/1972.
13. There had already been a major fire at Thulhiriya on October 6, 1970 caused by workers objecting to labour recruitment policies. *Tribune* (Colombo) 18/10/1970.
14. Rohan Wijeweera held that there was no Politburo or Central Committee, as claimed by 'Loku Athula' (see fn. 5 above). *Ceylon News* 14/6/1973. It is fairly clear that by April, 1971 there were rivals to Wijeweera's nominees in a number of places (particularly in Badulla) and that moves were beginning to take the leadership away from him altogether. See e.g. *Ceylon News* 18/1/1973.
15. Not a single non-Sinhalese was mentioned by 'Loku Athula' in the dozens of names he submitted to the police. The great majority of detainees were also Buddhists although there were some Christians as well. See Obeyesekere: *op. cit.*
16. *Sunday Observer* (Colombo) 23/8/1970. Interview with Mahinda Wijesekera.
17. H. A. I. Goonetilleke: "Higher Education after the April Insurgency"; *Nation* 5: 35, 20/6/1971, p. 5.
18. In 1971 Mrs. Bandaranaike's son Anura, while visiting Cuba, was able to extract support for his mother from Fidel Castro. *Daily Mirror* (Colombo) 1/5/1971.
19. Lenin and Mao had been extensively translated into Sinhalese and distributed in Ceylon through the Soviet and Chinese governments and associated bookshops. *Siri Laka*, an LSSP-oriented daily, translated Che Guevara's Diaries between August 25 and November 15, 1968. Sydney Wanasinghe, of *Young Socialist*, translated and published Guevara's *Guerilla Warfare* in three parts in 1968 and 1969. Premalal

Kumarasiri, a former Maoist, worked as a translator for the Cuban and North Korean embassies and was personally known to some JVP leaders. The Koreans spent substantial sums, including the purchase of full page advertisements in newspapers from 1969, to publicise the thoughts of Kim II Sung.

20. The summaries of lectures given here were supplied to me by a self-styled JVP lecturer in August, 1971. Other summaries appear in U. Phadnis: "Insurgency in Ceylonese Politics", *Institute for Defense Studies and Analyses Journal* (New Delhi) 3: 4, April 1971, pp. 595–9; Politicus (pseud.): "The April Revolt in Ceylon"; *Asian Survey* March, 1972 and R. N. Kearney and J. Jiggins: "The Ceylon Insurrection of 1971"; *The Journal of Commonwealth and Comparative Politics* XIII: 1, March 1975. As the lectures were not published their content varied according to who was giving them.

21. This meeting arose out of the Kennakelle Estate strike, which was supported by the Badulla JVP. See *Times of Ceylon* 19/11/1970 and Fred Halliday: "The Ceylonese Insurrection": *New Left Review* 69, September-October 1971, p. 80.

22. The Deshapremi Bhikkhu Peramuna. One monk, Ven. Minipe Sobitha of Vidyodaya University, gave evidence for the prosecution on his involvement with the JVP. Otherwise the participation of monks seems to have been exaggerated in contemporary accounts. *Ceylon News* 24/8/1972.

23. *Vimukthi* 20/12/1970.

24. *Vimukthi* 20/1/1971.

25. *Ibid.*

26. U. Phadnis: "Insurgency in Ceylon"; *Economic and Political Weekly* 6: 19 /8/5/1971.

27. E. Samarakkody: *Ceylon Youth in Armed Uprising*; Colombo(?) 15/5/1971.

28. *Ceylon Observer Magazine* 19/1/1971.

29. Nanayakkara was believed to be sympathetic to Dharmasekera rather than Wijeweera. See e.g. *Ceylon News* 5/7/1973.

30. E. Samarakkody: *op. cit.*

31. *Vimukthi* 30/9/1970.

32. Details of 23 of the 32 prime suspects in custody in July, 1972 show seven of them as previously unemployed, six as students or graduates, four as manual workers, 3 as clerical or professional, 1 as an army private, 1 a member of the Ceylon Administrative Service and 1 a former M.P. *Ceylon News* 27/7/1972. Their average age was 27. The Attorney-General named D. A. Gunasekera as "in charge of the trade union section". *Ceylon News* 17/8/1972. The main JVP stronghold was in the Land Development Workers' Union through its president J. P. P. Dhanapala who was tried before the CJC.

33. The key development was the Hyde Park rally of August 10, 1970 and the press conference of the same month at which Wijeweera proclaimed himself general secretary of the JVP. *Ceylon Observer* 11/8/1970. The Hyde Park rally was addressed by Wijeweera, Wije-

sekera, D. A. Gunasekera, Ven. Kahawila Devasiri and S. D. Bandaranaike.

34. *Daily Mirror* (Colombo) 20/4/1970.
35. *Sun* (Colombo) 2/9/1970.
36. *Daily Mirror* (Colombo) 28/2/1971.
37. Nine JVP leaders met at Vidyodaya University to plan the revolt on April 2, 1971. They were: S. V. A. Piyatilleke, W. P. Vittharana ('Sanath'), U. M. Jamis ('Oo Mahataya'), W. T. Karunaratne, Lionel Bopage, Susil Wickrama (ratne), W. M. Sunanda Deshapriya, B. A. R. Kurukulusuriya and W. D. N. Jayasinghe ('Loku Athula'). Evidence of 'Loku Athula' and *Ceylon News* 17/8/1972.
38. See e.g. the editorial in the *Daily Mirror* (Colombo) 19/4/1971.
39. For example in her speech to the 1970 May Day rally. *Daily Mirror* 2/5/1970.
40. *Tribune* 16/8/1970 and 23/8/1970.
41. *Ceylon Observer* 9/8/1970.
42. *Ceylon Daily News* 8/8/1970.
43. *Ceylon Daily News* 18/9/1970.
44. N. M. Perera in *Daily Mirror* 26/3/1971.
45. *Nation* 1/5/1971.
46. *Daily Mirror* 1/5/1970.
47. *Ceylon Observer Magazine* 16/8/1970.
48. Ministry of Defence Press Release 71/71; Colombo, 25/5/1971. Reproduced in F. Halliday; op. cit., p. 91; *Ceylon Daily News* 27/5/1971; and in *Ceylon: the JVP Uprising of April 1971*; Solidarity London Pamphlet 42; London, 1971; p. 47.
49. *Daily Mirror* (Colombo) 1/10/1970.
50. In a pamphlet *The Present Political Situation* issued in January, 1971.
51. *Nation* 1/5/1971.
52. *Times of Ceylon* 10/4/1971.
53. *Nation* 7/4/1971.
54. Batty Weerakoon in *Nation* 1/5/1971.
55. 'Akbar' in *Nation* 1/5/1971.
56. T. B. Ilangaratne in *Nation* 1/5/1971.
57. Trial evidence suggests that these arrangements were left to university students, most of whom did not appear at the rendezvous at Borella or were confused by the curfew. *Ceylon News* 6/7/1972.
58. *Ceylon Daily News* 25/4/1970.
59. *Sun* (Colombo) 7/8/1970.
60. *Nation* 16/3/1971.
61. *Nation* 23/3/1971.
62. *Ceylon Observer* 19/9/1971.
63. See the Bulletins of the Ceylon Committee and the Ceylon Solidarity Campaign published in London in 1972 and 1973.

64. Recommendations arising from Lord Avebury's Report submitted to the Prime Minister of Ceylon; Amnesty International, London; 18/11/1971. I am indebted to Miss Stephanie Grant of Amnesty for allowing me to consult the relevant documents.
65. *Sun* (Colombo) 21/7/1971.
66. *Vimukthi* 15/8/1970.

CHAPTER 11

From Ceylon to Sri Lanka

The passage from Ceylon in 1948 to Sri Lanka in 1972 is marked by contradictions. Democratic institutions were consolidated, only to be challenged by the first serious revolutionary movement for over a century. The welfare provisions were enlarged against a background of steadily deteriorating terms of trade, reserves and foreign indebtedness. State control of the economy was rapidly extended without appreciably lessening the social and economic gap between the upper and middle classes and the mass of the people. Foreign policy was reoriented towards China and the smaller revolutionary regimes of Asia and Latin America, without reducing dependence on trade, aid, tourism and eventually military assistance from the major capitalist states. Throughout the whole period Ceylon was consistently criticised by Western advisers for its social and economic policies, yet it managed at least to maintain the modest living standards of a population which doubled in less than twenty-five years.[1] There was certainly no 'takeoff' into industrialisation on the pattern of Singapore, Malaysia or Taiwan. Equally there was no decline into chaos as in Indonesia or stagnation as in Burma. Nor was social progress simply a charade, with the privileged hanging on to everything as in the Philippines. The Ceylon upper classes were politically and socially dominant but because of the country's economic position and the policies of SLFP governments, they were unable to enjoy the conspicuous affluence of their counterparts in much of Asia and Africa. An upper class which cannot acquire cars, cameras, electronic equipment or regular shopping trips to London, New York or Paris, is hardly masquerading behind a facade of socialism. Those who did, sometimes illegally, take advantage of their position to acquire personal advantages, were strongly criticised. By 1973 some, like the directors of Lake House or Hirdaramani's were facing trial for evasion of currency regulations[2] and in the following year Sir Oliver Goonetilleke and some of his relatives were successfully prosecuted for similar offences.

Political Development

To judge Sri Lanka's political development it is not enough simply to set up a number of arbitrary criteria and then to assess the degree to which these have been realised. Such criteria, whether they be the attainment of a 'modernised polity' or of 'socialism', tend to be imposed from outside and to require the acceptance of values which are not necessarily those of the actors within the situation being described. On a Western definition Sri Lanka has not yet established a fully effective modern democracy, or it would have been able to accommodate the grievances which broke out in revolutionary form. Equally it is not a socialist society or those grievances would not have arisen. Yet to accept either position uncritically is to impose ideal types on reality. In most institutional respects Ceylon was highly successful in adapting and developing democratic practices and attitudes. In terms of stabilising the parties, drawing the masses into electoral politics, avoiding military coups, bowing to popular pressures and defining the content of politics to accommodate those pressures, the political system provides a better model of a participatory democracy than many states of Europe or America. Experiments with Peoples' Committees after 1971, and with forms of workers' participation in nationalised industries, are further developments which may take Sri Lanka more rapidly along the path of formal democracy. These institutional devices, which are the logical outcome of a century of Western radical liberal thinking, have however been superimposed on a society which still largely accepts hierarchical notions arising from Sinhalese and Indian religion and philosophy and on an economic system in which realisable wealth is concentrated into very few hands even if formal property ownership is fairly widely spread. Moreover even if Sri Lanka were to become more egalitarian as a result of measures like the Land Reform Act of 1972, it would still have

great difficulty in meeting the demands of its people for jobs
and incomes. Liberal democracy rests on the assumption that
the economy is sufficiently expansive for popular demands to be
met. Such an assumption cannot automatically be made for Sri
Lanka.

Liberal democracy also assumes equal access to power,
although in all existing democracies, as in every other type of
political system, this does not prevail. In Ceylon, as in the
original British model, certain classes had much greater access
to parliament and the bureaucracy than did most of the
population. The status system of the society reinforced this
differential access. Lawyers and civil servants were not only the
two most politically powerful groups but their education,
background, language and ownership of landed property made
them socially dominant as well. The 'capitalist class' in a
Western sense was relatively weak, particularly as it was drawn
disproportionately from small minority groups like Borahs,
Sindhis or Christian Karawas. The most politically important
businessmen, such as H. W. Amarasuriya or D. R. Wijewardena
were, like the Senanayake, Bandaranaike and Ratwatte families,
part of the dominant Sinhala Buddhist culture and were thus
capable of exercising continued influence after independence
where other capitalist groups were on the defensive, mainly
through the political agency of the UNP.

The political system thus relied upon, and consequently
served the interests of, the Anglicised professional classes and
particularly those sections of them who were identified with the
Buddhist revival, rather than with Christian or British culture.
The 'emerging élite' proved to be this segment, together with
their natural allies, the 'new mudalalis', or Sinhalese businessmen who expanded their fortunes on the basis of the licensed
and controlled capitalism introduced by the first Bandaranaike
government. Neither they, with their dependence on government protection, nor the older established Sinhala Buddhist
plantation owners or businessmen, had any real interest in an
expanding private enterprise economy. The UNP was not
encouraged to develop as an entrepreneurial private enterprise
party but assumed the role of protecting existing businessmen
against further restriction, taxation or nationalisation. Both
major parties had an incentive to advocate state socialism. It

was electorally attractive to the mass of the voters who had little property and no privilege. At the same time, it need not seriously disadvantage the Sinhala plantation and business interests who were to be found equally in the UNP, the SLFP and the Marxist parties.

There was thus a fairly solid political and economic basis to the establishment of a consensus between the major Sinhalese parties. This consensus stood some chance of being acceded to by the two major Tamil parties which were equally dominated by the professional and socially superior sections of their particular community, and by the Christian and Muslim minorities whose leaders had enjoyed strong positions, in the professions and business respectively, since British colonial times. No politically important class had a strong incentive either to develop Ceylon firmly along Malaysian lines as a private enterprise economy attracting foreign capital, or to follow the Burmese road to Buddhist socialism in which foreign capital was excluded and domestic commerce was completely state owned. Nor, until 1971, did there seem to be any significant group wishing to follow a Chinese or Cuban road of revolution followed by drastic restructuring of society. All Marxist groups, including the radical Trotskyists and Maoists, were enmeshed in the established political system. The radical Left simply enjoyed a parasitical position upon the larger LSSP and pro-Soviet Communist Party. The potentially inflammatory situation among the Ceylon Tamils was always contained by leaders who were more conservative than their Sinhalese counterparts. The Indian estate workers were highly unionised but politically isolated under essentially social-democratic leaders who were, themselves, members of the business and plantation-owning classes. The DMK has so far proved to be an irrelevance in both Tamil communities and during 1971 there was not a single revolutionary incident involving them, despite a promise from the self-styled radical DMK leader Ilanchelian, that his supporters would rally to the JVP revolution.[3]

By most standards, then, the institutionalisation of parliamentary democracy was far advanced by the time the new constitution placed parliament firmly at the centre of political authority. A common commitment to democratic socialism bound together all the major Sinhalese parties, who also accepted the unitary state, the dominance of the national culture and religion and the desirability of a neutral foreign policy which would attract aid and support from all sides. There were major differences of emphasis within this consensus and without them the vigour of political debate would have been severely limited. There was a general acceptance of extended patronage as a motive force behind political allegiance and of the need to reform and politically control the bureaucratic administration. All parties encouraged candidates from the rural intelligentsia, the peasantry and the clerical, teaching and shopkeeping classes to run under their respective banners for local office. None was anxious, and only the SLFP proved able, to attract such people into positions of national influence. Rather, the parties committed themselves to restructuring the education system in such a way as to broaden the opportunities for the rural masses to elevate themselves to a position where they would eventually share power. In so doing successive governments greatly expanded the horizons of the young without at the same time being able to make any concrete provision for employing those who were being prepared for jobs which did not exist.

In trying to understand how such a seemingly successful political system contained within it an explosive potential which grows yearly, there is little to be learned from strict Marxist or Weberian approaches.[4] Ceylonese Marxists have consistently failed to understand or even adequately to describe their own society. Apart from some promising articles in *Young Socialist* in the 1960's and the individual contributions of Colvin de Silva, Doric de Souza, Hector Abhayawardhana and a tiny handful of other intellectuals, Ceylonese Marxism has been concerned with events outside Ceylon and largely irrelevant to it, or with factional disputes and expedient politics. None of this has produced a single meaningful analysis of the reality of such concepts as 'ruling class', 'capitalist class', 'compradore bourgeoisie', 'feudalism', 'neo-colonialism' or even 'proletariat' and 'peasantry'. All these terms are used in polemic but they have been given no specific local reference. To do so would produce rather embarrassing political conclusions. It might, for example, be argued that the entire welfare state rested on the backs of Indian Tamil estate workers through their contribution to the export economy and that, in one sense, the whole of Sinhalese and Ceylon Tamil society is 'exploiting' the estate workers as a whole.[5] It would be difficult to explain away the fact that many of the unionised wage-earners under Marxist leadership are white-collar employees of the state or of private commercial concerns and thus, strictly, also living off the 'surplus-value' produced by productive labour.

No satisfactory Marxist model has yet been applied to Sri Lanka and it is hard to believe that one will be. Maoism looks in vain for the social formations found in China, Stalinism searched for an almost non-existent industrial proletariat, Trotskyism can hardly advocate the building of socialism in one country though that was the aim of the Coalition government of Mrs. Bandaranaike. When the various Marxist groups desisted from denouncing each other as traitors they really had surprisingly little to contribute either to understanding Ceylon or to providing concrete solutions to its immediate problems. Hence the appeal of the JVP in 1971 to educated but underemployed youths who had waited for the results of the promised revolution only to find that it had not taken place. A major segment of the intelligentsia has been committed to some form of Marxism ever since Ceylon gained independence. This segment has filled some of the most influential roles in the political and administrative structure. Yet once in those roles most Marxists have fully accepted advice from the World Bank, the ILO, and visiting teams of Western economists. A major element in the political culture has been the expectation of a socialist revolution, an attitude which cannot help but threaten the stability of any political institutions established on existing bases. While the revolutionaries themselves become 'domesticated', their ideas are simply taken up by a younger and less easily accommodated section of the masses which sees less and less opportunity of benefiting from the existing social and economic arrangements.

Thus the ideological consensus is faulted and the basis of the system, in general satisfaction or apathy, becomes increasingly insecure. The masses of Sri Lanka are more effectively politicised than anywhere else in non-Communist Asia. Despite conservatism and deference the controllers of the political system cannot rely on apathy or indifference to provide a ballast. They can certainly not assume that only the urban working-class, over which the established Marxists still have organisational control, is likely to respond to revolutionary appeals. They cannot be sure that such appeals will come, as in the past, largely from members of the upper-middle classes who have a stake in stability. Nor can non-Marxists assume that effectively working liberal institutions guarantee stability. By raising expectations they might well have the opposite effect in the economic circumstances in which Sri Lanka finds itself.

Consensus Building

To maintain an effective parliamentary democracy there must be sufficient agreement on policies and appointments for the victors not to feel it absolutely essential to cling to power at all costs and for the defeated not to resort to revolutionary violence to redress the balance. Before 1971 this had been consistently the case, despite some hesitations in March, 1965 and the alleged but unproven complicity of the Opposition in the abortive coups of 1962 and 1966. The acceptance of defeat is a fundamental operating rule. If the system is to remain stabilised there must also be a fair degree of agreement among the competitors on major policy issues. When the government is changed, there should be basic continuity which allows it to be changed yet again without the whole system lurching from one extreme to another every few years. One element in this continuity can be provided by a non-partisan and expert administration. In recent years the parties have increasingly favoured patronage or selective transfers within the public service with the result that personnel no longer remains stable upon the change of government. The other element in providing continuity, a high degree of policy consensus among the major parties, therefore becomes increasingly important. Such a consensus has been maintained and even widened since 1956, despite the often repeated dichotomy which Ceylonese politicians stress between 'reaction and progress' or between 'democracy and dictatorship', when contrasting their party with its opponent.

This consensus has been built and maintained by many

features of the system which have already been outlined. The steady development towards a two-bloc party division meant that only the Tamils were left outside a trend which encouraged competition at the margin between the two major elements, competition which naturally tends towards the 'centre' where the swinging voter is believed to reside. Sri Lanka's electors have thrown out their rulers at every election since 1956 and this search for their loyalty is thus every bit as vital as in any other two-party system. Three quarters of seats have changed hands since 1956 and this volatility is most apparent in the Wet Zone Kandyan seats. As the electoral system makes these seats proportionately more numerous than their population would suggest, the consensus is built up on what the politicians, many of whom represent Kandyans, imagine the traditional peasant voter to want. The consensus is further maintained by the previous fluidity of partisan loyalties, which means that both the major parties have considerable segments who have belonged to other parties. There is a large ex-Marxist group in the SLFP and a large ex-SLFP group in the UNP, not to mention less important transfers between each and every one of the Sinhalese parties. Finally the consensus is bolstered by the common social and educational background of party leaders.

The consensus among Sinhalese politicians is not simply a form of words but reflects these features of the political system and particularly of the electoral situation. Although the two major blocs are verbally hostile and contain elements who speak openly of revenge or suppression against their enemies, they behave, and are forced by the electors to behave, in a manner which makes a major degree of mutual accommodation and tolerance unavoidable. Within each bloc there are further consensual elements in the need for smaller parties to accept the positions of their larger partners, who in turn must make some more limited accommodation to them. This mutual bargaining brings the Tamil element into the consensus to some extent. The UNP 'National Government' of 1965 balanced the Sinhala communalism of Philip Gunawardena and the Rajaratnas with the Tamil protectiveness of the Tamil Congress and the Federal Party, though this unnatural consensus broke down within a year or two. Both major blocs have come to arrangements with the two Indian Tamil estate unions, bringing even this alienated element into the system to some extent. The consensus is based on electoral necessity, coalition politics, compromise between communities and an appeal to the balance-holding Sinhala (and particularly Kandyan) peasantry. Not surprisingly the exercise needs a computer-like mind to manage it. It also involves endless policy adjustment, the rejection of once fundamental positions and a return to them again when the situation changes. The consensus is thus fragile and where it cannot be sustained, as between 1958 and 1962, the system itself may well become very fragile too. It is, further, a consensus which is acceptable only as producing concrete benefits. By 1971 a significant part of the youth no longer worked within the consensual agreements of their elders.

In general the SLFP dictated to others what issues should be agreed upon. This right it earned by the landslide of 1956 and its subsequent tenure of office for nine years. In 1955 the UNP had been clearly a conservative party, despite earlier attempts by Dudley Senanayake and others to commit it to nationalism and social democracy. The Marxist parties, particularly the LSSP, were opposed to Sinhala communalism and made a strong appeal in the Tamil and tea estate areas. They still asserted their revolutionary objectives. In foreign policy Sir John Kotelawala firmly committed Ceylon to the American alliance and allowed Britain to keep bases in Ceylon. There was very little consensus, either between the UNP and the SLFP, or between either of them, the Marxists and the Tamil parties. By 1970 there was agreement on so many more issues that parliament voted unanimously to become a Constituent Assembly for the creation of a new constitution, a policy once confined to the LSSP. The leaders of the LSSP and the Communist Party now sat in a government with a party which they had regarded as "petty-bourgeois" in 1955. In effect they accepted democratic socialism by abandoning a radical Marxist stance, just as the UNP accepted it by deserting its open free-enterprise liberalism. Naturally their interpretation of the term varies considerably. Twenty years before neither would have been prepared to use it at all.

The process by which this consensus was built can be traced through policies emerging over a long period of time. S. W. R. D. Bandaranaike was already elaborating the basic elements in the future programme of the SLFP through the Sinhala Mahasabha in the 1930's. The LSSP, too, committed itself by 1939 to policies which were later to come into operation and be accepted by all Sinhala parties. These included the gradual extension of the use of Sinhala and Tamil in the lower courts, the abolition of the village headman system, nationalisation of petrol imports, a ban on Indian estate labour immigration, bus nationalisation and a State takeover of education.[6] These were all to be implemented after 1956 by the SLFP, except for the ban on Indian immigration which was made effective as early as 1949. While the LSSP was to remain outside the consensus until the 1960's by advocating Marxist revolution and by its defence of the Ceylon and Indian Tamils, some of its attitudes had always been similar to those on the Left of the Ceylon National Congress. Within the Congress it was not simply Bandaranaike who pressed for *swabasha* and social reform but J. R. Jayawardena and Dudley Senanayake as well.

Through the Sinhala Mahasabha, Bandaranaike kept up this pressure after the foundation of the United National Party. At the 1949 UNP annual conference the SMS submitted resolutions on Sinhala, national dress, prohibition of alcohol and horse racing, the nationalisation of education and the promotion of ayurvedic medicine.[7] Even after Bandaranaike had left the UNP, resolutions in a similar vein continued to be moved. In 1954 conference reiterated "its decision to make Sinhalese and Tamil the official languages throughout the country in the shortest possible time." In the following year Dudley Senanayake and H. W. Amarasuriya moved again for the total prohibition of drinking and racing. At the same conference a resolution was submitted calling for "an over-all and co-ordinated Socialist programme."[8] Most of these resolutions were either sidestepped or passed but not implemented. However they suggest that on the Right as well as the Left there were some policy ingredients which could form the basis of a more rapid move towards consensus after 1956. At the time of Bandaranaike's victory the degree of consensus was small, though already perceptibly greater than in 1947 when the UNP ran against Marxists committed to revolutionary solidarity between all sections of the masses.

The building of consensus can best be traced on two issues,

the language policy and the adoption of democratic socialism. On both there were movements towards the SLFP position by the UNP and the Marxists. These bear out Bandaranaike's own assessment in 1952 that "our Party is a middle party."[9] On language all non-Tamil parties had been committed since before independence to *swabasha*, meaning the official use of Sinhala and Tamil as outlined in the State Council resolution of 1944 on conditions of parity and designed to replace English. An enquiry on implementation of this policy reported as early as 1946.[10] The adoption of "Sinhala Only and the reasonable use of Tamil" by the SLFP in 1955, coupled with the campaigns of the Basha Peramuna, changed the situation. Philip Gunawardena's VLSSP had already adopted a Sinhala Only policy in 1954. Agitation grew until the UNP changed its policy at Kelaniya in 1956. It was only the Tamil parties, the Communists and the Samasamajists who still supported parity. Marxist meetings were violently broken up in 1955. As the Communists admit in their official history "the two Left parties were temporarily isolated from the mass movement and the initiative passed out of the hands of the Left."[11] It was not until 1960 at a riotous delegate meeting during negotiations for a no contest pact with Mrs. Bandaranaike, that the LSSP finally voted for Sinhala Only. This had become essential not only electorally, but to make feasible the associated tactic of supporting the SLFP. Six years later the Left had moved over so far as to organise a mass strike against the Reasonable Use of Tamil regulations, which had been an integral part of Bandaranaike's original programme. These regulations were largely implemented to accommodate the Federal Party in its alliance with the UNP, suggesting that even the Federalists had *de facto* abandoned parity.

The shifting of the Left and Right on language away from parity and towards Sinhala Only was a clearcut and easily documented trend. The movement on democratic socialism is more complex as the term is vague and its implementation more complicated. Even G. G. Ponnambalam, at the foundation of the Tamil Congress in 1944, declared himself to be a socialist although the party programme does not mention the word.[12] The LSSP at its foundation had subscribed to the classic formula of "the nationalisation of the means of production, distribution and exchange." By its own account it was not until the expulsion of the Stalinist group that "a clear revolutionary programme" was adopted.[13] The Communists scarcely mentioned socialism in the manifesto adopted at their first congress in 1945 as they were still members of the National Congress and searching for a formula which would allow an "anti-imperialist" united front to be formed. At the same time Bandaranaike was saying of the Sinhala Mahasabha that it was "definitely socialistic".[14] This was not, however, an aspect that the United National Party was to stress on its formation, including as it did most of the leaders of Muslim business and Sinhala plantation owners. The UNP did very little that could have been called socialistic and its election propaganda in 1947 and 1952 was predominantly anti-Marxist.

The SLFP declared itself as Democratic Socialist from its foundation and was recognised as such by the Socialist International. The great bulk of nationalisation measures, in banking, insurance, trade, transport, oil and plantations were all undertaken by the Bandaranaikes. The United National Party's claim to be socialist depends much more on the creation of public corporations in previously unexploited areas and in the continuance of SLFP policies. Its verbal commitment to socialism became much more pronounced after 1956. In J. R. Jayawardena's opinion this marked one of the greatest changes in its policy.[15] In 1958 it incorporated Democratic Socialism into its programme and this has been reaffirmed at several party conferences. What this actually means is far from clear. In its 1965 manifesto the UNP laid great stress on liberty and democracy. Its only socialist pledge was "to continue to run the Ceylon Transport Board and the Port Cargo Corporation and the other nationalised undertakings." It also argued for the co-existence of the public and private sectors on the grounds that "what free enterprise can achieve in some sectors of the economy a Government Department or corporation cannot achieve except at greater cost and slower speed."[16]

If the UNP conversion to socialism is half-hearted, the Marxist conversion to democracy is more marked. The Communists at their Sixth Congress in December, 1960 adopted a thesis extending to Mrs. Bandaranaike's government "its wholehearted co-operation to implement the progressive

policies of the 1956 programme of the late Mr. Bandaranaike."
This went on to argue extensively about the parliamentary and
democratic nature of the party: "The Communist Party seeks
to establish full democracy and socialism in Ceylon by peaceful
means. It considers that by developing a mass movement, by
winning a majority in Parliament and by backing the majority
with mass actions, the working class and its allies can overcome
the resistance of reaction and ensure that Parliament becomes
an instrument of the people's will for bringing about fundamental changes in the economic, social and state structure."[17]
Apart from the brief period of 'ultra-Leftism' between 1948
and 1950 this has always been the Communist position. The
LSSP, in contrast, has moved considerably from the revolutionary Trotskyism of the 1940's because of the need to work under
the shadow of the SLFP. This it has achieved only with serious
splits and considerable confusion. The group around N. M.
Perera had to fight hard between 1960 and 1964 to get their
policy of alignment with the SLFP adopted and were often
defeated, particularly in 1962. As the Samasamajist intellectual,
Hector Abhayawardhana, argued at the time "the Left in
Ceylon cannot continue to function on the two planes of
parliamentarianism and doctrinaire revolutionism simultaneously."[18] An academic analyst had similarly prophesied in
1959 that "the traditional Marxist parties will have to become
increasingly social democratic or face the risk of greater loss of
electoral strength."[19]

Since the Coalition there has been little talk of revolution and
dictatorship in the LSSP. This has been confined to the 'Far
Left', the JVP, Maoists and Revolutionary Samasamajists.
Throughout her first period of office Mrs. Bandaranaike
stressed that the SLFP was a democratic socialist party and this
was fully accepted by her partners. While it might be argued
that the Left means something far more radical than the Right
by 'socialism', developments since 1956 give credence to the
notion that a greater degree of consensus exists on the shape
of the Ceylon economy than previously as well as on the
methods of attaining socialist ends. The same coming together
of extremes is notable in foreign policy, on the constitution and
on cultural and religious issues. In most respects the Tamil
parties have stayed outside the consensus but ceased resorting

to *satyagraha* and passive resistance, suggesting a higher degree of accommodation than in 1958-1962.

"Nationalising" Politics

That a consensus on particular issues has been established and maintained suggests that Sri Lanka's political élite has recognised certain common goals. The success of the system may be measured by the extent to which those goals have been achieved. Broadly the aims of partisans can be summarised under the one word 'decolonisation'. From 1915 to 1956 this meant transferring formal authority from the British to the Ceylonese. This was easily achieved, given the willingness of the British to withdraw from South Asia after 1945 and their earlier preparation of Ceylon for self-government under constitutional provisions more far-reaching and democratic than in any other Afro-Asian colony. The Ceylon élite naturally adopted the role into which it had been placed by the colonisers. Until 1956 very little changed. The last British Governor-General was replaced in 1954 by a Sinhalese Anglican Knight, appointed by Queen Elizabeth on the recommendation of a Cambridge educated Sinhalese Buddhist Knight. The Queen herself had visited Ceylon in the previous year amidst much jubilation. Despite the report of the Official Languages Commission in 1954, English continued to be the language of law, administration, intellectual discourse and policy-making. The 'vernaculars' were preserved for electioneering. The Westernised élite simply completed some unfinished business already begun before independence, including the disfranchisement of Indian Tamils. Over 90% of international trade and a large part of internal commerce and the plantation industry remained in British and Indian hands. British airmen and sailors were stationed at Katunayake and Trincomalee and the Queen's portrait hung in public offices.

In this first stage the system had only to adjust to dealing with foreign affairs, where the government aligned firmly with Anglo-American postures on all important issues except trade with China. The goal of formal independence had been reached. However decolonisation of a system effectively under European domination for several centuries proved a complex process.

Ceylon, rather than being a new nation, was a very old nation which had remained dormant in the countryside but by no means dead. Parliamentary democracy coped easily with the strikes and threats of revolution from its thoroughly Western-ised Marxists prior to 1956. Thereafter the system was placed under far greater strain, as the general goal of decolonisation proved much more elusive than the legalistic Ceylon National Congress and UNP leaders had imagined. When Bandaranaike spoke, in his first Reply to the Address on May 4, 1956, of a "new era", he was recognising that decolonisation included the ending of cultural and economic domination by foreigners.[20] To eliminate these obstacles was to be a longer task than simply becoming independent. It had not been completed by 1972.

The objective of cultural and economic decolonisation can be analysed into its component parts of communal readjust-ment, cultural reassertion and economic self-sufficiency. The first implied that the Sinhala Buddhist majority should also be a majority in all important areas of employment and power. The second involved restoring Buddhism to its 'rightful place', making Sinhala the national language, creating a national education system and loosening the hold of English culture in all significant areas of thought. The third alone included what Western sociologists and political scientists have seen as the major task of new nations, modernisation and industrialisation. Economic self-sufficiency meant not only ending the hold of British and Indian business upon the economy but also ending its reliance on trade with the former coloniser. This had endless ramifications, from foreign policy changes to alteration in the tenure of plantations. While Ceylon was highly successful in communal readjustment and relatively successful in cultural reassertion, it moved very slowly towards its economic objectives.

The political élite had already mastered the basic principle of communal adjustment during the State Council. The Soulbury Constitution, particularly in its electoral provisions, enshrined much that had been learned about asserting the rule of the majority while securing the acquiescence of the minorities. In every significant walk of life, except so far in commerce, com-munal adjustment has taken place. The system strained and almost collapsed between 1958 and 1962, when this process was at its height. By 1962 the goal had been largely achieved. Only where economic factors were pre-eminent, particularly on the plantations, was it impossible to declare communal adjustment fully effective. The painfully slow process of registering the status of Indian Tamils preparatory to their repatriation was not simply due to administrative incompetence. A government which can issue ration books and polling cards to all its citizens could, if it chose, have registered half-a-million aliens. Rather, it recognised that the whole basis of the economy still lay in tea export and that few but the Indian Tamils were likely to work on the estates.

In the field of cultural reassertion the policies laid down by the Buddhist Commission Report and adopted by Bandaranaike were carried out by 1962 in most cases. What "giving Buddhism its rightful place" actually means was never clear, although all Sinhalese parties have subscribed to it since 1956. The elevation of the two *pirivenas* of Vidyodaya and Vidyalankara to university status in 1959, the creation of the Ministry of Cultural Affairs and the temporary replacement of Sunday holidays by Poya Days in 1966 all suggest that a great deal has been done in this direction. Mrs. Bandaranaike's government claimed in 1962 that, with the setting up of the new Ministry, "Buddhism, the religion of the majority of the people of this country, was given its rightful place and a revival of national culture—dancing, literature, music, etc.—was actively promoted, encouraged and financed by the Government."[21]

Cultural reassertion in non-religious areas has been less successful. Once again, economic factors have proved fairly intractable. Despite constant agitation against South Indian Tamil films and magazines, their economic viability has preserved them.[22] The English language press continues to sell one-third of all daily papers and English is used by intellectual journals ranging from the official publications of the University of Ceylon to *Red Flag* of the Maoist Communist Party. Educational policy has had constantly to be modified to meet the reality that there are very few Sinhala texts and translations which are much use above the primary level.[23] *Swabasha* educated graduates have gone to swell the ranks of the unemployed simply because a knowledge of English is vital for a country engaged in international commerce.[24] Catholic schools have continued to exist in fact, although 'Manager Controlled' since 1960. Even the zoning of schools has not prevented ambitious parents from registering their addresses within the Royal College or Ananda catchment areas or giving donations to 'non-free' schools like St. Thomas's. The fact that an English-based education is still the key to public service positions has not been lost on the general public. Nor, although most parliamentary speeches are made in Sinhalese, has it ceased to be true that government publications are in all three languages, 'Sinhala Only' notwithstanding.

Controlling the Economy

Because the great majority of important politicians are both drawn from 'oral professions' like law and teaching and have had Anglicised upbringings, they have been less successful in 'renationalising' Sri Lanka than, for example, the Buddhist leaders of Thailand or Burma. Their attention has been focused on the symbolic aspects of cultural reassertion. In economic affairs even those with some expertise have been oriented towards Britain, a country notoriously incapable of solving its own economic problems. The goal of economic self-sufficiency has proved the most difficult to formulate, let alone reach. While a consensus has been established that democratic socialism is to be the method used, this is still differently interpreted by Left and Right. The mixture of the mixed economy has different components, depending on whether the UNP or the SLFP is in power. Both sides in politics are aware that there is a genuine difficulty in increasing savings and investment at the expense of consumption. Sri Lanka has the most elaborate welfare state in Asia and its electors and trade unionists regard its preservation as more important than sacrificing for a future which changing patterns of trade may well destroy in any case.

The goal of economic self-sufficiency is generally accepted as involving the Ceylonisation of the economy, import substitution to preserve the trade balance and constant expansion to absorb the rapid population increase and end dependence on foreign aid. The first of these, being related to the general goal of communal readjustment, has been achieved to a limited extent. With the exception of bus and port nationalisation most of the state intervention by the Bandaranaikes was aimed to some extent against foreign interests. Trade with the Communist countries, which expanded after 1956, was reserved for Ceylonese citizens. The Co-operative Wholesale Establishment greatly extended its trading powers in areas which had been Indian dominated. The restrictive importing measures introduced in October, 1962 gave the government a further opportunity to Ceylonise trade. Bank deposits by Ceylonese were restricted to the two nationalised banks although this restriction was later lifted by the UNP. The distribution of petroleum products was taken out of British and American hands in 1961. Despite these and many other measures, the SLFP government was forced to admit in 1962 that "the import and export trade of the country still continues to be dominated by foreign business houses."[25] In 1970 the Coalition took over control of the British agency houses which managed the export of primary produce. Even in domestic commerce it could still be argued in 1969 by the Sinhala Chamber of Commerce that "outsiders are far ahead of us in business enterprises."[26] Not until 1975 were the major tea estates finally nationalised with compensation paid to the British and Ceylonese owners.

It is difficult to assess in general terms success in achieving broad economic aims, as these are focused on constantly moving targets. There is a marked discrepancy between the optimism of successive Ministers of Finance and the pessimism of academic critics. The fullest academic analysis of the modern Ceylon economy concludes for the period up to 1965 that "it is the failure of economic policy makers to recognise and adjust to the profound changes in economic environment which took place over a period of time but were essentially conspicuous during the 1940's, that is largely to blame for the dissipation of the earlier opportunities and the deterioration of Ceylon's prospects. By failing to create a rapidly expanding yet externally balanced transitional economy they brought on the forced structural changes of the early sixties and the recent declines in consumption standards."[27] This judgement attaches blame to both major parties and to civil service advisers alike. An official of the Central Bank, writing in a personal capacity, also judged that "the governments led by D. S. Senanayake and S. W. R. D. Bandaranaike . . . were ineffective in taking decisions which were for the moment unpalatable but would have constituted the prophylactic to an ailing economy."[28]

Most economic analyses had concentrated on Ceylon's adverse payment balances and its consequent inability to expand living standards. The JVP rising in 1971 drew urgent attention to the growing unemployment among school-leavers, which was endemic in most post-colonial Asian societies. As a direct consequence of the rising, the government of Mrs. Bandaranaike co-operated with an inter-agency mission from the International Labour Office under Professor Dudley Seers as Chief of Mission. While its general conclusion was that "unemployment has now become chronic and intractable in nearly every developing country"[29] it made a number of proposals and implicit criticisms about the local situation. These elaborated upon standard Western doubts about the subsidised rice ration and dependence on plantation products. Strong local representations added the dimension of criticism of administrative processes, political institutions and the education system. Building upon Snodgrass' critique of policies in the 1950's, the report went on to argue for the 1960's that "the politico-economic system of Ceylon had shown marked unresponsiveness in the 1950's; now this became glaring."[30] The cutting back of imports and import substitution had not merely been failures but had inhibited growth and frustrated the Ten Year Plan. Locally generated investment had been exceptionally low and foreign investment was limited.[31] Such dynamic growth as had occurred in the 1960's was mainly in rice growing, which could not absorb educated youth.

This was a criticism not merely of SLFP governments, under which formal indices of growth had declined, but also of the UNP, under which they had risen quite rapidly. The report endorsed proposals for educational reform put forward by the Minister for Education in direct response to the 1971 rising. These included raising the age of school entry to six years, reforming the GCE 'O' level examination and reorienting education away from academic and towards technical and agricultural concerns. Noting that "there was never any occasion for a fundamental reshaping of the politico-administrative structure", the report goes on to criticise the growing interference of M.P.s in administrative decisions.[32] Here the imposition of British norms is most apparent, particularly as the report recommended a greater degree of public participation which, in the local context, would probably mean even more partisan involvement and patronage appointment. Recognising the cultural gap between administrators and intellectuals and the ordinary citizen the report calls for 'initiatives' from the public, possibly to be rewarded by prizes, and for an increase in local government powers. Again there is some tendency towards imposing Western solutions.[33] But there is a warning that "the emergency had marked the end of an era and underlined the need for fundamental changes in the future if the generations were ever to be reunited on a path of sustained development."[34] This was useful advice because of the smugness previously induced by provincial isolation.

In general, economists have accepted these critical judgements and are agreed that the level of real incomes and consumption dropped measurably between 1960 and 1964 and again after 1970. The earlier decline was not unconnected with the suspension of American aid in 1962, but more importantly reflected both a failure in government effectiveness and the impact of factors over which no government could have real control. The practice of planning, which had been strongly favoured by Bandaranaike, had become discredited by the failure of the various plans to be anything more than well-documented and sophisticated exercises in presentation. As in Britain, from which most economic inspiration continued to come, neither the politicians nor the civil servants were adequately educated in economic theory. Nor were the government machine and parliamentary process, geared to nineteenth century notions of balanced budgets and annual accounts, fitted to effective control of the economy. To some extent this began to be remedied after 1965, with the creation of the Ministry of Planning under the Prime Minister's direct control, and the growing influence of the Central Bank and, through it, of the World Bank. By 1968, with greatly expanded rice production and a rise in that year of 6.1% *per capita* real product, the crisis conditions of 1964 had receded. The Central Bank reported that "the high growth rate of real output was partly the outcome of the stimuli provided by the Government in recent years."[35] Progress was, however, accompanied by a marked rise in living costs and a regular increase in unemployment.

Ceylon soon built up an impressive corps of professional economic advisers from local and international sources. The decline in communalism as a central political issue since 1964 redirected attention to pressing economic issues, although these had never been totally neglected. The effectiveness of the system in improving the economy must be judged in the understanding that some of the most important restraints on growth are totally beyond the control of the local government as in all nations heavily dependent on international trade. Thus to say that economic growth has normally been modest, and sometimes negative is not necessarily to subscribe to the fallacy that democratic systems are by their nature incapable of promoting steady economic growth in underdeveloped countries.[36] In recent years many of the political factors inhibiting growth have become less important. The initial startling incompetence of the public corporations set up between 1956 and 1962 was due as much to lack of a managerial class, as to patronage, the placing of factories in Minister's constituencies or trade union recalcitrance. By 1968 the great majority of corporations were making a profit and contributing to import substitution.[37] As in most other countries launching a programme of rapid nationalisation, the government and managerial machines had to adjust over several years to new responsibilities.

The government has little control over the weather despite claims by rural politicians that typhoons are evidence of the gods' anger with current rulers. Nor can it effectively influence the bidding at the London tea auctions. Attempts to inaugurate birth-control campaigns have been inhibited by claims that these would reduce the strength of the Buddhists relative to other groups.[38] In November 1967 devaluation was forced by the actions of Britain, to which Ceylon still sent over one-quarter of its exports.[39] Changes in the prices of tea, rubber, coconut and rice, all affected by the weather and political conditions in Southeast Asia, are vital to the economy, yet largely uncontrollable. Subsidies on rice, which attempt to give incentives to producers without penalising consumers, are regularly criticised by World Bank advisers. Aid is affected by the vagaries of uncontrollable foreign governments.[40] Despite all this Sri

Lanka has still managed to maintain and periodically to advance its real living standards, to provide universal free education, free medical attention, rising agricultural productivity and the beginnings of industrialisation. To that extent the system has effectively moved towards the goals set it. Its slowness in doing so largely reflects the intractability of many of the problems which Sri Lanka, like all underdeveloped rural economies, faces in a world over which it has no significant influence. As has been argued in the context of Southeast Asia, "democratic regimes which must cater to the strong distributive pressures generated by their electoral clientele are thus particularly vulnerable to the vagaries of world prices for primary products on which their budgets depend."[41]

Modernisation or Sinhalisation?

It has become customary among academic political scientists to discuss the emergence from colonialism in terms of "modernisation theory." In general this holds that a number of processes are taking place which will have certain more or less predictable consequences. An abstract model of a 'modern society' is used, which while it derives from the writings of Max Weber and Talcott Parsons, has also been strongly influenced by American historical experience, culture and national ideology.[42] As elaborated in varying forms in the 1960's, from the work of Almond and Coleman[43] to S. P. Huntington[44], theories of modernisation were held to be generally applicable. Societies were moving along a continuum from 'traditional' to 'modern'. They were described as 'transitional' in the sense of moving from one ideal-typical pole to another. As they became 'modernised' so they approximated socially, economically and politically to the advanced Western societies. It was generally acknowledged that in the transition process there was no necessary and rigid congruence between the stages of measurable, economic development and the stages of political development. The Communist countries of Europe were clearly economically developed, yet they showed few signs of becoming participatory, competitive democracies. Some nations, and most markedly India and Ceylon, seemed to be stagnating in economic development and yet to possess most of the democratic

z

institutions common to advanced Western democracies. As scholarship became more intensive in regard to particular areas or nations, so the broad generalisations of modernisation theory became increasingly questioned.[45] So many modifications and exceptions needed to be introduced that the general theory was in danger of being swamped in a sea of specific exceptions.

That Ceylon was partly 'modernised' in many respects before the granting of independence can hardly be denied. The dismantling of Kandyan feudalism had been begun by the British in 1833 and the creation of a plantation economy based on the alienation of village lands was well advanced by the second half of the nineteenth century. The Ceylon economy had a 'traditional' aspect, based on paddy and coconut cultivation, and a 'modern' aspect based on tea, rubber, shipping and banking. The former was dominated by the Sinhala Buddhist majority, the latter by Indians, British, Christians and other minorities. Ceylon similarly had a 'modern' political system after 1931, lending credence to the notion of congruence between economic and political manifestations of the modernisation process. Universal suffrage brought with it demands for public education and social services. The majority of the population was literate at independence, a unique feature for any British or French colony gaining post-war freedom. The majority of citizens took part in elections after independence. The public was relatively well informed through the mass media and seemed genuinely interested in the electoral process. There were few respects in which Ceylon could not be described as politically modernised. Its electoral turnout was far higher than in the United States, as was its level of unionisation. A small number of fairly well organised parties dominated the political system and seemed, until 1971, to embrace all ideological positions canvassed in the nation. The revolutionary movement, again until 1971, seemed fully domesticated, a factor seen by most Western political scientists as essential to the stability of 'transitional' societies. While academic surveys continued to categorise Ceylon amongst 'transitional' societies, this was usually a mark of ignorance, based on the false assumption that a nation with such low living standards must, in some way, still be politically backward. Yet a rigorous application of the norms of 'modernity' can only lead to the conclusion that

Ceylon was every bit as modern in terms of political institutions and practices as the great majority of advanced industrial nations.

If Ceylon was already well on the way to complete political modernisation by 1947 it is necessary to characterise the process of creating Sri Lanka over the next twenty-five years as something other than a transitional stage from 'tradition' to 'modernity'. In some respects, most notably in the creation of viable permanent parties, such a transition was apparent. In others, and particularly in the enshrining of apparently traditional features such as an officially recognised religion, there seems little progress towards a modern, secular, bureaucratised society. In many respects Sri Lanka promises a greater degree of popular involvement in politics than did the polity created in 1947. There has been a marked movement from the British notion of 'good government', based on an élitist and Platonic civil service and political class, to a notion of 'popular government', based naturally on a greater degree of accommodation for the prejudices of the masses. In this respect Ceylon may be said to have moved from a 'British' to an 'American' concept of the purpose of politics. If 'modernisation' is taken to mean just such a movement, then the general theory requires no major modification. It could however be argued that the notion of 'modernity' in its original Weberian form was very firmly based on a movement in the opposite direction. Government would become more bureaucratised, more impersonal, less subject to patronage and nepotism, less influenced by popular attitudes. In all these respects Ceylon became progressively less 'modernised', as it became a more open and participatory democracy.

What seems to have happened in the transition from Ceylon to Sri Lanka fits few of the conventional specifications for a process of modernisation. Just as the social welfare system was built on an economic base which proved to be insufficiently expansive to support it, so the political system was built upon a social base which made it unlikely that change would be in a 'Western' direction. Ceylon remained a rural society. The electoral balance was held by the Kandyans, the least modernised sector. The Westernised Marxists and the UNP found it necessary to move towards a consensus with the SLFP which, despite its social democratic pretensions, was fully in the tradition of the Sinhala Buddhist revival. The most Westernised institutions (the bureaucracy, the judiciary and the military) were all subject to indigenisation. The changes in military leadership following the 1962 coup brought in elements beholden to the SLFP and limited the Burgher, Christian and Anglicised leaders to a large extent. The new constitution of Sri Lanka made the bureaucracy and judiciary potentially subject to patronage and thus, in the existing political atmosphere, to Sinhalisation. The legal profession, which has been the principal bearer of Western and specifically British, values in Ceylonese society, now has to conduct its business in Sinhala. The changes to the education system culminating in the struggle against Church schools in 1960, while they have created their own monsters, have also reduced the probability that the future generation of politicians will be anything like as Westernised as the present. The same should inevitably be true of future bureaucrats, lawyers, journalists and teachers. This is not to hold that the English-speaking élite has been displaced already. The grievances evidenced by the JVP rising strongly suggest that the *swabasha* educated are still heavily discriminated against in attractive employment. Rather it is to argue that there can be no simple connection between 'modernisation', 'democratisation' and 'Westernisation' in the future political development of Sri Lanka.[46]

In several important senses the movement away from Western attitudes and practices has been a necessary step towards modernisation and socialisation. British and Christian education instilled indifference or even contempt towards the ancient religion and history of Ceylon. It was an affront to many perfectly well-educated and modernised Ceylonese that this alien domination of education should continue. It was equally an affront to socialists that a replica of the British public school and Oxbridge system should be preserved long after independence, even if most socialists had been brought up within it. This was not a system which encouraged economic modernisation once it had created a large, prosperous and talented professional class. For that class turned to land rather to industry as a source of income but even more importantly, as a source of prestige. It was not simply the indigenous value system which encouraged the creation of an educated landed gentry and political élite, but the British upper-middle class traditions so effectively planted on Ceylonese soil by the schools and the university. It was not 'traditional' values alone which made the educated turn to clerical and administrative employment, but the hard fact that they provided the main avenues through which Sinhalese and Ceylon Tamils could maintain a reasonable income, property and pension. The values inculcated through the Westernised education system were just as antithetical to entrepreneurship and technology as anything inherent in the indigenous culture. The privileged class which arose in colonial Ceylon and continued to dominate politics after independence was only in some part a continuation of the Kandyan aristocracy. It was equally a replica of the knights of the shires, lords of the manor and justices of the peace of late Victorian England. Business enterprise was firmly in the hands of the various Indian groups and the Muslims or Karavas, who did not want a new class of businessmen to be formed from the Goyigama Sinhala or Vellala Tamil majorities. This specifically 'Asian' phenomenon was rationalised and defended by British attitudes which were contemptuous of trade and commerce and stressed the values felt desirable for the creation of a class of Platonic 'philosopher kings' who had no practical, technical or scientific knowledge at all. To move away from this part of the British inheritance was not only necessary for nationalists wanting to stress Lanka's ancient culture. It was also obligatory for socialists wishing to break down the inequalities inherent in the creation of the Anglicised minority and for modernisers who wanted to produce an innovatory drive which that class did not possess and could not possess so long as its gaze was firmly fixed on status, hierarchy and security—all the hallmarks of the Anglicised professional as of his British mentor.

As the Anglicised political élite reached out to the masses so it necessarily modified its alien character and, often consciously, became 'indigenous'.[47] This did not immediately change the reality of a denationalised élite ruling with the permission of an electorate steeped in ancient religions and cultures. Even after 1956 most of the political, judicial, administrative and journalistic leaders were either the same people as those who had exercised influence in the last days of the Crown Colony, or were their relatives or had very similar backgrounds. Several had 'Sinhalised' themselves in the manner of S. W. R. D. Bandaranaike, or Pieter Keuneman. The Marxist parties, in common with the SLFP and the UNP, had greatly reduced the amount of English-language literature produced and placed their emphasis on the indigenous newspapers like *Aththa* or *Janadina*. But policy debates were still conducted in an Anglicised setting. *Tribune*, *Forward* and *Nation* were the arenas in which ideas were canvassed and most of the sessions of the Socialist Study Circle, in which the Coalitionist intellectuals worked through their programme, were conducted in English. The English-established universities at Peradeniya and Colombo were still more influential than the former Buddhist *pirivenas* at Vidyalankara and Vidyodaya, although it was the latter which were to provide the student backbone for the JVP rebellion. What was happening was not a rapid displacing of the Anglicised from office, but a steady erosion of their influence which, nevertheless did not open up sufficient avenues to power and employment for the vastly expanded cohorts of *swabasha* educated youth. Just as the welfare and employment programmes of successive governments crumbled against the rock of declining terms of trade, so the promises made to the indigenous masses after 1956 turned sour in the reality of continued dominance by the small classes created by the colonial system.

'Modernisation' is a difficult term to apply to the progress of independent Sri Lanka, and 'Westernisation' is clearly inappropriate. 'Indigenisation' too, has its difficulties. For much of the 'return' to ancient ways is purely symbolic. The 'traditional' Sinhalese political institution was the *sangha*-advised monarchy, served by functional caste groups.[48] No ostensibly socialist politician would dream of reverting to arrangements which were already moribund by the arrival of the Portuguese. The pressure for a 'rightful' place for Buddhism came largely from the urban middle-class Buddhist revival groups which, as argued in Chapter Six, were a reaction to Christian domination and were oriented towards purified and modernised Buddhism. The political pressure from the Kandyan monasteries has been largely self-protective. The lands were to be left alone, the structure of the religion was to be free from state intervention and the political party was to be abolished as a divisive force in society. In the former two demands the *sangha* has been heeded against the Buddhist reformers of Colombo. In the latter respect they have been completely ignored not merely by the Westernised political élite, but also by the voters who have taken very readily to party politics. All parties with exclusively 'traditionalist' objectives have been decimated at the polls. Even the alleged traditionalism of the JVP, which was largely confined to its demands for returning Kandyan village lands alienated by the estates, went side by side with attacks on caste and even on the Buddhist clergy, all in the name of Marxist-Leninism.

Thus 'indigenisation' is not the same as a simple return to 'traditional' values. Buddhist revivalism came to Ceylon with Western liberalism and the revivalist and prohibitionist movements formed a driving force behind the liberal-democratic Ceylon National Congress. The origins of the LSSP in the Suriya Mal movement were 'indigenous' in using a local flower as a substitute for the Flanders poppy. The SLFP itself was founded by an Oxford graduate who had to relearn Sinhalese, had Christians and Muslims among its founding officers and declared itself to be social-democratic. Merely to reassert Sinhala Buddhist dominance is not necessarily to urge a return to traditional ways. Only the most conservative clergy and the most extreme communalists did so, and surprisingly little notice seems to have been paid to them by the rural masses. The JVP movement, the most unmistakably 'indigenous' major political force in Ceylon, drew many of its heroes from overseas and was led partly by cosmopolitan former students. 'Indigenisation' or 'Sinhalisation' need not be incompatible with modern political institutions and ideologies once the confusion between 'modernisation' and 'Westernisation' is recognised. In particular the increasingly socialist orientation of Ceylonese politics, culminating in a specifically socialist constitution for Sri Lanka, may be considered essentially a move in a modernising direction. Despite much Western theorising to the contrary, there is no necessary progress towards pluralist capitalism throughout the former colonial world. On the contrary socialism appears increasingly attractive

as a way of achieving democratic and egalitarian objectives in
stagnant or slowly expanding economies.

To move from a colonial society ruled by an Anglicised élite
with its economic and political base in alien institutions, to a
socialist democracy whose leadership pays increasing heed to
the indigenous masses, has been no simple matter. After the
events of 1971 it remains an open question whether the process
can continue peacefully without severe ruptures to the political
and social system such as have not been experienced for one
hundred and fifty years. Independence came so easily because
no substantial class was displaced other than the expatriate
British administrators. The managers of tea estates, commerce
and banking remained behind to be phased out on retirement.
The political élite had already been created before 1947 and was
easily able to restrain the Marxists and Ceylon Indian Congress
who seemed their only serious rivals. With each successive
shift in power violence and disruption broke out as newly
triumphant groups over-asserted themselves and minorities
losing their privileges fought back. The riots of 1956 and 1958
were a natural consequence of the assertion of Sinhala dominance. The chaos between 1959 and 1962 resulted from the
inability of the SLFP to agree on its socialist aims and the
resistance of Ceylon Tamils and Christians to its espousing of
Sinhala Buddhist dominance. The strikes of 1966 were a warning
that no government would be able to move backwards towards
accommodating the Tamils, even if their political strategy were
based on creating communal unity. Finally and most drastically,
the rising of 1971 showed that the generation born and brought
up under Sinhala political dominance expected its rewards in
concrete rather than spiritual terms. Political instability and
crisis has been most marked during the SLFP's terms of office,
not because that party was necessarily less competent than the
UNP, but because it was less conservative. By challenging
established interests it unleashed the resentments not only of
minorities but also of the majority. For despite all the socialistic
aspirations of Ceylon's governments, wealth and power remained unevenly distributed and disproportionately in the
hands of the Anglicised community and sections of the Ceylon
Tamils, the Muslims and the Indians.[49] Their remarkable ability
to hold on to their social position only exacerbated the resent-

ments of the rural Sinhala masses, which were fed and encouraged by politicians of all the Sinhalese parties.

Through all this turmoil the basic political institutions continued to function. Those which were threatened, such as the Senate or the press, were attacked for their Anglicisation and conservatism. Those which were strengthened, such as parliament itself, were maintained precisely because they gave power to the Sinhala Buddhist majority and allowed demands for social and economic reform to be articulated. Even during the many states of emergency which accompanied the crises referred to above, the degree of freedom remaining was substantial compared to that in most Asian and African nations.[50] Despite the attacks of its critics in the legal profession and among conservative politicians, the Coalition government elected in 1970 repeatedly pledged its intention to maintain a plural democracy despite a much criticised extension of the life of parliament for two years. Its promise to deal with the Lake House newspaper corporation was concentrated on the question of broadened ownership, rather than outright nationalisation. Even the controversial Criminal Justice Commission measure, designed to deal with insurgents and currency speculators, met with sustained criticism from within the Coalition. Suggestions that the Sri Lanka constitution was designed to be "a charter for constitutional dictatorship"[51] ignore the fact that the previous constitution also made possible a perfectly legal transition to dictatorship had a ruling party with a large majority wanted this. Whether Sri Lanka remains as effective a participatory democracy as was Ceylon is partly a matter of the intention of the ruling parties and the ability of its government to resist further revolutionary demands from rural youth. The new institutions of Sri Lanka offer more opportunity for 'popular government', even if they depart from the British notion of 'good government' enshrined by Soulbury. The virtual monopoly of power in the hands of the socially superior could conceivably be changed through the ballot box and through a consistent attempt by the radicals in Sri Lanka to broaden the social background of the politically active and to reduce the hierarchical divisions which have characterised social and political life for over two thousand years.

The Dilemmas of Sri Lanka

The political development of Ceylon into Sri Lanka raised a series of intellectual and ideological problems. The very uniqueness of Ceylon's experience and the extraordinary combination of apparent contradictions which characterises it, raise the issue of "Ceylon exceptionalism". Judged by formal "development theory" there existed a whole series of disjunctures. Society was overwhelmingly rural yet over half the workforce received wages or salaries. The major segment of the proletariat, the plantation labourers, were both highly unionised and politically neutered. The population was well educated yet not even the Westernised minority seemed responsive to scientific or innovatory impulses. Welfare provisions, based in the West on urbanisation and industrialisation, preceded both in Ceylon. Private capitalism was only imperfectly developed before it began to be replaced by state socialism. The rural masses were completely politicised and electorally mobilised, yet never threw off the control of their social superiors nor even seriously challenged it. The government structure was in contact with the people at far more points than in most of Asia and was constantly legitimised through elections and welfare provision. Yet it crumbled rapidly, if very temporarily, when attacked by ill-armed and confused teenagers and school children. Institutions created by the British lost their independence rather than becoming more autonomous and 'functionally specific' as Parsonian theory requires. The organised working class became a bastion against armed revolution, frustrating the expectations of Marxists once more. Politicians moved into the centre of the stage rather than giving way to professional bureaucrats and managers. Socialism, religion, language and history were the four pillars of a consensual ideology advanced by radical aristocrats and Westernised professionals and accepted by rural, middle-class opinion leaders. Deferential relationships were incorporated into a modern party structure. Traditional practices and myths supplemented the mass media as a means of rationalising modern practices to the rural masses.

The record of Ceylon may be used to challenge and test most available models of development. In particular there is little evidence of deliberate or even unconscious movement in a 'Western' direction. The most conscious modernisers in Ceylon were the Marxists who wanted to move away from entrepreneurial capitalism altogether. The dominant political force was Sinhala Buddhist revivalism which wished to create a system which would be both modern and indigenous. The ethnic minorities were preoccupied with protecting their interests against undue domination by the Sinhala Buddhist majority. The most Westernised major community, the Catholics, consciously 'Easternised' themselves in the 1960's and made their peace with the majority. The only totally Anglicised community, the Burghers, took the path of emigration which reduced their numbers by half. The alternative models of modernisation provided by Russia, China or Cuba had little concrete appeal except to those too young to be assimilated into the dominant political culture. In partisan rhetoric the 'imperialist nations' of Britain and America were denounced and the 'socialist countries' were praised. Aid from China was welcomed because it was felt to be less expensive and to carry less obligations than aid from the West. Yet the major political force favouring state socialism were the Samasamajists who had always been critical of the Soviet Union and whose analysis of Marxism was totally at variance with Maoism or Castroism. The model of state socialism adopted was that of a mixed economy with property relations in the rural sector largely untouched except by redistributive land reform and state-sponsored colonisation. There was very little concrete political influence from the Communist world.[52] If any important politicians hankered after a dictatorship, it was for one based on extending the Public Security Ordinances left by the British.

The creation of Sri Lanka raised the whole issue of the viability of liberal democracy in Asia. Ceylon and the Philippines were the poorest countries in the world regularly to change their government by elections. Ceylon was able to do so on five occasions without any of the chaos and dissension evident in the even poorer Indian states which also changed their governments. While the parties spoke of each other as enemies of democracy and quite genuinely suspected each other of conniving at or planning coups, no defeated government attempted to stay in office or to use force of any kind to prevent its defeat. The conduct of elections nationally remained beyond reproach and such violence, bribery or excessive expenditure as occurred locally was often severely punished. The rich were less able to buy electoral success than in the Philippines. Liberal democracy in all its classic dimensions flourished much more successfully than in half the countries of Europe. In every respect Ceylon after 1931 was a model for the peaceful transfer of power, both from the British and as between the major parties. There was no doubt, on Ceylonese example, that democracy could be fully established in a post-colonial Asian rural society provided there had been no enemy invasion, no armed struggle for liberation and no armed intervention from outside. The record of Ceylon cannot, of course, offer much guide for South East Asia, where none of those conditions prevailed. Through the difficult years which followed the collapse of the Korean War boom, the communal readjustment and the beginnings of socialism, liberal democracy continued to function with the increasing participation of the people. The more difficult question to answer is whether it can continue indefinitely in the face of the growing gap between manufacturing and primary producing nations, of a potential shortage of the goods and raw materials which Sri Lanka needs but does not possess and of a continuing and irreversible population explosion within a slowly moving economy.

The peculiar intractability of the problems facing Sri Lanka suggests that liberal democracy is continuously at risk. The 'modernising' school of developmentalists have in a sense issued a false prospectus by focusing on the need to stabilise and consolidate a participatory society and regulative institutions. Ceylon had already done that years before the JVP rising. Its administration needed to be made more efficient as in most modern states. In virtually every other regard it had built a working model of liberal democracy which should have satisfied anyone. Yet for more than three years after 1971 the country was ruled under emergency regulations which gave the government power to suspend most basic freedoms provided that its parliamentary majority gave approval. These powers were written into the new constitution. A democracy which can be legally suspended is always liable to wither away in the face of continuing economic and social crises. The key to assessing the viability of democracy in 'developing' and 'modern' societies is simply that the latter have *per capita* incomes twenty or more times those of the former and economies which expand more rapidly than their populations. By focusing attention on 'modernisation', 'system maintenance', 'functional specificity' and 'institutional autonomy', much Western social science loses sight of those very stark facts. The starkness is all the more menacing in Sri Lanka, where liberal democracy goes together with universal education, subsidised food, a national health service and mass unionisation. In such a political environment expectations do not simply rise. They explode.

Western governments, social scientists, politicians, advisers and bankers are all committed to the maintenance of liberal democracy. They expend millions of words and immeasurable quantities of money to establish their credentials. The experience of Sri Lanka suggests a hiatus between acts and intentions. It has not been a victim of 'imperialism' in the original sense of the term nor in the sense in which it is used within the country today. While the Kandyan peasants lost much of their forest land to the estates, the living standards of the whole population, their welfare and education provisions and their freedom from starvation and disease all rested on the surplusses built up by the plantation economy in the 1940's.[53] British soldiers left in 1957 never to return and British equipment was rapidly available in 1971 when requested. Ceylon suffered from a more insidious form of exploitation than anything contained in the classic Leninist calendar. With the withdrawal and running down of British investment in the 1960's the amounts being repatriated to the metropolitan country as dividends became a relatively insignificant item in the foreign exchange balance. British shippers were paying more to Ceylon for the use of harbour facilities than British investors were deriving from investment income. The classic form of exploitation by foreign companies had become relatively unimportant.[54] In its place Ceylon had become increasingly indebted to foreign borrowing for short-term loans and credits to bridge its external resource deficit. In 1968–70 it was raising more by this method than was made available in all forms of external aid. As 43% of its resource deficit was caused by capital repayments it was, in effect, borrowing from Western institutions to pay back other Western institutions who were creditors as the result of previous loans. As the ILO team of 1971 summarised it: "The Government turned more and more to suppliers' credits and short-term borrowing, with further sums then being borrowed to pay off earlier obligations. In 1968 the main source of short-term finance was overseas banks, but in 1969 and 1970 the Government had increasing recourse to commercial borrowing. This costs a great deal, not merely in terms of the nominal interest rate, but also because higher prices have often to be paid for goods financed in this way."[55]

Not only was the economic basis of democracy being eroded by unemployment and welfare demands at home. It was also being undermined by deteriorating terms of trade, expensive tied aid and rising rates of interest. While international economists and bankers advised that money spent on subsidised rice could be better invested in productive industry, money spent on debt servicing and repayment could not be spent either on feeding the population or on employing them. Resources were still being funnelled out of Ceylon but to lenders rather than investors. Governments and agencies of the capitalist democracies constantly acted in a manner which destroyed their credibility as patrons of democracy in the underdeveloped nations. The United States cut off aid for several years in angry reaction against the nationalisation of oil distribution services catering for a market less profitable than in the smallest American state. British aid rose from negligible proportions to a sum of £5 million per annum or rather less than had been paid for many years to support autocratic monarchies in Jordan and Muscat. Most glaring and politically explosive, was the annual military expenditure by the United States in Buddhist Vietnam of sums sufficient to finance Ceylon's external deficit many times over. Enormous resources were spent for the military defence of a democracy which did not exist while small sums were grudgingly made available, accompanied by suitable sermons on thrift, to a democracy which not only survived but enjoyed the active support of most of its people.

The fundamental dilemma for a democratic socialist Sri Lanka is whether the international economic system sustained by the industrial capitalist democracies makes possible the retention in primary producing countries of the institutions and attitudes exported from the metropolis. Political institutions in underdeveloped societies have to bear greater strains than in the vastly more prosperous and economically viable nations which transplanted the institutions and which regard with contempt or dismay their distortion and destruction. The form which democracy may take in Sri Lanka depends on the success of its rulers in overcoming the problems which arise from its dependent economy. The consolidation of Bandaranaike socialism will prove impossible if those basic problems are not overcome. If they deepen, resentment will naturally grow against the major industrial societies which dominate the world economy. It was the initial refusal of the United States to countenance oil nationalisation which began the process of restructuring international loyalties. The continued criticisms of welfare policies by the World Bank may have had a similar effect. Yet Sri Lanka will depend nearly as much as Ceylon on trade with and aid from Western capitalist democracies. A hard look at comparably small and dependent economies which have realigned with the Communist world is hardly inspiring to any of the parties which rule Sri Lanka. Cuba and Vietnam evoke ambiguous responses while South Yemen and Zanzibar are positively abhorrent. Sri Lanka's cultural links remain with the English-speaking world and nothing in the Sinhalisation programme has redirected them towards Russia or China. Sri Lanka faces a world which will not be any easier to function in than that confronted by Ceylon. If the trade programmes of Western industrial nations continue to discriminate against goods manufactured in the tropics, if the United States and Western Europe become more exclusive while the Communist countries become more expansive, then Sri Lanka's relations will change and the models to which its youth will look will also change. If revolutions spread in Africa, Latin America and South East Asia on the basis of guerilla tactics, then young radicals in Sri Lanka will continue to move away from the European ideologies of the established Marxist parties which will become even more enmeshed in the existing political system than before. All these factors are largely outside the control of indigenous politicians. However much they 'modernise', however sincere their democratic beliefs, however necessary and desirable the changes which they seek, the future of Sri Lanka's politics will be shaped as much by the world as by forces within the Island.

NOTES

1. The ILO Report (*Matching Employment Opportunities and Expectations*; Geneva, 1971) argued that "the emergence of chronic large-scale unemployment was due to the contrast between the fast growth of population and the inertia of the economy in the face of adverse trends in world markets" (p. 17).
2. Action was, of course, most likely to be taken against political opponents of the government. Supporters of the government were also warned against enjoying too high a living standard. Members of Parliament buying cars under a special import licence, for example, were obliged to have their names and the make and cost of the one car allowed to them, published in the newspapers. *Ceylon News* 28/9/1972.
3. Based on "Loku Athula's" deposition presented in evidence to the Criminal Justice Commission in 1973.
4. The argument that "both sociological and socialist *ideologies* tend to act as a brake on the development of a theory of social change" (Irving Horowitz: *Three Worlds of Development*; New York, 1966; p. 430) applies particularly well to Sri Lanka where even the Marxists have subscribed to the notion of "Ceylon exceptionalism" for many years.
5. For a version of this theory see Colvin R. de Silva: *Against Helotry*; Colombo, 1949.
6. G. F. Lerski: *Origins of Trotskyism in Ceylon*; Stanford, 1968.
7. *Agenda for the UNP Annual Sessions*; Colombo, 23/7/1949.
8. UNP: *Annual Conference Agenda and Commemorative Number*; Colombo, 1955.
9. S. W. R. D. Bandaranaike: *Speeches and Writings*; Colombo, 1963; p. 159.
10. *Sinhalese and Tamil as Official Languages*; S.P. XXII—1946.
11. Anon.: *Twenty Five Years of the Ceylon Communist Party*; Colombo, 1968; p. 68.
12. *Constitution of the All-Ceylon Tamil Congress;* Colombo, 1944; 2. Aims and objects.
13. Leslie Goonewardena: *A Short History of the Lanka Sama Samaja Party*; Colombo, 1960; p. 15.
14. S. W. R. D. Bandaranaike: *op. cit.* p. 103 and p. 220.
15. Interview with J. R. Jayawardena in August, 1969.
16. United National Party: *Manifesto 1965*; Colombo, 1965; pt. 12.
17. *Twenty Five Years of the Ceylon Communist Party*; p. 80.
18. *Times of Ceylon* 17/12/1962.

19. I. D. S. Weerawardena: *Ceylon General Election 1956*; Colombo, 1960; p. 225.
20. S. W. R. D. Bandaranaike: *Towards a New Era*; Colombo, 1961; pp. 766–82.
21. Department of Information: *Economic and Social Progress 1956–62*; Colombo, 1962; p. 64.
22. See the *Report of the Commission of Enquiry into the Film Industry of Ceylon* (S.P. II—1965; Colombo, 1965). In 1972 a National Film Corporation was created to control the import and distribution of foreign films.
23. One-fifth of all titles and one-eighth of all copies of books printed were still in English in 1965. (*Statistical Abstract of Ceylon—1966*; Colombo, 1969; Table 275.) Virtually all imported books are in English or Tamil.
24. The ILO Report (*op. cit.*) pointed out that "of youths aged 15 to 19 with O level passes, more than 90 per cent are seeking work." (p. 234).
25. Department of Information: *op. cit.* p. 54.
26. Sinhala Chamber of Commerce: *Sinhala Development Fund*; Colombo, (1969).
27. D. R. Snodgrass: *Ceylon—An Export Economy in Transition*; Homewood, Ill., 1966; pp. 235–6.
28. G. Uswatte Aratchi: *Why Ceylon Needs Foreign Aid*; London, 1968; n.p.
29. ILO Report; p. ix.
30. *Ibid.*; p. 14 where it is noted that "apart from Burma Ceylon was the only country in Asia earning less foreign exchange in 1968 than in 1958" (fn. 1) and that "few countries have shown a responsiveness at all adequate to the rapidly changing economic and political situation in the post-war period, but Ceylon's reactions have perhaps been especially weak." (fn. 2).
31. Malaysia, a comparable if more prosperous plantation economy enjoyed a capital inflow four times that of Ceylon and its exports were four times as valuable as those of Ceylon. ECAFE: *Economic Survey of Asia and the Far East*; 1970.
32. ILO Report; p. 149.
33. For a criticism of the Report for its 'ethnocentricity' and a defence of it see: David Wall: 'The New Missionaries' and Michael Lipton: 'Ceylon—the Role of the Inter-Agency Mission' in *South Asian Review* 5: 3 April 1972.
34. ILO Report; p. 245.
35. Central Bank of Ceylon: Annual Report for 1968; Colombo, 1969; p. 29.

36. Some comparisons with Malaysia (West) are: (ECAFE: *op. cit.*)

Growth rates in Gross National Product at current prices, per annum

	1960–65	1965–69
Ceylon	3·9%	6·1%
Malaysia West	5·9%	6·9%

Change in Gross National Product over previous year

	1968	1969	1970
Ceylon	8·3%	5·7%	5·3%(est.)
Malaysia West	5·8%	9·0%	n.a.

Increase in per capita Gross Domestic Product

	1950–60	1960–65	1960–68
Ceylon	0·5%	1·4%	2·4%
Malaysia West	0·9%	2·8%	2·7%

But note the ILO Report observation that much of the rise in the 1960's was due to increased rice production.

37. Central Bank of Ceylon; *Annual Report for 1968*; pp. 74–124.
38. By 1988 population may have tripled since Independence. *Statistical Abstract of Ceylon—1966*; Colombo, 1969; Table 26 gives a high projection of 21,484,000, a medium projection of 20,707,000 and a low projection of 18,517,000. Population in 1946 was 6,657,000.
39. 26·37% of exports by value were to Britain in 1965 and 28·87% in 1964. China is normally the second most important market but this is largely due to the rice for rubber agreements since 1953 rather than to open competitive trade. See *Statistical Abstract for 1966*; Table 163.
40. For example American aid ceased between 1962 and 1965 (SLFP government) as a response to nationalisation of oil installations, while Chinese aid ceased between 1965 and 1970 (UNP government).
41. J. C. Scott: 'Patron–Client Politics and Political Change in Southeast Asia'; *American Political Science Review* 66: 1 March 1972.
42. For a critique of 'modernisation theory' concentrating on its American moorings see D. C. O'Brien: 'Modernization, Order and the Erosion of a Democratic Ideal—American Political Science 1960–1970'; *The Journal of Development Studies* 8: 4 July 1972 pp. 351–378.
43. G. A. Almond and J. S. Coleman: *The Politics of the Developing Areas*; Princeton University Press; 1960 and the series of Princeton studies which it inspired during the 1960's. See also David E. Apter: *The Politics of Modernization*; Chicago University Press; 1965.
44. Samuel P. Huntington: *Political Order in Changing Societies*; Yale University Press, New Haven; 1968, in which a more complex analysis of development is attempted on the basis of current empirical work, with an emphasis on maintaining stability.
45. See for example: L. Rudolph and S. H. Rudolph: *The Modernity of Tradition*; University of Chicago Press, Chicago; 1967 (for India);

R. S. Milne: 'Political Modernisation in Malaysia'; *Journal of Commonwealth Political Studies* 7: 1 March, 1969; and S. U. Kodikara: 'Communalism and Political Modernisation in Ceylon'; *Modern Ceylon Studies* 1: 1 January, 1970.

46. For a discussion of 'Westernisation' and 'indigenisation' see J. Jupp: "Political Parties in non-Communist Asia"; *Political Studies* XIX: 3, 1971 pp. 284–293.

47. Marshall Singer: *The Emerging Elite*; Cambridge, Mass.: 1964.

48. See Ralph Pieris: *Sinhalese Social Organisation in the Kandyan Period*; University of Ceylon, Peradeniya; 1956 and Robert Knox: *An Historical Relation of the Island Ceylon (1681)*; Ceylon Historical Journal, Maharagama; 1958.

49. Though see the conclusion of the ILO Report *(op. cit.)* that 'the distribution of income in Ceylon appears from Table 11 to be much less heavily concentrated in the hands of a rich minority than in most developing countries' (fn. 1, p. 35).

50. Despite long periods of imprisonment awaiting trial, the defendants in the 'coup' cases of 1962 and 1966 were eventually all released. Notwithstanding legal criticism of the Criminal Justice Commission, those involved in the JVP rising of 1971 were also given open and very extensive trials. The only death sentences for 'political offences' were of those proved to be involved in the assassination of Bandaranaike in 1959, again after a lengthy trial. Two of the three sentences were later commuted to life imprisonment.

51. A. G. Noorani: 'The Draft Constitution of Ceylon'; *Tribune* (Colombo) 20/5/1972.

52. As distinct from rhetoric about China, Cuba or North Korea, the three systems apparently having most ideological appeal to Coalitionists in recent years.

53. Propaganda against land alienation always focused on the tea estates, which were largely foreign owned, rather than on rubber or coconut estates which are mainly owned by Sinhalese.

54. Of course, Ceylon had no control over profits arising from the packaging, wholesaling or retailing of tea once it reached the major markets.

55. ILO: *op. cit.* p. 16.

Epilogue

The landslide defeat of Mrs Bandaranaike on July 21, 1977 marks the end of many aspects of the Bandaranaike revolution, begun in 1956. Perhaps even more important for the future, it has left Sri Lanka without any Marxist parliamentarians for the first time in over forty years. A whole generation of LSSP, Communist and SLFP politicians was swept away, most of them at an age when prospects of a return to power seem dim. The Sri Lanka Freedom Party, the 'natural party of government' for the preceding twenty years, saw almost all its leadership decimated in a manner reminiscent of the defeat of the United National Party in 1956. Like the UNP before it, the SLFP had overlooked the punitive tendency so strong among Sri Lanka voters which has caused them to remove every government since 1956. By extending the life of parliament to seven years, the SLFP compounded the cumulative effect of adding new, young and largely unemployed voters to the register. By 1977 only a minority of voters had any personal recollection of the promise of popular power held out by Bandaranaike in 1956. Most simply witnessed the rise of the Ratwatte and Bandaranaike families, the increasing abuse of their growing powers by government M.P.s and the continued failure to improve a stagnant economy now affected by world-wide inflation. Rather than turning to the Left, which they saw as equally guilty by its association with the Coalition, young voters moved towards the alternative party, the highly organised and confident UNP.

As an historic event the elections of July 21, 1977 will be noted as ending the careers of many who had served public life since before independence. Seats which had been safe for twenty years or more were no longer so. The electoral pattern was altered as drastically as in 1956 and the great bulk of Members returned, as in that year, were totally new to office. Yet this was not a 'revolution' in the same sense. The UNP Members were drawn from social backgrounds not dissimilar to those of their SLFP opponents. The UNP itself was officially committed to a democratic Socialist programme which was ideologically very close to Bandaranaike's aspirations and which accepted most of the measures introduced after 1970. The political power of the rural Sinhalese Buddhist was in no sense diminished. Indeed the defeat of the Marxists removed a major Anglicised element from parliament. While still led by J. R. Jayawardena, a pre-independence politician, the UNP had been remoulded by him so as to capture the political and ideological ground long monopolised by the SLFP. That party was attacked and defeated, not for its programmes, but for its failure to carry them out in an appropriately puritanical and efficient manner. Rather than attacking socialism, as in the past, the UNP simply claimed that the SLFP government "lacked the moral strength vital for honest leadership and good Government." (*A Programme of Action to Create a Just and Free Society*; UNP, Colombo, 1977 p. 1)

Thus the basic proposition that a consensus has been established between the two major forces in politics, and that they fight on their record for the support of the rural Sinhalese, is strengthened by the results of 1977. Even more markedly than in 1960, the attempt by the Marxists to present themselves as an ideologically distinct alternative to both major parties, was humiliatingly crushed. The voters of Sri Lanka now think dichotomously and third party interventions are rejected. By removing the Marxists from the Coalition in 1975 and 1977 Mrs Bandaranaike consigned them to electoral oblivion. But by splitting the vote which had been united in 1970 she made it impossible to salvage much for her own party either. The long-term trend since 1956 had been towards some sort of permanent alliance between the Marxists and the SLFP, which if it had not been able to win in 1977 would have done much better than the United Left Front or the SLFP on their own. The dilemma for the SLFP was that in pushing ahead with the Coalition programme it inevitably antagonised precisely those social groups who had worked hardest for it and benefited most from its rule, the new class of Sinhalese businessmen, the owners of rural property and the dispensers of patronage. They became increasingly alarmed at the policies of LSSP Ministers and worked towards the break up of the Coalition. Yet only by maintaining the Coalition could the SLFP hope to win the 1977 election.

The elections confirmed that the middle-ground of Sinhalese politics is almost monopolised by the UNP and the SLFP. The Marxist constituency has remained stagnant since 1947 and despite the fielding of a number of former JVP leaders as candidates, there seems to be little electoral support for a position more radical than that of the two major Marxist parties. After July 1977 the only major electoral element remaining outside the consensus were the Ceylon Tamils, who voted solidly for the Tamil United Liberation Front, now pledged to separatism. But even the TULF was, for the most part, simply the cautious and constitutional Federal Party, goaded by its younger supporters into a more militant posture. With an overwhelming majority for one party in the National State Assembly, their classic tactic of holding the balance in return for concessions has no future for some years.

The Tamils were, however, able to nominate the leader of the opposition for the first time. An immediate response to the election results was a series of riots and communal killings reminiscent of 1958 although not on so large a scale. Coming immediately after an outbreak of political vengeance killings and the consequent declaration of a curfew, these events underlined once more the delicacy of the democratic balance and the inevitability of long periods of emergency rule to preserve public order and political stability. Democracy was further weakened by the landslide effect, as previously in 1956 and 1970. The SLFP was seriously underrepresented and a raw, new UNP contingent had absolute power in parliament, including the power once again to change the constitution. With the official opposition led by the Tamil United Front, pledged to separatism, with the previous government party only a small minority and the Marxists driven out of parliament altogether, the UNP were in a position where they could override the normal decencies of democratic life if they so chose. Their leadership remained drawn from those with considerable parliamentary and ministerial experience but the pressures upon them from the mass of the party came from rural politicians whose commitments to Western democratic processes still needed to be proved. The new UNP government immediately created an executive presidency under a constitutional amendment in October 1977. Under this system the president would be elected by popular vote, would have the right to dissolve the assembly but could only be removed by it on a two-thirds majority. He could nominate the Cabinet and appoint district ministers with executive authority over regional development. J. R. Jayawardena became the first executive president on February 4 1978, marking the most radical constitutional step away from British parliamentary tradition since independence. The UNP also began the rapid reversal of Sri Lanka's long established welfare system. Jayawardena thus instituted a strong government able to implement drastic economic changes and reverse welfare policies of the previous 30 years.

The elections of 1977 confirmed the allegiance of Sri Lanka's voters to the democratic process. At the same time they swept away many of those who had been most closely associated with that process in the past. The new constitution to which the United National Party has been committed since 1971 will, as adopted, create a strong president whose role may well be incompatible with the Westminster system. The tensions and frustrations which were revealed in the post-election riots suggest that many Sri Lanka voters are less than tolerant of political or ethnic enemies. The condition of the economy is such that the new government, despite its vast majority, will face the same problems as its predecessors. The Marxist Left will be faced even more acutely with the dilemma of how to repair its shattered support and whether to pursue parliamentary or revolutionary tactics. The Sri Lanka Freedom Party, despite its defeat, retained most of its electoral support and can certainly not be written off. Thus while the elections of 1977 changed the outward face of Sri Lanka democracy, the basic issues in local politics will remain the same for some years. These are essentially how to preserve a form of social democracy within an economy which seems incapable of supplying the rewards demanded by the electors at the ballot box.

APPENDIX I

Election Results by Party, Vote and Number of Seats and Percentage Turnout

1947			1960:		
	UNP	751,432....42		UNP	908,996....50
	BLP	113,193.....5	(March)	MEP	325,832....10
	TC	82,499.....7		CP	141,857.....3
	Inds	549,381....21		FP	176,492....15
	LSSP	204,020....10		Others	236,327.....9
	CP	70,331.....3		SLFP	648,094....46
	CIC	72,230.....6		LSSP	322,352....10
	Others	44,278.....1		TC	38,275.....1
				Inds	270,881.....7
		Turnout			Turnout
	TOTAL	1,887,364.61·3%		TOTAL	3,069,106.77·6%
1952:	UNP	1,026,005....54	1960:	UNP	1,143,290....30
	LSSP	305,133.....9	(July)	MEP	102,833.....3
	TC	64,512.....4		CP	90,219.....4
	Inds	326,783....12		FP	218,753....16
	SLFP	361,250.....9		Others	54,387.....4
	CP/VLSSP	134,528.....4		SLFP	1,022,154....75
	FP	45,331.....2		LSSP	223,993....12
	Others	64,084.... 1		TC	46,803.....1
				Inds	140,522.....6
		Turnout			Turnout
	TOTAL	2,327,626..74%		TOTAL	3,042,954.75·6%
1956:	UNP	718,164.....8	1965:	UNP	1,579,181....66
	LSSP	274,204....14		MEP	110,388.....1
	TC	8,914.....1		CP	109,744.....4
	Inds	289,491.....8		FP	217,986....14
	MEP/SLFP	1,045,725....51		Others	173,709.....6
	CP	119,715.....3		SLFP	1,226,833....41
	FP	142,036....10		LSSP	302,095....10
	Others	18,510.....0		TC	98,726.....3
				Inds	237,805.....6
		Turnout			Turnout
	TOTAL	2,616,759..71%		TOTAL	4,056,467..82%

```
1970:   UNP ...... 1,876,956 .... 17
        LSSP ........ 433,244 .... 19
        TC .......... 115,567 ..... 3
        MEP ......... 46,571 ..... 0
        Others ........ 23,914 ..... 0
        SLFP ...... 1,812,849 .... 90
        CP .......... 169,229 ..... 6
        FP .......... 245,747 .... 13
        Inds ......... 225,559 ..... 2
                                Turnout
        TOTAL ..... 4,949,616. 85·2%
```

Party Percentage Voting Support

	UNP	SLFP	LSSP	CP	BLP	MEP*	CIC	TC	FP	Inds.	Others
1947	39·81	—	10·81	3·73	6·00	—	3·83	4·37	—	29·11	2·35
1952	44·08	15·52	13·11	5·78	—	—	—	2·77	1·95	14·04	2·75
1956	27·44	39·96	10·48	4·57	—	—	—	0·34	5·43	11·06	0·71
1960(M)	29·62	21·12	10·50	4·62	—	10·62	—	1·25	5·75	8·83	7·70
1960(J)	37·57	33·59	7·36	2·96	—	3·38	—	1·54	7·19	4·62	1·79
1965	38·93	30·24	7·45	2·71	—	2·72	—	2·43	5·37	5·86	4·28
1970	37·92	36·63	8·75	3·42	—	0·94	—	2·33	4·96	4·56	0·48

All figures are based on the *Ceylon Daily News*: "Parliaments of Ceylon". Different but basically similar figures are contained in Department of Elections: *General Elections in Ceylon 1947–70;* CGP, Colombo; 1971

*In 1956 the description MEP covered all candidates here included with the SLFP. After 1959 the MEP was confined to the followers of Philip Gunawardena only.

Results of the Sri Lanka General Election of July 21st, 1977

PARTY	UNP	SLFP	LSSP	CP	TULF	Inds.	Others
VOTES	3,148,651	1,831,115	230,281	122,416	375,053	239,664	164,399
PERCENT	51·5%	30·0%	3·8%	2·0%	6·1%	3·9%	2·7%
MEMBERS	139	8	—	—	17	1	1
VOTES PER MEMBER	22,652	228,889	—	—	22,062	239,664	164,339
VOTES PER CANDIDATE	20,579	12,628	2,952	4,896	17,047	904	3,102
	(153)	(145)	(78)	(25)	(22)	(265)	(53)

```
                TOTAL VOTE:        6,111,579
                PERCENT TURNOUT    87·3%
```

NOTES: The Pottuvil two-Member seat remained vacant due to the death of a candidate before polling day.

'Others' include candidates of the Ceylon Workers Congress, the MEP and of the United Left Front (other than those listed as LSSP or CP). There is a considerable discrepancy between newspaper listings of

ULF candidates and those allocated the 'Star' symbol in the Extraordinary Gazette of June 20, 1977. The Gazette has been used as the basis for placing such candidates in the 'Others' category. One Independent with ULF support (Vasudeva Nanayakkara) has also been included with "Others". The total ULF vote, including the LSSP and the CP, on this basis was 432, 113 or 7% of the total.

All candidates previously in the Federal Party, together with some former Tamil Congress and Independent candidates, contested under the Tamil United Liberation Front symbol.

The communal composition of Members returned was: Sinhalese—136, Ceylon Tamils—18, Muslims—11, Indian Tamil—1.

These figures are provisional and are based on the *Sun* (Colombo) 23 July 1977 and the *Sunday Times* (Colombo) 24 July 1977, amended in accordance with the Extraordinary Gazette of the Republic of Sri Lanka for 20 June 1977.

APPENDIX II

Election results grouped by areas and type of constituency

NOTE: The elections of 1947, 1952 and 1956 are excluded from this analysis because the distribution of seats was quite different up to 1959. Also the consolidation of parties was in that period incomplete; there were large numbers of independents whose presence blurred the distinctions between regions which these tables are designed to show.

"**Urban Seats**" (18) (Those in which a majority of the electors live within City, Municipal or Town Council areas). Major occupations: Commercial, Clerical and Industrial.

Election	UNP	SLFP	Marxists	Others
1960 (March)				
Votes	156,083	42,960	120,733	144,178
Percentage	33·7%	9·2%	26%	31·1%
Seats Won	12	—	2	4
Votes per Candidate	13,007	4,773	7,102	2,773
1960 (July)				
Votes	195,301	73,552	134,150	78,454
Percentage	40·6%	15·3%	27·9%	16·2%
Seats Won	5	3	5	5
Votes per Candidate	15,023	14,710	19,164	4,358
1965				
Votes	270,210	92,950	114,702*	76,489
Percentage	48·7%	16·8%	20·7%	13·8%
Seats Won	11	1	2	4
Votes per Candidate	30,023	13,278	12,744	3,642
1970				
Votes	358,329	137,713	166,347	85,175
Percentage	47·9%	18·4%	22·3%	11·4%
Seats Won	8	2	5	3
Votes per Candidate	27,564	19,673	27,724	2,937

*Includes candidates of the LSSP(R) and Communist Party ("Peking")

Seats: Colombo North, Colombo Central (3), Borella, Colombo South (2), Kotte, Dehiwala—Mt Lavinia, Moratuwa, Kandy, Senkadagala, Akmeemana, Galle, Jaffna, Nallur, Trincomalee, Negombo

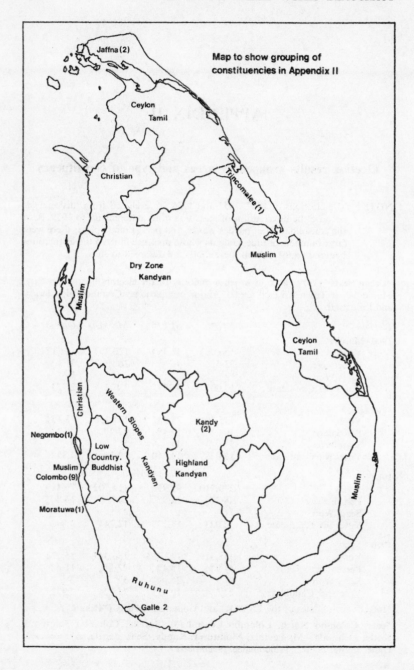

Map to show grouping of constituencies in Appendix II

Jaffna (2)

Ceylon Tamil

Christian

Trincomalee (1)

Muslim

Dry Zone Kandyan

Ceylon Tamil

Muslim

Western Slopes

Christian

Kandy (2)

Negombo (1)

Low Country. Buddhist

Kandyan

Highland Kandyan

Muslim Colombo (9)

Muslim

Moratuwa (1)

Ruhunu

Galle 2

"**Low Country Buddhist Seats**" (13): Over 90% Low Country Sinhalese and almost 90% Buddhist. Major occupations: Coconut plantations, rice farming, some industry.

Election	UNP	SLFP	Marxists	Others
1960 (March)				
Votes	112,252	94,562	40,945	107,077
Percentage	31·6%	26·6%	11·6%	30·2%
Seats Won	3	5	1	4
Votes per Candidate	8,634	10,506	3,412	2,677
1960 (July)				
Votes	124,927	173,317	5,856	43,985
Percentage	35·9%	49·8%	1·7%	12·6%
Seats Won	1	10	—	2
Votes per Candidate	9,609	13,332	5,856	2,932
1965				
Votes	151,679	215,426	29,445	66,114
Percentage	32·8%	46·5%	6·4%	14·3%
Seats Won	2	10	—	1
Votes per Candidate	16,853	19,584	14,722	2,543
1970				
Votes	178,332	293,478	56,392	38,431
Percentage	31·5%	51·8%	9·9%	6·8%
Seats Won	—	11	2	—
Votes per Candidate	16,212	26,680	28,196	4,270

Seats: Divulapitiya, Mirigama, Minuwangoda, Attanagalla, Gampaha, Mahara, Dompe, Kelaniya, Kolonnawa, Kesbewa, Kottawa, Homagama, Avissawella

"Ruhunu Seats" (27) (Southern Province and Kalutara District): Approximately 90% Low Country Sinhalese and 90% Buddhist. Major occupations: Rice farming, fishing, coconut, rubber and some tea plantations, some commerce and industry.

Elections	UNP	SLFP	LSSP	CP	Others
1960 (March)					
Votes	206,943	96,986	75,997	54,931	225,703
Percentage	31·3%	14·7%	11·5%	8·3%	34·2%
Seats Won	10	3	4	2	8
Votes per Candidate	7,665	4,408	4,222	3,433	2,376
1960 (July)					
Votes	266,913	206,902	70,523	26,510	81,549
Percentage	40·9%	31·7%	10·8%	4·1%	12·5%
Seats Won	2	14	5	2	4
Votes per Candidate	9,886	13,793	11,754	13,255	3,546
1965					
Votes	312,295	239,745	115,726	62,744	137,756
Percentage	36%	27·6%	13·3%	7·2%	15·9%
Seats Won	9	6	6	3	3
Votes per Candidate	15,614	14,984	16,532	15,686	3,723
1970					
Votes	375,892	333,258	178,895	87,100	48,321
Percentage	36·7%	32·6%	17·5%	8·5%	4·7%
Seats Won	1	14	8	4	—
Votes per Candidate	15,036	23,804	22,361	21,775	1,858

Seats: Horana, Bulathsinhala, Bandaragama, Panadura, Kalutara, Beruwala, Matugama, Agalawatta, Balapitiya, Ambalangoda, Bentara-Elpitiya, Hiniduma, Baddegama, Ratgama, Akmeemana, Galle, Habaraduwa, Weligama, Akuressa, Deniyaya, Hakmana, Kamburupitiya, Matara, Devinuwara, Beliatta, Mulkirigala, Tissamaharama

"**Western Slopes Kandyan Seats**" (25): Almost 70% Kandyan Sinhalese and over 80% Buddhist. Major occupations: Rubber plantations, with some coconut and tea, rice farming, mining.

Election	UNP	SLFP	Marxists	Others
1960 (March)				
Votes	156,206	142,309	82,529	105,996
Percentage	32·1%	29·2%	16·9%	21·8%
Seats Won	9	10	3	3
Votes per Candidate	6,508	6,468	2,579	1,277
1960 (July)				
Votes	197,173	191,875	45,079	49,886
Percentage	40·7%	39·7%	9·3%	10·3%
Seats Won	4	17	3	1
Votes per Candidate	8,215	10,659	7,513	2,169
1965				
Votes	305,005	239,481	70,669	35,602
Percentage	46·9%	36·8%	10·8%	5·5%
Seats Won	14	6	3	2
Votes per Candidate	12,708	13,304	11,778	913
1970				
Votes	308,094	357,319	99,141	10,843
Percentage	39·7%	46%	12·8%	1·5%
Seats Won	1	18	6	—
Votes per Candidate	12,324	18,806	16,523	571

Seats: Wariyapola, Bingiriya, Katugampola, Kuliyapitiya, Dambadeniya, Polgahawela, Kurunegala, Mawatagama, Dodangaslanda, Dedigama, Galigamuwa, Kegalle, Rambukkana, Mawanella, Yatiyantota, Ruwanwella, Dehiowita, Kiriella, Ratnapura, Pelmadulla, Balangoda, Rakwana, Nivitgala, Kalawana, Kolonna

"**Kandyan Highlands Seats**" (26): Approximately 50% Kandyan Sinhalese, nearly 60% Buddhist and over 30% Indian Tamil Hindus (Mostly unenfranchised). Major occupations: Tea industry, rice farming.

Election	UNP	SLFP	Marxists	Others
1960 (March)				
Votes	131,492	105,533	29,995	144,818
Percentage	31·9%	25·6%	7·3%	35·2%
Seats Won	9	13	—	4
Votes per Candidate	5,057	4,797	1,363	1,434
1960 (July)				
Votes	175,395	171,224	—	40,354
Percentage	45·3%	44·2%	—	10·5%
Seats Won	8	16	—	2
Votes per Candidate	6,746	7,444	—	2,374
1965				
Votes	248,508	221,806	—	72,344
Percentage	45·8%	40·9%	—	13·3%
Seats Won	17	7	—	2
Votes per Candidate	11,296	9,242	—	2,192
1970				
Votes	272,295	322,588	—	38,544
Percentage	43%	50·9%	—	6·1%
Seats Won	3	23	—	—
Votes per Candidate	10,892	13,441	—	1,752

Seats: Matale, Rattota, Wattegama, Akurana (2), Galagedera, Yatinuwara, Udunuwara, Senkadagala, Kundasale, Teldeniya, Minipe, Hanguranketa, Hewaheta, Gampola, Nawalapitiya, Kotmale, Nuwara Eliya, Maskeliya, Passara, Badulla, Soranatota, Uva-Paranagama, Welimada, Bandarawela, Haputale

"Dry Zone Kandyan Seats" (18): Approximately 65% Kandyan Sinhalese and 75% Buddhist. Major occupations: Subsistence farming, hunting, irrigation farming.

Election	UNP	SLFP	Marxists	Others
1960 (March)				
Votes	70,341	111,249	11,656	34,143
Percentage	30·9%	48·9%	5·1%	15·1%
Seats Won	4	13	1	—
Votes per Candidate	3,908	6,544	647	542
1960 (July)				
Votes	91,272	130,056	5,198	4,307
Percentage	39.5%	56·3%	2·3%	1·9%
Seats Won	4	13	1	—
Votes per Candidate	5,070	7,650	5,198	861
1965				
Votes	120,933	144,840	—	59,165
Percentage	37·2%	44·6%	—	18·2%
Seats Won	6	9	—	3
Votes per Candidate	8,062	8,520	—	2,275
1970				
Votes	195,457	232,717	—	40,169
Percentage	41.7%	49·7%	—	8·6%
Seats Won	1	16	—	1
Votes per Candidate	10,858	13,689	—	2,231

Seats: Medawachchiya, Anuradhapura, Kalawewa, Mihintale, Minneriya, Polonnaruwa, Amparai, Kekirawa, Yapahuwa, Nikaweratiya, Bibile, Mahiyangana, Laggala, Moneragala, Hiriyala, Dambulla, Walapane, Horowapotana

"Ceylon Tamil Seats" (17) (those in which Ceylon Tamil Hindus form the largest group in the population): Approximately 85% Ceylon Tamil, 80% Hindu and 7% Muslim. Major occupations: Irrigation farming, fishing, some coconut and rice farming.

Election	UNP	SLFP	FP	TC	Marxists	Others
1960 (March)						
Votes	5,587	1,265	153,776	38,275	37,596	81,867
Percentage	1·7%	0·5%	48·3%	12%	11·8%	25·7%
Seats Won	—	—	13	1	—	3
Votes per Candidate	5,587	1,265	9,611	4,784	2,211	3,275
1960 (July)						
Votes	22,031	4,614	180,744	40,229	17,366	27,283
Percentage	7·5%	1·8%	61·8%	13·7%	5·9%	9·3%
Seats Won	1	—	13	3	—	—
Votes per Candidate	22,031	4,614	11,296	5,747	4,341	3,031
1965						
Votes	25,750	5,536	183,675	92,842	26,917	45,229
Percentage	6·8%	1·5%	48·3%	24·4%	7·1%	11·9%
Seats Won	2	—	12	3	—	—
Votes per Candidate	6,437	2,768	11,479	6,631	2,990	2,380
1970						
Votes	47,293	23,864	220,980	115,507	15,032	58,969
Percentage	9·8%	4·9%	45·9%	24·1%	3·1%	12·2%
Seats Won	2	—	11	3	—	1
Votes per Candidate	11,823	5,966	12,276	9,625	2,147	2,457

Seats: Kayts, Vadukkoddai, Kankesanturai, Uduvil, Jaffna, Nallur, Kopai, Uduppiddi, Point Pedro, Chavakachcheri, Kilinochi, Vavuniya, Trincomalee, Kalkudah, Batticaloa (2), Padiruppu

"Christian Seats" (9) (those in which Christians form the largest group in the population): Approximately 70% Low Country Sinhalese and 50% Christian. Major occupations: Coconut plantations, fishing, some commerce.

Election	UNP	SLFP	Marxists	Others
1960 (March)				
Votes	72,262	41,914	18,446	46,279
Percentage	40·4%	23·4%	10·3%	25·9%
Seats Won	6	2	—	1
Votes per Candidate	9,033	5,239	2,049	1,543
1960 (July)				
Votes	90,757	51,398	22,165	10,230
Percentage	52%	29.4%	12·7%	5·9%
Seats Won	6	2	—	1
Votes per Candidate	11,345	8,566	11,082	1,461
1965				
Votes	131,392	56,517	25,566	18,052
Percentage	56·8%	24·4%	11%	7·8%
Seats Won	8	—	—	1
Votes per Candidate	16,424	9,419	12,783	1,805
1970				
Votes	142,476	116,764	—	27,038
Percentage	49·8%	40·8%	—	9·4%
Seats Won	3	5	—	1
Votes per Candidate	17,809	16,680	—	4,506

Seats: Colombo North, Wattala, Negombo, Katana, Ja-ela, Mannar, Chilaw, Nattandiya, Wennapuwa

"Muslim Seats" (9) (those in which Muslims form the largest group in the population): Approximately 45% Ceylon Moors. Main occupations: Commerce, rice farming, fishing.

Election	UNP	SLFP	Marxists*	Others
1960 (March)				
Votes	71,181	19,026	54,472	116,155
Percentage	27·3%	7·3%	20·9%	44·5%
Seats Won	3	—	1	5
Votes per Candidate	17,795	6,342	18,157	4,005
1960 (July)				
Votes	91,001	64,396	55,069	66,714
Percentage	32·8%	23·2%	19·8%	24·2%
Seats Won	2	2	1	4
Votes per Candidate	22,750	21,465	27,534	6,671
1965				
Votes	178,044	59,430	48,464	72,638
Percentage	49·6%	16·7%	13·5%	20·2%
Seats Won	4	1	1	3
Votes per Candidate	25,434	19,810	16,154	4,540
1970				
Votes	177,281	89,982	58,557	50,891
Percentage	47·1%	23·9%	15·5%	13·5%
Seats Won	4	3	1	1
Votes per Candidate	25,325	14,997	58,557	4,241

*Confined to Colombo Central.

Seats: Colombo Central (3), Mutur (2), Kalmunai, Nintavur, Pottuvil, Puttalam

Select Bibliography

1. Bibliographies and General Reference

Ceylon Daily News: *Parliaments of Ceylon*: Associated Newspapers of Ceylon, Colombo; 1947, 1956, 1960, 1965, 1970.
Ferguson's Ceylon Directory: Associated Newspapers of Ceylon, Colombo; Annual
H. A. I. Goonetilleke: *The April 1971 Insurrection in Ceylon—Select Bibliography;* Louvain, 1973
— : *Bibliography of Ceylon (1507–1967)*: Interdocumentation, Zug, Switzerland; 1970
Theresa Macdonald: *Union Catalogue of Government of Ceylon Publications*; Mansell, London; 1970
National Archivist's Office: *Ceylon National Bibliography*; Monthly
Richard F. Nyrop: *Area Handbook for Ceylon*; US Government Printing Office, Washington; 1971
Edith M. Ware: *Bibliography on Ceylon*; University of Miami Press, Miami; 1962

2. Official Publications—Ceylon and Sri Lanka

Administration Reports for each Government Department, Agency and Corporation; Ceylon Government Printer, Colombo; Annual
Anon: *Towards Socialism*; Department of Information, Colombo; 1958
F. Dias Bandaranaike: *Foreign Economic Aid 1950–62*; CGP, Colombo; 1962
(S. W. R. D. Bandaranaike): *The Official Language and the Reasonable Use of Tamil*; Department of Information, Colombo; 1961
Central Bank of Ceylon: *Annual Reports* and *Monthly Bulletins*
— : *Report on the Sample Survey of Consumer Finances*; CGP, Colombo; 1964
Ceylon (Constitution) Order in Council 1946; Government of Ceylon Legislative Enactments; CGP, Colombo; 1960
Department of Census and Statistics: *Census of Ceylon*; CGP, Colombo; 1953 and 1963 (continuous)
— : *Statistical Abstract of Ceylon—1966*; CGP, Colombo; 1969
Department of Education: *Proposals for a National System of Education*; CGP, Colombo; 1964

Department of Elections: *Results of the Parliamentary General Elections 1947–1970*; CGP, Colombo; 1971

Department of Information: *Use of the Tamil Language*; CGP, Colombo; 1958

Judgment of the Criminal Justice Commission (Insurgency) Inquiry No. 1 (Politbureau): CGP, Colombo, 1976

Department of National Planning: *The Short Term Implementation Programme*; CGP, Colombo; 1962

Director of Information: *Recommendations of the Sasana Commission*; CGP, Colombo; 1961 (in Sinhala)

Electoral Commissioner: *Administration Reports*; CGP, Colombo; Annual

M. D. H. Jayawardene: *Economic and Social Development—a Survey 1926–1954*; CGP, Colombo; 1955

Ministry of Planning and Economic Affairs: *Agricultural Development Proposals 1966–1970*; CGP, Colombo; 1966

National Planning Council: *The Ten Year Plan*; CGP, Colombo; 1959

(Parliamentary Debates)

House of Representatives Debates (Hansard); Colombo 1947–1972

Senate Debates; Colombo 1947–1971

National State Assembly Debates; Colombo 1972–to date

Parliamentary Series Nos 12 and 13, 15; 1958–1959: *First and Second Reports from the Joint Select Committee to Consider the Revision of the Constitution*; CGP, Colombo; 1958

Parliamentary Series 1956–1957 No. 6: *Report from the Select Committee to Consider the Working of the Provisions of the Ceylon (Parliamentary Elections) Order in Council*; CGP, Colombo; 1964

Parliamentary Series 1967–1968 No. 28: *Report from the Select Committee Appointed to Consider the Working of the Provisions of the Ceylon (Parliamentary Elections) Order in Council*; 1968

N. M. Perera: *External Economic Assistance 1950–1964*; Treasury Economic Affairs Division, Colombo; 1964

Proposals for the Establishment of People's Committee; CGP, Colombo; 1970

Report of the Commission on Constitutional Reform of 1945; (Reprint with additions of Cmd. 6677; London 1945); CGP, Colombo; 1970

Sessional Paper XIV—1944: *Reform of the Constitution*; CGP, Colombo; 1944

Sessional Paper XIII—1946: *Report of the First Delimitation Commission of September 1946*; SGP, Colombo; 1946

Sessional Paper XXII—1946: *Sinhalese and Tamil as Official Languages*; CGP, Colombo; 1946

Sessional Paper VI—1948: *Report on the First Parliamentary General Election of 1947*; CGP, Colombo; 1948

Sessional Paper XXII—1948: *Correspondence Relating to the Citizenship Status of Indians Resident in Ceylon*; CGP, Colombo; 1948

Sessional Paper XVIII—1951: *Report of the Kandyan Peasantry Commission*; CGP, Colombo; 1951

Sessional Paper XXII—1953: *Final Report of the Official Languages Commission*; CGP, Colombo; 1953
Sessional Paper VII—1961: *Final Report of the National Education Commission*; CGP, Colombo; 1961
Sessional Paper II—1962: *Report on the Parliamentary General Elections of 1960*; CGP, Colombo; 1962
Sessional Paper XI—1964: *Final Report of the Press Commission*; CGP, Colombo; 1964
Sessional Paper III—1965: *Report of the Bandaranaike Assassination Commission*; CGP, Colombo 1965
Sessional Paper XVIII—1965: *Report of the Committee on Citizenship by Descent*; CGP, Colombo; 1965
Sessional Paper XX—1966; *Report on the Sixth Parliamentary General Election of Ceylon*; CGP, Colombo; 1966
Sessional Paper XII—1966: *Report of the Commission on Broadcasting and Information*; CGP, Colombo; 1966
Sessional Paper VII—1971: *Report on the Seventh Parliamentary General Election of Ceylon*; CGP, Colombo; 1971
Sessional Paper I—1976: *Report of the Delimitation Commission 1976*; CGP, Colombo; 1976
Standing Orders of the House of Representatives of Ceylon; CGP, Colombo; 1959
Standing Orders of the Senate of Ceylon; CGP, Colombo; 1957

3. Official Publications—Other

India—Directorate of Commercial Publicity: *Ceylon Economic and Commercial Conditions*; New Delhi; Annual
International Bank of Reconstruction and Development: *The Economic Development of Ceylon*; Johns Hopkins University Press, Baltimore; 1953
— : *The Foreign Exchange Problem of Ceylon*; Ministry of Planning, Colombo; 1966
— : *Recent Economic Trends—Ceylon*; Ministry of Planning, Colombo; 1966
International Labour Office: *Matching Employment Opportunities and Expectations—a Programme of Action for Ceylon*: ILO, Geneva; 1971
UN-UNESCO-WHO: *Family Planning Evaluation Mission to Ceylon*; UN Development Programme, 1971

4. Books

A. C. Alles: *Insurgency 1971*; Colombo, 1976
S. Arasaratnam: *Ceylon*; Prentice Hall, Englewood Cliffs NJ; 1964
S. D. Bailey: *Ceylon*; Hutchinson's University Library, London; 1952
— : *Parliamentary Government in Southern Asia*; Institute of Pacific Relations, New York; 1953
S. W. R. D. Bandaranaike: *Towards a New Era*; Department of Information, Colombo; 1961

— : *Speeches and Writings;* Department of Broadcasting and Information, Colombo; 1963

Robin Blackburn (ed.): *Explosion in a Sub-Continent*; Penguin, Harmondsworth; 1975

Buddhist Commission of Enquiry: *The Betrayal of Buddhism*; Dharmavijaya Press, Balangoda; 1956

L. J. M. Cooray: *Essays on the Constitution of Ceylon*; Law Faculty, University of Ceylon, Colombo 1970

Gamani Corea: *The Instability of an Export Economy*; Colombo, 1975

K. M. de Silva (ed.): *History of Ceylon—Volume 3—From the Beginning of the Nineteenth Century to 1948*; Colombo Apothecaries for the University of Ceylon Press Board, Colombo; 1973

— (ed): *Sri Lanka—A Survey*; London, 1977

W. P. N. de Silva: *Industrial Law and Relations in Ceylon*; KVG de Silva; Colombo; 1964

D. B. Dhanapala: *Madam Premier*; Gunasena, Colombo, 1960

— : *Among those Present*; Gunasena, Colombo; 1962

T. D. S. A. Dissanayake: *Dudley Senanayake of Sri Lanka*; Colombo, 1975

Hans-Dieter Evers: *Buddha and the Seven Gods*; Yale University South East Asia Series, New Haven; 1968

— : *Monks, Priests and Peasants*; Leiden, 1972

B. H. Farmer: *Pioneer Peasant Colonisation in Ceylon*; Oxford University Press, Oxford; 1957

Hugh Fernando: *The Inside Story*; Author, Wennapuwa; 1965

J. L. Fernando: *Three Prime Ministers of Ceylon*; Gunasena, Colombo; 1963

S. E. J. Fernando: *The Law of Parliamentary Elections in Ceylon*; Lake House, Colombo; 1947

D. N. Forrest: *A Hundred Years of Ceylon Tea 1867–1967*; Chatto and Windus, London; 1967

Richard Gombrich: *Precept and Practice—Traditional Buddhism in the Rural Highlands of Ceylon*; Oxford University Press, London; 1971

K. Gough and H. Sharma (eds.): *Imperialism and Revolution in South Asia*; Monthly Review, New York; 1973

H. A. de S. Gunasekera: *From Dependent Currency to Central Banking in Ceylon*; Bell/LSE, London; 1962

Ananda Guruge (ed.): *Return to Righteousness—Selected Writings of Anagarika Dharmapala*; Ministry of Education, Colombo; 1965

F. Houtart: *Religion and Ideology in Sri Lanka*; Theological Publications, Bangalore, 1974

H. A. J. Hulugalle: *The Life and Times of D. R. Wijewardene*; Lake House Colombo; 1960

L. M. Jacob: *Sri Lanka—From Dominion to Republic*; National, Delhi; 1973

J. R. Jayawardena: *Selected Speeches*; Colombo, 1974

Kumari Jayawardena: *The Rise of the Labour Movement in Ceylon*; Duke University Press, Durham NC; 1972

Sir W. Ivor Jennings: *The Constitution of Ceylon*; Oxford University Press, Oxford; 1951
— : *The Approach to Self-Government*; Cambridge University Press, London; 1956
Sir W. Ivor Jennings and S. J. Tambiah: *The Dominion of Ceylon*; Stevens, London; 1952
Sir Charles Jeffries: *Ceylon—The Path to Independence*; Praeger, New York; 1963
— : *OEG—Sir Oliver Goonetilleke*; Pall Mall, London; 1969
H. N. S. Karunatilake: *Economic Development in Ceylon*; Praeger, New York; 1971
R. N. Kearney: *Communalism and Language in the Politics of Ceylon*; Duke University Press, Durham NC; 1967
— : *Trade Unions and Politics in Ceylon*; University of California Press, Berkeley; 1971
— : *The Politics of Ceylon (Sri Lanka)*; Cornell University Press, Ithaca; 1974
Sir John Kotelawala: *An Asian Prime Minister's Story*; Harrap, London; 1956
E. R. Leach: *Pul Eliya—a Village in Ceylon*; Cambridge University Press, Cambridge; 1961
G. J. Lerski: *Origins of Trotskyism in Ceylon*; Hoover Institution, Stanford; 1968
Y. Levy: *Malaysia and Ceylon—a Study of Two Developing Countries*; Sage Publication, Beverly Hills; 1974
Trevor Ling: *The Buddha*; Penguin, Harmondsworth; 1976
E. F. C. Ludowyck: *The Modern History of Ceylon*; Weidenfeld and Nicolson, London; 1966
P. Mason (ed.): *India and Ceylon—Unity and Diversity*; Oxford University Press, London; 1967
G. C. Mendis: *Ceylon Today and Yesterday*; Lake House, Colombo; 1963
J. Minattur: *Martial Law in India, Pakistan and Ceylon*; Nijhoff, The Hague; 1962
S. Namasiviyam: *The Legislature of Ceylon*; Faber, London; 1951
— : *Parliamentary Government in Ceylon 1948–1958;* KVG de Silva, Colombo; 1959
G. Obeyesekere: *Land Tenure in Village Ceylon*; Cambridge University Press, London; 1967
H. M. Oliver: *Economic Opinion and Policy in Ceylon*; Duke University Press, Durham NC; 1957
S. A. Pakeman: *Ceylon*; Praeger, New York; 1964
Urmilla Phadnis: *Religion and Politics in Sri Lanka*; C. Hurst, London, 1976
Ralph Pieris (ed.): *Some Aspects of Traditional Sinhalese Culture*; University of Ceylon, Peradeniya; 1956
D. M. Prasad: *Ceylon's Foreign Policy under the Bandaranaikes (1956–1965)*; S. Chand, New Delhi; 1973
M. D. Raghavan: *The Karavas of Ceylon*; KVG de Silva, Colombo; 1961

E. A. G. Robinson and M. Kidron (eds.): *Economic Development in South Asia*; Macmillan, London; 1971

M. S. Robinson: *Political Structure in a Changing Sinhalese Village*; Cambridge University Press, Cambridge; 1975

Saul Rose: *Politics in Southern Asia*; Macmillan, London; 1963

Bryce Ryan: *Caste in Modern Ceylon*; Rutgers University Press, New Brunswick; 1953

— : *Sinhalese Village*; University of Miami Press, Miami; 1958

N. K. Sarkar: *The Demography of Ceylon*; CGP, Colombo; 1957

N. K. Sarkar and S. J. Tambiah: *The Disintegrating Village*; Ceylon University Press, Colombo; 1957

R. A. Scalapino: *The Communist Revolution in Asia*; Prentice-Hall, Englewood Cliffs NJ; 1969

J. Schechter: *The New Face of Buddha*; Gollancz, London; 1967

Maureen Seneviratne: *Sirimavo Bandaranaike*; Colombo, 1975

Marshal R. Singer: *The Emerging Elite*; Massachusetts Institute of Technology, Cambridge, Mass.; 1964

D. E. Smith: *South Asian Politics and Religion*; Princeton University Press, Princeton; 1966

D. R. Snodgrass: *Ceylon—an Export Economy in Transition*; Richard D. Irwin, Homewood Ill; 1966

H. W. Tambiah: *Sinhala Laws and Customs*; Lake House, Colombo; 1968

A. J. Tresidder: *Ceylon*; Van Nostrand, Princeton; 1960

Theodor von Fellenberg: *The Process of Dynamisation in Rural Ceylon*; A. E. Bruderer, Berne, Switzerland; 1966

Tarzie Vittachi: *Emergency '58*; Andre Deutsch, London; 1958

L. G. Weeramantry: *Assassination of a Prime Minister*; Author, Geneva; 1969

I. D. S. Weerawardena: *Government and Politics in Ceylon 1931-1946*; Ceylon Research Associates, Colombo; 1951

— : *The Senate of Ceylon at Work*; University of Ceylon Press, Colombo; 1955

— : *Ceylon General Election 1956*; Gunasena, Colombo; 1960

I. D. S. Weerawardena and M. I. Weerawardena: *Ceylon and Her Citizens*; Oxford University Press, Madras; 1956

N. D. Wijesekera: *The People of Ceylon*; Gunasena, Colombo; 1965

(D. C. Wijewardena): *The Revolt in the Temple*; Sinha Publications, Colombo; 1953

A. J. Wilson: *Electoral Politics in an Emergent State*; Cambridge University Press, London; 1975

— : *Politics in Sri Lanka 1947-1973*; Macmillan, London; 1974

W. A. Wiswawarnapala: *Civil Service Administration in Ceylon*; Colombo, 1974

C. A. Woodward: *The Growth of the Party System in Ceylon*; Brown University Press, Providence RI; 1969

W. Howard Wriggins: *Ceylon—Dilemmas of a New Nation*; Princeton University Press, Princeton; 1960

W. H. Wriggins and J. F. Guyot: *Population, Politics and the Future of Southern Asia*; Columbia University Press, New York; 1973
Nur Yalman: *Under the Bo Tree*; University of California Press, Berkeley; 1967
Zeylanicus (pseud.): *Ceylon—between Orient and Occident*; Elek, London; 1970

5. Pamphlets and Leaflets

All-Ceylon Saiva (Hindu) Practices and Observances Protection Society: *Temple Entry Movement in the North*; T. Arumugaswamy, Tellippalai; 1968
All-Ceylon Tamil Congress: *Constitution*; ACTC, Colombo; 1944
Anon: *Companion to the Buddhist Commission Report*; Catholic Union of Ceylon, Colombo; 1957
Anon: *Catholic Action According to the Balavegaya*; Messenger, Colombo; n.d.
Anon: *Twenty Five Years of the Ceylon Communist Party*; People's Publishing House, Colombo; 1968
Anon: *Why Lake House Seeks to Destroy the Coalition*; Colombo; 1970
M. Banda: *The Logic of Coalition Politics*; Socialist Labour League, London; 1965
S. W. R. D. Bandaranaike: *Bandaranaike the Socialist (Selected Speeches)*; Socialist Study Circle, Colombo; 1965
Edith M. Bond: *The State of Tea*; War on Want, London; 1974
Catholic Union of Ceylon: *Companion to the Buddhist Commission Report*; C.U.C., Colombo; 1957
Ceylon Workers Congress: *Annual Reports*; CWC, Colombo
Christian, John: *What is Catholic Action?*; Tribune Publications, Colombo; 1964
Harindra Corea: *Freedom—What Then?*; Ceylon Economic Research Association, Colombo; 1960
G. de Fontgalland: *Barricades at the Temple*; Times of Ceylon, Colombo; 1968
Colvin R. de Silva: *Towards a Dictatorship*; LSSP (?), Colombo; 1938 (?)
— : *Against Helotry*; Bolshevik-Leninist Party, Colombo; 1949
— : *Hartal*; Lanka Samasamaja Party, Colombo; 1953
— : *Their Politics and Ours*; LSSP, Colombo; 1954
— : *The Failure of Communalist Politics*; LSSP, Colombo; 1958
J. A. L. Cooray: *The Revision of the Constitution*; Author, Colombo; 1957
— : *Some Aspects of the Constitution of Ceylon*; Institute of Chartered Accountants of Ceylon, Colombo; 1963
Federal Party: *Ceylon Faces Crisis*; FP, Colombo; 1957
J. L. Fernando: *Bandaranaike Legacies*; Times of Ceylon, Colombo; 1965
Lionel Fernando: *Press Freedom and Responsibility*; Tribune Publications, Colombo; 1972
Forward: *Ceylon Communist Party 25th Anniversary*; Forward, Colombo; 1968

Leslie Goonewardene: *Differences Between Trotskyism and Stalinism*; LSSP, Colombo; 1954

— : *What we stand for*; LSSP, Colombo; 1959

— : *A Short History of the Lanka Samasamaja Party*; LSSP, Colombo; 1960

Government Clerical Service Union: *Annual Reports*; GCSU, Colombo

G. Healy: *Ceylon—the Great Betrayal*; Newsletter, London; 1964

C. R. Hensman: *The Role of the Western Educated Elite*; Community Pamphlet No. 4 (1); Colombo; 1962

J. R. Jayawardena: *Buddhism and Marxism*; Gunasena, Colombo; 1950

V. Karalasingham: *The Way Out for the Tamil Speaking People*; Young Socialist; Colombo; 1963

— : *Politics of Coalition*; International Publishers, Colombo; 1964

— : *Senile Leftism—a Reply to E. Samarakkody*; International Publisher's Colombo; 1966

Pieter Keuneman: *The Fight for Left Unity*; People's Publishing House, Colombo; 1951(?)

— : *Forty Years of Socialism*; Ceylon Communist Party, Colombo; 1960

Lanka Samasamaja Party: *With the Masses into Action*; LSSP, Colombo; 1953

— : *The State Language Question*; LSSP, Colombo; 1955

Badiuddin Mahmud: *Muslim Dignity Restored*; ISF, Colombo; 1968

K. P. Mukerji: *Madam Prime Minister Sirimavo Bandaranaike*; Gunasena, Colombo; 1960

Basil Perera: *Pieter Keuneman—a Profile*; Ceylon Communist Party, Colombo; 1967

N. M. Pieris: *1956 and After*; Author, Colombo; 1958

S. Ponniah: *Satyagraha and the Freedom Movement of the Tamils in Ceylon*; Kandiah, Jaffna; 1963

E. Samarakkody: *Ceylon Youth in Armed Uprising*; Author, Colombo(?); 1971

Walter Schwarz: *The Tamils of Sri Lanka*; Minority Rights Group, London; 1975

N. Shanmugathasan: *A Marxist Looks at the History of Ceylon*; Author, Colombo; 1972

— : *A Short History of the Left Movement in Ceylon*; Author, Colombo; 1972

Sri Lanka Freedom Party: *Joint Election Manifesto of the United Front*; SLFP, Colombo; 1970

Statement of Ten Central Committee Members of the Ceylon Communist Party; Foreign Languages Press, Peking; 1964

United National Party: *The Manifesto and Constitution of the UNP*; UNP Colombo, 1947

— : *What we Believe*; UNP, Colombo; 1964

— : *Election Manifesto*; UNP, Colombo; 1965

S. A. Wickremasinghe: *The Way Ahead*; Lanka Press, Colombo; 1955

6. Articles in Journals

H. Abhayawhardena: "Categories of Left Thinking in Ceylon"; *Community* 4, 1963

C. F. Amerasinghe: "Legal Limitations on Constitutional Reform"; *Ceylon Journal of Historical and Social Studies*; 9; 1 January–June 1966
— : "The Legal Sovereignty of the Ceylon Parliament"; *Public Law*, Spring 1966

N. Amerasinghe: "An Overview of Settlement Schemes in Sri Lanka"; *Asian Survey* XVI: 7, July 1976

S. Arasaratnam: "Ceylon Insurrection of April 1971"; *Pacific Affairs* 45: 3, Fall 1972

N. Balakrishnan: "Sri Lanka in 1974—Battle for Economic Survival"; *Asian Survey* XV: 2, February 1975
— : "Sri Lanka in 1975: Political Crisis and Split in the Coalition"; *Asian Survey* XVI: 2, February 1976
— : "The Five Year Plan and Development Policy in Sri Lanka"; *Asian Survey* XIII: 12, December 1973

T. Balasuriya: "Sri Lanka—Period of Questioning"; *Economic and Political Weekly*; X, 25 & 26, June 21 and 28, 1975

Sunethra Bandaranaike: "Politics in Ceylon"; *Venture* (London) 22: 3, March 1970

A. Bharati: "Monastic and Lay Buddhism in the 1971 Sri Lanka Insurgency"; *Journal of Asian and African Studies* XI; 1–2, Jan–April 1976

Charles S. Blackton: "Sri Lanka's Marxists"; *Problems of Communism* XXII: 1, January 1973

Ceylon Journal of Historical and Social Studies 5: 1, 2, 3 & 4 July–October 1956: D. S. Senanayake Memorial Number

L. J. M. Cooray: "Operation of Conventions in the Constitutional History of Ceylon 1948 to 1965"; *Modern Ceylon Studies* 1, 1970

Doric de Souza: "Parliamentary Democracy in Ceylon"; *Young Socialist* 1 & 2 July and October 1961

Editorial and Documents of the LSSP Conference; *Fourth International* (London) 1: 2, Summer 1964

Hans-Dieter Evers: "Monastic Landlordism in Ceylon"; *Journal of Asian Studies* 28: 4, August 1969

B. H. Farmer: "Nine Years of Political and Economic Change in Ceylon"; *World Today* 21: 5, May 1965
— : "The Social Basis of Nationalism in Ceylon"; *Journal of Asian Studies* 24: 3, May 1965

T. Fernando: "Elite Politics in the New States: the Case of Post-Independence Sri Lanka"; *Pacific Affairs* 46: 3, Fall 1973

W. L. Fernando: "People's Committees—an Experiment in Grass Roots Democracy"; *Ceylon Today* XX: 7 & 8. July–August 1971

Fred Halliday: "The Ceylonese Insurrection"; *New Left Review* 69, September–October 1971

C. R. Hensman: *Organising for Development*; Community Pamphlet No. 7 Colombo; 1964

Sir. W. Ivor Jennings: "The Evolution of the New Constitution"; *University of Ceylon Review* 5, April, 1947
— : "The Ceylon General Election of 1947"; *University of Ceylon Review* 6, July 1948
— : "Ceylon's 1952 Election"; *Far Eastern Survey* 21, December 1952
— : "Additional Notes on the General Election of 1952"; *Ceylon Historical Journal* 2: 3–4, January–April 1953
— : "Nationalism and Political Development in Ceylon"; *Ceylon Historical Journal* 3: 1 & 3–4, July 1953 and January–April 1954
— : "Politics in Ceylon since 1952"; *Pacific Affairs* 27: 4, December 1954
J. Jiggins: "Dedigama 1973: a Profile of a By-election in Sri Lanka"; *Asian Survey* XIV, 11, November 1974
James Jupp: "Constitutional Developments in Ceylon since Independence"; *Pacific Affairs* 41: 2, Summer 1968
James Jupp and L. J. M. Cooray: "The Constitutional System in Ceylon"; *Pacific Affairs* 43: 1, Spring 1970
R. N. Kearney: "The New Political Crises of Ceylon"; *Asian Survey* 2: 4, June 1962
— : "New Directions in the Politics of Ceylon"; *Asian Survey* 7: 2, February 1967
— : "Ceylon—Political Stresses and Cohesion"; *Asian Survey* 8: 2, February 1968
— : "Sinhalese Nationalism and Social Conflict in Ceylon"; *Pacific Affairs;* 37: 2, Summer 1964
— : "The Marxists and Coalition Government in Ceylon"; *Asian Survey* 5: 2, February 1965
— : "Militant Public Service Trade Unionism in a New State"; *Journal of Asian Studies* 25: 3, May 1966
— : "The Partisan Involvement of Trade Unions in Ceylon"; *Asian Survey* 8, 1968
— : "Educational Expansion and Volatility in Sri Lanka: the 1971 Insurrection"; *Asian Survey* XV: 9, September 1975
R. N. Kearney and J. Jiggins: "The Ceylon Insurrection of 1971"; *Journal of Commonwealth Political Studies* XIII March 1975
S. U. Kodikara: "Communalism and Political Modernisation in Ceylon"; *Modern Ceylon Studies* 1: 1, January 1970
N. S. G. Kuruppu: "A History of the Working Class Movement in Ceylon"; *Young Socialist* 1, 3 and 4, 1961–2
G. R. T. Leitan: "The Role of the Government Agent in Sri Lanka"; *Journal of Administration Overseas* XV: 1, January 1976
G. J. Lerski: "The Twilight of Ceylonese Trotskyism"; *Pacific Affairs* XLIII: 3, Fall 1970
S. Namasivayam: "The General Election in Ceylon in 1956"; *Parliamentary Affairs* 9: 3, Summer 1956
G. Obeyesekere: "Religious Symbolism and Political Change in Ceylon"; *Modern Ceylon Studies* 1: 1, January 1971

Urmilla Phadnis: "Parties and Politics in Ceylon"; *Political Science Review* 5: 1, May 1966
— : "Agalawatte By-election—a Case Study of the Political Behaviour of Rural Ceylon"; *International Studies* 10: 3, January 1969
— : "Ceylon's Traditional Left"; *Venture* (London) 23: 10, November 1971
— : "Insurgency in Ceylon"; *Economic and Political Weekly* 6: 19 8/5/1971
— : "Trends in Ceylon Politics"; *India Quarterly* XXVII: 2, April–June 1971
— : "The UF Government in Ceylon: Challenges and Responses"; *The World Today* 27: 6, June 1971
U. Phadnis and L. Jacob: "The Constitution of Sri Lanka"; *India Quarterly* XXVIII: 4, October–December 1972
Bryce Ryan: "The Sinhalese Family System"; *Eastern Antropologist* 6, 1953
— : "The Sinhalese Village and the New Value System"; *Rural Sociology* 17: 1, March 1952
E. Samarakkody: "The Politics of a Coup d'Etat"; *Young Socialist* 5, June 1962
N. Sanderatne: "Sri Lanka's New Land Reform"; *South Asian Review* 6: 4, October 1972
— : "Tenancy in Ceylon's Paddy Lands—the 1958 Reform"; *South Asian Review* 5: 2, January 1972
M. D. Silva: "Sri Lanka: the end of Welfare Politics"; *South Asian Review* 6: 2, January 1973
— : "Why a New Constitution"; *Ceylon Today* XXI: 5 and 6, May–June 1972
Murray A. Strauss: "Childhood Experience and Emotional Security in the Context of Sinhalese Social Organisation"; *Social Forces* 33: 2
S. J. Tambiah: "The Politics of Language in India and Ceylon"; *Modern Asian Studies* 1: 3, July 1967
— : "Buddhism and This Worldly Activity"; *Modern Asian Studies* 7: 1, January 1973
J. M. van der Kroef: "Whose Lion? Whose Roar?"; *Far Eastern Economic Review*, July 20, 1967
— : "Ceylon's Political Left—its Development and Aspirations"; *Pacific Affairs* 40, 1968
— : "Many Faces of Ceylon Communism"; *Problems of Communism* XVII: 2, March, 1968
David Wall: "The New Missionaries"; *South Asian Review* 5: 3, April 1972
W. A. Warnapala: "Peoples Committees in Sri Lanka"; *Journal of Administration Overseas* XV: 2, April 1976
— : "The New Constitution of Sri Lanka"; *Asian Survey* XIII: 12, December 1973
— : "The Marxist Parties of Sri Lanka and the 1971 Insurrection"; *Asian Survey* XV: 2, February 1975

— : "Press and Politics in Sri Lanka"; *Journal of Constitutional and Parliamentary Affairs* IX: 2, April–June 1975

I. D. S. Weerawardena: "Minorities and the Citizenship Act"; *Ceylon Historical Journal* 1: 3

— : "Minority Problems in Ceylon"; *Pacific Affairs* 25: 3, September 1952

A. J. Wilson: "Minority Safeguards in the Ceylon Constitution"; *Ceylon Journal of Historical and Social Studies* 1: 1, January 1958

— : "The Governor-General and the Two Dissolutions of Parliament—December 5, 1959 and April 23, 1960"; *Ceylon Journal of Historical and Social Studies* 3: 2, July–December 1960

— : "The Sources of Power in the Ceylon Constitution"; *Young Socialist* 4, January 1962

— : "The Governor-General and the State of Emergency, May 1958–March 1959; *Ceylon Journal of Historical and Social Studies* 2: 2, 1959

— : "The Cabinet System in Ceylon 1947–1959"; *Indian Yearbook of International Affairs*, New Delhi; 1959

— : "Ceylonese Cabinet Ministers 1947–1959—their Political, Economic and Social Background"; *Ceylon Economist* 5: 1, March 1960

— : "The Tamil Federal Party in Ceylon Politics"; *Journal of Commonwealth Political Studies* 4, July 1966

— : "Oppositional Politics in Ceylon (1947–1968)"; *Government and Opposition*, Winter 1968

W. A. Wiswawarnapala: "The Formation of the Cabinet in Sri Lanka—a Study of the 1970 United Front Cabinet": *Political Science Review* (Jaipur) 12; 1 & 2, January–June 1973, pp. 121–33

A. L. Wood: "Political Radicalism in Changing Sinhalese Villages"; *Human Organisation* 23: 2, Summer 1964

Calvin A. Woodward: "The Trotskyite Movement in Ceylon"; *World Politics* 14: 2, January 1962

W. H. Wriggins: "Impediments to Unity in New States—the Case of Ceylon"; *American Political Science Review* 55: 2, June 1961

7. Monographs and Articles in Books

James Jupp: "Communalism in Ceylon and Malaysia" in A. Leftwich (ed.): *South Africa—Economic Growth and Political Change*; Alison & Busby, London; 1974

— : "Five Sinhalese Nationalist Politicians" in W. H. Morris-Jones (ed.): *The Making of Politicians—Studies from Africa and Asia*; University of London, London, 1976

R. N. Kearney: "The Marxist Parties of Ceylon" in Paul R. Brass and Marcus F. Franda: *Radical Politics in South Asia*; Massachusetts Institute of Technology, Cambridge Mass.: 1973

Bryce Ryan and Murray Strauss: "The Integration of Sinhalese Society"; *Research Studies of the State College of Washington*; 22, December 1954

Nur Yalman: *The Flexibility of Caste Principles in a Kandyan Community*; Cambridge Papers in Social Anthropology No. 2; Cambridge; 1960

8. Unpublished Theses and Papers

Y. R. Amerasinghe: *Trotskyism in Ceylon—the LSSP 1935–1964*; Ph.D. Thesis, University of London; 1974

T. R. Gamelin: *Ceylon's Political Parties in Three General Elections, 1960 and 1965*; Ph.D. Thesis, Duke University; 1968

Janice Jiggins: *Caste and Family in the Politics of the Sinhalese*; Ph.D. Thesis, University of Sri Lanka, Peradeniya; 1973

R. N. Kearney: *Ceylon—a Study in Political Change*; Ph.D. Thesis, University of California; 1964

Wilda Morris: *Patterns of Electoral Politics in Ceylon 1947–1970*; Ph.D. Thesis, University of Illinois; 1971

Michael Roberts: *"The Political Antecedents of the Revivalist Elite in the MEP Coalition of 1956"*; Ceylon Studies Seminar 1969–1970 Series, No. 11; University of Ceylon, Peradeniya; August 30, 1970 (Mimeo)

— : "Reformism, Nationalism and Protest in British Ceylon—The Roots and Ingredients of Leadership"; Unpublished paper to the Conference on South Asian Leadership, University of London; 1974

S. J. Tambiah: *The Process of Secularisation in Three Ceylonese Peasant Communities*; Ph.D. Thesis, Cornell University, Ithaca; 1955

A. J. Wilson: *"Sinhalese—Tamil Relationships and the Problems of National Integration"*; Ceylon Studies Seminar Papers No. 1; University of Ceylon, Peradeniya; 1968 (Mimeo)

9. Selected Newspapers and Periodicals

Published in Sri Lanka:

Asian Marxist Bulletin	*Modern Ceylon Studies*
Aththa	*Nation*
Ceylon Daily News	*New Law Reports*
Ceylon Daily Mirror	*Quest*
Ceylon Economist	*Red Flag*
Ceylon Journal of Historical and Social Studies	*Samasamajist*
	Sinhale
Ceylon Labour Gazette	*Siri Laka*
Ceylon News	*Siyarata*
Ceylon Observer	*Sun*
Ceylon Today	*Times of Ceylon*
Community	*Times Weekender*
Dawasa	*Tribune*
Dinamina	*Udaya*
Economic Review	*UNP Journal*
Forward	*University of Ceylon Review*
Janadina	*Vimukthi*
Janavegaya	*Virodaya*
Marga	*Weekend Sun*
Messenger	*Young Socialist*

Published Elsewhere:

Asian Review (London)
Asian Survey (Berkeley)
Ceylon Committee Bulletin
   (London)
Ceylon Solidarity Campaign Bulletin
   (London)
Eastern World (London)
Economic and Political Weekly
   (Delhi)
Far Eastern Economic Review
   (Hong Kong)
Fourth International (London)
Ginipupura (London)

Journal of Asian Studies (Chicago)
Journal of Commonwealth and
   Comparative Politics (London)
Modern Asian Studies (London)
Pacific Affairs (Vancouver)
Pacific Community (Tokyo)
The Parliamentarian (London)
Round Table (London)
Satana (London)
South Asia (Perth)
South Asian Review (London)
Sri Lanka Newsletter (New York)
United Asia (Bombay)

10. Interviews and Discussions (conducted at various times but mainly in 1969)

E. F. Dias Abeyesinghe—*Commissioner of Parliamentary Elections*
Hector Abhayawardena—*currently Chairman, People's Bank of Ceylon*
A. Aziz—President, *Democratic Workers' Congress; nominated MP*
Father Tissa Balasuriya—*Principal, Aquinas College, Colombo*
A Caldera—*Joint Secretary, All-Ceylon Buddhist Congress*
C. P. De Silva—*Minister of Lands 1956–1970; former Leader, SLFP*
Colvin R. De Silva—*LSSP Founder; Minister for Plantations since 1970*
Professor K. M. De Silva—*Professor of Ceylon History, University of Ceylon*
Doric De Souza—*Former LSSP Senator; Permanent Secretary, Minister for Plantations since 1970*
V. Dharmalingam—*Federal Party MP for Uduvil*
A. Dissanayake—*former Secretary, United National Party*
Lionel Fernando—*Permanent Secretary, Department of Peoples Committees*
H. A. I. Goonetilleke—*Librarian, University of Ceylon*
Leslie Goonewardena—*former General-Secretary, LSSP; Minister since 1970*
Prins Gunasekera—*former Secretary, MEP; SLFP MP for Habaraduwa*
Professor L. Hewage—*Joint Secretary, All-Ceylon Buddhist Congress*
T. B. Ilangaratne—*Vice-President, SLFP; Minister in all SLFP Governments*
J. R. Jayawardena—*Leader, UNP; Minister in all UNP governments*
Kumari Jayawardena—*Senior Lecturer in Economic History, Vidyodaya*
Lal Jayawardena—*Permanent Secretary, Ministry of Planning*
Badiuddin Mahmud—*President, Islamic Socialist Front; Minister for Education 1960–63 and since 1970*
Donovan Moldrich—*News Editor*, Times of Ceylon

Anil Moonesinghe—*Chairman, Ceylon Transport Board; Former LSSP Minister*
Susil Moonesinghe—*formerly Chairman, Ceylon Broadcasting Corporation*
George Nalliah—*formerly Federal Party Senator; Leader of Minority Tamils*
A. J. Niyathapala—*President, UNP Youth Leagues; former UNP MP and Senator*
N. M. Perera—*Leader, LSSP; Minister for Finance 1964 and since 1970*
Maithripala Senanayake—*Vice-President, SLFP; Minister in all SLFP governments*
Bernard Soysa—*General Secretary, LSSP; MP for Colombo South since 1956*
Bala Tampoe—*President, Ceylon Mercantile Union; Founder, LSSP (Revolutionary)*
A. Visvanathan—*LSSP Secretary, Jaffna*
Sydney Wanasinghe—*Editor, Young Socialist*
I. Wickrema—*former President, Government Clerical Service Union*
Herbert Wickremasinghe—*SLFP MP for Bandaragama; President, SLFP Trade Unions*
D. G. William—*former LSSP Trade Union leader and Senator*
Professor A. J. Wilson—*Professor of Political Science, University of Ceylon*

Various Officials of:

All-Ceylon Tamil Congress; Ceylon Federation of Labour; Government Clerical Service Union; Government Publications Department; Islamic Socialist Front; Lanka Samasamaja Party; Samasamaja Kantha Peramuna; Socialist Study Circle; Sri Lanka Freedom Party; Sri Lanka Nidahas Vurthiya Samithi Sammelanaya; Tamil Socialist Front; *Times of Ceylon*; United Commercial and Mercantile Union; United Motor Workers Union; United National Party; United Port Workers Union.

Index

(NOTE: The spelling of Sinhalese and Tamil names and terms varies in local English-language sources. The most common or most recent variants are used here. Note also that some organisations changed 'Ceylon' to 'Sri Lanka' in their title after 1972, but many did not. All organisations are indexed under the name used from their foundation.)

foundation, xiv, 74; in government, 17, 73, 334; ideology of, 8, 21, 76, 101, 123, 125, 127, 150, 263, 281, 304, 337, 338; leaders, 44, 80, 91, 93, 100, 102, 106–108, 128n, 171, 186n, 200, 298, 306; and other Marxists, xvii, xviii, 15, 74, 75, 79, 103, 107, 180, 296, 302, 312, 314, 329; organisation chart, 135; and trade unions, 74, 75, 94, 98, 106, 108, 178, 180, 181, 188n; Youth Leagues, 20, 107, 301; see also Coalition, Marxists

Communist Party ('Peking'), Ceylon, 47, 80, 297, 321n, 341; see also Maoists

communities, 2, 3, 28, 30–35, 38, 41, 50, 56, 102, 123, 136–161, 191, 193, 205–207, 236, 288n, 299, 334

consensus, 11, 62, 98, 122, 124, 139, 175, 250, 303, 329, 330–339 passim, 342, 349, 356, 367, 368

conservatives, 5. 7, 11, 16, 21, 58, 59, 62, 126, 137, 139, 146, 149, 151, 152, 158, 173, 204, 205, 214, 279, 294, 329, 334, 353

conservatism, 7, 18, 57, 121, 122, 125, 127, 138, 144, 152, 155, 157, 165, 200, 205, 220, 232, 269, 270, 312, 331, 354, 355; c. Buddhism, 36–37; c. institutions, 253

Consolidated Fund, 281

Constituent Assembly, xviii, 18, 159n, 219, 222, 230, 258, 259, 262, 265, 272, 275, 277, 280, 284, 289n, 290n, 334

Constitutions, 2, 4, 5, 18, 78, 170, 202, 219, 222, 223, 224, 239, 258–292, 334, 338, 358, 368, 369; reform and change, 4, 5, 258–292, 293; Constitutional Revision Joint Select Committee on, xv, 259, 274, 287n, 291n; Donoughmore Constitution (1931–1947), xiii, 2, 57, 220, 234, 235, 271, 278, 279, 282; Soulbury Constitution (1947–1972), xiv, 4, 5,

63, 136, 173, 190, 202, 221, 222, 225, 239, 243, 258, 259, 266–271 passim, 280–286 passim, 289n, 294, 340, 355, s. 29 of, 267, 272, 274, 275, 288n, 289n, Ceylon Constitution (Amendment) Act of 1959, xv, 260, C. (C.) Order in Council of 1946, xiv, 271; Sri Lanka Constitution of 1972, xviii, xix, 20, 23, 141, 176, 183, 185, 190, 216n, 222, 229, 230, 236, 269–287, 287n, 289n, 290n, 291n, 292n, 329, 350, 353, 355, Constitutional Court, 167, 169, 269, 280, 284, 285, 289n, 290n, 291n; see also administration, Constituent Assembly, electoral system, Government, Ministerial system, Parliament, Republic

co-operatives, 21, 126, 162, 184, 220, 251

Co-operative Wholesale Establishment, 66, 241, 343

Cooray, J. A. L., 267–272 passim, 274, 289n, 290n

Cooray, L. J. M., 287

Cooray, Cardinal Joseph, 37, 148, 149

Corea, Gamani, 16, 224, 255n

Corea, Ossie, 25n, 160n

corruption, 115, 192, 218, 219, 237, 243, 248, 249, 250, 252, 256n, 265; see also bribery

coups, attempted, 20, 318, 319, 327, 332, 357; of 1962, xvi, 13, 25n, 69, 70, 141, 148, 164, 241, 252, 268, 284, 316, 350; of 1966, xvi, 17, 26n, 241

courts, 247, 248, 252, 270, 273, 274, 285, 286, 317, 335

Criminal Justice Commission, xviii, 21, 55n, 247, 252, 253, 256n, 285, 317, 321n, 323n, 355, 365n; CJC Act, 128n, 225, 257n

Criminal Law (Special Provisions) Act, xvi, 14, 252

Cuba, 88n, 111, 123, 188n, 302–